Politics and Society in the Third World

Politics and Society in the Third World: An introduction

Susan and Peter Calvert

Department of Politics,
University of Southampton

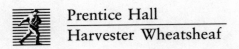

Prentice Hall
Harvester Wheatsheaf

London New York Toronto Sydney Tokyo Singapore
Madrid Mexico City Munich

First published 1996 by
Prentice Hall Europe
Campus 400, Maylands Avenue
Hemel Hempstead
Hertfordshire, HP2 7EZ
A division of
Simon & Schuster International Group

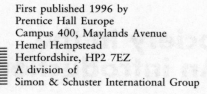

Typeset in 10/12 pt Sabon
by Photoprint, Torquay, Devon

Printed and bound in Great Britain by
T.J. Press (Padstow) Ltd

Library of Congress Cataloging in Publication Data

Calvert, Susan.
    Politics and society in the third world : an introduction / Susan and
Peter Calvert.
        p.   cm.
    Includes bibliographical references and index.
    ISBN 0–13–355231–4
    1. Developing countries – Social conditions. 2. Developing countries
– Politics and government. I. Calvert, Peter. II. Title.
HN980.C328 1996   95–37428
306′.09172′4–dc20   CIP

British Library Cataloguing in Publication data

A catalogue record for this book is available from the British Library

ISBN 0–13–355231–4

1   2   3   4   5   00 99 98 97 96

Contents

Figures

Tables

PART I
The Third World

1 What is the Third World?

THE THIRD WORLD: WHAT IS IT?

This book is intended as an overview of the Third World and a guide to its political and social problems. It is interdisciplinary, because the subject is so large. No one academic specialism poses all possible questions, let alone gives possible answers to the two main themes with which we shall be concerned: environment and development. Both are very much current issues, and much of the material on which we draw therefore comes from current sources: newspapers, magazines and TV and radio programmes. The principal task is to bring all this material together in a series of topic areas which make sense in themselves and also relate to one another. Before turning to the way in which the book is structured, however, we should first define its subject: the Third World.

What is the Third World? There is no getting away from the fact that there is no consensus on how it should be either defined or categorized. This lack of agreement is tending to increase with time, and already many specialists prefer to use a different term or to avoid it entirely. But the term is so widely known and so convenient that it is as widely used now as it was 20 years ago. Most writers, too, would have no difficulty coming to a broad agreement as to which regions of the world and which countries within those regions the concept covers. Chapter 2 therefore deals with the physical structure of the Third World and the way in which geography and climate have shaped it. Yet many important questions remain.

'Third World' is frequently seen as having been coined by the French demographer Sauvy in 1952. It is believed to derive from the French term, the 'third estate', which was used to signify the commoners as against the aristocracy and the clergy. But this is perhaps looking for a degree of precision in the term's origins which is somewhat suspect. The idea of some kind of third alternative to the rapidly developing post-war division between East and West does not really require much explanation. For example, General Juan Domingo Perón in Argentina had before 1948 identified what he saw as the extremes of exaggerated individualism and state collectivism which called for the pursuit of a 'middle way', and by the following year the 'Third Position' between capitalism and communism had become a central plank of his doctrine of 'Justicialism'. As Perón anticipated, during the Cold War the problems of definition were somewhat simpler in that the very idea of non-alignment suggests a three-way division.

The 'Third World' has evolved into a concept of development (Worsley 1967). However, this is problematic for different reasons. First of all, levels of development vary so much. Hence the term has different meanings to different people and organizations. Different institutions use different indicators of different types of development. In any case it is unlikely that any two states will exhibit comparable levels of development on all indicators.

To define the Third World in terms of poverty is even more problematic. It is true that even the least developed country of western Europe, Portugal, is better off in terms of per capita income than any country in Latin America. But this is a single indicator and there are many people in Latin America who have lifestyles which the poor of Portugal – or indeed of an advanced industrialized country such as Germany or the United States – would envy. The global poor, wherever they live, have been identified as a 'fourth world', but the more usual use of this term is that of the World Bank, which has since 1978 talked of a 'Fourth World' of the very poorest countries. At the same time, the World Bank has taken some of the oil-rich Middle East out of its Third World category. A different problem is posed by the relatively well-developed but still poor Newly Industrializing Countries (NICs).

However, even with these reservations we can say that the Third World shares problems, though the same ones do not necessarily apply in all the countries of a region, let alone world-wide. Among these are geography (Bangladesh), lack of infrastructure (Burkina Faso), war/famine (Somalia) and a burgeoning population in some areas without economic growth to compensate for the additional demands this makes on the economy (Africa South of the Sahara generally). Third World nations may be seen to share economic dependency and relative backwardness. They are socially and economically disadvantaged. As Clapham says: 'What distinguishes the third world is its peripherality. Economic peripherality has meant separation from, and subordination to, the dominant industrial economies which have developed especially in Europe and North America' (1985: 3).

Such economies are part of the world economy, but they became part of it in the first instance through the supply of primary products, and the global system they joined was created by and is sustained by the industrial economies. Development in the Third World thus depends on access to First World technology, and this actually enhances the gap between the developed and the developing worlds. The NICs have been successful both in obtaining this access and in making use of it, which is not by any means the same thing. But for the rest of the Third World the big question is: where will investment come from, will it be just displaced pollution or market access investment?

Inheriting a colonial economy determines the pattern of infrastructure available to a newly independent state. Since 1945 there has been an increase in the number of independent countries in the world from around 50 to nearly

200. Naturally this complicates the idea of a single category to embrace some two-thirds of the states, but at the same time this process has made consideration of this group of countries more vital than ever.

COLONIZATION

Nearly all Third World states are former colonies. Three exceptions are China, Thailand and Iran, each of which was subject to considerable pressure from colonizing powers, but ultimately maintained its independence as a result of conflict between two or more potential colonizers. A fourth, Ethiopia, escaped colonization in the nineteenth century only to fall victim to the imperial ambitions of Mussolini.

However, the historical experiences of colonization in different parts of the Third World are in fact very different. They vary according to the following factors:

- The stage at which colonization took place and the economic development of the colonial power involved.
- The different policies and practices of the colonial powers. French colonial rule emphasized cultural superiority, while British rule stressed racial superiority. Once colonies adopted French culture, they became part of France, and one in particular, Algeria, was actually incorporated as part of metropolitan France. Britain's ideology of superiority clearly would not permit such incorporation, but on the other hand it made rejection easier to take. When the French left Sekou Touré's Guinea, they smashed everything that they could not take with them.
- The nature of indigenous societies. In much of Latin America there has been a far longer period of independence and there was much less traditional society to supersede and/or absorb. In Asia colonial rule was shorter, independence was more recent and colonial absorption of existing political systems was much more variable and sometimes much less complete. 'Protectorates' such as Egypt, Morocco, Vietnam and parts of Malaysia, Nigeria, etc. were least affected.

However, the colonial experience might include a number of common features:

- The establishment of arbitrary territorial boundaries, notably in the interior of Africa. This was penetrated late and then not for settlement, which was mainly coastal.
- The imposition of a political and administrative order ultimately based on force, although often legitimized locally by superior technology and the mystique of power.
- Centralized, authoritarian administrative systems. All colonial rule, even that of a democratic country like the United States, which was the colonial power in the Philippines and (briefly) Cuba, is authoritarian.

INDEPENDENCE

Most of Latin America became independent at the beginning of the nineteenth century, much earlier than the rest of the Third World. Thus Argentina was effectively independent in 1810 and formally so after 1816, although it was not recognized as such by Spain until 1853.

Independence came to the rest of the European empires much more recently. The Second World War destroyed the myth of invincibility which helped make colonial rule acceptable, and it encouraged the growth of nationalism in the Third World. Invariably such nationalist movements were led by western-educated individuals such as Kwame Nkrumah in the Gold Coast (Ghana). After 1945 the will to hold the colonies no longer existed among large sections of the élite of the exhausted western powers: Britain, France, the Netherlands and Belgium. At this point there was much less contradiction than there had been previously between the values of the colonial power and the ideal of independence. With independence, however, these perceptions were to change rapidly, as the new state's identity was defined.

However, in all cases the institutions created by the colonial power for its own purposes become the state at independence. This makes the newly independent state at once strong and weak. It is strong in so far as it is intact, functioning and usually centralized. Only Argentina, Brazil, Mexico, India and Nigeria emerged into independence as true federal states, and in each case the struggle between federal and state governments has gone on ever since with varying outcomes. This independent state is weak in that it is inflexible and subject to nationalist criticism that its forms are inappropriate. It is associated with a small ruling clique and not with society as a whole, and so lacks legitimacy. This lack of legitimacy feeds corruption, which in turn contributes to the lack of legitimacy.

Westernized élites, who see themselves as heirs to colonial overlords, may seek to milk the state for all it is worth. This distorts development. Government does not plan for development and in any case cannot pay for it. The benefits accruing from control of the state so far exceed those available from other sources that desperation to control the state results, at best, in an undignified scramble which undermines its already tentative legitimacy and, at worst, in the suppression of opposition and the use of clientelism to reward political supporters. The illegitimate state often does not build that legitimacy slowly through evolution. Rather there is a tendency to frequent changes of constitutions and other superficial attempts to enhance the legitimacy of the state.

Internal insecurity goes hand-in-hand with external insecurity, which may be summarized as vulnerability due to lack of autonomy. Such weaknesses would exhibit themselves in the world market and also in the lack of power in institutions like the International Monetary Fund (IMF). US domestic policy can hit Third World states, as in the 1980s when interest rates were at historically high levels. But Third World states are also much more susceptible to natural disasters, as is evident from the very different capacity to manage flooding in Bangladesh and the Netherlands, for example.

THE 'END OF HISTORY' AS THE END OF THE THIRD WORLD?

The triumphalism of Francis Fukuyama (1992), who asserts that the liberal democratic state is the ultimate form of human social organization, is reminiscent of the unwarranted optimism of early modernization theories. These were shaped on an implied long-term blueprint based on western industrial capitalism, achievable through the operations of the global marketplace and the benevolence of the Group of Seven (G7) nations. The more mundane arguments surrounding the impact of the collapse of the Soviet Union on the continuing relevance of the concept of a Third World are twofold:

- The most obvious point is that the term's literal meaning ceases, and without a Second World the term is obsolete.
- If it is to be retained, its use is complicated by the liberation of the former Second World states from that category, and their varied and sometimes ambivalent relation to the remaining categories of First and Third Worlds. Where do the Central Asian Republics fit, the Ukraine, Russia? If they do fit in, will it be where they feel they belong, with the developed countries, or as part of the new Third World? Will the whole situation be the same in, say, two years' time anyway?

A number of points may be raised to counter such arguments:

- There is the pragmatic argument that the discipline of the Cold War and its alliances may have been a stabilizing force. This now removed makes the Third World a far more important area of study and concern, since it now constitutes in many ways a greater threat to the stability of international relations.
- There is a sense in which the collapse of the Eastern Bloc might be seen as concentrating the Third World, in that there ceases to be anywhere else to go. There are no alternatives to being poor in a western-dominated system, and, in so far as the Third World ever was polarized into two ideological camps, a division of the Third World has disappeared.
- On the other hand, the end of the Cold War does not really make much difference to the concept of a Third World, in that the term was one of self-definition for poorer states whether within the ambit of one

of the main power blocs or not. The earliest tentative moves towards the establishment of the Non-Aligned Movement (NAM), notably the Bandung Afro-Asian Solidarity Conference in 1955, included states on the basis of their independence not their ideological leanings. Cuba, despite its strong Cold War alliance with the former Soviet Union, was a leading member of the Non-Aligned Movement, as was Pakistan, despite its clear pro-western orientation.

- Most importantly, as the emphasis on self-definition suggests, those common elements which gave rise to the term 'Third World' remain valid as indicators despite the end of the Cold War. The operations of global markets may enhance the opportunities for some Third World states as First (and élite Third) World investors are attracted by potential profits from 'emerging market' funds. Thus the economic diversity of the Third World may be increased. But free markets will not end global poverty and the evidence thus far (see NICs below) is that escapees will be the exceptions.

SOCIAL AND OTHER INDICATORS

Since many concepts used routinely in political discussion, such as development, are very complex, social scientists are used to employing indicators of various kinds to measure them. Thus it has long been traditional to measure economic development in terms of a single indicator, per capita GNP: that is to say, the gross national product (GNP) of a country divided by its population. In Tables 1.1 and 1.2, selected figures for 1988 and 1992 are given. They show not only how wide is the gap between the most developed nations and the rest, but, more worryingly, how it is tending to open up, as the Third World itself is 'pulling apart'. In 1992 there was no real difference between the highest low-income country, Indonesia, and the lowest middle-income country, Côte d'Ivoire. Owing to a statistical revision, Chile, the highest lower-middle-income country, is recorded as having a higher GNP per capita than the lowest upper-middle-income country, South Africa. But not only had Saudi Arabia fallen out of the high-income category, but a substantial gap had already opened up between Saudi Arabia with a GNP per capita of $7,510 and the lowest high-income country, Ireland, with a GNP per capita of $12,210, roughly on a par with Israel.

In recent years, however, there has been increasing dissatisfaction with the crudity of this measure. To start with, comparisons of per capita GNP were rendered very difficult indeed by wide variations and wild fluctuations in exchange rates, so that the figures – if taken literally – would mean that in many countries people could not stay alive at all. Second, the indicator in itself does not show how the economic resources generated are actually used. Unless they are being channelled back into investment or social welfare, they

Table 1.1 *GNP per capita of selected states, 1988 (US$)*

Range	Population 1988	GNP per capita 1988 ($)	Growth 1965–88	Life expectancy	Adult illiteracy
Low income	2,884.0	320	3.1	60	44
1 Mozambique	14.9	100	–	48	62
17 Nigeria	110.1	290	0.9	51	58
21 China	1,088.4	330	5.4	70	31
22 India	815.6	340	1.8	58	57
29 Ghana	14.0	400	−1.6	54	47
31 Sri Lanka	16.6	420	3.0	71	13
Lower-middle income	741.7	1,380	2.6	65	27
43 Bolivia	6.9	570	−0.6	53	26
57 Thailand	54.5	1,000	4.0	65	9
60 Jamaica	2.4	1,070	−1.5	73	–
65 Turkey	53.8	1,280	2.6	64	26
71 Mexico	83.7	1,760	2.3	69	6
76 Brazil	144.4	2,160	3.6	65	22
Upper-middle income	326.3	3,240	2.3	68	24
80 S. Africa	34.0	2,290	0.8	61	–
84 Argentina	31.5	2,520	0.0	71	5
88 Trinidad	1.2	3,350	0.9	71	4
90 Portugal	10.3	3,650	3.1	74	16
91 Greece	10.0	4,800	2.9	77	8
93 Libya	4.2	5,420	−2.7	61	33
High income	784.2	17,080	2.3	76	–
97 S. Arabia	14.0	6,200	−3.8	64	–
100 Israel	4.4	8,650	2.7	76	5
104 Australia	16.5	12,340	1.8	76	a
105 UK	57.1	12,810	1.8	75	a
112 France	55.9	16,090	2.5	76	a
118 USA	246.3	19,840	1.6	76	a
120 Japan	122.6	21,020	4.3	78	a
121 Switzerland	6.6	27,500	1.5	77	a

a = UNESCO data, illiteracy less than 5%.
Source: World Bank (1990).

cannot generate further development. To give a clearer picture of what is going on, therefore, more indicators are required. Economic indicators include the actual purchasing power of the currency in terms of daily necessities, the rate of saving, the level of investment in industry and inequality of income and wealth. Social indicators include life expectancy, infant mortality rate (imr), the number of persons per doctor, the proportion

Table 1.2 *GNP per capita of selected states, 1992 (US$)*

Range	Population 1992	GNP per capita 1992 ($)	Growth 1980–92	Life expectancy	Adult illiteracy
Low income	3,191.3	390	3.9	62	40
1 Mozambique	16.6	60	-3.6	44	67
18 India	883.6	310	3.1	61	52
21 Nigeria	101.9	320	-0.4	52	49
27 Ghana	15.8	450	-0.1	56	40
28 China	1,162.2	470	–	69	27
32 Sri Lanka	17.4	540	2.6	72	12
37 Indonesia	184.3	670	4.0	60	23
Lower-middle income	1,418.7	2,490	-0.1	68	–
43 Ivory Coast	12.9	670	-4.7	56	46
44 Bolivia	7.5	680	-1.5	60	23
68 Jamaica	2.4	1,340	0.2	74	2
75 Thailand	58.0	1,840	6.0	69	7
80 Turkey	58.5	1,980	2.9	67	19
85 Chile	13.6	2,730*	3.7	72	7
Upper-middle income	477.7	4,020	0.8	69	15
80 S. Africa	39.8	2,670	0.1	63	–
92 Brazil	153.9	2,770	0.4	66	19
99 Mexico	85.0	3,470	-0.2	70	13
100 Trinidad	1.3	3,940	-2.6	71	–
102 Argentina	33.1	6,050	-0.9	71	5
107 Greece	10.3	7,290	1.0	77	7
108 Portugal	9.8	7,450	3.1	74	15
109 S. Arabia	16.8	7,510	-3.3	69	38
High income	828.1	22,160	4.3	77	–
110 Ireland	3.5	12,210	3.4	75	–
112 Israel	5.1	13,220	1.9	76	–
116 Australia	17.5	17,260	1.6	77	a
117 UK	57.8	17,790	2.4	76	a
124 France	57.4	22,260	1.7	77	a
127 USA	255.4	23,240	1.7	77	a
131 Japan	124.5	28,190	3.6	79	a
132 Switzerland	6.9	36,080	1.4	78	a

a = UNESCO data, illiteracy less than 5%.
* = revised upwards from 2,510.
Source: World Bank (1994).

of children in school and the percentage of adults who are able to read and write. Political indicators include governmental instability, the frequency of elections and the tendency to military intervention.

In 1990 the UN Development Programme published the *Human Development Report*, which used for the first time the Human Development Index (HDI). This ranked countries by a single measure which included social indicators such as life expectancy and adult literacy, but also included economic/social aspects like basic purchasing power. Since then the HDI has been refined to take account of early criticisms, but the basic principle that the general well-being of a country's population can be expressed in terms of a very small number of key indicators has stood the test of time (United Nations Development Programme 1994).

Some general conclusions emerge very clearly from Table 1.3, which is based on figures from 1988. Comparison with Table 1.1 shows how, with the effects of exchange rates taken out, the differences within countries can be seen to be as important as, if not more important than, the differences between them. The percentage in poverty is highest in South Asia and Africa South of the Sahara. South Asia has 30 per cent of the world's population, but nearly half the world's poor. Average life expectancy is 76 years in the developed world, 56 years in South Asia and 50 years in Africa South of the Sahara. Moreover, these effects are reflected in wide disparities within Third World states – in Mexico (where average life expectancy in 1992 was 70), life expectancy for the poorest 10 per cent is 20 years less than for the richest 10 per cent.

THE FUTURE

The view of the future of the Third World can be either optimistic or pessimistic. The optimistic view is as follows:

- Third World economic growth is good if we compare such countries with the condition of the now-developed nations when they were at the same stage of development.
- Third World manufacturers are increasing their share of the developed world's markets.
- Third World countries are experiencing rising life expectancy, literacy, etc.

However, according to the pessimistic view:

- The income gap between the Third World and the First World is still colossal. GNP per capita of Switzerland is $36,080 per year. This is 13 times that of Brazil, but 601 times that of Mozambique (*World Development Report, 1994*, 1992 figures). But although the economy of Brazil is growing rapidly, that of Mozambique is stagnant, so at present it seems to have little hope of catching up even with Brazil, let alone

Table 1.3 *HDI of selected states, 1988*

Range	Life expectancy	Educational attainment	Adj. real GDP/capita	HDI	GNP/capita minus HDI rank
Low HD	55.8	1.55	1,170	0.355	
173 Guinea	43.9	0.60	500	0.191	44
170 S. Leone	42.4	0.53	1,020	0.209	−7
159 Mozambique	46.5	0.78	921	0.252	14
139 Nigeria	51.9	1.12	1,360	0.348	6
135 India	59.7	1.16	1,150	0.382	12
134 Ghana	55.4	1.50	930	0.382	−1
Medium HD	68.0			0.649	
94 China	70.5	1.93	2,946	0.644	49
90 Sri Lanka	71.2	2.26	2,650	0.665	38
113 Bolivia	60.5	1.85	2,170	0.530	6
54 Thailand	68.7	2.14	5,144	0.798	28
65 Jamaica	73.3	2.32	3,670	0.749	22
68 Turkey	66.7	1.88	4,840	0.739	10
63 Brazil	65.8	1.91	5,142	0.756	−11
93 S. Africa	62.2	1.86	3,885	0.650	−33
79 Libya	62.4	1.57	5,207	0.703	−38
67 S. Arabia	68.7	1.54	5,289	0.742	−36
High HD	74.1			0.886	
37 Argentina	71.1	2.53	5,120	0.853	6
35 Trinidad	70.9	2.48	5,234	0.855	11
42 Portugal	74.4	2.15	2,252	0.838	−5
25 Greece	77.3	2.34	5,221	0.874	10
19 Israel	76.2	3.69	5,307	0.900	6
7 Australia	76.7	2.78	5,339	0.926	11
10 UK	75.8	2.76	5,337	0.919	9
6 France	76.6	2.78	5,345	0.927	7
8 USA	75.6	2.81	5,371	0.925	1
3 Japan	78.6	2.70	5,347	0.929	0
2 Switzerland	77.8	2.75	5,370	0.931	−1
1 Canada	77.2	2.80	5,347	0.932	10

Source: United Nations Development Programme (1994).

Switzerland. The irony is that the best Third World growth rates are to be found in the richest Third World countries, and in all the major regions of the world there are the same huge variations. In Africa, for example, Botswana has one of the fastest growth rates in the world, while much of the rest of the region falls into the 'least developed' category and has stagnant or declining economies. There are striking variations within countries too. For example, in Indonesia Java is rich, and Sumatra poor.

- The energy gap between the rich countries and the poor ones is so vast that the only remedy for it seems to be to discover oil or natural gas.
- The social gap, whether in life expectancy/health, education/literacy or otherwise, is increasing within the Third World if not between the average of Third World and First World states.

This 'pulling apart' has contributed to the idea that the concept of the Third World no longer has any value, and not simply because of the 'disappearance' of the Second World (see Chapter 14). We can summarize the arguments for and against the question of whether the concept of a Third World is any longer valid as follows.

Those who believe that it is still valid point first and foremost to general social indicators. Third World countries, for them, are those that have a lower per capita income, a higher percentage living in poverty, lower life-expectancy, higher imr and less access to education and other social services. Geographically, they are located in 'the South', and suffer from climatic disadvantages not accompanied by the economic and/or technological means to resolve them. Most but not all have undergone colonization and have become independent quite recently. During the Cold War, however, they were located outside the main power blocs despite possible alliances and the risk of superpower intervention. Hence they have exhibited the tendency to self-definition in terms of a 'third bloc', such as the Group of 77 and NAM. They retain a peripheral position in a global economic system created and sustained by the industrial economies.

Critics of the notion of a Third World point first to the massive disparities within the Third World, even if the oil-rich states are taken out and a 'Fourth World' of the very poorest states is created within regions of the Third World and within states. Geographically, they are also very diverse in advantages/disadvantages of location – compare the rich grasslands of Argentina and the semi-desert regions of Ethiopia. Historically, their experiences were totally different, not only in different colonizing powers' agendas, but also in variations in how and when independence was achieved. Different local traditions and attitudes of national leaders resulted in very diverse experiences of the Cold War. Last but not least, the very economic criteria that once seemed to unite them seem no longer to apply. Economic systems are seen to be constantly changing, in particular with the rise of the NICs and the 'pulling apart' of the Third World in the 1980s. There have been massive gains in East Asia, some gains in South Asia, some loss of development in Latin America, and near total disaster for many countries of Africa South of the Sahara. These arguments can be summarized in tabular form (Table 1.4).

The old order is changing, although as yet the nationalist perception of the world survives, continuing to recognize obsolete categories and to obscure the

Table 1.4 *Arguments for and against the validity of the concept of a Third World*

For	Against
Economics	
Lower per capita income, higher percentage living in poverty, lower life expectancy, higher imr, less access to education and other social services.	Massive disparities both within Third World and within states, even if oil-rich states taken out and Fourth World of poorest created. Vague concept which obscures more than it illuminates – all societies contain their own 'Fourth Worlds'.
Geography	
Location in 'South', climatic disadvantages not accompanied by the economic/tecnological means to resolve them.	Very diverse in advantages/ disadvantages of location – compare rich grasslands of Argentina and semi-desert regions of Ethiopia.
History	
Few exceptions to colonial experience, resultant distortions in economies, national boundaries, etc. Cold War location outside main power blocs, despite possible alliances; hence self-definition, e.g. Group of 77 and NAM, but subject to consequences of superpower struggles, e.g. Somalia.	Experiences totally different, not only in different colonizing powers' agendas, but also in variations in how and when independence was achieved. Variations in perceived strategic importance. Different location traditions and attitudes of national leaders resulted in very diverse experience of the Cold War.
Marginality	
Peripheral position in the global economic system created and sustained by the industrial economies.	Economic system constantly changing, e.g. rise of the NICs, 1980s pulling apart of Third World with massive gains in East Asia, some in South Asia, some loss of development in Latin America, disaster for many countries of Africa South of the Sahara.

real inequalities, such as those between the rich of India and the poor of the southern United States. Nigel Harris exemplifies this view:

Thirdworldism began as a critique of an unequal world, a programme for economic development and justice, a type of national reformism dedicated to the creation of new societies and a new world. It ends with its leading protagonists either dead, defeated or satisfied to settle simply for national power rather than international equality; the rhetoric remains, now toothless, the decoration for squabbles over the pricing of commodities or flows of capital. (1986: 200)

PERSPECTIVES

An optimistic view of the future of the Third World tends to be associated with a political perspective which might generally be considered 'right-wing'. Central among such thought is the neo-liberal or neo-classical school. Many who hold neo-liberal or neo-classical views of economics believe that the operation of the global 'invisible hand' will eventually advantage the Third World, enabling it to break out from its present impoverished position.

'Disadvantage' theories, often known as 'cumulative disadvantage' theories, hold that disadvantage compounds disadvantage, although better results can be obtained, at least in part, by better understanding of the process of development, including the judicious use of interventionist measures by Third World governments, often part of policies of import substitution. These measures were, of course, the developmental solutions advocated by some early dependency theorists (notably Raúl Prebisch).

The free operation of markets, thought by neo-liberals to be the means to overcome the rigidities holding back the Third World, is viewed as pessimistically by the Left now as it was in the 1960s before the ascendancy of the neo-liberal school. (Thus an anti-free-trade position is both initiative and response in relation to the neo-liberal position.) The problem remains the same for nations not advantaged during the nineteenth century. Free markets create unequal exchange and advantage the most powerful. A social-democratic or reformist position accepts these difficulties, but argues that they can be overcome by a combination of self-imposed limitations by the advanced industrialized countries and concerted action by the UN and other agencies.

However, others argue that the assumption that trade will grow in the absence of controls (so evident in the debate over the Uruguay Round of the GATT – see Chapter 11) will not, as hoped, eventually overcome poverty and enable comparative advantage to equalize the situation, because the rich countries have 'weighted the dice'. They did not and will not themselves rely on the free play of the market and risk losing those advantages. Such an argument is sometimes labelled 'structural'. In some ways this term is as misleading as terms such as neo-liberal or orthodox, because all market arguments stress some structure or another, sometimes the structure of world trade, sometimes the structure of global capitalism. Usually 'structuralism' is a term specifically applied to the Marxist/neo-Marxist school and dependency theories, which can be both Marxist/neo-Marxist and non-Marxist.

The way forward for the Third World, and what development is, are differently perceived by the different schools. For neo-liberals the main rigidities or obstacles to development are the deadweight of traditionalism and state interference, which function to limit the dynamic forces of personal initiative and competition. There are echoes here of the theories of Talcott Parsons and Seymour Martin Lipset, US sociologists who sought to identify specific characteristics of traditional and modern society.

Most schools accept industrialization as what development is. Only radical schools question it. Among these we can single out, for their originality and special interest, the 'greens' and feminist thinkers, although they question it for very different reasons. The greens want smaller-scale, less damaging technologies and are forced by the logic of their own argument to question the assumption of growth itself. Feminist writers distrust the very nature of industrial society as it currently exists. They reject its masculine values and they see no possibility of balanced development without the full participation of women in the development process. Again we can sum up the various positions of the rival schools in tabular form, provided we do not take them too rigidly as definitions (see Table 1.5).

THEMES OF THE BOOK

The twin themes of this book, therefore, are environment and development. Environment has shaped, and is continuing to shape, the politics and society of the Third World. At the same time, the impact of development is increasingly changing the environment in ways that look likely to test to the limit the human capacity to adapt.

Third World countries generally see industrialization as the key to development, and with good reason. It is what the advanced industrialized countries have that they do not have. But times have changed and the capital for development will come from abroad: thus in the 1980s China encouraged foreign investment in industrialization. The disadvantage of this is the extent to which this will simply mean some limited development in a Third World country rather than the development of that country, since development of a country holds little interest for foreign companies investing there. Effective development must incorporate some genuine improvement in the quality of life for the majority of a country's population and not just for a western-oriented élite. Those countries that have been most successful at development in recent years are precisely those in which wealth is spread most widely. For reasons which will be discussed later, the quality of development must include all aspects of development: political and social as well as economic. Displaced First World pollution or continuing western-supported authoritarian rule cannot be seen as development.

Table 1.5 Perspectives compared

	Liberal/neoclassical	Disadvantage	Structural/dependency	Social democratic/reformist	Ecological-green	Religious world-view	Feminist
Proponents	Rostow, OECD	Myrdal	Baran, Amin, various schools	Brandt, UNCTAD	Brundtland, Greenpeace	John Paul II, the Ayatollahs	V. Shiva, E. Boserup, etc.
Optimistic/pessimistic	Optimistic – trickle-down	Generally pessimistic	Degree of pessimism varies, non-Marxist most	Cautiously optimistic	Generally pessimistic	Millenarian	Generally pessimistic
Emphasis on	The operation of markets, equilibrium	Development economics	World capitalist system, global class structure	North-South division; basic needs	Sustainable development	Personal salvation	Role of women in development process
View of TNCs	Transfer advantages	Good for thriving region, not others	Exploit Third World	Advanced industrial countries need to control	Destructive beyond redemption	Foreign, therefore suspect	Male, therefore suspect
Vulnerable groups	Will eventually benefit	Third World generally	Peripheries	South	Ultimately all living things; immediately the world's poor	Poor, meek, downtrodden	Women
Development solution	Break-out is inevitable	Possible escape with overflow from advantaged countries	Structural inequality; escape only possible with (a) fall of capitalism or (b) independent form	North-South dialogue; concerted action by UN agencies	Restrict growth, control pollution, encourage return to pastoral state	God	Women
Environmental problems	Irrelevant – the market will resolve when the time is right	Exported pollution from developed countries	By-product of capitalism; remedy social revolution	Tends to rely on technological 'fix'	Supreme crisis of humanity in one lifetime	The Lord will provide	Created by men

In the rest of Part I, Chapter 2 looks at the natural environment, the shape and structure of the Third World and the geographical factors that give it a distinctive identity. In Chapter 3 the nature of the crisis that confronts the Third World will be examined in more detail.

In Part II we turn to the human environment, and the economic (Chapter 4), social (Chapter 5) and cultural (Chapter 6) context of Third World states and their decision-makers will be examined in turn.

Part III deals more specifically with the politics of the Third World, with the problem of state-building (Chapter 7), political participation (Chapter 8), the special role of the armed forces (Chapter 9) and the international pressures that shape Third World life and society (Chapter 10).

In Part IV we return to policy issues: the right to development (Chapter 11), the role of women and of indigenous peoples in a developing world (Chapter 12), and the international politics of the environment and the growing North–South divide (Chapter 13). Finally, in a concluding chapter (Chapter 14) we speculate about the immediate future.

2 The shape of the Third World

PHYSICAL LOCATION

Christopher Clapham defines the Third World, as usually regarded, as comprising 'the Americas south of the United States; the whole of Africa; Asia apart from the Soviet Union, China and Japan; and the oceanic islands apart from Australia and New Zealand' (1985: 1). This does not make for a neat conceptual package in geographical terms. The Third World is not a geographical unit, but a state of mind.

Yet some kind of division has to be made and the rival term, 'the South', is no less misleading in the geographical sense. As can be seen from the map which illustrated the Brandt Report and which familiarized many people with a non-Mercator projection for the first time, the line which demarcated 'the South' meanders across the northern hemisphere before plunging southwards to exclude Japan, Australia and New Zealand (see Figure 2.1).

There are also more specific questions that could be raised about the definition as it stands. Even in 1985 the inclusion of South Africa in the Third World was a little odd. China is not included because it was part of that Second World which was perceived to exist before the collapse of the USSR. Its size makes it virtually impossible to ignore, but its inclusion (or exclusion) may distort our view of other Third World countries. (Similarly, generalizations about South Asia are distorted by the sheer human weight of India.) In 1995 we would need to distinguish between the different parts of the former Soviet Union if trying to apply Clapham's definition.

Last but not least, the meaning of 'the oceanic islands' is far from clear, and is certainly not the same as the islands of Oceania, which is what most people would probably expect it to mean.

As regards map projections, Mercator's, used in Europe since the sixteenth century, exaggerates the relative size and hence the visual impact of the North. Only at the Equator is latitude correct in relation to longitude. The distortion becomes infinite at the poles, turning the Antarctic into a white smudge round the bottom of the map. The effect is even more dramatic with a polar projection such as that which graces the flag of the UN itself. Exaggeration has its value – a circular map of the world centred on New Zealand places Antarctica in the near foreground, which says much about the relationship between the two territories. But it transforms Spain and Portugal

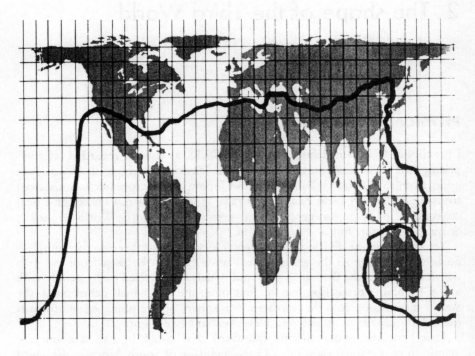

Figure 2.1 *The North–South divide according to Brandt.*

into a thin brown line round the edge. The currently favoured Peters Projection (used by Brandt), which distributes the distortions between the Equator and the poles, renders more accurately the proportions between the more and less densely inhabited parts of the earth. It is more appropriate than older projections, therefore, to enable the viewer to understand the relative importance both of the Third World as a whole and of individual countries within it. Unfortunately, it would be of little or no use in helping you to get from one part of the Third World to another, unless you wanted to go due North–South or East–West.

Redrawing the map of the world to reflect, in terms of relative area, non-geographical variables such as wealth or political power is, unfortunately, impossible without distorting spatial relationships to a point at which they become completely unrecognizable. However, any map of the world that differentiates countries by, say, their place in the World Bank classification by per capita income, is a useful corrective to the simple North–South model, if only because it shows up very clearly the secondary concentration of wealth in the oil-rich countries of the Middle East (see Figure 2.2).

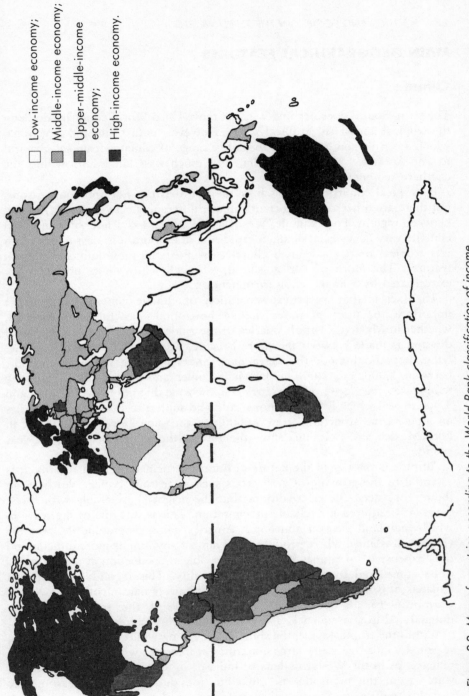

Figure 2.2 *Map of countries according to the World Bank classification of income.*

Low-income economy;

Middle-income economy;

Upper-middle-income economy;

High-income economy.

MAIN GEOGRAPHICAL FEATURES

Climate

The term 'South' does not imply it, but most Third World countries do lie in the tropical and/or sub-tropical zones. However, both Chile and Argentina, which are truly southern, span the entire range of climates from sub-tropical to sub-Antarctic. Outer Mongolia, and much of China, falls within the northern temperate zone.

In tropical countries there is little division between hot and cool seasons, but there are other very important climatic differences between countries and between regions. For example, West/Central Africa has a hot wet equatorial climate, very heavy rainfall and a rapid rate of evaporation. East Africa has a wet tropical or dry savannah climate, owing to its mountain and plateau features. The Horn of Africa is arid, although many of its problems are exacerbated by human action (or inaction).

The fact is that a vertical separation of climate zones is often more important for most purposes than a horizontal one. In Latin America, whether in Mexico, Central America or the Andean countries, the traditional division is made between the *tierra caliente*, below 1,000 m, which is low-lying, hot and humid; the *tierra templada*, lying at a moderate altitude, between 1,000 and 2,000 m, which is cooler and so capable of growing temperate zone crops; and the *tierra fría*, the zone that lies between 2,000 and 3,000 m and which is mountainous, cold and subject to frost. Above that lies an alpine zone stretching from 3,000 m to the snow-line over 4,500 m. In both Mexico and Colombia snow remains on the highest peaks all the year round.

Altitude is the key to the nature of human settlement in such regions. It is essential to the growing of cash crops such as tea and coffee. Not only do these crops need cooler conditions, but the height – preferably with forest cover – is required for reliable precipitation. This is just one of the ways in which mainland Central and South America gains geographically over the Caribbean islands, where production of almost anything is more difficult and thus expensive. Of course, if cost is of no object, production at the margin is often considered to be of the highest quality. This is said of Caribbean bananas; it is indisputably true of Blue Mountain Jamaican coffee. Low-lying Caribbean islands lack moisture, and many of the smaller ones are uninhabited in consequence. The Bahamas rely on imported water.

Within the tropical zone, the shifts in prevailing winds bring the monsoon, seasonal winds that carry large quantities of moisture with them; hence local reliance, as in the Western Ghats of India or in Sri Lanka, on the storage of water from the monsoon in 'tanks' to use during the dry season. The complexity of the patterns involved even in a small area like Sri Lanka (which is about the same size as Ireland) is shown by the fact that the north-east (mid-October to mid-February) and south-west (April to June) monsoons affect different parts of the island: part of the island, notably the main city Colombo, gets both, and other parts get neither and are arid. The Sinhalese monarch Parakramabahu I (1153–86) ordered the construction of tanks with the well-known phrase: 'Let not one drop of water reach the sea without first serving man' (Insight 1986: 27). So assiduous were the workers that in 1904 11,200 tanks could still be counted, many feeding dense networks of irrigation canals. The largest, the Parakrama Samudra, is bounded by a wall 9 miles long and of an average height of 40 ft.

If a country uses less than 10 per cent of its annual renewable water resources, it is unlikely to experience shortages of water. China and most of southern Asia use more than this, but not more than 20 per cent, so shortages, when they do occur, occur on a regional rather than a national basis. But of the 25 countries using more than 20 per cent of their resources, 11, in the Middle East, are already using more than half, and over the next 25 years the most critical area for freshwater supplies is expected to be Africa (UNFPA 1992). Access to water resources is likely to become more problematic and more subject to international disputes in the very near future (Thomas and Howlett 1992).

Relief

There are major geological fault lines under both developed (Japan, the western United States, Iceland, Greece, New Zealand) and Third World countries (Iran, Indonesia, Philippines, Peru, Colombia, Mexico). The relative geological stability of much of the United States, Canada, northern Europe and northern Asia is undoubtedly an asset to economic and social development, although Japan, a model for much of today's world, is spectacularly unstable and experiences on average 700 earthquakes a year. However, as we shall see later, the incidence of natural disasters may be the same, but the impact of them is much less in developed states.

The massive block of the Himalayas determines much of the geography, as it does much of the climate, of a sizeable section of the Third World. They are high enough to interrupt the orderly circulation of winds in the Indian Ocean that takes place in the Pacific, and the result is the monsoon. In South America, the Andes, the highest and longest major cordillera of young fold mountains, are geologically extremely active. Extensive trough faulting gives stepwise topography, and volcanoes and earthquakes attest to continuing upward movement of strata, as do the raised beaches along the coast which helped the formation of the great nitrate fields. The Andes, like the Himalayas, are a major climatic barrier, and it is now thought that the formation of both ranges was responsible for ending the relative warmth of the Tertiary era and bringing about the onset of the Ice Ages.

Today mountains still have a great importance for human beings. They establish political boundaries, structure communications, source major rivers, yield important minerals, and provide temperate foothills and low uplands where human settlement is safer and more comfortable than on the plains. Even smaller mountain ranges have a regional/local significance. The only frontier between the First and Third Worlds which consists of no more than a line on a map is that between the United States and Mexico. Otherwise the Mediterranean, the Dardanelles, the Caucasus Mountains and other features act as natural barriers.

Mountain-building (orogenic) processes continue under water, A celebrated underwater fault line encloses the Caribbean, stretching from the Virgin Islands by way of Puerto Rico to the Dominican Republic, where west of the Cordillera de Cibao it forks, giving to the north the northern peninsula of Haiti, the Sierra Maestra of Cuba and the Cayman Islands, and to the south the southern peninsula of Haiti and Jamaica. Though relatively quiet at present, the volcanic origin of the Lesser Antilles has been accompanied by dramatic evidence of its continuing importance, notably the explosion of Mont Pelée on Martinique in 1902. Vulcanism in both Indonesia and the Philippines, similarly, has had a regional and indeed global significance.

Rivers

Great river basins have everywhere been the seat of the earliest known human civilizations, both in the Middle East (the Nile and the Tigris/Euphrates) and in East Asia (Yangtse, Hoang Ho, Mekong). Great rivers formed the major routes both into and out of new areas in Europe and North America (St Lawrence, Mississippi–Missouri, Rhine, Danube) in the era before wheeled land travel became a reasonably convenient alternative to transport by water. The celebrated amber route from the Baltic to Byzantium ('Middlegarth' to the Northerners) followed the rivers. In Asia, the Jordan, Tigris–Euphrates, Indus, Ganges–Brahmaputra, Irrawaddy, Salween, Mekong, Yellow River and Yangtze have all helped shape the distribution of human settlement.

In North America, the two great navigable river systems account for the growth of and still serve Canada and the United States. Mexico has to share the waters of the Colorado and the Rio Grande with the United States. Neither is navigable and heavy use has reduced the Rio Grande to a muddy trickle. Most of Mexico's rivers flow directly and seasonally from the Sierra Madre to the sea.

In South America, on the other hand, the situation is very different. The Magdalena, Orinoco and Amazon, and the Parana, which with its tributaries and the Uruguay flows into the estuary called the Rio de la Plata, are all navigable, while others, the Tocantins and São Francisco in Brazil, and the Colorado, Negro and Chubut in Argentina, fulfil other important local needs.

In Africa, apart from the Nile, the Zambesi, Orange, Congo–Zaire, Niger and Senegal rivers have similarly acted as traffic routes since well before the age of colonial penetration. Of all the major regions of the world, only Oceania lacks major river systems, with the rather doubtful exception, perhaps, of the Murray River in Australia.

The value of navigable river systems lies, above all, in their connection with the sea. However, the sea links not only navigable rivers, but coastal and island civilizations, such as Japan, China, Korea and Taiwan. The sea has the distinctive property of joining all coastal points on the globe with one another, without the need for the navigator to go through territory controlled by others.

All fresh water comes ultimately from the sea in the form of precipitation. The sea is also the great motor of climate. Recently scientists have begun to realize, now that they can measure them more accurately and over the whole of the world's surface, that changes in sea temperature and current have massive effects on regional climates. It had long been known that 'El Niño' affected the flow of the cold Humboldt Current northwards along the west coast of South America, causing the fish harvest to fail. Only in the last few years has it become clear that the shift in this current, which has its beginning in the positioning of some relatively small islands some 3,000 km out in the Pacific, has a direct effect on climatic conditions not only in South America generally, but in North America as well, leading, for example, to the hot summer of 1994. Global warming poses a serious threat to the Third World, especially where, as we shall see, the effects of drought are amplified by the degradation of the land through overuse. Drought in turn causes changes in river use. The controversial Sardar Sarovar dam on the Narmada River in India was designed to cope with the droughts in Gujarat occasioned by the failure of the monsoon (Vajpeyi 1994).

Human action has the greatest impact on river systems. The most recent human use of rivers is for the generation of hydroelectric power. This is quite possible even where rivers are not navigable, as in the case of the Bumbuna Falls project in Sierra Leone.

Boundaries

Frontiers are influenced by and in turn influence geography. In some parts of the world, notably in Europe, international boundaries have not only been agreed, but are formally demarcated by the placing of posts, fences or checkpoints. In the case of Third World countries, this is often not the case.

The major influence on present-day international boundaries in the Third World has been colonial expansion. Time and again the frontiers between colonial empires were settled by diplomatic conferences by people who had no first-hand knowledge of the areas and features to which they were referring. In addition, only occasionally were they formally demarcated.

Hence unless they follow the lines of rivers, they often cut across the territories of indigenous peoples or tribes. A classic example of this is in West Africa, where British settlements in The Gambia, Sierra Leone, Ghana and Nigeria adjoin states that were formerly part of French West Africa. Prescott quotes a Yoruba chief in Dahomey (now Benin), separated by the colonial frontier from the majority of his tribe in Nigeria, as saying: 'We regard the boundary as separating the French and the English, not the Yoruba' (Prescott 1965: 63). The same may be said of East Africa, where Uganda exemplifies the arbitrary nature of colonial boundaries. An even odder example is to be found in southern Africa, where Namibia's boundaries are extended eastwards into the narrow Caprivi Strip running between Angola and Botswana to Barotseland in what is now Zambia. This illogical feature was originally intended to allow the former colonial power, Germany, to build a railway to link its East and West African territories.

The potential for boundary disputes is great and is not helped by the fact that many colonial-period treaties did not refer to identifiable physical features, but assumed the existence of a boundary that was well known to all concerned at the time.

AGRICULTURAL ACTIVITY

Land tenure and production

Inequality in land ownership is not confined to the Third World. Australia, an advanced industrial country, has one of the most unequal land distribution ratios in the world as measured by the Gini index, the standard measure of land inequality. However, the Third World is distinguished by the survival of traditional cultivation, even if this is now often under threat. It is important to distinguish between peasants – cultivators who have traditional rights to land – and plantation workers on large estates, who work for wages.

Peasants have (1) access to land, (2) family labour, (3) small-scale technology and (4) ability to generate surplus in a cash economy. Even small-scale technology requires cash for purchase and maintenance. Peasants make up some 80 per cent of farm workers in the Third World.

Traditional peasant cultivation was balanced between the need to produce for subsistence and exchange, and the need to conserve. The key requirement is production for subsistence. This is conditioned by the nature of the crops available, and there are three major variants based on the following crops:

- Wheat (sub-tropical, temperate) – Europe, North-West Africa, Middle East, 'Southern Cone' of South America.
- Rice (tropical, humid) – South, South-East and East Asia, West Africa.
- Maize (sub-tropical, dry) – Americas, East Africa.

Production for subsistence is based on traditional knowledge and understanding of the needs of the soil. It is therefore resilient and, because of its varied nature and limited expectations, forms the best possible protection for the poor against the possibility of famine. The big problem with subsistence farming is that, as population expands, the land areas cultivated are subdivided until production is often barely adequate, implying that large sectors of the population must be malnourished. Because peasants are producing large-bulk, low-value crops in the main, they are also not very productive in monetary terms, which leads their contribution to be underestimated by those in the so-called modern sector of the economy.

With rising population, too many people in the Third World are working too little land. There are two possible 'solutions': land reform by redistribution, which is politically difficult with the vested interests involved, and land colonization. The latter is, of course, only possible where land is available. Increases in the 1970s in the land area cultivated in Latin America, China, and South and South-East Asia have been considerable, although at the cost of damage to marginal land and its fragile ecosystems. The 'carrying capacity' of the land – that is to say, the number of people a given area can support – has also been increased at least temporarily, as a result of the 'green revolution', involving the use of high-yielding strains and chemical fertilizers. On the other hand, there has been a marked decline in the production of both wheat and maize in Africa, despite (or because of) the increase in production of cash crops for export, such as tobacco and cotton.

The most successful way found so far to increase the carrying capacity of land is by the wet cultivation of rice. Techniques developed thousands of years ago have proved capable of being used over long historical periods without degrading the land: the silt brought down by the irrigation water acting to replenish the soil and the conditions of cultivation helping to maintain neutral acidity. Where conditions are extremely favourable, in Sumatra, the technique produces as many as three crops of rice a year. Two are normal in the south of China, where there is and has been for centuries extensive use of vegetable composts, green manure and both animal and human wastes ('night soil') to maintain and enhance the fertility of the soil. However, the normal pattern is one crop of rice, alternating with other crops such as sweet potatoes or vegetables, which may be grown without irrigation during the dry season.

Wet rice cultivation has spread from its original heartland in Asia to West Africa (Ghana, Nigeria) and Latin America (Brazil, Guyana), not to mention the USA (South Carolina). It requires level, well-watered soils which can be rendered watertight by 'puddling'. It is also very labour intensive, although it can in favourable conditions ensure the necessary security for farmers to grow a wide range of more speculative crops for market. A drawback is that rice production by this method accounts for a significant increase in the production of methane, one of the 'greenhouse gases'.

Estates vary a great deal. They have existed in their present form in Latin America since the sixteenth century, and Brazil has experienced three successive 'boom' periods in sugar, rubber and coffee respectively. In South Asia, plantations have been established since the nineteenth century, producing tea and cotton. In tropical Africa, plantation agriculture often dates only from the beginning of the twentieth century, and crops produced include cocoa, peanuts and palm oil. Of course, a considerable part of plantation production is consumed within the Third World itself (for example, before the Gulf War Iraq was the major consumer of Sri Lankan tea). Nor are all plantation crops necessarily in direct competition with local food production. Tree and shrub crops such as tea and coffee usually occupy a relatively small part of a country's cultivated land. Even bananas, which as a cultivated crop are very wasteful of land, are largely grown for consumption within the Third World.

Land colonization has a detrimental effect on the land, usually resulting in permanent land clearance. Initially the methods are very similar to that of traditional 'slash-and-burn' agriculture. This is still practised, usually in tropical rainforest, sometimes in savannah. The main locations which have been significant in recent years have been Central America, Western Amazonia, West/Central/East Africa, the Philippines, Malaysia and Indonesia. A fresh site is selected, trees are cut down, larger tree stumps are left in place and then branches, twigs and bushes are burnt, leaving the charred landscape covered with a layer of wood ash, which acts as a fertilizer. Intercropping of species is normal, and the system, which was devised for local crops such as manioc and cassava, has successfully assimilated crops introduced from elsewhere.

However, when intensively practised the results are very different. 'Slash-and-burn' cultivation can be used successfully over very long periods provided not too much is asked of the land. But the fertility of the thin forest soils falls off rapidly, and yields in the third year are normally only half that of the first. The success of the method therefore depends on cultivation of relatively small patches which are shifted every two or three years. One or two years of crops in Brazilian/West African/South-East Asian rainforest are followed by periods of fallow varying between eight and fifteen years, during which secondary vegetation is re-established and the forest begins to regenerate. It is impossible to accelerate this cycle without damage, but this is in effect what the new settlers are trying to do. Land clearance opens up areas to permanent settlement. Population growth leads to a reduction in fallow periods. Global demand leads to the sale (or usurpation) of the land by large landowners or corporations, followed by intensive cultivation by mechanical and chemical means, and attempts to realize increased profit, in particular by the introduction of ranching after the initial decline in fertility. The result is the permanent degradation of the land, resulting over time in a general decline of its carrying capacity in the face of rising demand.

Paul Harrison gives the example of the village of Ambodiaviavy, near Ranomafana in Madagascar (Harrison 1992). This was carved out of the forest in 1947 by eight families, numbering in all 32 people, who settled on the valley bottom. Between 1947 and 1980 a combination of the natural growth of population and the arrival of new settlers from the overcrowded plateaux raised the population of the village to 320. With the best land already occupied in the 1950s, cultivation gradually spread up the hills on both sides of the valley. However, at the same time existing family holdings were subdivided to give new plots to children at marriage, so most of the plots of the 36 families resident in 1980 were too small to feed the family. Families responded in a variety of ways. Some sold part of their plot, making their situation worse rather than better. Others tried to carve out new plots from the steep forest land higher up the mountain. Not only was this land relatively unproductive, but in a short time their need for food forced them to cut down on the vital fallow period needed for the land to recuperate, with the result that its capacity to regenerate was being permanently impaired. In a single generation the families had gone from relative affluence to poverty.

Madagascar is a big enough island still to be able in theory to feed all its inhabitants. However, the Food and Agriculture Organization (FAO) has identified a number of 'critical zones' where land resources were already inadequate to feed their 1975 populations. Most of these were areas subject to severe land degradation, where the natural carrying capacity of the land was already seriously impaired, and their total population was in excess of a billion (Higgins *et al.* 1982).

Marketing and supply

The development of towns was initially the result of grain cultivation and the need for protected storage. Towns soon found themselves forced into alliance or conflict with local big landowners for political power. Towns need a rural hinterland to ensure their feeding. The long-term trend everywhere has been first the expansion of towns and then the urbanization of the countryside. The concentration of wealth in the towns made them a tempting target, and an alliance with local landowners offered them necessary protection for their markets, in return for a considerable profit for the landowners. The growth of populations was accelerated by irrigation and the development of wet rice farming where this was possible.

Getting products to market, however, implies some element of food preservation. The traditional methods developed in the neolithic era were drying (pulses, tubers, meat), smoking (meat, fish) and the use of salt or brine (fish, meat). Canning uses more modern technology, but still does not rely on the availability of a power supply for storage. Refrigeration, first developed in the mid-nineteenth century but much extended in the past 40 years, opened up the possibility of marketing high-quality products. The success of the application of preservation and marketing techniques to agriculture, or 'agribusiness' as it is now often known, is that it creates added value in the end product and ensures its marketability. Bananas and other soft fruit depend for almost all their very high value in the shops on the measures that have been taken to get them there.

Speeding up transport makes the preservation and marketing of food much easier. Since the traditional overland routes from Europe to the East were blocked by Turkish expansion, first the Portuguese and then the Spaniards sought the way to the East by water. The Portuguese empire was built on the spice trade, and though later disputed by Dutch and English traders, it will, when Macau reverts to China in 1999, have lasted just over 500 years. Fast clipper ships brought tea to Britain in the nineteenth century; in the twentieth century the steamship made tropical produce available widely for the first time. In recent years it has become possible for Third World produce to be sold in the advanced industrial countries competitively even at the time of year at which their own produce is in season, while even a slight variation of the harvest season enables Mexican fruit to be sold in the United States when direct competition with Florida and California might make this seem impossible. Many Third World countries' dependence on an external market is reflected in the nature and orientation of their communication links, by land or water.

Mining

If the Portuguese empire was built on the spice trade, the main motivating factor in Spanish colonial expansion was the search for gold and silver. However, by the end of the 1980s the major producers of gold were two oddly matched but relatively developed states, South Africa and the former Soviet Union. Meanwhile, Third World states had been the scene of colonial and post-colonial rivalries over access to a whole variety of mineral deposits, and the latest gold rush has been taking place in the northern part of Brazilian Amazonia.

Brazil is also a major producer of a more dangerous metal, uranium. UN intervention in the Congo (now Zaire) in 1960 was at least partly fuelled by concern at the strategic importance of the mineral deposits of Katanga Province to a nuclear or potential nuclear power. Since that time, however, it has become clear that uranium is in fact distributed quite widely on the earth's surface. Though this lowers its strategic importance to individual Third World states, it also has the incidental disadvantage of making nuclear proliferation in Third World countries much harder to control (see Chapter 9).

As in the development of the Soviet Union under Stalin, but with less drastic methods, early attempts to develop Third World countries were based on the traditional 'smokestack' industries of coal and steel. Hence in Brazil primacy in the 1930s went to the creation of an indigenous steel industry, centred on the massive Volta Redonda project. In China during the 'Great Leap Forward', an attempt was made to substitute labour for investment by encouraging the creation of 'backyard' blast furnaces. What metal these succeeded in producing, however, proved to be of such poor quality that the experiment was allowed to lapse, although not, unfortunately, before it had created considerable environmental damage. More recently, competition from the NICs and from Japan has driven down the world price of steel to the point at which there is now a substantial oversupply of basic steel products.

Though there is much less demand for steel as such than there was, it still remains central to successful industrialization. In the developed world, for a variety of uses ranging from metal window frames to car bodies, it has been superseded by aluminium. Aluminium is one of the commonest elements in the earth's crust, and in the form of bauxite it is found throughout the world. However, it is such an active chemical element that its separation from the ore involves a very high input of electrical power. This takes place in a two-stage process by which the ore is processed into alumina, and then the alumina is processed into finished aluminium. Hence only where there are considerable quantities of bauxite and a very considerable surplus of power available at low cost, as in developed countries such as Canada, is aluminium production economic. An additional problem is that the fabrication of aluminium alloys involves relatively expensive techniques if it is to be successful, thus limiting the spread of technology from the advanced industrialized countries into the Third World.

The result is that only a quarter of world production comes from the Third World, from Guyana, Jamaica and Suriname. In the case of Jamaica, it is the island's sole mineral resource, and in 1980 Jamaica was still forced to sell most of its unprocessed bauxite for a relatively meagre return (Dickenson *et al.* 1983: 136–7). In Sierra Leone bauxite is mined by Sieromco, part of Alusuisse of Switzerland. The effect of mineral extraction there has been to create huge areas of devastation.

The high bulk and low value of most minerals exported in this way means that some of the abundant mineral resources of the Third World have not been exploited at all. Those deposits most readily accessible by river or sea have generally speaking been opened up first, and certainly remain most competitive on the world market: for example, the copper of Chile or Peru, or alluvial tin in Malaysia and Indonesia. However, world economic conditions can change rapidly as mining from a country like Chile demonstrates, and the ability of transnational corporations (TNCs) to switch production from one part of the world to another makes the negotiating strength of Third World governments much weaker than their nominal sovereignties would suggest. The collapse of the world price of copper has dealt a severe blow to the economies of Zaire and Zambia.

The fate of Guatemala's dealings with International Nickel over its subsidiary Exploraciones y Explotaciones Minerías Izabal (Exmibal) is instructive. No sooner had the government of the day realized that the nickel ore was there than it hastened to 'renegotiate' Exmibal's 1968 contract, giving the government a 30 per cent share in the proceeds. However, with oil accounting for one-third of the cost of production, Exmibal's nickel plant at Chulac-El Estor in Guatemala did not begin operations until 1977. It never worked at more than 20 per cent of capacity until production was suspended in 1981 in adverse world economic conditions (Calvert 1985: 150–2).

The situation does not seem to be much better for a small Third World country that happens to have a really unusual resource. Sierra Leone is not just a producer of bauxite, it is also one of the few places in the world where there are substantial deposits of rutile, the black sand from which the space-age metal titanium is extracted. Since 1983 Sierra Rutile Ltd, a subsidary of the US multinational Nord Resources Corporation, has extracted 150,000 tons of rutile worth more than $80 million each year. Sierra Rutile is the country's largest employer, but wages are still meagre. Conditions are even worse than before the transnational moved in. Often mining gives rise to other infrastructural developments. This has not been the case for Sierra Leone. Representatives of the mining companies blame the corruption of the Sierra Leone government and the people for not throwing the rascals out, and not the terms of trade which they have had to accept. Successive IMF structural adjustment packages (SAPs) have failed. The government agreed to float the Leone, which devalued 25,000 per cent against the dollar, and to cut subsidies on fuel and food. Sierra Leone was virtually bankrupt, even before half its national territory was occupied by rebel forces from Liberia.

HUMAN SETTLEMENT

Population

One person in four in the world lives in China. Three out of four live in the Third World. Over the past 40 years, the population of the Third World has grown exponentially, leading some (including, notably, the Chinese and Indian governments) to place control of population at the centre of their strategy to achieve a reasonable standard of living for their people. *The State of World Population Report* (UNFPA 1992) called for 'immediate and determined action to balance population, consumption and development patterns: to put an end to absolute poverty, provide for human needs and yet protect the environment'.

But what is a balanced population? The distribution of population in the world is far from even (see Table 2.1), and to make more sense of it, it is necessary to look at it according to the principal regions into which the world can be divided.

Table 2.1 *Most densely populated countries, 1991 (inhabitants per square kilometre)*

Country	Population density (persons/km^2)	Percentage below poverty line
Bangladesh	803	86
Bahrain	759	
South Korea	432	16
Netherlands	402	–
Japan	327	–
Belgium	296	–
Rwanda	273	85
Sri Lanka	262	–
Lebanon	260	
India	259	48
Trinidad and Tobago	253	–
El Salvador	252	27
Haiti	234	76
United Kingdom	234	–
Jamaica	227	–
Israel	221	–
Germany	218	–
Philippines	208	58
Vietnam	202	
Burundi	202	83
United States	27	–
Russia	9	

Source: *Third World Guide 93/94* (1992).

First of all, however, a note of caution. Censuses even in the First World can be controversial. Accurate information about the size of families and the ages of family members may be even harder to obtain elsewhere, especially where the majority of the population is illiterate.

According to the UNFPA report, world population in mid-1992 was 5.48 billion. It would reach 6 billion by 1998, by annual increments of just under 100 million. Nearly all of this growth would be in Africa, Asia and Latin America. Over half would be in Africa and South Asia.

Asia is more than four times as heavily populated as any other part of the Third World. With a population of 3.11 billion in 1990, its density of population is nearly eight times that of North America excluding Mexico (United States 249.2 million, Canada 26.5 million) or the former USSR (288.6 million). It also includes seven of the ten largest countries by population: the largest, China (1088.4 million), the second largest, India (815.6 million),

Indonesia (174.8 million), Japan (122.6 million), Bangladesh (108.9 million) and Pakistan (106.3 million). Of these only Japan is an advanced industrialized country.

Latin America is relatively sparsely populated. With a total population in 1990 of 448.1 million, it includes another country, Brazil, that has a population of more than 100 million (150.4 million) and Mexico which, with 88.6 million in mid-1990, was getting near it. But as the fifth largest country in area in the world after Russia, Canada, China and the United States, Brazil is not at all densely populated, and the only country on mainland America that approaches European standards in terms of population density is tiny El Salvador, in Central America (with a population of 5 million). Many Latin Americans quite reasonably regard their countries as being underpopulated. Argentine public policy, for example, still favours 'peopling the pampas'.

Africa too is sparsely populated. However, although population statistics for its poorest countries are notoriously unreliable and overall estimates therefore have to be approached with care, its estimated 642.1 million population is growing at an average rate of 3 per cent a year. This may not seem much, but it would lead to the population of the continent being nearly three times as large by 2025. The second largest country by area in Africa, Nigeria, has the largest population. This is currently estimated at 108.5 million. However, as the results of the 1962, 1963 and 1973 censuses had to be set aside owing to political unrest, there is considerable doubt as to whether these more recent figures are in fact correct.

Oceania, by contrast, has accurate statistics, but is the most sparsely populated region. Apart from developed Australia and New Zealand (20.3 million), only some 11 million people are scattered over its vast area: 5.2 million in Melanesia, 3.9 million in Papua New Guinea, 0.8 million in Fiji, 0.6 million in Polynesia and 0.4 million in Micronesia. Many of them live on very small island states where the distinctions we make elsewhere between town and countryside are of relatively little use.

As a result of population pressure in the Third World, increasing numbers of migrants are crossing national boundaries in search of work. In the 1980s, an average of 603,000 immigrants entered the United States legally every year, and an equivalent number went to Canada and Australia. In Europe, politicians played on the fears of voters to push through legislation restricting legal immigration, and the British colonial government of Hong Kong forcibly repatriated Vietnamese who were described as economic migrants not political refugees.

Of the 57 countries in the world which by 1990 had passed laws to reduce immigration, no fewer than 43 were themselves developing countries. Until 1982 Nigeria, the largest country in Africa, enjoying an oil boom, welcomed migrant labourers. With the recession in 1983, its military government summarily expelled a million Ghanaians, who were left to make their way back to their own country on foot, by bus or by car, as best as they could.

Refugees: the case of Rwanda

In 1994 the world was shocked by news of the large-scale massacres in the tiny Central African state of Rwanda. Before April 1994 Rwanda was the most densely populated country in Africa, with more than six million people farming the fertile land. But the country was divided between two antagonistic ethnic groups: the Tutsi, traditionally the warrior class, and the Hutu, traditionally the labourers. The spark that ignited the conflict was the death of the country's first Hutu president in a mysterious air crash. Hutu slaughtered Tutsis. The Tutsi army retaliated, leaving half a million people dead and up to a million Hutu languishing in refugee camps in Zaire. By the end of August, Rwanda was looted and largely deserted.

Having failed as a peacekeeper, the UN faced formidable difficulties in mounting a successful relief effort. The French government, which had its own agenda, tried to establish a safe area within the country, but soon withdrew. The Zairean camps were unable to cope: the water supply was polluted by corpses and the volcanic ground was too hard to dig graves.

Traditional rural settlement

The duality of many Third World economies is well recognized. The modern formal sector can be contrasted with the traditional informal sector, and the urban with the rural. However, the distinctions are neither clear nor separate. The one depends on the other.

Standard poverty measures ignore subsistence production. Hence it is very difficult to determine accurately levels of poverty in rural areas, although it is clear that they are generally poorer than urban areas – hence the direction of migration. Lower levels of participation in the economy, whether as producer or as consumer, are found among the poor in all parts of society, but especially among the rural poor.

It is said that the degree of rural inequality in India is declining. This is questionable, although evidence from Indian government surveys does show increasing diversification of the rural economy. India's overall economic growth is impressive (*c.* 5.5 per cent p.a.), and it is now the seventh largest economy in the world. However, its growth is mainly urban and consists largely of the secondary production of consumer durables for the urban élite (which is, of course, very large in absolute terms on account of the massive size of Indian society). There is also one major achievement in rural development: self-sufficiency in cereal production was achieved during the 1980s. However, at the same time, in many rural areas, population is growing rapidly, agricultural production is stagnant, unemployment is high and consumption is down. Inequality in land-holding, as measured by the Gini index, has increased, and, more critically, so has the proportion of holdings that are too small to be viable.

Among regional variations, it is in the South and East that there has been the slowest growth in agricultural output. The Central, South and East also record the highest proportions of rural poor, and the highest mortality rates are to be found in the Central and East. By contrast, urban poverty has been declining as a proportion in urban areas, although it is still growing in absolute terms (Ghosh and Bharadwaj 1992: 140–6).

The survival of the traditional rural sector was seen in the nineteenth century by classical liberals as an obstacle to development. It is still seen as such by neo-liberals today, although at the same time the greens offer a sharply contrasting interpretation, arguing that traditional rural lifestyles are the way forward to sustainable development.

Land reform

Land reform is one means by which the state can act to help the poorest sectors of society by the redistribution of property. It can take various forms; the three most common of which are as follows:

- The distribution of land to the landless poor.
- Legislation limiting the size of estates, forcing the sale of 'surplus' holdings.
- Rent control.

Land reform is often opposed (especially by landowners) on the grounds that it will lead to a fall in production. In the state of Kerala in India, as in the NICs, there is a much greater degree of equality in land-holding, however, than there is in semi-feudal Pakistan, for example.

However, land reform is far from easy to carry out. The power of existing landowners to resist any serious land reform by political pressure and legal obstruction is frequently reinforced by the inclusion within their ranks of senior army officers. In Latin America major land reform programmes have either followed or been accompanied by high levels of violence. In Mexico land reform was made possible by the alliance forged between rural interests and the leaders of the Mexican revolution (1910–40). In Bolivia it followed the revolution of 1952 which placed the National Revolutionary Movement (MNR) in power, and in Cuba it was a consequence of the Cuban revolution of 1959. But in Chile between 1970 and 1973 the government of Salvador Allende was unable to overcome a strong alliance between the local landowners and the armed forces, supported by the United States, and land reform in the Dominican Republic, though pressed by the Carter administration in an attempt to avert revolution, was successfully killed by military opposition.

Even where a government has the strength to carry out land reform, the technical problems are immense. First, land is by no means a homogeneous commodity that can be shared out at will. Its varying quality, the availability of water and transport, and its nearness or otherwise to the market, all affect its utility. Second, it is not always easy to agree who should get access to land. Those who already work it regard themselves as having a prior claim. But what of the needs of the landless? Should those who have worked the land be made to share their good fortune with strangers? In the Mexican case, serious conflict between the competing claimants played into the hands of the traditional owners.

Collectivization seems at first sight to be an ideal solution. In Latin America, where land had been traditionally regarded as the property of the state, the pioneering experiment was that of Mexico, where limits were placed on the size of estates that could be held, and in the 1930s co-operatives (*ejidos*) were endowed with the land that had been expropriated, which was declared inalienable. Working practices varied, the earlier ejidos, broadly speaking, being divided into equal-sized plots worked by separate families, and the later worked in common by all the families settled on them. These ejidos were strongly criticized by their political opponents as inefficient and unproductive, but the evidence is that, having regard to the nature of the land in each case, they were as efficient as privately owned land. Not until 1992 did a Mexican government actually challenge the nature of the land reform carried out by its predecessors.

In Africa, land has not normally been expropriated as private holdings. Tanzania from the beginning saw collective ownership as traditionally African as well as socialist. Critics of the Tanzanian experience, however, remark that after some 30 years of a socialist economy it remains one of the poorest countries in the world.

Communists and some socialists regard such measures as half-hearted. Disputes over ownership, for them, can be simply resolved by the state assuming ownership of all land. It is then for the state to create collective institutions by which individual farms can be managed by those who work them. However, after the initial impetus given by mechanization, and despite the social benefits of community centres, health clinics and the rest, Soviet collective farms proved to be unable to meet their country's needs for basic foodstuffs, while in the Third World the record has been similarly ambiguous. In China, collectivization after 1949 has led to a level of production sufficiently high to end hunger, but has failed to provide funds for industrialization. In Cuba, attempts at diversification and industrialization failed, and after 1970 the country returned to its traditional dependence on the large-scale production of sugar, although for the Soviet rather than the American market.

Urbanization

The most striking feature of Third World countries is rapid urbanization. In 1950 only 29 per cent of the world's peoples lived in cities; in 1990 three times as many people did so, although the proportion had only risen to 43 per cent. But, more strikingly, in 1950 only about half the world's urban population was in Third World cities. By the year 2000 the population of cities in the Third World is expected to outnumber that in the rest of the world by more than two to one: 2,251.4 million to 946.2 million (Hardoy *et al.* 1992: 29).

However, Hardoy *et al.* identify three inaccurate assumptions about urbanization in the Third World which tend to be repeated: namely, that 'most of the problems (and much of the urban population) are in huge mega-cities', that 'the high concentration of population and production is a major cause of environmental problems' and that these problems are accurately documented in the existing literature (1992: 31).

It is hardly surprising that in the First World people tend to think of urban areas in the Third World as megacities (see Table 2.2). In 1950 there were only two cities, London and New York, with a population of more than eight million. In 1990 there were 20 such giant cities, and 14 of them were in the developing world (UNFPA 1992: 16). However, it is also true that in 1990 only a third of the urban population of the Third World lived in cities with more than one million inhabitants. In fact, in many of the smaller and/or less populous countries, half the urban population lives in cities with populations of less than 100,000. Such smaller cities have also grown very rapidly in recent years, and it is this rapid growth, rather than the overall size of the cities, that is associated with the problems of urbanization.

Table 2.2 *World's largest cities, c. 1988*

City	Country	Population
Mexico, DF	Mexico	20,000,000
São Paulo	Brazil	16,800,000
Rio de Janeiro	Brazil	11,100,000
Buenos Aires	Argentina	9,967,825
Seoul	South Korea	9,639,110
Jakarta	Indonesia	8,800,000
Moscow	Russia	8,642,000
Tokyo	Japan	8,354,695
New York, NY	USA	7,353,000
Shanghai	China	7,220,000
London	UK	6,775,200
Beijing	China	6,710,000
Tientsin	China	7,390,000
Chungking	China	6,200,000
Tehran	Iran	6,022,029

Source: Adapted from *Third World Guide 93/94* (1992).

The problems which urbanization brings do not stem purely from the overall level of urbanization, which as it happens varies a great deal from one region to another. The most urbanized part of the developing world is Latin America (41 per cent), which is comparable with Europe (48 per cent), but has some way to go before overall it reaches the level of North America (65 per cent). Other parts of the Third World are much more rural, urban East Asia is only 24 per cent, urban Africa 18 per cent, and South Asia 17 per cent, but this is not likely to last long. Bangladesh is rural and has only 13 per cent of its population living in cities. But it has in fact a higher population density ($756/km^2$) than the Netherlands ($400/km^2$), the most densely populated country in Europe, which has 88 per cent of its population living in cities. What is most worrying, undoubtedly, is that countries that have the fastest rate of population growth overall also tend to have the fastest rates of growth of urban populations.

The main features of Third World cities are as follows:

1. One large city, which is usually but not necessarily both the capital and the main commercial centre, predominates, containing anything up to a quarter of the entire population. The disproportion can be striking. The extreme case is the city-state of Singapore (100 per cent urban), but Montevideo, capital of Uruguay, contains half the country's people; Buenos Aires, capital of Argentina, some 23 per cent. The feature is equally marked in Africa, where it is often attributed to colonialism, but this can hardly be the case in Latin American states that have been independent for a century and a half. Dependency theorists would argue that the size of cities is linked to their role as a point of contact with the world economic system, but this seems rather to understate the role of government. Occasionally there are two large cities of roughly equal size, such as Rio de Janeiro and São Paulo in Brazil, Ankara and Istanbul in Turkey, Cape Town and Johannesburg in South Africa, Beijing and Shanghai in China. Where this happens one either is or has been the capital, the other the major commercial centre (Gamer 1976: 131–9).
2. Other cities are surprisingly small. In Mexico, Mexico City is some ten times as big as the next largest city, Guadalajara. Traditionally, migration has taken place over relatively short distances, owing to the difficulty of transport, although disentangling these flows is difficult because in the Third World as in the First there is, of course, also a substantial amount of movement from one city to another in search of work. Hence these smaller, regional centres act as 'way stations' for migration to the capital/ largest city, and indeed at one time this may have been the case everywhere. However, in modern times the evidence is that in Latin America at least the main migration flows are direct from the countryside to the largest city.

3. Third World cities are swollen by heavy recent immigration. China is an exception, probably only because until recently movement from place to place has been rigorously controlled by the authorities. In Africa and Asia the cities attract an excess of young men in search of work, while women often stay in their villages and keep their farms or plots going for subsistence. In Latin America and the Caribbean young women predominate in the burgeoning cities and towns. In both cases many migrate as part of an existing family unit.

4. Migration places the maximum strain on the infrastructure (roads, transport, housing, utilities, education, health and other public services). However, city governments tend to spend very little on housing or other services for the poor, partly because they do not want them to come in the first place, partly because they do not get much from them in the way of taxes. In all but the most favourable times, much of the urban area of Third World cities consists of shanty towns.

5. Shanty towns, perhaps unexpectedly, are not always very densely populated, and many of the worst urban conditions develop in older-type properties which have been allowed to fall into disrepair and are then subdivided. In Brazil these overcrowded tenement slums are called 'beehives'. Living in them consumes the greater part of a new immigrant's resources and offers little in the way of services. It is not very surprising, therefore, that people soon move out into the shanty towns. By definition shanty towns seldom, if ever, have reasonable mains services, although some Brazilian *favelas* have been established for so long that they have some mains services laid on. The absence of piped water and sanitation for such areas would be a dangerous combination in any circumstances. But shanty towns tend to congregate in the least favoured areas, and there are more immediate dangers when a shanty town locates close to factories or other sources of employment. Hundreds died in February 1984 when petrol (gasoline) leaking out of a fractured pipe exploded under a shanty town at Cubātão in Brazil, but this was only the most spectacular evidence of an environment so heavily polluted by unchecked industrial development that children had to go to hospital daily to breathe unpolluted air (Hardoy *et al*. 1992: 85–7). Though some effort has been made to clean up Cubātão since this incident, more recently a similar leak into another city's sewers destroyed several blocks in Mexico's second city, Guadalajara, in a series of explosions over three days. Three thousand were killed by toxic gas and 200,000 were evacuated following a release of methyl isocyanate from a chemical plant at Bhopal in India (Hardoy *et al*. 1992: 92). Despite this, cities are, by contrast with the countryside, seen as favoured places to live, especially by young people.

6. Above all, in Third World cities, industrial activity is unable to provide jobs for all the immigrants. Production is dominated by TNCs which, by the standards of the society, are capital-intensive and employ relatively few

people. The main job opportunities come in the disproportionately large services sector, in which government employment predominates. Much of the population is therefore unemployed or underemployed, and links with the home village are maintained as much out of economic necessity as out of family loyalty. This is quite the opposite of what is usually intended, as, for example, in Africa, where tribal identity is very strong and urban workers send remittances to their families, expecting in due time to return to the village.

Provided that urban areas are well governed, they have important advantages. It is much easier and cheaper to deliver efficient public services where distances are short and costs relatively low. Properly planned transport systems can make it easy for citizens not only to get to work, but also to enjoy a good range of recreational and other facilities – the rich have always liked to live in cities. Policy-makers are urban-dwellers and in their decisions they tend to favour what they know best. It is, of course, in the city that democratic politics originally evolved, and there is widespread agreement that a satisfactory environment can only be attained in Third World cities by the empowerment of those directly affected.

COMMUNICATIONS

The impact of air travel

In some ways, the new ease of air travel in the age of the jumbo jet, which has compressed space and time, has helped widen, not close, the gap between the First and the Third Worlds and perhaps more importantly between the more developed countries of the Third World, where infrastructure is sophisticated, and the poorer countries, where it is often virtually non-existent.

Because of the special conditions of Latin America, air travel was taken up with particular interest and enthusiasm. Avianca, Colombia's flag carrier, is the second oldest in the world. This is no coincidence. Owing to the incredibly broken terrain, Colombia's surface transport network remains fragmented and inadequate, and air freight has played and continues to play a significant role in its economic development (Hilling 1978: 91). Air travel has also helped make possible a degree of unity in Malaysia, Indonesia and the Philippines. Otherwise it is an expensive luxury for a Third World country to have its own airline, particularly when, as with Pluna in Uruguay, it has 4,000 employees and only one aircraft. But there are not many ruling élites who have been able to resist the temptation. In recent years, some have been seeking to divest themselves of the expense through privatization, only to find that there are relatively few players willing to buy. Such is the internationalization of the air industry that in the holiday season you can easily find yourself travelling from Buenos Aires to Montevideo on an aircraft chartered from Royal Jordanian Airlines.

Railways

Transport systems that were developed during the colonial period (or in Latin America during the early national period) were very basic. Given the limits of technology, there was little difference between those for local use and those oriented towards export. Railways had a prehistory of some two centuries or more in Britain. It was the application of steam power to locomotive propulsion that turned them into both a practical means of transport and an instrument of colonial expansion, particularly in its last phase, the scramble for Africa. Cecil Rhodes' dream of a 'Cape to Cairo' railway was never realized, but an African transcontinental railway was eventually completed, although the engineers who surveyed it were lucky enough to arrive on the scene only a few days after the end of the Ashanti Wars. It was the railway which made a united India possible. To this day, railways continue to form a significant means of transport in South, South-East and East Asia.

Even with the coming of the railways, national rivalries vitiated notions of rational planning. Dennis Austin wrote in 1978 of the 'marvellously clumsy chain of profit and control' that linked South-Central African states to the world market:

> How marvellous were the ways of capitalist enterprise and how tortuous! Between Maputo and Beira in Mozambique, for example, the railway still runs for part of its way outside the country through Rhodesia. But the major line of rail in southern and central Africa ran from Durban through Natal and the Transvaal northward, under Rhodesian management through Botswana into Rhodesia, then up over the great railway bridge (high above the Victoria Falls) across the Zambesi river into Zambia; out again from Lusaka through the Copper Towns into Zaire, when it became the *Chemin de Fer du Bas Congo et Katanga* until it entered Portuguese territory, where wood-burning locomotives carried the freight through central Angola as the Benguela Railway, owned by a British company, to the Atlantic coast at Lobito. (Austin 1978: 86)

Railways have considerable advantages as a means of transport in the Third World. They can shift very heavy loads relatively cheaply, and carry large numbers of passengers and their belongings in safety, using a minimum of expensive imported fossil fuel per passenger kilometre. The path they require is narrow and interferes very little with the natural environment now that wood-burning locomotives are no longer used (it was the need to feed them which, far more than any other single cause, was responsible for the deforestation of the United States). Once the infrastructure is in place, too, it is relatively easy to maintain: even if a bridge is washed away by floods, it is much easier to replace it for a train than for road transport.

Against this, of course, there is the problem of inflexibility: goods have to be transhipped to train or lorry for eventual delivery to their destination. Such inflexibility often reflects the purpose for which Third World countries were originally linked into the global economy. Railways built to serve the transport needs of colonial or semi-dependent production are quite often no longer in the right place for modern centres of population. Examples of this can be found in the radial pattern of the railways on the pampas of Argentina and in the short railways feeding the hinterland from a variety of ports in West Africa. Many of these have proved useless for modern conditions and have been closed.

More generally, from the 1960s onwards, rail has had to contend with an unfavourable political climate. Increasingly for long-distance passenger travel, not least by politicians and the staffs of development agencies, trains have been superseded by aircraft. Cheap motor vehicles became available in large numbers, and for people in the Third World they offered a freedom of movement that they had never previously enjoyed. Four-track vehicles offered a reasonable ride on the worst of surfaces. The high cost of building and maintaining roads was borne not by the passenger, but by the state. So rail networks were run down and in some countries disappeared altogether.

This had significant social consequences, as an example will show. Some colonial railways did come to benefit the independent nations. Though built originally with strategic defence of the Protectorate in mind, the Sierra Leone Government Railway had since its opening become a major factor in knitting together the country's many tribes and providing employment. Its closure was the price paid by Siaka Stevens' government for IMF support. Today few signs of it remain and at Magaburaka, once an important centre but now lying off the main road, it is almost impossible to trace the outlines of what was once the station yard. The only railway in the country is a recently constructed mineral line carrying iron ore from the mines down to the harbour at Port Loko. Being electrified (in a country where parts of the capital only get four hours' electricity a day!) it employs very few people, and having no other function it makes no useful impact on the surrounding countryside. Instead both passengers and freight have to contend for space on the country's few roads, even fewer of which have anything which might be termed an all-weather surface. Not surprisingly, anyone who can afford it, or can get someone else to pay for it, drives a Mitsubishi Pajero (Shogun).

In the First World, since the launch of the Japanese 'bullet train' and the building of the French TGV network, rail has been making a comeback. In fact, although only 30 per cent of the world's population live in the developed countries, they still account for 88 per cent of the rail traffic. Some Third World countries are building new lines or extensions of old lines as part of their development strategy. Most are intended primarily to open up significant new ore deposits to the world market, but although the rolling stock comes from Japan, the bogeys from Switzerland, the signalling equipment from Germany, and so on, a new line still generates a significant amount of local economic activity. Examples include Brazil, Cameroon, China, Nigeria, South Korea, Uganda and post-war Vietnam.

Road

Much of the traffic of West Africa is still carried by the 'mammy lorry', an improvised bus on a truck chassis. Many if not most of these are brightly painted with surprising but sometimes all too appropriate slogans, often with a religious flavour. Similar improvisations, notably the ubiquitous 'jeepney' in the Philippines, are to be found with local variations in many other Third World countries. However, the enthusiasm for these picturesque vehicles often shown by First World visitors should be tempered with a greater realization of their environmental disadvantages. In the countryside these may not be so apparent. But badly tuned diesel engines are one of the biggest problems of Third World cities, pumping out vast quantities of toxic fumes which constitute the major element in polluting the atmosphere in cities as far removed as Calcutta, Cairo, Lagos or Mexico City, and overall increase the concentration of greenhouse gases and contribute to global warming.

Roads of a sort are not hard to build, and they have the great advantage that improvements can be phased in as funds or labour becomes available. In addition, road-building is labour-intensive and requires relatively simple skills. It therefore makes an important input into a developing economy. However, good roads are expensive to build and difficult to maintain. In West Africa heavy rains can bring flash floods that can wash away whole sections of surfaced road. Not surprisingly, Africa is very short of surfaced roads: in fact Africa and Latin America together have only 7 per cent of the world's surfaced road. At least a third of all World Bank loans have consistently been for road projects, and in June 1971 the UN Economic Commission for Africa took the initiative to set up a permanent bureau to construct a Trans-African Highway, to stretch 6,393 km from Mombasa to Lagos, linking a number of existing 'growth areas' and using for the most part existing roads. These roads were to be upgraded to an approved standard by their respective national governments (Hilling 1978: 88–9).

The military government of Brazil (1964–85) placed the building of access roads at the centre of its strategy to open up Amazonia. The move of the capital to Brasília in 1960 had been accompanied by the building of an access road from Belem to Imperatriz and thereafter up the valley of the Tocantins, opening up a large sector of Eastern Amazonia. In the mid-1960s Rondônia was opened up by a new road from Cuiabá to Pórto Velho, again linking with the highway from Braslia via Goiana. But the centre piece of its National Integration Programme of 1970 was the Transamazonian (Rodovia Trans-amazônica), a massive project to connect the coast to Humaita and thence to

Porto Velho, while at the same time facilitating land colonization along a 10 kilometre strip on either side of the proposed route (Hilling 1978: 90).

The work of 'opening up' Amazonia was to be continued subsequently by the building of an even longer strategic road, the Rodovia Perimetral Norte, round Brazil's northern frontier, connecting up with feeder roads into all the neighbouring countries of the Amazon basin. Such alarm has been created at the environmental implications of effectively unrestrained logging, and the impact this has had on Brazil's Indian communities and the wildlife of the area, that most of the original plan remains on the drawing board. However, the northern section has been constructed to link up with the road northward from Manaus, and work is currently about two-thirds complete on a link road from this down the Essequibo valley towards Georgetown in Guyana.

SMALL ISLAND DEVELOPING STATES

While transport across the enormous distances of the continental Third World remains a central problem, some parts of the Third World exhibit very different needs. The global problems of climate change and the potential rise of mean sea-level have, at least for the moment, called attention to the special problems faced by Small Island Developing States (SIDS).

There are two major areas in which such states are to be found: in the Caribbean, in close proximity to larger mainland states, from which they owe their independence to the accidents of colonial rivalry; and in the Pacific, where their isolation gives them a natural geographical identity. At Barbados in 1994, under UN auspices, an organization was formed to defend their common interests.

- SIDS are particularly vulnerable, owing to their small size and frequent dependence on a single export crop, to natural and environmental disasters. In the long term, their extremely limited supplies of land are easily exhausted. In what is now the Republic of Nauru, mining for phosphate in the colonial period had left one-third of the small island state a waste of dead coral, with its 5,000 population crowded into the part that remains. Biological diversity on the remaining land is minimal. Although, as points of access to our maritime environment, the islands offer particular advantages, their capacity to absorb significant increases in tourism, their only obvious source of additional revenue, is very limited. As a result of the need to import food etc. for tourist consumption, the island state of St Vincent in the Caribbean actually loses money on its tourist industry.
- Their dependence on fishing makes their immediate maritime environment particularly sensitive to disturbance. Their traditional habit of discharging wastes into the sea therefore has to be superseded as a

matter of urgency by effective management of wastes and care of irreplaceable coastal and marine resources. This is at once a threat from the tourist influx and a threat to the attractions that bring them. Chief among these are the living corals of which many of the Pacific islands are composed.

- Many of them are low-lying and depend on infrequent rains for freshwater supplies.
- Their geological structure, rising from the deep sea bed, means that for energy resources they are for the present extremely dependent on the import of fossil fuels, although in the long run the harnessing of solar, wave and wind power are all practical 'renewable' alternatives.
- Some of them are so remote that their dependence on the outside world for transport and communication is total.

THE BALANCE SHEET: ASSETS AND PROBLEMS

To sum up, therefore, Third World countries other than the SIDS mostly have a complex balance of assets and problems. Let us consider their assets first.

On either side of the tropics, there is plenty of sunshine and a generally reliable and predictable climate pattern, although in the tropics themselves mist and haze can persist well into the morning, lowering the overall temperature but raising humidity. In the sub-tropical zones, there is generally a considerable annual surplus of rainfall. In conjunction with the great rivers as sources of irrigation, this has enabled these regions, through the wet cultivation of rice, to develop some of the world's largest concentrations of population, and, although there is considerable argument about how far the earth's capacity to produce food can be extended, some expansion at least does appear to be a reasonable possibility. In the case of rice this would happen by extending the area cultivated and not by increased productivity.

The tropical rainforest, if it survives, offers the most spectacular possibilities for the development of new and valuable products from its rich biodiversity. But the amount of information that has to be gained first is so great that conservation is of vital significance if this asset is ever to be realized.

Many Third World states have significant mineral deposits, many of which are still unexploited. Yet owing to the development of satellite sensors, the location of key minerals can now be made by those having access to space technology, which means, in practice, a small handful of advanced industrialized countries and the TNCs they shelter. Third World governments that can get access to this information and bargain effectively could, if the companies were willing to let them, plough back the proceeds of these irreplaceable resources, as Venezuela initially did and Kuwait (until the Gulf War) continued to do with its oil, either into infrastructure or long-term investment, or both.

With their large populations, Third World states also have vast human resources. Many of their citizens already have to be very resourceful simply to survive. But countries, such as those of the East Asian 'powerhouse' (see Chapter 4), that set out systematically to unlock the potential of their citizens by promoting education, particularly for women (see Chapter 12), are likely to find that their investment is very well spent in terms of the general betterment of society.

On the other side, however, there are also deep-rooted and persistent problems. Poverty is the root of many of the most persistent problems of the Third World. Floods, drought and hurricanes all threaten human life and pose serious challenges to governments. However, people are much more vulnerable to these emergencies if they live in inadequate shelter and lack the economic resources to protect themselves against them. Such disasters have already become a matter of concern at least to individual citizens and groups in the advanced industrialized countries.

Population growth may not of itself be a problem, but population growth coupled with the compelling pressure to achieve First World standards of living undoubtedly is. A child born today in an advanced industrialized country will, it is estimated, consume around 40 times the natural resources that a Third World child will consume before it reaches adulthood. This contrast is not only unethical but also unstable.

The pessimists who have warned of the coming exhaustion of land and mineral resources have so far generally proved to be wrong (though mineral deposits can and do run out and the dire state of Bolivia's tin industry is there to prove it). However, mineral deposits are not infinite and agricultural land once lost, whether to neglect, to urbanization or otherwise, cannot easily be replaced, if indeed it can be replaced at all. So it would be prudent to assume that at some stage shortages will act in a way not at present predictable to check development in some if not all Third World countries.

3 The crisis of the Third World

POVERTY AND BASIC NEEDS

One billion people in developing countries – or one in five of the world's population – live in poverty. Their basic needs remain to some degree unmet. Basic human needs are universal. The manner of organizing to meet them varies with circumstances.

These basic needs are as follows:

- Clean water.
- Good food.
- Proper sanitation and health facilities.
- Reasonable housing.
- Education.

They are, of course, interrelated, but the most important of all is clean water. We shall look at each of the five basic needs in turn, and then consider how they are likely to be affected by two factors linked to economic development: population growth and environmental degradation.

Where basic needs are not met, the effects can be devastating. For example, a major world effort is needed to break into the cycle of infection and reinfection which in recent years has led to millions of deaths in countries in Africa South of the Sahara (SSA). In 1995 an outbreak of the Ebola virus in Zaire led to headlines throughout the developed world featuring its terrifying consequence, acute haemorrhagic fever leading in over 80 per cent of cases to death through the dissolution of the patient's internal organs.

Generally speaking, where population is high relative to the resources available to sustain them, the basic needs are most difficult to meet and the most marked forms of poverty and vulnerability are likely to occur. Aspects of material poverty as experienced in the Third World include undernutrition, malnutrition, ill health and low levels of education. However, a complicating factor is that poverty is not experienced by whole countries. Even in very poor countries (as measured by GDP per capita) there is a rich élite, although élite lifestyles also vary. Moreover, the relative importance of the different factors making for poverty (physical, national past and present, international past and present) varies over time and from place to place.

Stressing the meeting of basic needs as the primary driving force towards development, sometimes imaginatively termed the 'basic needs approach', emphasizes that health and education are motors for productivity and that the basic needs of all sectors must be met. This approach was expressed in the ideological framework of UN conferences in the early 1970s, when it confronted the older emphasis on the eventual trickling down of the benefits of development and a development agenda in the 1960s stressing employment and income distribution. In other words, this new approach saw qualitative change as the vital first step, not as something achievable through initial quantitative change. Such an approach was not then and is not now universally accepted.

In First World countries the 1970s saw the emergence of ideas associated with neo-liberalism, and in the 1980s these were adopted in most parts of the Third World. Neo-liberals have argued that, for example, emphasizing the meeting of basic needs slowed down growth in Sri Lanka in the 1960s and 1970s, impeded the development of Jamaica in the 1970s (as witness the fiasco of the sugar industry there), and proved detrimental to that of Tanzania, still, after several decades, one of the poorest countries in Africa.

The fact remains that the meeting of basic needs depends on the continued provision of funding, and that the only way this can be done with certainty is by a system of financial transfers from the better-off to the poor at international, national and subnational levels. Third World countries, however, tend to lack internal transfers as safety nets for the poorest sectors. Shifting resources to the poor is a cost to the non-poor, and it is they who are likely – all other things being equal – to have a greater say in political and economic decision-making. In an extreme case, the wealthy backed by the armed forces were able to prevent the introduction of income tax to Guatemala until the early 1970s. When, finally, it was introduced, the top rate was only 4 per cent.

On the other hand, it is always difficult to target benefits for the poor. First of all, the poor often have an all too well-founded suspicion of government. Censuses do not pick up all of the poor. Officials are always suspect and census-workers are no exception. Non-governmental organizations are better at targeting aid to the poor than are governments, but they often lack the resources. Most effective may be a process of self-selection: that is to say, making available benefits that have no interest for those that are not poor, such as low-paid, public-sector employment. However, economic orthodoxy frowns on creating employment in this way, no matter how socially desirable it might be, and governments that have got into financial difficulties may find themselves compelled to cut the size of the public sector regardless of the inevitable social consequences.

External aid and assistance tends to be directed to middle- or high-income countries for political reasons. In 1988, 41 per cent of all foreign aid was to such countries, which are more likely to be politically useful allies. They are also certainly more likely to be the target of private overseas investment, generating in turn a greater degree of political commitment to protect that investment. Although modern Great Powers no longer send gunboats to force small countries to pay their debts, at least one of the reasons why they do not is that they do not have to. The modern financial system leaves a poor country very little alternative but to comply with the conditions laid upon it (see Chapter 4). Moreover, developed countries do still use 'gunboat diplomacy' for other purposes.

WATER

Fresh water is less than 3 per cent of the world's water and it is not evenly distributed. The majority of Third World populations live in rural areas where only some 15 per cent have access to clean water. Even in urban areas of the Third World most households do not have running water. In India, for example, 70 per cent of all surface water is polluted. The *World Development Report 1992* estimates that globally one billion (a thousand million) people are without access to clean water and 1.7 billion do not have proper sanitation. The combination of inadequate water supply and no sanitation is a guaranteed recipe for the rapid spread of water-borne illnesses. The World Health Organization (WHO) says that the number of water taps per thousand population is a better indicator of health than the number of hospital beds.

Not only is water scarce in the Third World, but it is getting scarcer. Growing population, increasing urbanization (which lowers quality through sanitation problems as well as increasing demand), rapidly rising demands from industry and the increasing pollution of watercourses by both solid and liquid wastes, all combine to make potable water a rarer and therefore more valuable resource. Indeed water is also required for a variety of purposes other than drinking: washing and cleaning, irrigation for crops and, in more recent years, the generation of hydroelectric power (HEP).

Like food, water can be used as a political weapon, with devastating effect. Elaborate irrigation works were constructed in ancient times in Mesopotamia, now Iraq. These canals and dams fell into decay in the time of the Romans, leaving desert in the upper reaches and marsh in the lower region between the Tigris and the Euphrates. In the past few years, Saddam Hussein has drained the marshes in order to destroy the habitat of his Shi'a opponents, the Marsh Arabs. The result of this is likely to be the further desertification of what was once the most fertile country in the Middle East, as the old term 'the Fertile Crescent' attests.

In ancient times the natural annual rise and fall of the Nile inundated the surrounding land and made the development of advanced civilization possible in Egypt. However, the first dam on the Nile at Aswan was constructed as long ago as the end of the last century. In the 1930s the taming of the

Tennessee Valley in the United States achieved world-wide attention. In the immediate post-war years, the availability of large contracting firms with earth-moving equipment and the increasing sophistication of reinforced concrete technology made it possible for countries all over the world to seek to solve their water problems by constructing large dam projects both for irrigation and for hydroelectric power. This was the era of the 'superdam' and many of these massive constructions are still being built.

However, the construction of large dams has proved to have important unwanted consequences. The flooding of ever larger tracts of land has caused significant problems of displacement of populations. At the same time, blocking the flow of large rivers seems increasingly likely to cause significant environmental damage. Not only does silt rapidly settle in the newly created artificial lakes, but the lakes themselves are liable to eutrophication (biological damage). The technical problems connected with irrigation have now in themselves made such simplistic solutions suspect.

In western India a dam on India's holiest river, the Narmada (see Gita Mehta's *A River Sutra*), will displace 250,000 people. The World Bank was funding the dam, but withdrew its support under pressure from both local and international groups. It is too late to stop this project, but other superdams are likely to be stopped. The environmental, social and economic costs are now perceived to exceed expected economic benefits in most cases. The cost of Itaipu, for example, comprises a significant part of Brazil's massive international debt. It was on these grounds that the President of the World Bank decided in August 1995 to withdraw support for the controversial Arun III project in Nepal (*The Guardian*, 16 August 1995).

However, stopping such projects is no easy task, as there are powerful forces operating in their favour. The Sardar Sarovar dam, also on the Narmada River, is the biggest dam project in the world and brought the World Bank as funding agent an unprecedented number of protests. It was subject to years of delay because Gujarat could not reach agreement with other neighbouring states on how to share the power from the dam. However, it is the displacement issue which makes this project so controversial. The protesters argue that the dam is being built to a western model; it is being built for the rich who will use its power, not for the poor tribal people who are being displaced and who are losing their once clean river and their way of life, often having to seek work in local cotton factories. The land given in compensation to those displaced is not comparable with that which they are losing. Stony, marginal land cannot compensate for prime land farmed effectively for years. The water situation there is much more difficult. The loss of forests for traditional medicines and fuelwood cannot be replaced.

Under pressure from NGOs, the World Bank sent an independent assessor. The assessor was critical of the role of the Indian government, and the World Bank withdrew its funding. But this was not the end of the project. The government of India has assumed responsibility for funding the project and work continues. Millions need the dam as well. India must double its food production and for this it needs water. However, objectors argue that the water will go to the richest areas, that India suffers from poor water management and consequent high costs, that 141 smaller-scale dams are still incomplete while funds are sought to build superdams, that low-tech alternatives are available (e.g. ridges to trap rainwater and halt soil erosion), and that the real reason for superdams is that bureaucrats are used to large projects and engineers want glamour. There is a lot of truth in these arguments.

The Tehri dam, being built to provide drinking water in the upper waters of the Ganges, will be located in the foothills of the Himalayas in an area with much seismic activity. It suffers from a shortage of funds and poor construction techniques, and a burst would cause a tidal wave to kill millions. The town of Tehri was the capital of an ancient kingdom, and it has been home to 20,000 people who have enjoyed facilities such as a hospital and university, but it is next to the dam. Hence the town will be displaced from the mild valley bottom where it never snows to the hillside, which is snow-covered for a full two months every year. The people will receive compensation, but the sum awarded to each family will not cover the cost of one of the new houses. Moreover, the dam-builders were supposed to have planted the sides of the valley below the Tehri dam to stop silting downstream, but they have not done so. The valley is the main source of food for the whole region. Since rice cannot be grown in quantity on hillsides, the production of food for the region will necessarily fall.

The Victoria dam on the Mahaweli River in Sri Lanka was partly funded by the British taxpayer. It was planned in 1978 and built in six years. The dam provides power for Sri Lanka's burgeoning textile industry, boosted to the level of a national economic ideology by the late President Premadasa. It also supplies irrigation from the wetter west of the island for the drier east. Rice production was increased fivefold using the dam's potential for irrigation. Sri Lanka used to import food; now it exports. The turbines of the Mahaweli project provide not only the power for textile production, but also electricity for the towns of Sri Lanka; not the villages yet, but that is expected by the end of the century.

There were health problems, especially with malaria and hepatitis at first for those who were displaced and resettled, but these people soon developed immunity. Social considerations were given priority in the displacement process. Whole villages were moved and their biggest problem remains what it was before the move: marauding wild elephants. On the negative side, environmental issues were not given the priority they might properly be accorded now; they were simply not seen as so important. There has been a loss of biodiversity: Sri Lanka's rich wildlife has been diminished. There is also some evidence that cutting the forest in the region of the dam may have made the local climate hotter.

When considering the damaging effects of superdams, one should also keep in mind the following facts:

- About three billion people in the world do not have electricity. It would be very difficult to argue that they do not have a right to it.
- The world's food production must double over the next 40 years. There is no realistic way this can be achieved except by continuing to expand the wet cultivation of rice.
- There is water rationing in Delhi. There they naturally want both the water and the power that the Tehri dam could provide, and it is in Delhi that national decisions are taken (*Assignment*, 'Lands of the Dammed', BBC Television, 1993).

Water is in addition such a key resource that it is becoming a serious security issue and potential source of international tensions. The diversion of the waters of the Jordan by the Israelis has been a significant ground for contention between that state and Jordan, which has lost out. Syria has been grumbling over Turkey's control of the headwaters of the Euphrates. Bangladesh is concerned about India's control of the Farraka barrage on the Ganges. And the waters of the Colorado River are so saline by the time they leave the territory of the United States that Baja (Lower) California, one of Mexico's most fertile farming areas, is threatened.

Currently it is confidently expected that water resources will become a major issue in international politics by the end of this century, when, it is argued, resource-based conflicts may provide new roles for underemployed armed forces. In one sense they have always done so. Water is so crucial to human life that access to it has always been a matter for the whole community. The present-day figures are sobering. Global water usage doubled in the 40 years from 1940 to 1980, and is expected to do the same again before the end of the twentieth century.

Existing imbalances are very marked. China, with 25 per cent of the world's population, has access to only 5 per cent of the world's water. So many people need access to water that 35 to 40 per cent of the world population lives in multinational river basins. Fifty countries have more than three-quarters of their territory in such basins.

Within a river basin system, there is a great advantage to the countries that lie upstream (the 'upstream riparian'). Hence it is frequently not the polluter who bears the cost of contaminating watercourses, as in the case of United States pollution of the Colorado River, which reduces its value for irrigation downstream in Mexico.

The main problem is the increased salinity of water when it has been used for irrigation. Other major problems created by human beings include contamination by the excessive use in agriculture of fertilizers and pesticides (less than 1 per cent of all pesticides used reach a pest), by biological waste from human beings themselves and by industrial waste, particularly from large cities, but also from mines and other installations (Postel 1989).

Inappropriate irrigation schemes, often devised with good intentions as part of the Green Revolution, destroy through waterlogging or salinity the usefulness of some 12 million hectares each year. In addition, irrigation schemes like dams are actively creating new water-borne health hazards, which are very hard to control. Both create large areas of slow-moving water. In the Nile Valley the construction of the Aswan High Dam put an end to the age-old cycle of inundation (the natural annual flooding of the land as a result of rains far upstream). As an unplanned result, it has created the ideal conditions for the spread of the snails which are hosts to bilharzia parasites. In India the World Bank's decision to fund the Narmada dam was criticized so much that environmental concerns were made part of the project remit.

Water is not just for consumption. For millennia it has provided transport and access to remote areas. However, today waterways are being damaged by overuse, which erodes the banks, or by increased silting: for example, that of the Panama Canal due to run-off increasing after deforestation in the 1970s.

FOOD

In the 1930s Third World countries collectively exported some 12 million tons of grain. By the late 1970s they were importing some 80 million tons.

However, these figures conceal two paradoxes. First, world food production overall is sufficient even in the 1990s to feed all the people in the world to a reasonable standard. UN Food and Agriculture Organization (FAO) projections show that it is possible to feed all our present population enough to provide 3,600 calories per person. But in 1972 the US government paid farmers $3 billion to take 50 million hectares out of production while millions starved in the Sahel for want of a harvest (Bradley 1986), and under the EU's Common Agricultural Policy (CAP) land is being 'set aside' to keep prices up. Second, there are increasingly severe grain shortages in the Third World at the same time that an increasing proportion of world cereal production is being diverted to animal feed. In 1972 the heavy sales of wheat to the Soviet Union which helped raise the world price went to the production of meat. By the end of the 1970s, in Mexico more basic grains were eaten by animals than by 20 million peasants (*International Herald Tribune*, 9 March 1978; quoted in Frank 1981).

About 30 per cent of the world's land is potentially arable. About half of this is under cultivation. Half of the land under cultivation is in the Third World, but it is inhabited by three-quarters of the world's population, and the disproportion is even more marked in individual countries. Inequality of land distribution contributes to overfarming and underproduction. Some 80 per cent of the land in Latin America is held by less than 10 per cent of the population. The environmentalist George Monbiot (1992) cites the case of Brazil where farmland extending to the size of India lies uncultivated because it is held by its owners as an investment. Brazil's richest 1 per cent own 15 times as much land as the poorest 56 per cent. Under Brazilian law, land idle for more than five years may be legally occupied by any of Brazil's ten million landless peasants. Landowners, not surprisingly, have a variety of means to resist such occupations. They are quite prepared to use violence if necessary.

More than 500 million people are seriously malnourished. Malnutrition is not just an evil in itself. It lowers resistance and so exacerbates the problem of disease. Poor nutrition in mothers causes underweight babies, and low birth weights are increasing in some areas. Some 60 per cent of children in rural Bangladesh are underweight. Low birth weight is the factor most strongly correlated with later health problems. Hence directly or indirectly malnutrition causes the death of 40,000 children under five years old every day.

Food aid can make things worse. Critics have particularly targeted the sending of infant feeding formula as part of aid packages, as there is evidence that both this and the aggressive marketing of artificial babymilk powder to Third World mothers by companies like Nestlé is resulting in many unnecessary deaths. The formula itself is not the problem, but it has to be made up with clean water in sterile equipment, and, even where mothers understand the need for hygiene, the facilities are often inadequate. More often the formula is made up with dirty water and diluted to make it go further, so that if it fails to contract gastroenteritis or dysentery, the child is of low body weight and so less well equipped to resist other challenges to its immune system. Breast feeding is by far the safest method for Third World babies, particularly since it conveys a degree of immunity against local diseases. In Sierra Leone, where 180 children per 1000 die before the age of one and nearly a quarter of all children die under the age of five, babies often thrive until weaned.

Undernutrition has been exacerbated by the tendency of some Third World countries to cease to be self-sufficient in staples and to become importers of food they used to produce. This is a common phenomenon in Africa, due to urbanization, changing consumption and production patterns, and the 'demonstration effect' fostered by the mass media. Even Mexico, where maize probably originated, is no longer self-sufficient in the basic staple of its diet. In fact it now exports fruit and vegetables to the United States and imports wheat in return. When Third World countries get into financial difficulties, their plight is often because of the need to maintain a high – some would say excessive – level of imports of grain and other basic foodstuffs. Importing food and food products increases Third World vulnerability anyway, because of the need to deal in scarce convertible currency, but the imposition of austerity measures, along with currency devaluation, hits imports of all kinds, food included.

There are important domestic consequences too. Agribusiness is 'modern'; it seeks to gain efficiency by mechanization, and by a sad coincidence it is the best arable land that is easiest to subject to mechanization. The occupation or purchase of these lands displaces settlers on to marginal lands. Hence it is, ironically, often the free market in land rather than population pressure that can be seen creating refugees and/or hunger. In the case of the Philippines, the marginal workers have been driven into the forests, where they in turn displace indigenous peoples, with disastrous consequences for the environment and lost lifestyles.

The most severe form of food deficit is famine, which differs from undernutrition in its acuteness and in the accompanying increase in deaths associated with the crisis. Famine is, sadly, becoming such a common sight on First World television screens that people have come to take it very much for granted. There is one good consequence: that many individuals give generously to famine relief. But whether they should have to give and, much more importantly, whether the poor of Third World nations should continue to experience famine, is a morally debatable question. It should not be forgotten that the greatest achievements in surviving famines are local, the result of community and family efforts in the affected areas. Famine is not simply a natural disaster and it is no accident that it is currently associated with Africa South of the Sahara, and especially with the Sahel region and the Horn.

Famine was also commonplace in India historically. However, the most recent famine in India was the Bengal Famine of 1943, during the Second World War, when both government and the transportation network were strained to the limit. There has been none since independence in 1947, thanks to a public food distribution system, although chronic hunger persists in India and claims many lives as a matter of course. On the other hand, China has since the revolution greatly reduced chronic hunger as a routine condition of the population, but has nevertheless suffered famine, most notably at the end of the 1950s during the turmoil of the Great Leap Forward. The fact is that the cause of famine is not necessarily a lack of food, but rather whether food gets to those who need it – the question of the difference between access and entitlement.

As Dreze and Sen point out, 'it has to be recognized that even when the prime mover in a famine is a natural occurrence such as a flood or a drought, what its impact will be on the population depends on how society is organized' (1989: 46). Even in a country stricken with famine, most sectors do not suffer famine as such: Sen estimates only 2–3 per cent. Most sectors have entitlement based on their capacity to produce their own food, to trade some other product for food, or to earn a wage with which to buy food. The rich do not go hungry even in famine. Urban areas tend to draw resources from marginal areas, as was the case in Ethiopia, where government food purchases for the cities contributed to rural famine. In 1988 it was a time of reasonable food availability in Somalia, and the famine that shocked the world was the result of human agency. In the civil war, crops had been burnt, resulting in a flood of refugees without reserves or mutual support networks and no 'entitlement' to food. In 1994 in Rwanda the flood of refugees was so massive that in only three weeks a major disaster was created (see also Wijkman and Timberlake 1984).

Climatic factors are not, therefore, the causes of famine in any real sense. Rather, like wars and political crises, they are trigger factors. Droughts have occurred year after year in Africa South of the Sahara in the past, but have not necessarily been accompanied by famine (see Schmandt 1994). Much of the United States is arid, but it does not suffer from famine, as it has the complex infrastructure to ensure that in emergencies resources are more equitably distributed. This infrastructure is vital to reduce vulnerability. But in their former colonies, traditional defence mechanisms were often dismantled by European colonizers, as Gita Mehta describes in *Raj* (Mehta 1990). Famine therefore emerged as an unintended consequence of the ways in which local economies were restructured to meet the needs of the colonial powers. The most productive land was taken for settlement or plantations, reducing land available for production to meet local needs. Competition frequently destroyed local artisan production which could earn funds for times of food shortage.

Unhappily, food aid, though an essential humanitarian response to short-term crisis, can very easily be exploited as a political weapon. In 1974, for example, US government disagreements with Bangladesh led to a reluctance to release food aid in a time of famine. Even when food aid arrives at its intended destination, as in Somalia in 1993, it may be hijacked by local warlords or power blocs and used by them to reward their own political supporters. Lastly, the availability of free food drives down the price of staples on the local market. If the supply of aid goes on too long, therefore, the incentive to plant for the new season is eliminated and the cycle of deprivation is set to continue. In this way food aid has ironically and tragically acted to prolong the effects of drought in Ethiopia.

At present one-quarter of the earth's population is not getting enough food. Malnutrition begins before birth, as is shown by declining birth weights in many individual cases and over some areas. In Africa South of the Sahara, deaths of the under-fives contribute 50–80 per cent to the total mortality of the population, compared with 3 per cent in Europe.

Africa South of the Sahara was a food exporter until 1960. According to Shiva (1988) the region was still feeding itself as late as 1970. But by 1984, 140 million out of 531 million Africans were being fed with grain from abroad. As noted above, the main reason for this is that export-oriented cash crop production has replaced subsistence farming.

Much was made at the time of the so-called Green Revolution, which from 1940 onwards did so much to increase world food production. But the 'miracle' seeds of the Green Revolution (financed by the Rockefeller Foundation in the 1940s and the Ford Foundation in the 1960s) were high yield varieties (HYVs), which, as they were intended to, produced massive increases in marketable surpluses, especially of wheat and rice. There were two problems for Third World farmers. The new seeds were hybrid. They did not breed true, and new supplies had to be bought each year, thus making the farmer dependent on cash purchases. They also needed huge volumes of water and high levels of chemical fertilizers, pesticides and fungicides. These things consumed scarce foreign exchange, increasing the national debt in the process and adversely affecting water supplies. Hence the benefits of the Green Revolution, and there were many, were in practice skewed to the wealthier sectors because they were only easily available to larger landowners. They therefore inadvertently helped increase the serious disproportion in access to land and wealth in Third World societies.

SANITATION AND HEALTH

Clean water and sanitation are functional not just luxuries. Since 1992, beginning with Peru, South America has been experiencing its first cholera epidemic for more than a hundred years. The cost of the Peruvian cholera epidemic in terms of lost tourism and agricultural exports has already exceeded by far what it would have cost to avoid the problem.

The estimate of the number of cholera infections each year is enormous, some six million. Cholera breeds in the gut and is spread by contaminated food and water. It hits hardest at the weak, the old and the young. Convulsions, vomiting and diarrhoea produce dehydration which can kill in four hours. Yet years of neglect made Peru highly susceptible to this disease. For Peru it is a man-made disaster. Cholera was brought by boat to Chimbote in 1990–1, where the Peruvian preference for raw fish and the absence of simple sanitation (communal latrines and contaminated water supplies) combined to pave the way for an epidemic. Chimbote should be a prosperous place with an adequate infrastructure for the general health of its population. It is the world's largest fish-meal producer. But the European-descended élite who control the profits from fish-meal do not get cholera. They do not invest in infrastructure, arguing that this is the government's job and its absence the government's failure. Like their counterparts in other Latin American countries, the Peruvian élite prefers to keep its money abroad in more stable countries.

Within weeks the epidemic had spread to five neighbouring states and it is now again endemic in South America. Mountain villages have been hit by cholera too, although they might have been assumed to be healthier places, because the rivers which are their main source of water are also their sewers. The main exception was in areas controlled by the guerrilla movement

Sendero Luminoso. Where the building of latrines was ordered by Sendero, and those who did not use them were threatened with death, there was no cholera (*Assignment*, 'Peru in the Time of the Cholera', BBC Television, 1993).

One good thing has come out of this: schools are now teaching basic hygiene for the first time. But most such education and other assistance has been left to the aid agencies – Peru's hospitals have been totally overwhelmed. However, it does not take an epidemic to overwhelm Third World hospitals. Poverty has the same effect, if more slowly.

Poverty is the main reason for poor health. Health improved dramatically in Europe in the nineteenth century by the provision of public water supply and sewerage, and this long before there were significant advances in the ability of medicine to cure illness. Many diseases in the Third World today were once as common in the now developed world, but public expenditure solved the problems that gave rise to them. Economic development, therefore, is the quickest and surest way to better health for all.

However, aid agencies have continued in recent years to seek to increase economic growth through large-scale industry and agribusiness, knowing full well that this would primarily benefit the health of the already fairly healthy higher-income sectors. The touching belief remained that the benefits of this development would in time 'trickle down' to the poorer sectors of society. But in practice the health gap between rich and poor continued to widen. In 1978, therefore, the 134 countries which attended the WHO conference of that year agreed on behalf of their peoples to seek as a conscious goal the target of 'Health for All'. In 1981 health was identified as fundamental human right by WHO and the year 2000 was set as the target date for 'Health for All' (Thomas 1987: 106).

Primary health care was identified as the main means through which the target could be met. Social indicators were to be used for monitoring the success of health programmes. But health care could not be made effective without the active co-operation of members of the public. Stress was therefore to be placed on accessibility, participation and health education, in the design of health programmes. The main policy initiatives were to be in the following areas:

- Adequate food.
- Safe water.
- Family planning.
- Immunization.
- The provision of essential drugs.
- The treatment of common injuries and illnesses.

The technology was certainly available to ensure that for the most part the target was met, but many inappropriate policies were followed through lack of foresight and co-ordination, and in addition there was a generalized failure to take on board the fact that socioeconomic and political factors compound health problems in the Third World. The essential preconditions for the success of 'Health for All' were two: political commitment to the target on the part of Third World governments, and the willingness to decentralize health provision to local communities to enable participation. This was by no means always easy to achieve.

Some countries were noticeably more successful than others in achieving the objectives they set themselves, and there were a number of different reasons for failure.

China was seen as generally successful. Its government took the view that health should be possible at any level of income and stressed the role of education. Health care was relatively equitably distributed. However, there were some weaknesses. The programme did relatively little for rural women. Moreover, the country's economic liberalization opened it up to penetration by the international tobacco companies, with serious long-term consequences for the rise of lung cancer and respiratory ailments. Another socialist country, Cuba, was also fairly successful with an ideology of social justice and nationalized health services, but in a very centralized, relatively 'high-tech' health system, medicine was overdependent on professionals and was still not meeting the needs of the poorest. Tanzania too adopted a centralized system and its urban élite are disproportionately advantaged. In Mali massive foreign aid for health facilities soon became unsupportable – a new good cause replaced it! In many poor African countries, aid has been severely constrained. Corruption has consumed funds needed to maintain services at colonial-period levels, and health care is often limited.

By 1985 it was clear that the achievements in health care varied enormously and the early optimism had waned. At this point the Rockefeller Foundation published *Good Health at Low Cost*, an investigation into the successes of China, Sri Lanka, Costa Rica and, perhaps most notably, the state of Kerala in south-western India. In all of these areas, residents have life expectancies of more than 65 despite the fact that, as their low per capita GDPs demonstrate, these areas are all very poor indeed by world standards. Four factors were found which reduced the infant mortality rate sufficiently to raise life expectancies to developed country levels:

- An ideological commitment to equity in social matters.
- Equitable access to and distribution of public health care provision.
- Equitable access to and distribution of public education.
- Adequate nutrition at all levels of society.

The logic is clear. Malnutrition, aggravated by infectious diseases spread by poor sanitation and polluted water supplies, causes the bulk of Third World mortality, especially in children under five. Of the 15 million unnecessary

Table 3.1 *Children's health, 20 poorest states*

Country	U5MR (per 1,000 live births)	% of U5s underweight
Mozambique	297	57
Afghanistan	292	
Angola	292	
Mali	284	31
Sierra Leone	257	23
Malawi	253	24
Guinea-Bissau	246	23
The Gambia	238	
Guinea	237	
Burkina Faso	228	
Niger	221	49
Ethiopia	220	38
Chad	216	
Somalia	215	
Mauritania	214	31
Equatorial Guinea	206	
Liberia	205	20
Rwanda	198	28
Cambodia	193	30
Burundi	192	38

Source: *Third World Guide 93/94* (1992).

infant deaths each year, four million are from one or more of six cheaply immunizable diseases, and a further five million result from diarrhoea preventable by oral rehydration therapy, the salts for which cost next to nothing. The cost of just three weeks of what the world's governments spend on arms would pay for primary health care for all Third World children, including ensuring access to safe water and immunization against the six most common infectious diseases (see Table 3.1).

Infant mortality rate (imr), defined as the number of children per 1000 who die in the first year of life, varies strikingly between the major regions of the world. The world average is 81 per thousand. This compares with, on the one hand, Europe, where the average is 16, and Africa, where it is 114. These figures also conceal striking variations within regions. Likewise imrs are always higher in rural areas, which are less likely to have the same levels of access to medical services, female education, potable water and proper sanitation, or indeed the incomes necessary to achieve adequate levels of nutrition. Malnutrition has a serious effect on the unborn child and, in serious cases or if continued throughout development, can lead to irreversible impairment. Surveys in East Africa and South Asia show that children under five are moderately malnourished in some 15–30 per cent of cases, and the same percentage of children have low birth weights, indicating probable malnourishment during pregnancy. At the same time, poor hygiene and unsafe storage conditions make food poisoning a serious danger for both children and adults.

Where urban conditions are grimmest and overcrowding most marked, the differences between urban and rural imrs still exist but are less pronounced. At the beginning of the 1990s the world's highest rate was for Sierra Leone, at 180, but the rate for Equatorial Guinea was almost as bad. Since many more small children die after the age of one, there is an increasing tendency among agencies involved in development to prefer under-five mortality rates (U5MRs) to imrs as indicators. Using these rates, UNICEF's 1988 figures (UNICEF 1990) suggest that Mozambique has the worst rate (298). Such statistics are not surprising for the poorest countries of Africa, but what is perhaps most interesting and hopeful is the very low rates being achieved now by some still very poor countries. China and Sri Lanka both have U5MRs of 43, compared with India's 149, and Cuba, at 18, is comparable with many wealthy First World nations.

A high infant mortality rate is the main reason for low life expectancy at birth. In most parts of the Third World, if you survive childhood, you have a fair chance of living almost as long as people do in Europe or the United States. Again, because of the high infant mortality rate, many of the worst life expectancies are to be found in Africa South of the Sahara. These figures are usually broken down by gender, since almost invariably women live longer than men, and in some societies, Japan being the most obvious example, there is such a wide a gap that it calls for explanation. Male/female life expectancy gaps do tend to be smaller in poorer countries, though, and the gap is non-existent in Bangladesh, for a variety of reasons which are dealt with later in Chapter 12. For Africa some representative figures are as follows:

Western Sahara: (female) 41, (male) 39
Chad: (female) 41, (male) 39
Guinea: (female) 45, (male) 41
Angola: (female) 46, (male) 42.

Not all low life expectancies are to be found in Africa. The lowest in Asia is that for Afghanistan, where, unusually, the average female life expectancy of 43 is actually less than the male 44.

Although, when things go wrong, there is no substitute for good medical help, the least important factor in general good health is the provision of good medical services. Medical solutions tend to be rich-world solutions: they are generally expensive and involve technology. However, they would include vaccination, which is relatively cheap and simple to administer, and, while poverty may be the factor most intimately bound to the health of the population, levels of immunity to infectious diseases are also important to public health. Paradoxically, one of the growing problems of the Third World is not that drugs are not available, but that there are too many of them. Some 30 major companies control some 50 per cent of the world pharmaceutical trade. External regulation of them by Third World countries is often weak, since they lack both the resources and the expertise to control what is sold. Pharmaceutical companies are big foreign exchange earners, so restrictions in their home countries in the developed world may not be too tight either. The market is very competitive – the merger of Glaxo and Wellcome in the UK in 1994 created the world's largest drug company, but it still accounted for only 6 per cent of the world market. The World Health Organization (WHO) itself is only an advisory body and its advice is not always followed. It is frequently found that drugs banned in the developed countries are either tested in developing countries or left on sale in developing countries long after they have been withdrawn from sale elsewhere.

Drug companies need to make money to recoup development costs as well as to keep shareholders happy. To do this, they want to sell not generic drugs from which the returns are relatively low, but specific branded products over which they can claim the right of 'intellectual property'. Through heavy advertising they promote the sale of branded drugs where generics would do. Their prices are so high and Third World health budgets so low that what they sell has virtually no additional therapeutic value, except possibly to the élite in the main urban centres. WHO has identified 200 cost-effective tried and tested drugs seen as basic and indispensable to any country's health needs, but in the name of free trade the developed countries can offer strong and successful resistance to any attempts to limit provision in this way.

However, drug regulation legislation has been proven to decrease reliance on expensive imported drugs. Sri Lanka established a National Formulary as early as 1959, and in 1972 the government of Mrs Sirima Bandaranaike established the Sri Lanka Pharmaceutical Corporation to produce generic drugs at low prices. Following independence in 1975, Mozambique established a central purchasing organization and an effective national formulary, although the circumstances of the country did not allow it to establish its own national drugs industry. In 1982 Bangladesh replaced its 1940 Drugs Act with a detailed National Drug Policy, banning many branded drugs altogether and establishing tight controls over the activities of TNCs in the country. Though this policy had strong support in the region, the United States government threatened reprisals on grounds of free trade, regardless of the ethical implications of forcing high-cost products on the population of one of the poorest countries in the world (Thomas 1987: 106–14).

At best, the power of the international drug companies can mean that Third World markets are flooded with branded cough medicine, but penicillin and other key drugs are unobtainable. Generally, it can mean the widespread availability of suspect products banned in the USA and Japan. At worst it means that a flourishing black market in prescription drugs grows up, and through their overuse, valuable antibiotics and anti-malarial drugs cease to be effective because germs and parasites develop resistance to them.

As seen above, health care in the Third World is often disproportionately used by the wealthy. As elsewhere, the rural poor are the group least likely to have access to it. Not only is it more difficult for logistical reasons to provide reliable health care in rural areas, but Third World governments, in this area as in others, often prefer to put their limited resources into large visible expenditures on urban hospitals, rather than devote it to primary health care, still less to essential health education.

While circulatory diseases are the main killers in the First World, infectious gastroenteric and respiratory diseases are more important in the Third World. It is, however, the rural populations who still suffer disproportionately from largely preventable infectious diseases (Danida 1989). For example:

- Over 400 million people in the world suffer from malaria.
- At least 225 million have hookworm (infestation by parasitic roundworms of any of several species of the genus Nematoda).
- 200 million are sick with schistosomiasis (infestation by blood flukes).
- 20 million suffer from sleeping sickness (trypanosomiasis, an endemic disease caused by a protozoan parasite carried by the tsetse fly).
- 20 million are afflicted by 'river blindness' (onchocerciasis, a nasty condition, prevalent in West Africa, in which a water-borne filiaral parasite enters the skin, usually in the lower body; it migrates through the body into the eyes, ultimately destroying the optic nerve and resulting in irretrievable loss of sight). Other preventable causes of blindness in tropical countries include trachoma, chronic infection of the conjunctiva by the bacterium *Chalmydia trachomatis*, and xerophthalmia, loss of sight through a simple deficiency of Vitamin A.
- 1.5 million children under five die each year from measles, a condition which is rarely fatal in the developed world, although it can and occasionally does lead to serious complications.

Case study: malaria

One of the worst of these scourges is malaria. It is also one that could be relatively easily rendered harmless, if sufficient resources could only be delivered to the task on a co-ordinated basis. The tiny West African state of The Gambia, until the 1994 coup an increasingly popular 'long-haul' tourist resort, was long known to sailors as the Graveyard Coast, and with good reason. In their villages, Gambians can expect an average of three bites per night from malaria-bearing mosquitoes. Mosquito nets would be considered an expensive luxury by most Gambians. Nor can most Gambians afford malaria preventatives; if they reach adulthood, they build up resistance. However, malaria is a real problem for children, who have not yet had time to develop resistance. Cerebral malaria, the kind found in The Gambia, attacks and destroys the brain. Hence not only do a million children under five die in Africa from malaria each year, but those who do not die may still suffer irreversible mental impairment. That malaria may soon become virtually untreatable is a real prospect by the year 2000. New, at present untreatable forms are developing, and new drugs are not being developed as quickly as they were.

Early work by the World Health Organization in the 1950s was mainly an attack on the carriers, the mosquitoes. DDT was extensively used until it was banned, but it turned out to be unnecessary. Simply covering stagnant water with a thin film of paraffin was enough to deter the mosquito from breeding. The campaign was therefore very successful. For example, the number of cases in Sri Lanka was reduced from thousands to an average of only 17 a year. Sadly, the campaign was not carried through to its logical conclusion. Residual cases remained and from these malaria parasites were transmitted again, with greater frequency once the mosquitoes had become immune to the pesticides being used against them and resources were no longer devoted to spraying the ponds and lakes. By the 1970s the war was lost. Ninety per cent of malaria cases today occur in Africa, where over 200 million people get it each year.

And it is not only in Africa that drug-resistant forms are re-emerging and presenting a formidable challenge to the resources of the major drug companies. Along the Thai/Cambodia border among prospectors the strains are virtually untreatable. The Thai operate mobile clinics along the border, but parasite resistance is encouraged by the abuse of anti-malarial drugs. The problem is the availability of drugs in Thailand, where malaria is under control, and their use as prophylaxis in Cambodia, a country dislocated by 20 years of war, where they promote resistance. Already the effects of chloroquine are diminishing. Aid workers have been seriously concerned at the absence of medical advice when Cambodians buy malarial treatments. As a result this area now has the most virulent form of malaria in the world.

The problems presented by malaria are not only medical but social. People move much further than mosquitoes, and in great numbers too in an area with refugees such as Thailand/Cambodia. The dispersal to the rest of the world of the 22,000 UN troops formerly in Cambodia, many of whom will have been sent from malarial areas, will not help either as they will take resistant strains home with them. But US military interest in developing malaria preventions is diminishing as it is now much less likely that US troops will be put in large numbers into South-East Asia. Instead malaria is losing out in the competition for funds as the money available goes into AIDS research. The toll of lives from malaria is more than 20 times greater than deaths from AIDS, but the victims of malaria are generally from poor countries. There is no money in tropical medicine and the big drug companies do not even bother to send their representatives to international conferences on tropical diseases – the WHO does all the cajoling, but often to little effect (*Assignment*, 'Fatal Latitudes', BBC Television, 1993).

Three out of five Third World governments spend more on arms than they do on health. Although there are marked variations, the *World Development Reports* suggest that this tendency is actually stronger in the low-income developing countries than it is in others. Two-and-a-half hours is all the time it takes for world military spending to consume the equivalent of the entire annual budget of the WHO. The cost of eradicating smallpox world-wide was only $83 million, the same as the cost of just one strategic bomber. But work against malaria was delayed due to 'shortage of funds' and the battle was lost.

Tuberculosis

The most recent epidemic to reappear, after several decades during which it had been possible virtually to ignore it, is tuberculosis (TB). According to WHO (1993), the number of people infected with TB in Africa is 175 million, in Latin America 115 million and South-East Asia 420 million. Tuberculosis is still treatable, but the proportion of these populations with access to treatment is in Africa only 25 per cent, in Latin America 42 per cent and in South-East Asia 45 per cent. Eight million new cases are reported every year. Since in the last few years the disease has been spreading like wildfire in the big cities of the United States, among the population deprived of welfare services by the free market philosophy of the Reagan years, there is ironically some hope that in the end something may be done about it.

In the meantime Dr Arati Kochi of WHO's TB Programme has said: 'Tuberculosis is humanity's greatest killer and it is out of control in many parts of the world. The disease, which is preventable and treatable, has been grossly neglected' (quoted in *The Guardian*, 4 May 1993).

Kerala

However, all is not doom and gloom. The goal of Health for All by the year 2000 has been missed, but, where efforts have been made, achievements have been remarkable. The state of Kerala, a densely populated state of some 30 million people in south-west India, is a good example of what can be achieved with limited resources. Although the state contains substantial Muslim and Christian minorities as well as Buddhists and the majority Hindus, Kerala has long been a relatively tolerant and harmonious backwater.

In 1957 a Communist state government was democratically elected. Since that time a variety of broadly leftist coalitions have held power. These governments have included communist and socialist elements as well as

Congress (S) and Janata Dal, but all have been kept on their toes both by pressure from Delhi and by the alternative, the return to power of a centre coalition. Such a coalition, including Congress (I), has been in power in the state since 1991. A major target for left-wing governments has been the traditional unequal distribution of land in the state. Needless to say, land reform was strongly resisted at first, but it was finally achieved in the early 1970s. As intended, it has resulted in a radical redistribution of wealth. Nine out of ten Kerala families now own their own home and smallholding. The amount of land which may be owned by a single family is severely constrained, to a maximum of 8 hectares. There is strong protection for workers through unions whose origins lie with the followers of Gandhi, who operated in the north of the state in the 1930s and 1940s. State legislation results in redistribution of income too, with a strong emphasis on social programmes especially in health and education.

The result has been a marked rise in life expectancy. Keralans enjoy a much higher quality of life than people in the rest of India, although the state has a lower than average per capita GNP. State control of aspects of food distribution and subsidies on basic foods ensure that the very poorest sectors are not malnourished. The average family size is two, not four as elsewhere in India. As well as good nutrition, the better education of women and good public health care contribute to lower the infant mortality rate. This stands at 20 compared with 95 for India as a whole, and a Keralan can look forward at birth to an average life expectancy of 70, compared with the all-India average of 56.

HOUSING

Two main aspects of this problem are important: the quality of housing and its location. For the first, one hundred million people have no shelter at all, and a further one billion are inadequately housed. For the second, most of the world's population still live in rural areas. However, many of them are landless, or nearly so, and hence have little to hold them there. Their natural course is to migrate to the big cities. By the end of the century nearly half will live in urban areas.

In 1990, 22 Third World cities had a population of more than four million. By 2000 there will be 60 in this position. Ten of the 13 most populated cities (more than 13 million people) will be in the South, with Mexico City and São Paulo still at the top of the list. It is already difficult adequately to describe the extent of the pollution in downtown Mexico City. The air is thick with photochemical smog generated by cars, diesel engines and industrial machinery. Since the city was build on a dried-up lake bed, the city centre has sunk by some 5 metres and sewage has to be pumped uphill to get it out of the way. With such serious problems of pollution, the future could be horrendous.

In rural areas, poverty facilitates the spread of sicknesses often unknown to the urban dweller. Thus in rural Argentina dirt floors allow the spread of Chagas disease, a tick-borne parasitic illness. However, overcrowding, most likely in urban areas, enormously increases the spread of air-borne diseases such as TB and diphtheria. It is even possible to contract hepatitis 'A' in Mexico City from the windblown faecal dust from the city's sewage farms.

EDUCATION

At first sight, education might not appear to be as essential a need as water, food or shelter. However, education plays a vital role in enabling human beings to become part of and work within modern society. It is, of course, inseparable from health issues, in particular family planning and thus population growth. As the British trade union slogan has it: 'If you think education is expensive, try ignorance.'

The availability of education is measured in various ways: by the percentage of children who attend school, by the mean number of years' schooling they receive, by the proportion of government expenditure devoted to education and, above all, by 'literacy' – the percentage of the population that can read and write, although this is not an easy figure to determine accurately (see Table 3.2).

In the developing world, 30 per cent of children aged 6–11 and 60 per cent of youngsters aged 12–17 do not attend school. However, much depends on the policies pursued by national and state governments. Thus in the state of Kerala in India there is 87 per cent adult female literacy, compared with only 29 per cent for India generally, and 94 per cent adult male literacy, which is much higher than in any other low-income region or country. In middle-income Brazil, where only 3 per cent of government expenditure goes on education, less than a quarter of primary school entrants successfully complete their courses. This compares very unfavourably with a much poorer country such as Sri Lanka, which spends a far greater proportion on educating its children and where nearly 9 out of 10 successfully complete their primary school courses. Hence in Sri Lanka, literacy rates are much higher than they are in Brazil, and this is reflected in Sri Lanka's far better performance on all the social indicators (see Table 1.3).

POPULATION GROWTH

In April 1992 a UN report saw population growth as the greatest threat to humanity. This view was shared by many of the world's leaders, notably the Prince of Wales, who said that same month: 'we will not slow the birth rate

Table 3.2 *World's lowest literacy rates, 1990*

Country	Percentage literate	Men (%)	Women (%)
Djibouti	12		
Solomon Islands	15		
Somalia	17	27	9
Burkina Faso	18	28	9
Sierra Leone	21	31	11
Benin	23	32	16
Guinea	24	35	13
Nepal	26	38	13
The Gambia	27	39	16
Sudan	27	43	12
Niger	28	40	17
Afghanistan	29	44	14
Chad	30	42	18
Mali	32	41	24
Yemen	32		
Mozambique	33	45	21
Mauritania	34	47	21
Bangladesh	35	47	22
Cambodia	35	48	22
Pakistan	35	47	21

Source: *Third World Guide 93/94*, p. 39.

much until we find ways of addressing poverty; and we will not protect the environment until we address the issues of population growth and poverty in the same breath'.

However, leaders from the First World were unsuccessful in their efforts to make population control a central theme of the Earth Summit. Their argument stemmed from the Malthusian view, which had become received wisdom in the western industrial nations, that increased population will at some stage confront finite world resources. It was publicly resented by much of the Third World, and a great deal of time was wasted on a sterile debate about whether Third World population or First World consumption was a more serious threat. Since the two are not mutually exclusive, the debate as such cannot have an outcome.

Population growth is highest in the countries of the Third World, as the figures for average population growth by continents show: Africa 3.1 per cent per year, North America 1.6 per cent, South America 2.2 per cent, Asia 2.6 per cent, Europe 0.6 per cent. Population growth places serious strains on the ability of Third World countries to feed, clothe and house their populations. But population is also a resource: where capital is scarce, labour is cheap

(Boserup 1981). So the balance from a purely economic point of view is not clear-cut. In any case, two much more immediate reasons for population control that are usually cited in Malthusian lines of argument are harder to dispute. Population control directly acts to raise the quality of women's lives. By facilitating the spacing out of families, it also indirectly contributes to the better health of children.

Population growth in the South is an issue in the North because it threatens northern lifestyles through environmental pressures. Perhaps more seriously, it promotes a fortress mentality in response to refugees' desire to escape, whether from persecution or from poverty.

There has in recent years been a vigorous debate as to whether poverty stimulates population growth. However, recent evidence is that, although birth rate drops dramatically once imr is reduced, it is not poverty as such, but the availability at a reasonable cost of means of artificial birth control, that has the most immediate relevance to population growth. Thirteen (rich) nations have already achieved zero population growth. But 3.5 billion people or 77 per cent of the world's population live in the Third World today, and on current trends this proportion will be 80 per cent by 2000 and 84 per cent by 2020. The Third World has 90 per cent of the world's population growth. Hence the world population, growing by 100 million people a year at present, is expected to double by 2050 to around 10 billion. Without natural disaster or human intervention or both, it will probably not level off until it reaches 14 billion, nearly three times today's level.

Interpreting the consequences of this growth, however, is more problematic. The present rate of population growth in the Third World alone would mean a 75 per cent increase in Third World energy consumption by 2025, even at present inadequate per capita levels. It is also possible to argue that population is only a problem in relation to the use of the world's resources. Since the Third World only uses about 20 per cent of the world's resources, it is if anything underpopulated, so population is not an issue. The population of the Third World is not expected to grow enough to consume as much as the North in the foreseeable future. Hence population will probably never have the equivalent environmental impact of consumption, since the South's consumption is not increasing at a sufficient rate to do so.

If we look at contribution to global toxicity, then we find that the population of rich countries is contributing some ten times the per capita municipal/industrial waste of those of the developing countries. In fact if I = impact on the environment, P = population, A = affluence and T = technology, then $I = P \times A \times T$ (*New Internationalist*, September 1992: 8). Although the linear equation may seem simplistic at first glance, it does seem reasonable to suppose that affluence and technology operate as multipliers, because consumption increases with affluence and because increased access to advanced technology increases the use of natural resources.

On the other hand, up to a point, affluence can increase the carrying capacity of land: that is to say, the numbers which can be supported without threatening an area's capacity to do so in the future. So its absence increases the problems of population increase to much of Third World. Population increase is a problem in Africa South of the Sahara because the carrying capacity of its land is low, not because population density is particularly high – in Africa South of the Sahara population density is less than 20 persons per square kilometre, while that of the Netherlands is more than 400 persons per square kilometre. However, the case of Africa South of the Sahara is also illuminating because it demonstrates that the question of population distribution is vital to any consideration of the matter. Africa South of the Sahara has overpopulated regions where carrying capacity is less than the population seeking a living there, especially in its vast and growing cities, in crowded coastal areas and in the most marginal highland ecosystems. At the same time there are enormous uncultivated and underpopulated fertile tropical areas with as yet underutilized carrying capacities.

There are a number of factors that can be shown to reduce population growth:

- Urbanization, which raises the cost of child rearing at the same time as reducing the pressure for child labour.
- Health care (including family planning).
- Female literacy.
- More earning opportunities for women, which tend to delay marriage as well as giving incentives to have smaller families.
- Reduced infant mortality rate, especially when resulting from better access to clean water.

Only 30 per cent of couples in the developing world outside China who wish to use artificial methods of birth control have access to contraceptives. In China the regime has tried to enforce a single-child policy, with various sanctions against couples who produce two children. However, this has created a new social problem, that of overcossetted offspring and the potential problem of later dependency ratios.

ENVIRONMENTAL DEGRADATION

Most scientists would agree on one thing, that life on earth depends on the very precise situation of the earth in the solar system. Life as we know it can only survive within very narrow temperature limits, where water can be made available to plants and animals in liquid form. James Lovelock, for one, has found the atmosphere of the earth to be so improbable in biochemical terms that he has concluded that only a regulatory process could explain it and that process was life itself. His 'Gaia Hypothesis' (from the Greek word for the earth) states that it is the collective interaction of all living things and inanimate matter on earth that gives stability (Lovelock 1979, 1986).

Though most scientists would not agree with this, many of them would identify in their respective fields of study evidence that the limits of tolerance of the ecosystem have been reached or are likely to be reached in the near future:

1. First of all, there is the quantity of the earth's resources being consumed. The human population of the world has tripled since 1910, but the consumption of natural resources has increased twentyfold.
2. The question of whether or not the earth is getting warmer (global warming) is disputed. What is not in doubt, however, is that since industrialization began the proportion of carbon dioxide in the atmosphere has risen significantly and that it is continuing to rise, along with the proportion of other gases such as methane. These gases are collectively referred to as the 'greenhouse gases', since they share the common property of allowing more of the sun's energy to enter the earth's atmosphere than they allow out. Unless some other factor acts to counteract this effect (such as the greater activity of plants in a warmer atmosphere to use the CO_2 and release more oxygen), the average temperature of the earth must rise.
3. The air is also polluted by increasing levels of harmful products of the combustion of fuels, whether in industrial plants, power stations, homes or vehicles. Some of these would act to assist global warming, some would counteract it to some extent by screening out the sun's rays. However, the motor car is the main problem. Concentrations of its exhaust gases are reaching such levels in big cities that they are a major contributor to the rise of asthma and other serious respiratory diseases. But many of the world's big cities are in the Third World, where there are weak controls on exhaust emissions and diesel engines are seldom well maintained. One-fifth of the world's population breathes air more polluted than the WHO minimum standards. All children growing up in Mexico City are likely to suffer some degree of mental impairment in consequence, and the situation in São Paulo, Calcutta or Manila may be even worse.
4. A special problem is presented by ozone. Ozone is an isotope of oxygen, found both near ground level, where it is a harmful irritant, and in the upper atmosphere, where it performs a vital role for all plant and animal life in screening out much of the ultraviolet light emitted by the sun. In 1982 scientists observed, to their surprise, that at high latitudes in the Antarctic the vital ozone layer was being heavily depleted during the winter, and, as their observations continued, they found that towards the end of the coldest period it was disappearing altogether (the 'ozone hole'). The cause was then traced to the production and release into the

atmosphere of stable chlorine-based compounds, in particular the chloro-fluorocarbons (CFCs) used in refrigerators, and halons, used in electrical transformers and fire extinguishers. Harmless at low altitudes, in the upper atmosphere these substances combine rapidly with the available ozone, and, since there is so little of it, soon use up all the available supply. Not only does this increase dramatically the risk of damage to skin and eyes for human beings and other animals, but there is evidence that it also disturbs the growing cycle of the very plants on which we rely.

5. Intensive farming of land with a high input of energy through the use of fertilizers and pesticides is 'efficient' in the narrowly economic sense of that term. But only in the short term. In the long term it is already clear that it can and does lead to serious degradation of the soil. And older problems are recurring: the drying-out of the soil leading to desertification, and the concentration of salts in the soil through irrigation. Some 97 per cent of our food comes from the land and 35 per cent – about a third – of available arable land has already been irreversibly (on any meaningful timescale) degraded. We are now foreclosing options for the future, and any further attempt to increase growth by increasing inputs, the method favoured by the governments of the rich northern countries, would speed this process of degradation up.

6. The general quality of water sources gives rise to serious concern (see earlier in this chapter and Chapter 13).

7. More than a thousand species are being irretrievably lost every day, as forests are cleared, fields ploughed up and the natural habitat of birds, animals, plants and fungi destroyed. Scientists have had time to evaluate the properties of no more than a few of the many plants of the tropical rainforest. But the loss of biological diversity (biodiversity) has more serious implications even than that. Human beings are becoming more and more reliant on only a few strains of certain cereals and fruits. Genetic mutation or the emergence of new crop diseases could threaten the whole structure of mechanized agriculture with catastrophe, and with it the whole human species.

8. Non-renewable sources, oil and natural gas provide at present some 60 per cent of global energy and there are only 50 years of proven reserves of these fuels. Though fossil fuels are often to be found in the Third World, it is the advanced industrialized countries which consume most of them. Fossil fuels give 78 per cent of the energy consumed by the United States. This represents some 26 per cent saving compared with 1973, but there is scope for much more. Japan has no oil or gas, although it does have abundant reserves of coal, at least in the short term. However, its industrial output is up by 81 per cent since 1973 without any increase in energy consumption. The USA could cut its energy consumption by half using only existing technologies, but until recently the use of fossil fuels has been seen as a matter of military security. The North's annual military

consumption of fossil fuels alone is twice the consumption of all African countries combined (Guimaraes 1991: 55).

9. The developed world is producing so much solid waste, much of it highly toxic, that already some states and companies are looking to the Third World for landfill sites. For example, Germany has been burying nuclear waste in Mongolia, and the USA disposing of its toxic products in Guinea-Bissau. However, the Nigerians have refused to accept industrial waste from Italy and such sites are becoming increasingly scarce at any price. Meanwhile, despite an international convention aimed at ending the practice, some 6.5 billion tons of refuse are dumped in our seas each year, with Britain one of the worst offenders. The long-term consequences of this irresponsible practice can only be guessed at. But we already know that pollution of the shallow and largely land-locked Baltic Sea has reached unacceptable levels, and that of the totally enclosed Caspian Sea has reached the point at which the survival of the celebrated (and extremely profitable) sturgeon fisheries of Russia and Iran is threatened.

The problem in almost all of these respects is that it is overconsumption in the rich countries that is most important in pushing world consumption to its limits. The richest 20 per cent of the world's states consume 70 per cent of the world's commercial energy. The rich countries make a disproportionate contribution to environmental damage. They do so because they enjoy disproportionate benefits from it. Hence they must in justice bear a disproportionate share of costs; they must help the South develop in a way that is sustainable indefinitely, if only because if they do not do so, the South can in a negative way ensure that international agreements are inoperative.

It was Mahatma (Mohandas K.) Gandhi who, when asked if independent India would achieve British standards of living, replied: 'It took Britain half the resources of the planet to achieve this prosperity; how many planets will a country like India require?' (De la Court 1990, cited by Thomas 1992: 15). The same problem has been expressed less elegantly, but with more precision, by Mostafa K. Tolba, the Director of the UN Environment Programme:

> the two basic causes of the environmental crisis are poverty and misused wealth: The poor in the world are compelled over the short run to destroy precisely the resources on which their long-term subsistence depends, while the wealthy minority makes demands on the resource base, which in the long run are unsustainable – thus making the poor substitute victims. (quoted in Guimaraes 1991: 53)

But the irony is that hunger and poverty are not the future nightmare scenario of environmental crises for many in the Third World, as they are for people in the developed world. They are here-and-now reality. One billion people, or about one-fifth of the world's population, live on less than $1 a day. In these circumstances, poverty may be more important than environment for much of the Third World. At first sight, to redress the balance looks well-nigh impossible. Either massive and unprecedented world economic growth (500–1,000 per cent) would be needed to cure poverty – and as presently understood this would not be sustainable – or there has to be substantial income redistribution from the First to the Third World coupled with early population stability – which is not politically viable. This dilemma has been seen as a confrontation between 'environmental realism' and 'political realism', and it is the latter that must change (UNESCO 1991).

Given their traditional orientation towards development, Third World and some East European governments still have to be converted. For them in the short term, sustainable development is unlikely to replace conventional economic development, which is perceived as delivering the following benefits:

- National power in the global stratification system.
- Retention of office through the support of the population or, at least, key actors within it.
- Personal material rewards.

Certainly the problems of the here and now are too great to contemplate the problems of future generations. Meanwhile the obligation to aid this conversion through the transfer of resources has not been seen as politically viable in the First World. A long-term perspective does not sit easily with national, or indeed with international, politics, and this is especially true for new states which feel themselves to be reacting rather than free to act in a system not controlled by themselves.

PART II
Social and economic contexts

4 The economic context

INTRODUCTION

Agricultural earnings traditionally form the basis of Third World export economies. The most important thing about them, however, is that they rest on so few products and that these show a strong regional concentration. For example, two-thirds of the exports from Africa South of the Sahara (SSA) are coffee and cocoa. Nearly three-quarters of all exports from Latin America consist of three crops: sugar, coffee and soya beans. The situation is even worse for certain individual countries, whose reliance in extreme cases may be on a single crop: in the case of Cuba, sugar, and of Bangladesh, jute.

The drive to find and exploit crops for export has resulted in a world-wide move from the growth of foodstuffs for subsistence to the production of cash crops for export. Such cash crops now occupy more than a quarter of the cultivable land of the Third World. This shift has serious consequences. First of all, it increases people's vulnerability to famine because personal reserves of food no longer exist (see Chapter 3). Second, for the individual family, it introduces a new kind of vulnerability/dependency on macroeconomic changes. The periodic fall in commodity prices, which previously would have affected only a few, now acts to reduce the country's foreign exchange earnings and hence its capacity to buy staple foodstuffs which are no longer locally produced in sufficient quantities.

There are even more serious long-term environmental consequences, the full effects of which are only just beginning to be recognized and have yet to be addressed by governments. The move into cash crops takes up much of the best, most fertile land, and subjects it to intensive cultivation of a single crop. Traditional patterns of crop rotation, which have kept the land in good condition for decades, if not for centuries, are abandoned. To compensate for the resulting deterioration, the land is subjected to heavy doses of fertilizers and pesticides. Since these have to be imported, as does much farm machinery and the equipment for irrigation, the new agriculture consumes most of the country's scarce foreign exchange. Meanwhile the soil suffers serious and potentially irreversible environmental damage, as in the case of the creation of the American dust-bowl or the desertification of Iraq, Ethiopia and the Sahel.

Turning Third World products into commodities (commodification) has indisputably linked the countries of the Third World to the global economic system. How this linkage works, what the impact is of unequal relationships and what are the prospects for the future all remain vigorously disputed.

MODERNIZATION

The Cold War resulted in the USA taking a direct interest in some parts of the world almost for the first time, especially but not exclusively to fill the gap left by the dismantling of the European colonial empires. Its initial approach was based on the notion of modernization.

The attraction of the United States for the rest of the world was that it represented modernity. There was little initial resistance, therefore, to the US belief that the rest of the world was destined in time to follow the example of the United States. Indeed, this view has, in the longer term, turned out to be at least partly true.

What was termed 'modernization theory', though, derived from two influences: the structural-functionalism of Talcott Parsons, based on the work of Herbert Spencer and Emile Durkheim, and Max Weber's work on values and attitudes. McClelland and Inkeles concentrate on values and take up the theme of evolution in their tendency to see growth towards equilibrium. Some of the early work of the structural-functionalists now seems almost naive in its touching belief in stability and pluralist consensus. Almond's work combines elements of Parsonian social theory and David Easton's political system analysis.

The best-known example of the school is the work of the American economist W.W. Rostow (Rostow 1971). Rostow's five stages of development – traditional society, preconditions for take-off, take-off, sustained growth and mass consumption – represent stages in the process of development in the United States. As with *Industrialism and Industrial Man* (Kerr *et al.* 1960), this was seen as a unilinear process leading to an end-state akin to that of the United States in the 1950s. For these writers, modernity implied liberal democracy and pluralism. Hence political development was virtually synonymous with modernization. It was a concept largely sustained by Ford Foundation finance and it expired with the grant in 1971.

The early modernization theorists saw traditionalism and modernity as two poles and in zero-sum relationship with one another. Later material acknowledges the survival of the traditional alongside the modern. The persistence of ethnic distinctions, clientelism, etc. would exemplify the survival of traditional patterns, likewise the continuing importance of caste in Indian elections. Traditional, however, did not necessarily mean static. Traditional culture was not internally consistent, and traditional societies were not necessarily homogeneous in social structure nor were they always in conflict with modern forms and therefore liable to be destroyed by change.

The failure of the first, optimistic modernization theories results in more sophisticated 'modernization revisionism'. Huntington, who coined the term, stresses the importance of indigenous social structures, but also the need for strong government. Unlike early modernization theory, which was optimistic in an era of assumed progress, modernization revisionism exuded a new pessimism and saw modernization itself as a force for the breakdown of order and the development of praetorianism. The process of development mobilizes social groups previously neglected or ignored and temporary disorder must be contained until institutionalization restores stability.

Ensuring order during the development process rests on strengthening the government and state. Its techniques often include repression, co-optation and ideological penetration. Huntington himself laid a strong emphasis on the value of the military as modernizers. Some modernization revisionists, such as J.J. Johnson, take the role of the military one step further. They argue that the military is a substitute for an effective middle class as an agent of developmental change.

DEPENDENCY

An economic emphasis characterizes work in the 'dependency' school, whether it be of the ECLA-derived dependentista type (see Prebisch 1950) or André Gunder Frank's 'development of underdevelopment'. The dependency thesis originated with the Marxist analysis of Third World economies by Paul Baran (1957). It was Baran who first distinguished Third World economies as being on the periphery of the world economic system, whose centre was in Europe and North America.

As the term 'dependentista' would suggest, the dependency thesis was developed and popularized in Latin America, by a variety of writers not all of whom were Marxists (Jaguaribe 1967; Cardoso[1] and Faletto 1979, first published 1969; Dos Santos 1969, 1970; Cardoso 1972; Furtado 1970; Sunkel 1969; Ianni 1975) and in a very similar version has since been widely adopted in other regions of the Third World (Amin 1990a, 1990b). The term is derived from the view that, because Third World economies are on the periphery of the world capitalist system, they have become dependent on the advanced industrialized countries. It rejects the developmentalist view that Third World states can in time undergo the same form of development as the existing industrialized states, for at least as long as the capitalist system exists in its present form. The reason, its adherents argue, is that the 'centre', the advanced industrialized countries, sets the terms on which the system

[1] Cardoso made a long, slow journey rightwards and, after a spell as Senator from São Paulo, became President of Brazil in January 1994.

operates. As a result, the terms of trade are unfavourable to Third World countries and the flow of capital is asymmetrical, tending to flow from the periphery towards the centre. This outflow is a structural constraint that ensures that the states of the 'periphery' are weak, open to penetration from the centre and with little or no scope for autonomous action (Bonilla and Girling 1973).

Most of these authors as well as the relevant international institutions and non-dependency theorists would accuse early modernization theorists of stressing the political to the exclusion of the economic, and would charge revisionists with ignoring the international dimension. These are the key elements of dependency theory. Dos Santos (1969) writes that underdevelopment

> is a conditioning situation in which the economies of one group of countries are conditioned by the development and expansion of others. A relationship between two or more economies or between such economies and the world trading system becomes a dependent relationship when some countries can expand through self-impulsion while others being in a dependent position can only expand as a reflection of the expansion of the dominant countries.

The duality of co-existent modern and traditional sectors found in modernization revisionism made life easier for the development of dependency theory, but it has its roots in two sources:

- The non-Marxist nationalism of Latin American structuralism. This school was exemplified by the UN Economic Commission for Latin America (ECLA) and its best-known representative, Raúl Prebisch. ECLA, established in 1949 at the request of the Latin Americans, who wanted 'a Marshall Plan for Latin America', criticized the theory of comparative advantage. The ECLA theorists divided the world into centre and periphery and argued that the oligopoly of markets in the centre leads to a long-term tendency towards declining terms of trade and to the concentration of industrial production in the centre and, in turn, to Latin American dependence on imports. As a result, sustained development depends on the nationalist bourgeoisie promoting industrialization – at first through import-substitution industrialization (ISI).
- Marx's distinction between core and periphery. Though Marx saw the exploitation of the Third World as part of the inevitable development of industrial capitalism, he argued also that imperialism breaks up traditional societies and creates new markets for industrial goods. Baran, Frank, Cardoso and Faletto were all influenced to some extent by this argument, but pointed out that things did not go thereafter entirely as Marx had envisaged. The fact was that capital did not accumulate in the Third World to be invested *in situ* to the benefit of the state.

Instead it was repatriated to the centre, thus accentuating its dominance in terms of capital formation.

The notion of the development of underdevelopment is associated particularly with the work of Andr Gunder Frank (1966, 1967, 1969). Frank argues that developed countries were formerly 'undeveloped' but they have never been 'underdeveloped'. Underdevelopment for Frank is a process of structural distortion. The economies of underdeveloped countries have been partially developed, but in a way that enhances their economic value not to their own citizens, but to the advanced industrialized countries. In this process, he, in common with other dependency writers, ascribes a special role to two agencies. The first is what he terms the 'lumpenbourgeoisie', otherwise generally known as the national bourgeoisie or, for the Maoists, the 'comprador' bourgeoisie (from the Portuguese word for a merchant – Frank 1970, 1974). The ruling classes in peripheral states actively encourage the outflow of wealth from their countries by using their 'control of state power to protect the interests of multinational capital' (Kitching 1982). It is they who find their economic interests best served by an alliance with the second agency, the foreign corporation, to exploit their own fellow-countryfolk.

Thus for Frank development in metropolis and underdevelopment in its satellites are two sides of the same coin. The metropolitan centres were once undeveloped but never underdeveloped. It is capitalist penetration which causes underdevelopment, and development in the satellites is only possible when they break away from their metropolitan exploiters. This is rarely possible and only takes place in moments of major crisis, such as war or severe economic depression.

Hence for Frank differing levels of development are the product not of different historical stages of development, but of the different functions the areas concerned perform in the international system. Production in colonies was determined not by the needs of those colonies (except colonial settlers 'needing' luxury goods), but by the needs of the colonial power. Hence unequal power relations have developed and continue to be maintained both between First and Third World countries (metropolis and periphery) and within Third World countries (city and 'camp', élite and mass). The worst off are the masses of the Third World, since they suffer from 'superexploitation' by both their own élite and that of the metropolis. Such inequality is known as 'structural heterogeneity' and stems from the fact that the local political élite are the agents of the international class and the state is their instrument.

Dependent economies are subjugated to the needs of the world economy by foreign (metropolitan) control of markets and capital, as well as by ownership of concerns which have competitive advantages over local firms, leading to the further continued outflow of capital. This has two causes: the need for capital-intensive foreign technology and imported capital goods on the one hand, and endemic balance of payments problems on the other. It is the reliance on the export of primary products hit by fluctuating prices that leads to balance of payments problems and thus to reliance on foreign direct investment and aid. The repatriation of profits, technological dependency and the dominance of multinational corporations all serve to undermine sovereignty. Tied aid and loans are examples of capitalism's need to continue its penetration of the Third World.

The third subdivision usually distinguished within the dependency school – Wallerstein's world-systems analysis – also lays stress, as would be expected, on economic factors. Wallerstein's world-systems model assumes that a peripheral position in the world economy by definition means a weak state, whereas being part of the core means having a strong state (Wallerstein 1974). However, this is just not true. Wallerstein's argument is reversed by those who see late industrializers as developing under the protection of a strong state. Late industrializers such as Japan have been able to develop through the leadership of a strong state bent on the objective of economic development. The case of the NICs is still controversial and will be discussed later.

In recent years there have been a variety of criticisms made of the dependency/dependentista school. The most important is that its theories do not fit the historical facts. As Laclau (1977) points out, Frank's historical analysis of the origins of capitalism is not accurate. Smith (1979) in *World Politics* describes dependency theory as 'theoretically logical but empirically unsubstantiated'. The next most important criticism is that national differences are neglected or even ignored altogether. Dependency theory does have a tendency to ignore differences between states. The global economy is the key, and national characteristics such as political parties and military establishments are, if not incidental, at least very secondary. The theory was developed to 'explain' the case of Latin America and is not really relevant elsewhere.

If there are strong criticisms from the empirical point of view, there are equally strong criticisms of the theoretical concepts employed by dependency writers. Their work fails adequately to define 'development', and their use of terms such as 'class' is inconsistent. It relies on 'latent conspiratorial assumptions' (Kamrava 1993) rather than a realistic perception of how business executives and politicians actually think. Much of the debate within the dependency school has been an internal Marxist squabble about the past which offers no hope for the future.

However, not all dependency theory is Marxist (see Chilcote 1978: 61; see also Chilcote and Edelstein 1974), and dependency theorists are no longer as simplistic or depressing as they have been in the past. They would not now accept a simple core–periphery split, but would want to introduce intermediate categories such as semi-periphery (a category which would include a large and powerful state like Brazil) and sub-metropolis. Cardoso and others recognize internal forces as making choices and decisions that impact on development, although their options are limited by external factors; this is 'national underdevelopment' (Cardoso and Faletto 1979: 21). Some internal groups wish to maintain dependent relations. Others oppose them. So dependency is not simply an external variable.

These writers have moved on from the early work of André Gunder Frank in seeing some kind of development as possible within capitalism, even if it is dependent development. Thus they may be seen to take some account of the emergence of the NICs. There is an alternative suggestion from Bill Warren within a Marxist framework that development is possible, although it will be of a distorted kind. For Warren capitalist imperialism functions to drag the Third World with it, thus promoting economic development. However, there is a nagging suspicion that some of these questions involve a tautology. Dependency is not separately defined; it consists merely in being dependent (see Dos Santos above).

CLASS AND STATE

Those concerned with the role of the state in the process of development have stressed either political or economic aspects. 'Class/state politics' (for further details, see Randall and Theobald 1985: 137–78) stresses both in either of the following frameworks:

- A Marxist framework, such as is to be found in the writing of Roxborough (1979). His frequent stress on 'modes of production' shows in the choice of term the Marxist base, and the use of the plural indicates the importance of individual national histories and states which are, of course, essentially political.
- A non-Marxist schema such as that found in the works of Stepan (1973, 1978), Schmitter (1979) or O'Donnell (1988).

Later neo-Marxist post-dependency explanations make class alignments within dependent states and the relative autonomy of the state central to their analysis. More emphasis is placed on examining indigenous structures. Obviously class formations are central, but so too is the political role of the state, not just as a representative of the dominant class, but as a participant in its own right. Pre-existing (i.e. pre-capitalist) modes of production survive in peripheral economies subjected to the capitalist mode (this idea is found in the work of Laclau). Indeed several modes of production may co-exist, and the role of the state is vital in determining the role of the national bourgeoisie (e.g. Roxborough 1979).

By comparison with old-fashioned Marxism, these explanations are flexible. Maoist influence can been seen in the fact that peasants are recognized as being a potentially revolutionary force (see also Colburn 1994). However, those they seem to have in mind are not peasants in the true sense, who remain a very conservative stratum, but those who constitute a 'peasantariat' like the plantation workers for TNCs such as Del Monte.

Conversely, there is a belated recognition that, far from being a powerful force for change, the industrial proletariat may constitute a small privileged élite in the Third World, as, for example, in Mexico, where the trade union sector forms one of the three pillars maintaining the dominance of the Institutional Revolutionary Party (PRI). On the other hand, nitrate and copper miners in Bolivia and Chile were left wing, while the urban working class in Brazil and Argentina followed Vargas, Goulart and Perón, populist figures of the centre-Left.

The view that the state is not simply part of the superstructure and an instrument of the dominant class has obvious sources within Marxist thought, especially the work of Gramsci. The state is seen as above squabbles by fractions of the ruling class pursuing their own short-term interests. There is a non-Marxist emphasis on the state from those, such as Stepan and Schmitter, who see an authoritarian stage as an historic necessity, not actually desirable, but something that unfortunately cannot be avoided at a critical stage of development.

O'Donnell developed the widely used concept of 'bureaucratic-authoritarianism' to describe the situation when, in a post-populist society constrained by the limits of industrialization, civil and military technocrats ally with foreign capital to demobilize or repress popular movements. However, O'Donnell's model not only is not generally applicable to Latin America, but fits very narrowly the very specific case of Argentina between 1966 and 1973. For this reason 'military developmentalism' may be a more widely acceptable term to describe the common features of the repressive military regimes of the 1960s and 1970s.

NEWLY INDUSTRIALIZING COUNTRIES

The possibility of a late start to development was first exemplified in Japan, Germany and the former Soviet Union. In the period since 1945 the dramatic growth of these economies and, more recently, the rise of the Newly Industrializing Countries (NICs) have certainly exacerbated the many problems of conceptualizing the Third World (Dicken 1986). The problem of Third World variety requires us to take account of the varying degrees of economic autonomy that may be possible within the global economy.

The term 'Newly Industrializing Countries' already has a slightly dated look. The new term that seems to be coming into vogue is 'New Industrial Economies' (NIEs), which is in any case more accurate since the 'core group' of NICs always includes Hong Kong, which is not a 'country'. South Korea, Taiwan and Singapore have already 'made it' from the Third World to fully industrialized status, and along with the colony of Hong Kong they constitute the 'Gang of Four' or the 'Asian Tigers'. Thailand, Indonesia, Malaysia, Argentina, Brazil and Mexico are on their way, possibly to be followed by the Philippines and Mauritius. However, there is less agreement on which other countries should be included in this category. Different institutions and different authors express different opinions about what constitutes an NIC.

Specifically, the question arises whether the NICs are a symptom of the changing order which signifies what Harris has called 'the end of the Third World'. As Harris points out (1986: 102), as recently as 1960 North America and western Europe had 78 per cent of the world's manufacturing output. By 1981 their share had fallen to only 59 per cent. At the same time, manufacturing output of the NICs and other middle-income countries had risen from 19 per cent to 37 per cent, while that of low-income countries, including Africa South of the Sahara, had remained virtually the same.

However, the impact of development is sometimes glaringly obvious even on the simplest of indicators. For example, in 1967 Indonesia was much poorer than India in terms of per capita income. In 1970, 60 per cent of the population of this vast, sprawling archipelago lived in what the World Bank defined as 'poverty'. By 1990 this figure had dropped to 15 per cent. Asia is the most significant area when it comes to dramatic economic growth precisely because of the huge numbers of human beings involved. Between 1970 and 1990 the number in absolute poverty more than halved despite rapid population growth. There can be no more dramatic evidence of the massive market expansion in that region, which has accompanied its rapid industrialization. Both the IMF and the World Bank expect the majority of growth in world output over the remaining years of the twentieth century to be predominantly Asian. This growth even on their own assumptions will far outstrip the paltry amount which its proponents argue will result from the conclusion of the Uruguay Round and the transformation of the GATT into the World Trade Organization (WTO).

It is hardly surprising that the relatively advantaged and diversified middle-income countries should seek to increase their share of global markets, but only a small proportion of them have done so. The NICs represent *the* most important blurring of the Third/First World division to date, as they have set out successfully to challenge the developed nations, both on their own traditional bases of industrialization (e.g. iron, steel and heavy industry) and also in the new consumer markets.

This can be seen by closer examination of the recent economic histories of the 'core' NICs – those on which there will be general agreement. South Korea and Taiwan will be taken as examples.

South Korea

South Korea was hard hit by the Second World War and the division of the peninsula between East and West. Korea had developed a significant manufacturing sector before the First World War, but most of its industry was located in the North. Hence despite the flight of many North Korean entrepreneurs to the South, South Korean industry had to establish itself with few resources and a dense population dependent on what it could produce. However, although manufacturing in 1945 constituted less than 10 per cent of the South's output, and exports and the savings rate were both low, native enterprise initially benefited from the distribution of confiscated Japanese property. Then came a major setback, the Korean War (1950–3), which devastated the country and caused major hardship. The war, however, marked a turning-point, since US aid, given to maintain a strategic ally in the Cold War, was used to pay for infrastructure and spent on roads, railways, ports, communications, power supplies, etc.

South Korea met the first oil shock by borrowing oil surpluses from private commercial banks. Its overall borrowing in the 1970s and 1980s was already high. However, this borrowing was not wasted, as so often occurs, but was put to work for developmental purposes. There was a strong emphasis on education. There were strict if not harsh labour laws, but popular disaffection with growth at the cost of poor conditions and low pay did not really surface until the military lost control in the wake of President Park's assassination in October 1979. The land reform which was part of liberation had led to the emergence of much small-scale rural enterprise. The period from the late 1960s to the end of the 1980s was a period of high real per capita growth, averaging more than 6 per cent per annum. This period, initially characterized by high savings and investment rates, gave way to a period of artificially suppressed interest rates which attracted low domestic savings. This further stimulated borrowing abroad. Debt prompted the seeking of a World Bank structural adjustment loan, and IMF encouragement along with US pressure based on the US desire for reciprocity of markets led to liberalization.

Everywhere the role of the state was apparent at least until this liberalization in the 1980s, and the interplay of government policy along with a culture of work and saving is often seen as the source of South Korean development. Initially export-led development of labour-intensive manufactures was given every possible assistance with exports from the new industries protected by subsidies, use of selective tariffs and protective quotas against imports to develop a home market for indigenous goods. Foreign exchange manipulation was employed to retain an export advantage. It is true that the 1970s saw the beginning of the liberalization of the South Korean economy. However, far from this process liberating hitherto unrecognized potential, it is in fact not yet complete. The South Korean economy still exhibits many of the features of its early origins. Wages are still low, hours long, working conditions poor and strikes common. Structural weaknesses are its over-dependence on a few products and especially on the US market for them.

Harris points out that neoclassical explanations will not do for South Korea. The importance of the role of the state is far too clear. But nor will explanations based on the massive civil and military aid from the USA. Accelerated growth came after the period of high inputs of aid and was in part the result of attempting to compensate for its loss. Foreign investment tended to concentrate in certain sectors only, and to follow rather than precede growth, and it was in any case less than that enjoyed by many other places which did not experience comparable levels of growth (Harris 1986: 44–5).

Taiwan

Taiwan had been colonized by Japan from 1895 to 1945, a much longer period than South Korea. It was densely populated and to this it added in the 1950s *emigré* Chinese nationalists, many of them entrepreneurial in ideology, who ruled it virtually as a colony in the name of the government of nationalist China. In 1949 it was poorer than the mainland, although it did have a small established industrial base dating from the 1930s. Between 1949 and 1955 land reform limited the size of individual holdings, although generous compensation was given to the larger landowners who used the funds to start their own businesses. High interest rates encouraged high domestic savings, and foreign borrowing was unnecessary.

However, because of its strategic location Taiwan did get an enormous amount of US aid, which again was used for infrastructural development and education. Given its military orientation, Taiwan came naturally to adopt a model of state-led economic growth. The authoritarian and effectively colonial government undertook the largest industrial enterprises and used high levels of tariff protection for its infant industries (though this was being reduced by the 1980s). It also controlled exchange rates.

Taiwan, having been less indebted, was in some respects more successful than South Korea. Exports showed massive growth to some 60 per cent of GNP and much of that was heavy industrial. However, there was a downside. Despite egalitarian income distribution, conditions for labour remained poor and Taiwan's overreliance on the US market made it vulnerable to shifts in US policy. Again Harris is clear that neoclassical explanations fail in the case of Taiwan's accelerated growth: government action, especially in keeping down labour costs, is seen as too important to the process. For Taiwan, 'The invisible hand was more of an iron fist' (Harris 1986: 53).

What both South Korea and Taiwan along with the other Asian Tigers have achieved is a specialized role in the world economy. They have done so from different starting points with different resources available to them and by way of different policy decisions.

If this variety exists among the small rapid developers of East Asia, it is quite obvious that their respective routes out of the Third World will be totally different from those of the Latin American NICs with their much larger and more diversified economies, utilizing far richer endowments of natural resources and state-dominated industrialization aimed at providing for an expanded domestic economy. (For further economic details of 'the modernization of Asia', including a wealth of comparative figures and graphs, see *The Economist*, 30 October 1993.)

It can be seen that, unlike Japan, many NICs were originally penetrated economies. There are therefore four ways NICs could encourage development in the wider Third World:

- As an example to others.
- As suppliers of technology and skills.
- As a market for Third World goods.
- As providers of development capital.

The NICs are seen by some as indicative of a genuine shift of economic power away from the First World. They are the first Third World countries to make the transition to fully developed status. China, what the World Bank has recently begun to call the eight 'high-performing economies' – Japan, Taiwan, Hong Kong, South Korea, Singapore, Malaysia, Indonesia and Thailand – and possibly Vietnam, have now developed to the point at which they are no longer strongly affected by fluctuations in the US economy. In the most recent recession, when between 1991 and 1993 most of the OECD economies were static, all but Japan continued to grow strongly.

Certainly the OECD countries (less Turkey) are no longer overwhelmingly dominant in the world economy. By local exchange rates they still account for 73 per cent of world output, as against less than 18 per cent for the developing countries and only 2 per cent for China. But by assessing the relative strength of economies by purchasing power parities, the IMF has placed the relative strength of the OECD and the 'Tigers' in a very different perspective. By this measure the OECD countries (less Turkey) account for only 54 per cent of world output as against 34 per cent for the developing countries and 6 per cent for China, making the Chinese economy in absolute terms the third largest in the world after the United States and Japan.

But there are many questions still to be answered. Having 'made it', will the NICs be more sympathetic to their former companions of the Third World, or will they simply join the rich-world clubs (OECD, WTO, IMF, World Bank) in accepting the burdens they lay on the less fortunate? Moreover, they made the transition under specific circumstances, with in each case a good balance of payments situation at a crucial moment, with closed markets and (often though not always) authoritarian regimes. Nor can independent states hope to replicate the unique circumstances of the British colony of Hong Kong.

By joining the rich world, the NICs accept – at least on paper – the prevailing ideology of market liberalism, and certainly in the case of Hong Kong the private market did act effectively without government action. However, for the rest, in the 1990s, the NICs are still in the process of democratizing and of liberalizing internal markets. Under the terms of the Uruguay Round, they will be expected to comply with the GATT by ending systems of export incentives, upholding intellectual property rights protection, guaranteeing foreign investment, eliminating tariffs and non-tariff barriers to trade, and liberalizing government procurement policies, services and exchange rates. It remains to be seen how far in practice they will comply with these standards and, if they do, what effect it will have on their ability to compete. For, up to now, the most striking thing about them is what the World Bank terms 'pragmatic flexibility', combining government support for infrastructure and heavy industry, directed credit for specific industries especially in the field of new technologies, free enterprise in manufacturing and distribution, and (contrary to prevailing models in the developed countries) a policy of promoting rapid wage growth to create a strong internal market as a basis for export success.

Existing NICs had advantages of cheap labour giving a potential for surplus, but not too many other costs to prevent such a surplus being accumulated and therefore to dissuade investors. It is precisely the advanced nature of many NICs and the size of their internal markets, especially in Latin America, which have attracted investment from the outside world, including the NICs themselves.

Other LDCs hope that manufacturing costs will now rise for NICs as they get richer, and that others will be able to take their places at the top of the Third World pile. They expect that their capital accumulation will, as with the industrialized countries, be limited by their need to distribute to a more demanding labour force with raised expectations. The present NICs would then become the markets for the kind of LDC product which they grew rich on, while moving on to more high-tech, capital-intensive production themselves.

The opinion is widespread, however, that the NICs' export success is unlikely to become much more general in the Third World. Moreover, if it did, the response of the developed countries might be protectionism. In any case, who would buy the quantity of manufactured products made by all the other countries of the Third World if they were in a position to export at the rate of the existing NICs? The price in terms of environmental degradation could also be unsustainable. As noted above, the sort of free trade envisaged by the makers of the GATT would work against the kind of advantages existing NICs enjoyed during their period of most rapid growth. Circumstances today are not only different, but they are very different for different regions. The ability to generate manufactured exports seems to have been vital to the success of all the NICs. Yet less than 10 per cent of all LDC manufactured exports come from Africa South of the Sahara. Where will Africa South of the Sahara begin to find the money for the levels of infrastructural investment it needs? On paper, thanks to the use of flags of convenience, Liberia is one of the great maritime nations of the world. In practice, it is an extremely backward country devastated by civil war. Who is going to invest in Liberia after its recent dismal history? How many years will it take for malnourished, ill-educated generations to be replaced by healthy and bright successors? Can the ruling military élite transmit its advantages to its successors? Does it know how to do so?

DEBT

Developing countries generally made social and economic progress relative to developed countries between 1945 and 1975. Then there was a decline, followed by a world recession lasting from 1980 to 1983, after which the developed countries have been pulling away again, despite a further decline and plunge into another recession, led by the United Kingdom in 1989 (see also Hayter 1983; Adams 1993).

The demonstration effect resulted in the 1950s and 1960s in a headlong rush to industrialize. Political independence in the Third World was to be accompanied by economic independence, and it looked as if it might happen in the 1970s with high demand for many Third World products and raw materials alongside growth fuelled by international lending organizations. Ironically, precisely this increased participation in world trade contributed to the destabilizing of prices, and the resulting decline in the terms of trade encouraged more borrowing. By the mid-1970s, the banks in the industrialized countries found themselves holding very large amounts of available capital in the form of oil surpluses, thanks to the OPEC countries' preference for keeping their revenues in liquid form. The banks' need to invest this capital led them into an active policy of extending access to loans to Third World states such as Brazil, Mexico and Indonesia. As a result, since 1972 the large commercial banks have again become main actors in North–South relations.

Industrial sectors grew. Encouraged by their respective national governments, in general with the active participation of the TNCs, the larger countries such as Brazil, India and China moved into the production of capital goods. By the end of the boom years, some Third World countries had become significant competitors in the world trade in manufactured goods.

The impressive growth in almost all Third World countries between the 1950s and the late 1970s was accompanied by a decline in the proportion, though not the numbers, of Third World populations living in absolute poverty. Agriculture was modernized to some extent almost everywhere by the so-called 'Green Revolution'. Public health and educational provision improved.

However, the boom ended as dramatically as it had begun. The trigger was the first 'oil shock' of 1973–4. The sudden increase in the price of oil hit Third World countries as well as the advanced industrialized ones. Unlike the industrialized countries, the former were in a weak position to meet the challenge. By the early-1970s private capital flows had far outstripped aid to the Third World and amounted to nearly 70 per cent of the net bilateral flows from industrialized to developing countries. This reflects the growth of transnational corporations as well as the process of recycling the oil revenues of more than 500 private banks, including the very largest in the United States, Japan, Germany, France and the UK. As a result, the 1980s saw net debt transfers of some $40 billion per year from developing to developed countries, a figure in excess of colonial repatriation and more than Third World spending on health and education (Adams 1991).

Foreign investment did encourage some modernization, which was sometimes extended through linkages to the rest of the economy – though it more often promoted the development of 'enclaves' of advanced technology in a generally backward economy. These limited gains have to be set against outflows in the form of profits, fees and royalties, payments for imported inputs, and losses due to transfer pricing by transnational corporations.

Geographical catastrophes added to economic crisis for some of the Third World. There was drought in Africa and hurricanes in the Caribbean. It was not just First World greed and incompetence which caused the devastating impact of the 1980s downturn on the Third World, but also Third World unrealistic hopes and expectations as well as corruption and incompetence.

Dollar surpluses from oil had been loaned to the Third World. They were spent either, as in the case of Mexico and Venezuela, on producing oil, the price of which then collapsed, or, as in the case of Argentina and Nigeria, on arms. Between 1975 and 1985 military expenditures accounted for 40 per cent of the increase in debt. By the end of the 1980s, annual world military expenditure was of the order of $1,000 billion. Of this 15 per cent was being spent in the Third World, where average military spending was 30 per cent more than expenditure on health and education. Often these massive expenditures were being incurred by military governments which had never been elected by their people. For many people this raises an important ethical question. It is hard to see why the mass of the civilian population should later have to pay back the debts contracted by military governments.

In 1981–2 Argentina's military government postponed its debt service. However, debt did not really become a big issue and the term 'debt crisis' did not appear until in August 1982 the two biggest debtors (Brazil and Mexico) suspended interest payments with the risk that in time they might actually default. It was this possibility that shook the stability of the world economy. In 1982, within two days of Mexico's announcement that it could not service its debt, the US government was already putting in place emergency measures. The government of Mexico almost at once agreed to terms that enabled it to reschedule. Financial support came through the IMF with the backing of the US government, worried about the political and financial stability of its southern neighbour. IMF support, however, was supposed to be backed by long-term adjustment through 'reforms' proposed by IMF technical advisers in consultation with the Mexican government of President Miguel de la Madrid.

These measures included the devaluation of the peso, import liberalization to force local prices down, and 'stabilization': that is to say, cutting the endemic budget deficit which had led to printing money and therefore to inflation. As in other cases, the IMF recommended that the government balance its books more by reducing expenditure than by increasing revenue, with the rationale that tax rates had to be kept low to encourage compliance and reduce the burden on the most dynamic sectors. However, the Mexican government for political reasons balked at the advice that subsidies (on water and electricity) were not targeted and therefore could be safely reduced and a more limited safety net put in place to support the very poorest sectors. Nor initially did it welcome the advice to embark on a far-reaching programme of privatization, starting with the most obvious assets, the state airlines.

This package became the model for dealing with subsequent cases, in most of which, as in Mexico, governments found themselves able to comply with only part of the strict conditions laid upon them. However, the anxiety of the world financial community was such that when this happened, further adjustments were made and new packages agreed, although inevitably with further costs. Some 25 countries were in arrears a year later, but through the co-operation of the debtor nations the creditors had already achieved 15 renegotiations. The process did not always go easily. The new civilian government in Argentina signed a deal with the IMF in 1984, but proved quite unable to meet its targets. In 1985 the incoming government of Alan García in Peru refused to pay more than 10 per cent of its export earnings. Brazil for a time suspended payment to force debt relief, but did not get it.

On the other hand, this case-by-case handling prevented the debtor countries co-operating with one another, still less, as the banks feared, forming a 'debtors' cartel' (Roett 1985). The fact is that debt empowers creditors and does *not* empower debtors – unless they are very large debtors and act in concert (see Table 4.1). Individual debtor countries did call for debt relief, but did not combine to challenge creditors because they wanted to keep contacts with the world financial system in order to be able to arrange new loans. Most of all, they did not want to be pariah states denied all access to outside funds and so forced to borrow internally in their own currency. (The only country that has an advantage in this respect is the United States itself. Since 1986 net US debt has been the largest in the world, but this debt is in its own currency so overseas creditors do not have same power to ensure that it can be repaid.)

Weaknesses in commodity markets coincided with the effects of tight monetarist policies in the industrialized countries and net resource flows were reversed. Africa South of the Sahara was most heavily indebted and hardest hit by interest rate rises. Most of the 26 most severely indebted nations are in

Table 4.1 *Total external debt of selected states, 1992 (US$)*

Range	External debt 1992 ($m)	Debt per capita 1992 ($)
Low income		
1 Mozambique	4,929	298
18 India	76,983	87
21 Nigeria	30,959	303
27 Ghana	4,275	270
28 China	69,321	59
32 Sri Lanka	6,401	367
37 Indonesia	84,385	457
Lower-middle income		
43 Ivory Coast	17,997	1,395
44 Bolivia	4,243	565
68 Jamaica	4,303	1,792
75 Thailand	14,727	253
80 Turkey	54,772	936
85 Chile	19,360	1,423
Upper-middle income		
80 S. Africa	–	–
92 Brazil	121,110	786
99 Mexico	113,378	1,333
100 Trinidad	2,262	1,740
102 Argentina	67,569	2,401
107 Greece	–	–
108 Portugal	32,046	3,270
109 S. Arabia	–	–
High income		
100 Ireland		
112 Israel		
116 Australia		
117 UK		
124 France		
127 USA		
131 Japan		
132 Switzerland		

Source: World Bank (1994).

that region. The Group of Seven (G7) Toronto Protocol allowed rescheduling for these countries and the IMF has similar arrangements, but repayments are still massive in proportion to resources. Now, to make matters worse, half of them are the francophone countries hit by French withdrawal of financial support and resulting forced devaluations in January 1994.

The consequences have been drastic. Africa may have lost as much as 30 years of development. For Latin America the 1980s were a 'lost decade'. Net transfers had been positive for Latin America (i.e. new funds borrowed exceeded debt repayments) until 1983, but the 1980s saw inflation without growth in most of the region. South Asia had borrowed heavily, but repayments were more manageable in proportion to its growing economies. Some East Asian countries, on the other hand, enjoyed favourable balance of payments situations, and were largely unaffected by the crisis.

The poorest countries export a narrow range of primary products. They have limited resources and many of those that they do have are not exploited to their benefit. Their people suffer from poor nutrition, low standards of education and other problems, all exacerbated by a high rate of population growth. They have little hope of ever being able to pay off their debts (see Table 4.2). Compare the favoured situation of middle-income countries which have natural resources, skilled labour and industrial bases. In sum they have flexibility of choice which the poorer Third World states do not.

Debt has many adverse consequences. It contributes to the pulling apart of the Third World, focuses attention on big debtors to the exclusion of small ones (Costa Rica was unable to get rescheduling on its small debts and was summarily ordered to pay up or face the consequences), and results in a vast increase in poverty accompanied by surrender of economic sovereignty (see Table 4.3). Other factors acting against a satisfactory resolution of the debt problem as far as the Third World is concerned include the policies of TNCs, the growing cost-effectiveness of labour-saving manufacturing technology, the bias of the world trading system against primary products, protectionist measures by developed countries, and the policies of the IMF and World Bank, through which creditor countries may intervene in debtor economies to ensure debts are serviced.

The ultimate irony was that private banks boosted profits for several years in the mid-1980s and have already been repaid many times over, not least because the money loaned often returned to the lending banks on deposit from the Third World élites to whom it had been lent. Their lending was irresponsible: since borrowers were not necessarily elected by their people but the money was loaned to a country with the assumed security that implied, much of the money was squandered or purloined by the borrowers. It is morally wrong to ask people who had nothing to do with the contracting of the debts to repay them – debt is not a national problem for debtor countries, but rather a burden which falls disproportionately on the poorest and weakest sections of Third World societies (see Structural Adjustment Packages below and Chapter 12).

As Susan George (1993) points out, it is also 'bad news' for all but a few people living in the creditor countries. The general population of the creditor countries gives tax relief to private banks on their bad debts and finances tax concessions when they write off debts. A further economic cost to the North

Table 4.2 *Debt in US$ and as a percentage of GNP, selected states, 1992*

Range	External debt 1992 ($m)	Debt as % GNP 1992
Low income		
1 Mozambique	4,929	494.8
18 India	76,983	25.9
21 Nigeria	30,959	108.4
27 Ghana	4,275	39.1
28 China	69,321	12.8
32 Sri Lanka	6,401	41.0
37 Indonesia	84,385	61.9
Lower-middle income		
43 Ivory Coast	17,997	191.0
44 Bolivia	4,243	61.2
68 Jamaica	4,303	131.7
75 Thailand	14,727	35.2
80 Turkey	54,772	47.8
85 Chile	19,360	48.9
Upper-middle income		
80 S. Africa	–	–
92 Brazil	121,110	31.2
99 Mexico	113,378	34.1
100 Trinidad	2,262	45.7
102 Argentina	67,569	30.3
107 Greece	–	–
108 Portugal	32,046	39.0
109 S. Arabia	–	–
High income		
100 Ireland		
112 Israel		
116 Australia		
117 UK		
124 France		
127 USA		
131 Japan		
132 Switzerland		

Source: World Bank (1994).

is the unemployment consequent upon the loss of sales to Third World countries, which cannot afford to buy so many First World products. There are social costs too. Notably, drugs are a major foreign exchange earner for heavily indebted countries, and not only does this have serious social

Table 4.3 *Countries having total identified external debt in excess of US$20 billion at 31 December 1986 compared with 1992 figure (high-income countries in italics)*

Country	1986	1992
Mexico	108.3	113.1
Brazil	106.3	121.1
South Korea	57.7	43.0
Argentina	49.9	67.6
Indonesia	37.2	84.4
Egypt	37.0	40.0
India	36.4	77.0
Venezuela	29.3	37.2
Israel	28.8	n.a.
Philippines	28.6	32.5
Greece	24.9	n.a.
Turkey	23.8	54.7
Chile	22.3	19.4
Portugal	21.6	32.0
Algeria	21.8	26.3
Malaysia	21.5	19.8

Source: World Bank, *World Debt Tables*, March 1987, and *World Development Report*, 1994.

consequences for the developed countries, but in financial terms this again hits the developed country taxpayer. For those who fear rather than welcome immigration, this may be seen as a social problem for the wealthy countries of the world; it certainly is for the refugees ('economic' or otherwise) who flee the poverty and dislocation of their indebted homelands. For many, flight is the only prospect in conflicts exacerbated by debt. These conflicts result in instability and this in turn impacts upon us all, as weapons purchased with borrowed funds are deployed against the lending countries or those under their protection. Finally, and perhaps most importantly, indebtedness heightens exploitation of natural resources. The free market policies which have hit the weakest and most vulnerable people are doing the same to the most delicately balanced ecosystems (on 'debt for nature' swaps, see Chapter 13).

George leaves us with the sobering thought that since 1982 the North has received the cheapest-ever raw materials from the South. Who then is the real debtor?

BRETTON WOODS

Rightly or wrongly, many attributed the failure of peace in the inter-war years to the defects of the world financial system. Hyperinflation in Germany, Austria and Hungary destroyed middle-class savings and made the victims eager recruits for fascism.

In 1944 the United Nations established what became known as the Bretton Woods system. The two key institutions of the new order were the International Monetary Fund (IMF) and the International Bank for Reconstruction and Development (IBRD – now commonly known as the World Bank). The timing of its creation reflected the perception that among the causes of the war was economic nationalism. Hence the free market principles that from the beginning underlay the work of the IMF.

Today even many free-marketeers would argue that markets operate less efficiently in conditions of poverty, and that theories of markets and movements to equilibrium are not entirely appropriate for application to the Third World. However, the majority of the present-day Third World states did not exist as sovereign entities in 1944 and had to fit in later with a system not designed for their benefit. It was a system essentially designed to help the industrialized countries avoid the problems they had faced pre-war. The main objectives of the Bretton Woods system were therefore twofold:

- To promote stable exchange rates.
- To encourage the growth of world trade and facilitate international movements of capital.

As far as the developed countries were concerned, it has long been generally believed that the system was successful. However, this view has recently come under attack from Sir Alec Cairncross (1994):

> The popular idea that Bretton Woods accounted for the prosperity of the post-war years has little substance. Thoughout its first 10 years the International Monetary Fund did very little and the World Bank contributed only a small part of the total flow of capital into international investment. The international monetary system was managed, not by the IMF, as was envisaged at Bretton Woods, but by the United States.

The fact was that most of the so-called evils of the pre-war system – devaluations, inconvertible currencies, exchange controls, trade restrictions – proved very resilient and lingered throughout the classical period of the Bretton Woods system, which ended with the devaluation of the dollar in 1971.

THE INTERNATIONAL MONETARY FUND

The purpose of the International Monetary Fund (IMF) is to assist countries in maintaining stable exchange rates – it is not primarily intended to promote economic growth and in practice it often does not do so. It is particularly important to the very poorest countries in the same way that the World Bank extends most of its loans to those countries which do not receive commercial bank loans.

The IMF is a mutual assistance society or club. The amount paid in by members is determined by a formula which broadly reflects their relative positions in the world economy. These quotas also determine the number of votes the country concerned can exercise and its maximum potential borrowing. The USA, UK, Germany, France and Japan together have 41 per cent of the votes. With the other two members, Italy and Canada, thrown in the G7 countries control over 50 per cent. Although the US quota is now down to 20 per cent, this is enough (given the large sums that it pays in) to ensure that the US government always has considerable influence. It is the only country that commands enough votes to be able to veto the key decisions that require 85 per cent majorities.

The theory behind the IMF – and in particular its Compensatory Financial Facility (CFF), which was set up in 1963 to give support during foreign exchange crises – is that borrowing temporarily can help a government to resolve the problems of deficits, by giving it a breathing space in which to carry out adjustments to its economy. If this were the case, it would be very convenient for Third World states, as it would enable them to make adjustments without surrendering control over their economies.

Unfortunately, in practice Third World relations with the IMF have not been happy ones. The Fund, rightly or wrongly, is not perceived as enhancing Third World security. Third World states see themselves as lacking influence within the IMF. At the same time, the IMF is seen as imposing on them an economic orthodoxy which is against their interests and indeed violates their sovereignty through the conditions it attaches to loans ('conditionality'). In 1980 African states meeting at Arusha in Tanzania expressed their frustration and called in the Arusha Declaration for the creation of a new system.

The problem is that the ideology of the IMF favours orthodox economic explanations of the need for stabilization. Those who work for the Fund think of it as being an organization which is concerned only with the technicalities of maintaining that system. Consequently, to borrow from the IMF, countries have to take measures which will as far as possible free up world trade regardless of the consequences for themselves. They will be faced with the following specific requirements:

- To reduce budget deficits through an immediate reduction in public expenditure.

- To eliminate all forms of price and wage control, including the removal of subsidies on basic foodstuffs, which often form an essential part of the bargain between Third World governments and key interests.
- To control the money supply.
- To devalue the currency in order to promote exports and reduce imports.
- To remove tariffs and quotas which protect infant Third World industries.

These requirements are collectively referred to as Structural Adjustment Packages (SAPs).

The shared resources of the fund are in theory available to all members with increasingly stringent conditions. The first and second tranches are available unconditionally, but amount only to taking out again some of the membership fee paid in. For many Third World countries it is the subsequent loans that are paid out in hard currency, and therefore have to be repaid usually over a period of 3–5 years in the same form, which are the ones on which they have come to rely. The IMF sees its role as technical (relating to short-term, non-structural economic problems) and argues that where the effects of structural adjustment fall is an internal political decision. What it has only recently come to recognize, at least in part, is that its free market orientation is political too.

The austerity measures which are an inevitable requirement of loans in excess of 50 per cent of quotas are supposed to boost exports, to reduce imports, usually through devaluation, and to lower government expenditure by constraining wages and welfare. Thus they tend to increase unemployment and to make the domestic working class pay for what is often a problem deriving from changes in world terms of trade. Such international fluctuations in any case hit the poorest sectors and disadvantaged groups hardest (see Chapter 12). Primary producers are more at the mercy of the international system than those who produce exportable manufactured goods, so countries that rely heavily on primary exports are most likely to get into balance of payments difficulties and therefore have to resort to IMF help. But at the same time they are those countries least likely to have the resources to be able to meet the welfare needs of their people.

Conditionality is part of the ideology of stabilization. But the IMF resists rescheduling of debts for the same reason, that its system of loans is supposed to be short term and repayments need to be available to be reloaned elsewhere. Third World countries wanted IMF principles to stress Third World development specifically. However, the USA and the UK argued that this was role of the World Bank not the IMF, and hence development in all member states was given equal consideration. They were, of course, right that this was the original objective, but even for the World Bank the reconstruction of Europe and Japan came first. With the IMF in its present form, short-term loans simply to rectify balance of payments problems and the equal treatment of unequal members simply combine to produce circumstances which favour industrialized nations.

The IMF will help fund debt purchase by Third World countries. However, if those countries have already accepted Structural Adjustment Packages and then defaulted, their past default will give them little prospect of future loans. Worst of all, the IMF's position as banker of last resort means that, if the IMF will not lend to them, no one else will do so either.

The effects of the debt crisis, in fact, were to lead to some enhancement of the role of the IMF. The first response was the development of special facilities requiring detailed programmes of reform. These were rejected by India and China, and almost all the SSA countries, where the drying up of funds resulted in increased harshness of conditions. There were riots at the proposed austerity measures in Bolivia, Brazil, Egypt, Venezuela and Zambia, and governments ousted partly for dealing with the IMF included those of both Ghana and Nigeria. On the other hand, the failure to deal with the IMF or to meet its conditions were to lead to defaults by the governments of Liberia, Somalia, Peru, Sierra Leone and Zambia, among others.

THE WORLD BANK

The World Bank has since its foundation been seen as the main source of multilateral lending to countries for individual capital projects. It established the International Development Association in 1960 to give loans on easy terms to the poorest countries, and certainly since 1973 the World Bank has distinguished between relative and absolute forms of poverty at personal and national levels, has stressed investment in the poor, and has funded projects concerned with small-scale production.

However, in the same year that the then President of the World Bank, Robert McNamara, said, 'it is clear that too much confidence was placed on the belief that rapid economic growth would automatically result in the reduction of poverty', the 1977 World Bank (IBRD) report on Africa said that aid should only be given where subsidies were abandoned, even if this meant food riots.

The evident failure of the IMF to deal with the problems of Third World debt has led the World Bank, too, to offer Structural Adjustment Packages to specified countries. One of their attractions originally was that there was no cross-conditionality. For example, a World Bank loan to Argentina has been unsuccessfully opposed by the IMF. But during the 1980s an informal or tacit cross-conditionality has become increasingly evident.

IDEOLOGY AND PRACTICE

The 1980s was generally a period of movement towards a market ideology. The oil price rise of 1973–4 had been successfuly absorbed by the wealthier countries. But the rise of 1978–9 produced recession in industrialized nations. This led in turn to a fall in commodity prices, increased protectionism, higher world interest rates, a scarcity of private loans and stagnating aid. Hence in the end it was the poorer and weaker Third World nations that were the main losers.

When Third World countries turned to the IMF for help, the advice they received in return was consistent. SAPs were based on the premise that the country's economy was fundamentally sound and that what was needed was adjustment to a temporary balance of payments crisis. SAPs placing emphasis on markets and exports at times of depressed commodity prices might seem suspect, and flooding the market would depress prices further. Debt repayment under SAPs also contributes to First World unemployment, it should be noted, as debtor nations must restrict imports and this means that their markets for imported goods from the First World are reduced.

SAPs advantage TNCs as well as local élites who have business interests by lowering wages and reducing the power of labour to demand a fair return from their employers. Local élites have benefited from privatization pro-grammes and do not share the pain of SAPs. They keep their money abroad in hard currencies, so devaluation just makes them relatively richer when they are at home. They do not use the public services which get cut, and certainly do not want to pay for them.

Free market policies have not resolved the debt problem, although with the passage of time over the past 12 years governments have in the main successfully 'muddled through'. George (1993: 27) notes that, despite shelling out some $1,300 billion between 1982 and 1990, debtor countries were still 61 per cent more indebted at the end of the period than at the beginning. Worst of all, Africa South of the Sahara's debt had increased by 113 per cent, although world interest rates had at last begun to fall back towards historically more reasonable levels.

SOUTH–SOUTH TRADE

South-South cooperation can provide important new opportunities for develop-ment based on geographical proximity, on similarities in demand and tastes, on relevance of respective development experience, know-how, and skills, and on availability of complementary natural and financial skills ... South–South cooperation offers developing countries a strategic means for pursuing relatively autonomous paths to development suited to the needs and aspirations of their people. (South Commission 1990: 16)

The assumption behind the stress on South–South trade is that, if widespread, South–South trade relations would break the stranglehold of dependency. Dependency on the North would be ended if the North could no longer control the terms of trade. However, some would argue that there is an infrastructure of northern domination, that the global institutions and the monetary system and the transport system are dominated by the North, and that in consequence dependency would not come to an end with the ending of the conditions that gave rise to it in the first place.

As well as enhancing the South's bargaining power against that of the North, South–South co-operation might enable the South to benefit from economies of scale. Complementary and supportive neighbours would enhance the possibilities of development. However, working against the development of South–South linkages is the existing preoccupation of the LDCs with North–South negotiations. The greater the concern with relations with the North, the greater the tendency to place South–South co-operation on the back-burner. A second cluster of causes is the disagreements, hostilities and sometimes even wars which reduce co-operation between Third World states. These become much more likely where very similar economies see themselves as being in competition; single- or very limited product economies force their members to be constantly aware of their dependency on the goodwill of their northern customers.

The diversity of the South at once militates against South–South co-operation and makes for economic complementarity with the North. Some LDCs have capital (Brunei, Saudi Arabia, the United Arab Emirates) and/or energy surpluses. Indeed these and other OPEC members such as Kuwait have made development loans available at preferential rates to less fortunate Third World states. Others, such as Mexico and Brazil, are technologically advanced relative to their neighbours and their technology may be more accessible and more appropriate to other LDCs than that of the North. The Volkswagen Beetle, for example, withstands the tough conditions of South American roads, and the Morris Oxford is again in production in Sri Lanka, where its relative simplicity and ease of repair make it much more appropriate to local conditions than more recent models.

Some countries rich in capital but lacking technical skills have made good this deficit by importing LDC nationals. Examples are Iraq and Kuwait. China has numerous technical and scientific exchange programmes with a variety of countries all over the world, and has undertaken thousands of development projects in LDCs. Some countries, such as India, have enormous manufacturing capability; others, such as Zaire or Namibia, are rich in various natural resources. Collectively they have the components for a bright future if only the many political difficulties that stand in the way of co-operation can be overcome.

In the 20 years between 1955 and 1975, trade among developed countries grew faster than trade either among LDCs or between developed countries and LDCs. But LDC exports to developed countries increased much faster than developed countries' exports to LDCs, suggesting that interdependence has been enhanced. Yet it remains true that the main developed country market is other developed countries, and that they also provide the main market for LDC products. The character of developed country imports from less developed countries is more vital than in the reverse case. Either they are mainly non-renewable or developed countries cannot produce them due to their properties of climate, etc. This gives less developed countries strength in the long term through import-substitution industrialization. Japan and the EU are more dependent on LDC imports than the United States, which is the most self-sufficient of all developed countries, but projections suggest that US import dependence will increase with time.

Another possibility, already tried in some cases, is cartelization. To create a producer cartel in some products is possible, but the very poverty of Third World nations and their need for funds to tide them over in the short term works against success. Oil is the best-known case. But oil was an exception in that it is the essence of modern production, it would cost a great deal to substitute, and a high proportion of supplies were held by OPEC members which had surplus resources to strengthen their position. There are few if any other products that would qualify under all these headings. And indeed since the beginning of the 1980s, many of the best-known producer cartels have collapsed, not least the International Tin Agreement (ITA) (Crabtree 1987), while OPEC itself no longer controls the greatest share of traded oil and is nothing like as powerful as it was in the 1970s.

CONCLUSION

In economic terms, what Third World countries have in common is a tendency to be exploitable, although the extent to which this actually happens varies a great deal. Interpretations of why this is and how it might be changed have dominated theories of development. The position of the NICs and the extent (and impact) of Third World indebtedness are key issues in the current debates about the economic prospects for Third World nations.

5 The social context

INTRODUCTION

The impact of the process of, first, colonization and then development on Third World social structures may vary a great deal in form, but it will always be a key to understanding those societies.

At its most basic level, this impact affects the most fundamental of social factors, the size of the population. In pre-modern society, the balance between birth rate and death rate is variable. When there are too many children the population is controlled, if necessary by infanticide (Firth 1936; cited by Goldthorpe 1975: 21). In modern society the introduction of public health measures such as clean water and sanitation means rapid population increase as fertility remains high and mortality falls. Goldthorpe (1975: 23) notes, however, that there have been considerable differences between actual societies. One thing is clear, the act of colonization often means a sudden catastrophic population fall as new infectious diseases are introduced. This was conspicuously the case in Spanish America and has continued to be a problem until recently in very isolated communities with only sporadic contacts with the outside world, notably Easter Island.

IMPACT OF DEVELOPMENT ON DISADVANTAGED GROUPS

Development has a particular impact on groups such as children, the aged and indigenous peoples.

Development should have a positive impact on children by increasing the possibilities of education and opening up a greater variety of life chances. However, there are problems. In the first phase of development, rapid population growth means a greatly increased burden on the financial resources available for education, particularly in rural areas, and enhances the urban–rural divide. There can be considerable resentment in rural communities too at what they see as state educational provision being directed towards the concerns of the town, and thus being remote from their own needs and interests.

At the same time, integration into the world culture of film and television has presented Third World societies with an almost unattainable image of the good life, as lived in penthouse flats in Los Angeles or New York. Young people are likely to feel most keenly the disparity between their ideal and their actual circumstances. This and the pressure of population drives youngsters to seek work in the town, joining the tide of migration.

For the aged, development also brings some good: the possibility of better medical care; access to wider horizons through public transport, radio and television; some labour-saving devices. Migration to towns and splitting up of families, however, either takes the elderly away from the village community, where their skills are of use, or leaves the elderly a charge on rural relatives who, by definition, are less likely to be able to carry the burden.

Indigenous peoples are most vulnerable to the impact of development, not least because many governments intent on rapid development of their countries see the traditional lifestyles of indigenous people as a drag on progress and modernity (see Chapter 12).

GENDER AND SOCIETY

Stratification by gender is to be found in most Third World societies, and separate organizations for men and women exist in most, if not all, societies. Though in some societies these are tighter and more formal groupings, in Africa secret societies play a major role in gender differentiation.

In Sierra Leone, where male secret societies were the dominant organizations before colonization, the Poro still operates and retains considerable power today, especially among the Mende tribe, where it originated, and the Sherbro Bullom and the Temne, to which it later spread. Significantly, female secret societies also exist, and are known to be central to training girls in the social roles they are to assume as women. It was through her membership of the Sande (*bundu*) society that Madam Yoko (*c.* 1850–1906), later to be chief of Moyamba and ally of the British in the Hut Tax War, acquired her initial fame which led to an influential marriage (Foray 1977). As this example shows, in precolonial times women could and did hold political power in West Africa, and indeed were to take an important role in asserting the right to retain African dress and their African identity, but marriage formed an important key to their possibility of social advancement.

The tradition of 'bride price' in Africa reflects the traditional attitude of male society to women as a commodity – though a commodity which does retain some rights and in some tribes can attain positions of considerable power. It is part of the role of women in rural society to cultivate land to provide food (see Chapter 12), and this tradition survives, modified, in the urban context. Andreski notes that in urban Ghana an artisan will typically provide his wife with capital to trade on her own account, and, while not expecting her to feed him, does expect her to feed herself and her children (Andreski 1968: 50–1). Two traditional occupations for urban women are market trading and prostitution, although the latter did not originally carry the social stigma it does in Europe and often does not do so today, despite the efforts of both Christian and Muslim missionaries to change this perception. In Africa women have yet to reach the highest political positions.

In Asia the position of women varies greatly. In China, on marriage a woman ceases to be part of her birth family, symbolized by the physical removal of herself and her possessions to her husband's home. In rural areas the planting and cultivation of wet rice is regarded as women's work, and on any building site in China and Vietnam the bulk of the unskilled labour is provided by women. The ageing government of the People's Republic is unusual today for the almost total absence of women in high office. In Thailand and the Philippines, on the other hand, women retain their identity and in recent decades have emerged into important managerial and political positions. In Burma, Aung San Suu Kyi has been denied by the armed forces the position of leadership to which she had been elected. However, in South Asia, where Mrs Bandaranaike became the world's first woman prime minister in Sri Lanka in 1960, her daughter is now President, and both Pakistan and Bangladesh have women leaders.

In other parts of the Third World the situation is very different. In Latin America only one woman held political office in some 300 years of colonial rule and that for only three days. Nevertheless since women obtained the franchise, beginning in Ecuador in 1929, the situation in the region has steadily improved. In Mexico and Chile today the status of middle-class women can be very high. In Argentina, María Estela (Isabel) Martínez de Perón became the world's first woman executive President and since then Lidia Gueiler has served as President of Bolivia and Violeta Chamorro has been elected President of Nicaragua. However, although the UN declared 1975 International Women's Year, with a major conference held in Mexico City, in Mexico, as elsewhere, the majority of women are still poor and still work extremely hard. They may do so out of economic necessity or they may do so because of social expectation. They do not do so because of legal bonds, since although the population is nominally Catholic, the majority of poor people are not formally married (Lewis 1962).

ETHNIC CLEAVAGES

All societies are socially stratified, although in the most homogenous societies divisions remain those of gender and age-sets, membership of the latter often being determined by the particular batch of initiates into adulthood with which a young man or woman shared the appropriate tribal rituals. Stratification implies a horizontal division, which is registered in the power structure in the form of superordination vs subordination. However, one can differentiate between *horizontal* and *vertical* systems of stratification. In the former, other characteristics are spread across each band in a way that cuts across the main axis of stratification; in the latter, they tend to form the basis of stratification (Horowitz 1971). These are ideal types: in practice several different criteria usually work together. Ethnic differences are not clear cut: they tend to be expressed in terms of religion, language or shared common culture. Hence we must also differentiate between *rigid* and *flexible* systems of stratification.

Most areas subject to colonization were in fact already inhabited. Hence from first encounter, there arose a sense of ethnic differences. The annexation of land created new class structures. Local inhabitants were used to work the land, and where they were insufficient or failed to survive the rigours of forced labour, new workers were brought in. Slavery made a deep impact both in Africa and after 1517 in the Americas, but a century after emancipation both in Brazil and Cuba the experience has become historical and old divisions have had time to be eroded. It is worth remembering that slavery was not formally abolished in Mauritania until 1980 and that involuntary servitude in various forms is still prevalent in the Middle East and is believed to be on the increase in the 1990s.

Wherever ethnic differences are conspicuous, the tensions generated by them do remain socially significant; and where they are of more recent origin, the tensions can be considerable. In a number of territories once part of the British Empire, such tensions have been generated by the importation of Indian contract labourers, whose descendants today constitute a significant minority. In 1968 the government of Kenya deported the Asian minority who had contributed a disproportionate share to the government and entrepreneurial skills of the country. In 1972 President Idi Amin of Uganda did the same, attracting much international criticism.

Fijians today still share their island with a minority which is almost as big as the majority. But they do so on their own terms, since they bitterly resent pressure for equal access to power from the descendants of Indian indentured labourers. When an Indian-backed party won political power, it was excluded by force and Fiji withdrew from the Commonwealth rather than accept the right of the descendants of immigrants to take power.

In Guyana the descendants of Indian labourers form about 50 per cent of the population. Those of African descent account for a further 30 per cent, and the division between these groups is the major social cleavage in Guyana. Since 1957 the country's first ruling party, the People's Progressive Party (PPP) has been dominated by the Indo-Guyanese. But serious communal violence in 1963–4 led to the adoption of the proportional representation system, which had the effect of transferring power to non-Indians in the form of the People's National Congress (PNC), led first by Forbes Burnham and subsequently by Desmond Hoyte.

The existence of a substantial minority, however, does not of itself mean that they will be politically as opposed to socially significant. In Sri Lanka the

'Indian Tamils' form an encapsulated society in the tea-growing highlands and remain largely aloof from the struggle between a Tamil separatist movement, the Liberation Tigers of Tamil Eelam (LTTE), and the Sinhalese-majority government. The Tamil Tigers, as they are generally known, represent the aspirations of elements among the 'Sri Lankan Tamils', who have lived in the Jaffna Peninsula and in other parts of the North and East of the island at least since the eleventh century.

Not all importations of indentured labour have led to conflict, one such exception being the island state of Mauritius, a former British colony, named after a Dutchman and speaking French. But most Third World countries contain significant ethnic minorities of indigenous origin. In some countries, such as Burma (Myanmar), they are so numerous as seriously to call into question the central government's ability to control outlying areas. In others, ethnic differences have been fanned by populist leaders and the result has been large-scale social conflict and open civil war. Examples in Africa have included Burundi (1966–72 and 1994), Chad (1966–84), Nigeria (1967–70), Angola (1975–84) and Rwanda (1993–). In yet others, such as Laos and Vietnam, ethnic differences have been targeted by external powers as a way of influencing national politics.

Similar hostilities have been directed at the Chinese minority, descendants of traders and settlers who can be found throughout South-East Asia, notably in Myanmar, Indonesia and the Philippines, and against the Vietnamese in Thailand. In the former British colony of Singapore, founded in 1824, they form a majority. Tension between this Chinese majority in Singapore and the Malay ruling establishment of Malaysia led to Singapore's peaceful secession from the federation.

CLASS AND STATE

The colonial state maintained the structure of class dominance/subordination. Significantly, pre-revolutionary Ethiopia, which was not effectively colonized, retained the indigenous semi-feudal structure, which elsewhere had to a greater or lesser degree been modified by the colonial experience. However, it is important not to see the concept of class in the Third World through the prism of Marxist concepts, which were based on Europe at a particular stage of historical development. Class structures are *endogenous* – they arise from the particular nature and circumstances of the country concerned. And in Third World states they remain largely *traditional*, with the impact of industrialization etc. being in the main accommodated to traditional patterns of dominance and subordination. Thus in post-colonial Senegal, politics continued to be dominated by noble and freeborn families, while the descendants of slaves continued to be effectively excluded from power

(Crowder 1967: 110). Though in India the former ruling families have been deprived of their traditional powers, both there and in Pakistan and Bangladesh (to say nothing of Sri Lanka) they have used their social standing to pursue the democratic route to power as a very successful alternative.

The impact of settlement, moreover, varied a great deal and is very hard to generalize about. Countries where settlement supplanted almost all traces of the indigenous populations include Argentina and Uruguay as well as First World countries like Australia, Canada and the USA. Countries where settlement incorporated substantial indigenous populations without exterminating them, but at the cost of many of their native cultural traits, include Mexico and Peru from the Third World, and New Zealand from the First.

Invariably where there was substantial settlement the settlers displaced the ruling class and established cultural hegemony. However, there was most often some form of alliance between settlers and the colonial authorities, not a simple forced identity of views. Settlers could come to resent colonial dominance, and in time they would seek independence, as in the United States, most of Latin America, South Africa and Zimbabwe (then Southern Rhodesia). The most important legacy has been the plantation economy. There are essential differences between the farm and the plantation as a basis of economic organization, and this is reflected in the social structures that accompany each. Where the plantation has predominated, there has been a strong tendency to horizontal stratification of ethnic groups.

The post-colonial state has often incompletely adjusted. In Kenya and Zimbabwe, the settlers and/or their naturalized descendants keep their lands and have adjusted to the new post-colonial order; in South Africa, so far, the intention seems to be to take the same course. In Sri Lanka tea plantations were nationalized and the planters allowed to repatriate only part of their compensation; in Indonesia summary nationalization took place, but was followed by extensive corruption (Myrdal 1968). In West Africa plantations were corporately owned and there were few settlers. Only in northern Nigeria and Senegal did traditional rulers retain their powers, in both cases because the colonial powers did not seek to control the production of peanuts, and in the case of Senegal the right of eminent domain was abolished in 1964 (O'Brien 1971: 201–2). In southern Africa traditional rulers retained their powers in Lesotho (formerly Bechuanaland) and Swaziland, and in the case of the Zulus, some limited autonomy within the homeland system as the notional 'state' of KwaZulu.

The oligarchy

In place of settlers, in Africa, as earlier in Latin America, there has arisen an indigenous oligarchy. However, in Africa only in the case of Côte d'Ivoire has a local oligarchy emerged which is based on land-holding. Elsewhere the new basis for power has been power itself, which gives access to valuable economic returns. In Asia, where settlers were few and indigenous societies complex, no single oligarchy has emerged: although the dynastic basis of power is often very clear, different élites control the basis of economic wealth.

In Africa, the alliance between state functionaries and the propertied classes has taken different forms in different countries. Dr Jomo Kenyatta, an anthropologist trained by Bronislaw Malinowski, established himself as a chief of chiefs and made fellow Africans socially dominant within independent Kenya, allowing free rein (on conditions) to private entrepreneurs. In neighbouring Tanzania, Dr Julius Nyerere established a system in which state enterprise was dominant. Dr Kwame Nkrumah failed to do the same in Ghana and ultimately was unable to retain his power. In Uganda the government of Milton Obote drove out the Kabaka of Buganda, burnt his palace and suspended the Lukiko (traditional assembly), only to be displaced in turn by a military coup led by Idi Amin.

The oligarchy has preponderant economic power, generally enhanced by its alliance with key foreign interests. It is the dominant patron–client network, to which all subordinate patron–client networks are attached. Ethnic cleavages, if they exist, are only one among a number of ways in which society can be stratified in the interests of maintaining dominance. Wealth can give access to the highest levels in most societies, enabling its holders to exercise influence if not power. Religion and education form alternative axes of stratification. Ethnic allegiances can cut across class differentiation by wealth or power. Hence in Nigeria no single ruling class emerged. Power passed into the hands of the armed forces, whose representatives have continued, despite lip-service to the ideals of democracy, to retain as tight a control over the country as they can.

In Latin America the term 'oligarchy' has strong emotive meaning as a key term in the populist/leftist critique of the landowning élite. Nevertheless the term fits very well the situation that was general in Latin America until the twentieth century, and which continues to some extent in Peru and Colombia. Landowners remain an important element in the section of Latin American society which is so wealthy that it remains undisturbed by domestic economic dislocation and/or political unrest (see 'Peasantry' below).

The bureaucracy

The higher ranks of the civil service form a key part of this élite. They are very well paid indeed compared with both lower civil servants and the general run of the population, especially when other privileges are taken into account. In Africa university teachers and doctors are also very highly regarded, and although their advantages have declined with time, they can still be regarded as members of the upper class rather than of an intermediate middle class, with the small size of the élite giving them incomes in the top 1 per cent of the population. The importance of a university degree itself has declined with time, but is still disproportionate. In an extreme case, the former Belgian Congo, now Zaire, there were only a handful of graduates at independence in a population of over 13 million, and no strong landowning élite to form the core of an indigenous ruling class.

But in Ghana, as in many other African states, a significant number of senior civil servants who had served the colonial government continued to work for the Nkrumah regime, and, on his fall, were retained by the successor governments for precisely the same reason: their specialized knowledge. In addition to senior civil servants, a considerable number of expatriate advisers and technicians continued to hold important positions in the former British colonies well after independence: in 1966, for example, 4,668 expatriates still worked in the civil service in Zambia. In the former French colonies, French *assistants techniques* continued to manage key branches of the economy, justice, interior, agriculture, transport and public works and public health ministries, to say nothing of defence and internal security (Bretton 1973: 189).

Inevitably there are close links between the government of the day and the entrepreneurial or business class. As Bretton emphasizes, the economies of African states are so fragile that the the public sector élite, both politicans and civil servants, cannot exist independently of their outside earnings:

> For a few among the higher echelons, the payoff from rule or from public office below the level of rule may be satisfaction of lust for power; for the majority, the payoff is personal wealth and economic security or both. Satisfaction of lust for power without substantial material benefit accruing to the powerful is an improbability in the real world. (Bretton 1973: 176)

The National Reformation Council report in 1968 on the assets of former government ministers in Sierra Leone is one of a number of such documents produced by successor regimes in Africa which give chapter and verse (Sierra Leone NRC 1968). Such problems continue, and under the National Provisional Ruling Council (NPRC) government led by Captain Valentine Strasser considerable publicity has been given to the results of investigations into the financial affairs of high-ranking civil servants and other functionaries who had served under the Momoh regime. *West Africa*, 27 September– 3 October 1993, reported that the Justice Laura Marcus-Jones Commission of Inquiry had found that the former President himself had acquired 'a sizeable collection of real property' and 'was in control of pecuniary resources and property disproportionate to his past official emoluments'. The NPRC therefore ordered these to be forfeit to the state.

In Latin America public functionaries enjoy considerable prestige and the senior ones are very well paid indeed.

Entrepreneurial/business class

At independence, many (though clearly not all) of the colonial civil servants went home. Their business and financial counterparts stayed on, and their role became more important. At the same time, with varying degrees of success, a new indigenous business class began to emerge. On the impact of landlordism in the expanding cities of West Africa, Andreski writes:

> In the new towns, or the newer parts of old towns – that is to say everywhere where the settlement is not by clans – labourers have to pay about one-fourth or even one-third of their wages for a dingy cubicle without water or sanitation, or even for a corner in a room. The newly-rich owners of the rentable property (most of whom acquired it with the proceeds of graft) expect to get their investment amortised in five or even three years. In Freetown most of the property belongs to the old established 'creole' families; while in Accra (which has expanded so much recently) the biggest owners of property are still the heads of the so-called royal lineages, though much property has been bought by wealthy cocoa farmers and market women; and the same is probably true of Kumasi. (Andreski 1968: 28)

The new entrepreneurs, however, are often incomers. In South-East Asia it is the Chinese who perform the role of entrepreneurs; also Indians in the case of Malaysia and Singapore. The emergence of a new Malay business élite has been the objective of the Malaysian government's *bumiputra* policy – a policy of favouritism to the 'native people' or indigenous population, which has proved successful.

In Africa South of the Sahara, other than in Zanzibar where they formed the ruling élite, Arabs formed a similar entrepreneurial group, linking Africa North and South of the Sahara. In keeping with this tradition, in West Africa a new group has emerged, the Lebanese, to perform the role of traders and entrepreneurs and to be presented as scapegoats for economic failure. In Ghana business partnerships outside the tribe have often tended to founder on mutual suspicions that the other partner was secretly salting away part of the proceeds. There too Lebanese and Indian entrepreneurs have come virtually to monopolize medium-scale trade, and in Kenya and Uganda the dominance of trade by Indian immigrants was so much resented that they were summarily expelled by post-independence governments. Friction between traders and government has, however, been commonplace in African states, although until recently it has not taken a markedly ideological form.

In Latin America the traditional structure of a family owned conglomerate is slowly yielding to a new business élite, among whom recent immigrants, including Italians in Argentina, Germans in Brazil, Japanese in Peru and Lebanese in Ecuador, are prominent. The inability until recently to engage in almost any kind of trade without a multiplicity of forms and permissions has, as ever, ensured that close links with government were essential and has afforded a fertile field for corruption.

Peasantry

In 1970 the majority of inhabitants of the new states were still peasants. The attention of the world at the time was grabbed by occasional insurrection and civil warfare, and many in the industrialized world came to regard the peasantry as a revolutionary force (e.g. Wolf 1969; c.f. Scutz and O'Slater 1990; Kamrava 1992; Colburn 1994). However, in fact the main characteristic of peasants as a class is their extreme conservatism. This is understandable when it is remembered that, living as they do on the margin of subsistence, their entire being is taken up by the need to earn a living (Scott 1976). Foster (1976) calls the cultural expression of this the model of *limited good*. Peasants, he says, see their environment as a closed system, with insufficient resources. They are aware that there are more resources outside their immediate environment, but they do not see these resources as being normally available to them: 'To guard against being a loser, peasants in traditional communities have developed an egalitarian, shared-poverty, equilibrium, status-quo style of life, in which by means of overt behavior and symbolic action people are discouraged from attempting major change in their economic and other statuses' (Foster 1976: 35–6).

It is in Latin America that there is the longest tradition of study of the peasantry in Third World states. The most celebrated example is that of the Cornell Peru Project, which was organized in 1951 and began operations at Hacienda Vicos, Department of Ancash, which belonged to the state and was leased at ten-year intervals. The purpose was to engineer rapid social change among indigenous inhabitants by altering the local power structure. Based on the social theories of Harold D. Lasswell and colleagues (Lasswell and Kaplan 1950, Lasswell and Holmberg 1966), it sought to create change through 'participant intervention'. The project replaced external supervision of work by outside employees by that of indigenous leaders, abolished free services (labour tax) in favour of paid labour, invested the returns from peasant labour in improved agricultural practices, encouraged the setting up of a body of elected leaders to plan further changes, and initiated weekly meetings of the whole labour force to review progress (Holmberg 1971). It is therefore not only one of the most striking examples of the use of the experimental method in social sciences other than psychology, but a pathfinder for 1990s notions of the social *empowerment* of deprived groups (see Chapter 8).

The major characteristic of Peruvian peasants was powerlessness, and this was not only a characteristic of the group but, because of their position at the bottom of the Peruvian social hierarchy, a determining characteristic of Peruvian society as a whole, where they constituted over 50 per cent of the population. Hence changes on the local and national levels (and indeed on the international level) were interlinked. 'The Vicosinos were not only part of the national society in 1951, they were in their condition essential to it – a necessary subordinated complement to the dominant oligarchy' (Dobyns, Doughty and Lasswell 1971: 17).

The Vicos peasants wanted one thing above all: land reform. Conservatives blocked local expropriation of land as well as national plans to take over lands of the Cerro de Pasco Corporation, but the elected government of Manuel Prado Ugarteche (1956–61) approved direct sale before being overthrown by a military coup. The Vicos project led to emulation by peasant movements elsewhere in the country, and the government of Fernando Belaúnde Terry (1963–8), under pressure from peasant occupations of land, was able to secure passage of agrarian reform legislation, which, however, was not implemented. The military government of General Juan Velasco Alvarado (1968–75) nevertheless instituted 'Peasant Day' on 24 June 1969 and subsequently expropriated the large coastal estates from which the former oligarchy drew much of their wealth.

Here as elsewhere in Latin America, however, lineages remain strong. Old families have found new outlets for their wealth, and have successfully incorporated newcomers. Whether in Mexico, Costa Rica or Colombia, a striking proportion of those holding political power will be descended from or incorporated by marriage into one or other of the ancient lineages. At the same time, these show a pronounced tendency to marry among themselves. Meanwhile, in the 1980s, in opposition to the intransigence of the old families, many Peruvian peasants took to various forms of action on their own behalf, including participation in the Marxist rural insurgent movement Sendero Luminoso.

In Africa, on the other hand, a striking consequence of the fluidity of the class structure is that many members of the upper and middle classes come from peasant families, or themselves started life as peasants (Andreski 1968: 168). The peasantry remain the largest single class in many countries, but the African peasantry has been generally passive. Only in the disputable case of Kenya and in the Portuguese African territories did peasants play a major role in movements of national liberation, and then under the leadership of middle-class intellectuals such as Holden Roberto and Eduardo Mondlane. Since independence, peasant organizations have been generally weak.

Various factors appear to account for the relative powerlessness of the African peasantry. Given strong tribal and kinship ties, it has been difficult for a sense of class identity to develop in peasants as such, and the absence of a traditional landowing élite means that there is no easy focus for their hostility. Africa is relatively sparsely populated compared to other parts of the Third World, hence the struggle for land has not reached the degree of intensity that it has in, say, Guatemala or Peru. Linguistic divisions and low levels of literacy are also cited as reasons why peasant organization in Africa has failed to develop. Such divisions make it relatively easy for the élite to divide and rule, by buying off incipient leaders.

Lacking organization, peasants have tended to resist impositions upon them either by passive resistance or in rare instances by a form of *jacquerie* – a spontaneous, localized revolt against intolerable conditions. Maladministration and tax increases led to such a revolt in Chad in 1965 (Decalo 1980). Occasionally such revolts have been more organized, but they have similarly been directed towards and focused on local grievances. Examples are the peasant revolt in the Kwilu province of Zaire in 1964 and the Agbekoya rebellion in Nigeria in 1968 (Beer and Williams 1975).

Urban workers

Latin America became independent and was urbanized before industrial development arrived. New railways, notably in Argentina, offered a strong base for labour organization. But movements in Peru, Chile and above all Bolivia centred on mines and so were extremely vulnerable to military repression, leaving the scattered remainder to be subjected to various forms of restriction on their joint action. In practice, therefore, urban workers in Latin America have generally been targeted by populist leaders as one of the main elements in a multiclass alliance (see Chapter 8).

African states, on the other hand, generally had some industry at independence. Though African cities have grown considerably since 1950, however, the working class remains only a small fraction of the total population. The strength of state power, moreover, has led to incipient trade union movements being either captured by the ruling élite or suppressed by authoritarian governments.

In a number of single-party states, unions have become active partners with government in seeking to increase work rates and hold down pay claims. However, this has not always been successful. In 1961 a major strike broke out among the railway and port workers at Sekondi-Takoradi in Ghana, protesting at the corruption of the élite and the increasing authoritarianism of the CPP government. In 1971 a series of strikes in Dar es Salaam showed rising discontent with the growing authoritarianism of the Tanzanian government. In Nigeria, the imposition of military government was strongly resented and in 1971 there was a series of strikes in Lagos and Kano, then the main centres of industrialization. 'In Zaria and Ibadan, where factories are fewer, and opportunities for self-employment for strangers less, there were few incidents' (Williams and Turner 1978: 165).

In several former French African colonies, notably Congo (Brazzaville) and Dahomey in 1963 and Upper Volta in 1966, strikes have helped to bring about the fall of an unpopular government at the hands of the armed forces. By contrast, in Senegal 'Senghor's government since independence has indeed been periodically threatened by urban rioting, notably at St Louis in 1960, at Dakar in 1963 and again in the later 1960s, but the regime ever since 1960 has enjoyed a crucial external support in the detachment of French soldiery posted to the nation's capital' (O'Brien 1978: 180).

In states already under military government, strikes have been firmly discouraged, but workers have responded by a variety of covert means of resistance, including absenteeism, going slow, sabotage and theft, and sometimes by open rebellion, as in Ghana where the mining industry was in continuous turmoil from 1968 to 1970.

THE FAMILY

Family, marriage and kinship are basic social institutions. Kinship is both diverse and important. Marriage is universal. Though it takes very different forms, its contractual basis as an economic institution is usually very clear. Within marriage, the division of labour is normally clearly marked. In traditional as opposed to modern societies, the central role in social provision falls to the family.

What counts as a family is a difficult and important question. The nuclear family of northern and western Europe is distinctive and rather unusual. It is bilateral and hence forms a rather weak basis for larger structures such as clans and lineages. It is monogamous, and related households do not regard themselves in the main as having any special claim to the resources of each other. This pattern is also characteristic of Japan.

The pattern much more characteristic of the Third World is that of the extended family. This is usually unilateral. In India, as in China, a bride makes the physical journey to her husband's house and ceases on marriage to be regarded as a member of her former family. (This can have consequences much more significant than for a family alone: in Pakistan, for example, her mother has attempted to shunt aside Benazir Bhutto from her leadership role in favour of her brother, saying that, after all, she is no longer a Bhutto). It can be characterized by both forms of polygamy, either polygyny (as in some Arab countries) or polyandry (as in Nepal), neither of which works to the advantage of women. Even where the extended family does not co-exist in one household, several generations can live together in the same complex and a very carefully graded system of relationships is recognized.

The locus of authority within the family differs from society to society. Also characteristic of some societies is respect for the wishes of the child: in Thailand parents will not insist on a child taking medicine if he or she does not want to do so (Philips 1965; cited in Foster 1976). In India patterns can be particularly complex, and even among adults those holding authority in a family may refuse permission for treatment even though those immediately concerned have been convinced of its efficacy.

The family is not only the basic organizing unit of society, it acts as a basis for all social provision. Mutual obligation in traditional communities is particularly characteristic of extended family groups. A member of the family who acquires wealth is obligated to provide for other family members. Other family members can call upon him for support. Obviously the effect of this system, as it is among the Gilbertese (now part of the Pacific state of Kiribati), is to prevent any tendency towards hoarding or conspicuous consumption. Among the Tonga of Malawi, the family could be relied upon to provide for the wives and children of those seeking contract work in South Africa, and they in turn benefited from the remittances the workers sent home.

Both individuals and families are similarly linked by patterns of *dyadic* (two-way) *exchange*. In many cases these obligations are so well developed that they form a very satisfactory way of structuring time and so are not easily surrendered. Brown found that both Samoans and the Hehe of Tanzania placed such a high value on performing a wide range of social and political obligations, that they had a strong resistance to working for money (Brown 1957). However, a strong solvent of these traditional relationships is to be found in the urban market for cash crops.

Sociologists have paid particular attention to the tendency for the breakdown of the extended family in the face of modernization (Goode 1970). Here the dominant influence has been that of the social theorist Talcott Parsons (Parsons 1964), who argued that what he termed the 'isolated nuclear family' was the typical form in modern industrial society because modernization implied a process of 'structural differentiation'. By this he meant a tendency for institutions progressively to shed functions, so that in the case of the family its economic, political and religious functions have long since to a greater or lesser extent been assumed by specialized agencies, and latterly the job of caring for the old, the young and the unfit has also been assumed by the state or by commercial enterprises. At the same time, the *ascribed* status derived from the traditional family structure is replaced by *achieved* status based on one's own efforts and/or achievement.

Modernization in the Third World means above all that the family ceases to be the main economic unit of production and is replaced by the workshop or factory. Parsons argued that the demands of factories for labour called for the mobility and flexibility associated with the nuclear family; however, in the case of migrant workers into, for example, South Africa or Israel, the family unit itself seems in many cases to have disintegrated, the workforce being largely composed of individual young males living together in hostels. Goode (1970) argued that the disintegration of the extended family had in fact been more rapid than could have been expected were Parsonian assumptions correct. He suggested that the spread of the nuclear family had been accelerated by the image presented by the advanced countries, which was attractive in Third World countries because of the freedom it appeared to offer. In Africa migrants from the countryside welcomed town life because of the fact that it freed them from the obligations of the extended family (Little 1965).

It has also been suggested that it was not industrialization in northern Europe that brought about the decline of the extended family; it was the decline of the extended family that facilitated industrialization. If this is the case, this decline in the Third World might be expected to have a similar effect.

On the other hand, the extended family remains very much part of Indian society, and Somjee (1991) argues that the economic success of the Patidars of Anand in the State of Gujarat owed much to it. While they were barred by the Indian Land Tenancy Act from increasing the size of their land-holding, they were able to gain an increased return from it by growing cash crops such as sugar cane, bananas, cotton and later edible oilseeds, and benefited from the absence of tax on agricultural income. However, while retaining his interest in agriculture, it was also open to a Patidar to leave the cultivation of the land to a brother or cousin and move into Anand itself, to seek work in commerce or industry. The availability of this work came, of course, from other factors stimulating the growth of Anand, especially the rapid development of the transport system, which brought into the town a wave of new educational, government and other institutions, and with them a wave of professionals wanting new products and services.

> While in undertaking such ventures a Patidar no doubt took some risk, nevertheless he also had his land to fall back upon just in case the commercial or industrial venture did not succeed. The closely knit extended family, together with the facility for absentee agriculture, provided the Patidars with a sense of security for new ventures. (Somjee 1991: 94–5)

SOCIAL FACTORS FAVOURING DEVELOPMENT

The early modernizers thought in traditional terms: in terms of piecemeal change over long periods of time. They recognized that the same land would have to provide food for their children and grandchildren, and they acted accordingly. By contrast, the late modernizers have been driven by the urge to create visible results during the brief period of a political mandate. Many Third World countries have significantly changed their economic structures since independence, especially in the cases of Latin America, where independence came early, and Asia, where governmental responses have been particularly flexible. However, agriculture is a complex process and it takes a long time for the full consequences of changes to be either felt or understood.

The structure of Third World economies often exhibits glaring divisions, especially those between urban and rural, or between the formal and the informal sectors. The main cause of this has been rapid urbanization. Urbanization may either precede or follow rapid industrial development.

Hence urbanization levels vary a great deal. As noted in the first chapter, they are high in Latin America generally, but especially so in the Southern Cone. This is in part the result of Latin America's colonial history, where the creation of towns was the key element in the success of Spanish settlement. Many of the world's largest cities are in Latin America, including the largest, Mexico City, whose population of 18.7 million forms some 22 per cent of Mexico's total population. Urbanization, on the other hand, is relatively low in Africa South of the Sahara.

There is, however, a strong urban bias among most Third World policy-makers, in Africa as elsewhere. Coming as they do from urban or would-be urban backgrounds, they prefer urban to rural and favour strategies of industrial development, which result in further urbanization. Urbanization hitherto has been seen as essential for rapid economic growth and certainly has always accompanied it, as witness the striking growth of big cities in the NICs and in China. However, large cities have to be fed. Bread riots were a feature of life in Mexico City or Lima in the colonial period, when the local hinterland was no longer able to supply the needs of a rising population. And in the case mentioned by Somjee, the important point was that the Patidars were successful where the merchant caste, the Banias, who lacked their close connection to the countryside, were not (see also Baker 1990).

Urbanization has profound social consequences. Public services tend to be concentrated in urban areas, thus making them even more attractive to rural dwellers. The most able and the most mobile (that is to say, young unmarried adults) migrate to the towns, in the process further disadvantaging the rural areas. But towns are not well adapted to receiving them. Squatter settlements are found on all continents.

In-migration to the big cities has even wider implications, bringing in its wake an awareness of social change. Social change gives rise to cultural confusion. Uncertainty gives rise to new tensions and reinforces existing ones. Informality gives way to formality. A relatively static existence is changed by transport. Extended kinship, as Parsons noted, is replaced by the nuclear family. Social complexity increases, and there is an association between social change and political instability. The problem of unproductive urbanization arises, and when in-migrants compete for scarce resources and temporary or part-time jobs, friction and scarcity lead to 'unregulated petty strife'. However, in African society clan structures survive and clan members form groups sharing the proceeds of petty crime (Andreski 1968: 41); and where clans do not survive, 'gangs' emerge to perform the same organizing role.

At the same time, the other side of the coin of urbanization is rural poverty. Poverty in the countryside is not a new phenomenon, and it could almost be expected in drought-prone and degraded environments such as that of the Sahel or of the Horn of Africa. In fact, as Redclift points out, the problem in both these areas owes much to the structure of land ownership. The rich soil of Bangladesh is not a degraded environment. However, Bangladesh has an exceedingly unequal distribution of land, such that one-third of the people of this heavily populated country are poor peasants cultivating less than one hectare of land or share-croppers dependent on others for work (Redclift 1984: 74–5).

MAINTAINING SOCIAL PROVISION IN AN EVOLVING SOCIETY

With rapid social change come also a whole range of problems associated with the provision of housing, health and other social services. Gaps in social provision in the growing towns can be filled in a variety of ways, by (1) a church or sect; (2) other voluntary organizations; (3) occupational provision; or (4) the state.

The effects of migration are felt very differently in town and country. Typically in a plantation economy the main basis for housing provision other than the individual has been occupational: housing for the workforce. The relatively high standard of housing provided by the banana corporations in Honduras, for example, is a significant deterrent to unrest. However, such provision is relatively rare in towns, the assumption being that the cost will be picked up by the worker or by the state. In the town, the major problems of housing concern housing for young adults, and these can be and are met in a variety of ways by the adults themselves. However, unless an agency such as the state steps in to ensure provision, there are costs. The need to work impedes both education and training, tending to reinforce low expectations and to create a large semi-skilled labour force. For the individual it results in an unfamiliar (significant word) need to rely on groups other than the family.

For those in towns, occupational provision may or may not be made for crèche facilities, education and training schemes. Even if legally required, it may well not effectively exist or be capable of being enforced. For those left behind in the country, the remoteness of the young adults results in additional problems in the care of both the very young and the aged, which has traditionally devolved on the youngest unmarried daughters of the family, thus reinforcing their dependence on the family unit and leading to very marked differences in the experience of education between men and women. In rural areas, provision of schools is much more basic, too, and once children are of an age to work they will be in demand in the fields; their attendance then becomes spasmodic and soon ends altogether. Authorities on Japan, the most successful non-western society to achieve advanced industrialization, lay particular emphasis on the distinctive role of education in its economic development. By the end of the First World War, Japan had already achieved near universal literacy – something that is still far from being achieved in Central America, South Africa or Bangladesh, and is already on the decline in Britain and the United States.

Workers in modern companies enjoy access to up-to-date health provision, and large cities in the Third World can often boast of medical facilities that are as good as anything in the world. However, in rural areas many peasants and their families still depend on traditional healers, whose services are well known and trusted, and who also have the great merit of being relatively cheap. Obviously they cannot cure everything and the reputation of modern medicine for miracle cures has created a demand world-wide for access to modern treatments. But assumptions of health in the Third World can be very different from those in developed societies. Just as the overall figures for the number of people served by each doctor do not reveal the sharp contrast between town and country, so they do not reveal the hard calculation that goes into considering which service to use. In the Mexican village of Tzintzuntzan, a government health clinic was accepted in time, despite cultural and other barriers. But the cost of treatment in the neighbouring town of Pátzcuaro, though very low, was noted to be a significant deterrent (Foster 1967).

The other thing that distinguishes Japan is a very strong and universal conception of fairness (Dore 1987). Japanese industrial society has retained the very strong family and personal ties of traditional society and used them as the basis of a distinctive system of co-operative labour–management relations. Japanese companies in East and South-East Asia have successfully communicated to their workers the same ethos of egalitarian co-operation as is maintained at home. From this it appears that a sharply stratified society may not be essential to rapid economic growth, or, contrary to what Huntington (1965) suggests, a developing society may not have to trade off egalitarianism, democracy and economic growth for one another.

The need to get social services to those who require them explains why workers in the field of development have been taking increasing interest in the idea of 'empowerment' of local communities. Put simply, empowerment means showing people how to take their destinies into their own hands, and this in the Third World means community action. The formation of base communities (*comunidades de base*) within the Catholic Church in Brazil, and the growing impact of the evangelical movement there, has gone along with the rise of a much more active political participation among the poor, both in the countryside and in the shantytowns. These organizations are not simply religious, although Bible readings and public worship are both central aspects of their activities. They also often establish production co-operatives in the *favelas* and classes to teach basic literacy. They often have close connections with trade unions and with the Workers Party (PT), and this ensures that, despite their religious origins and orientation, they are in conflict with the Catholic Church establishment, which sees them as Marxist.

In India, disillusion with the failure of the initial model of state-led economic growth based on the western concept of the individual helped encourage a new emphasis on Gandhian ideas and fresh encouragement for the *panchayat* movement, which had created institutions before the demand existed for them. Obviously there are limits to what such action can achieve unless new resources can be made available, and empowerment is of no value if it simply enables the poor to manage their own poverty.

CONCLUSION

There are so many things that could be said about the social context of the Third World that any selection will be, to some extent, arbitrary. Stratification systems and institutional structures are the most vital underlying features of society in the Third World, as in the advanced industrial countries. However, a consistent pattern is the great gulf that separates the rich from the poor, and the central role of the state in articulating the relationship between them.

6 The cultural context

INTRODUCTION

The term 'culture' has many meanings. For the sociologist, the important thing is that it is the way in which group life is realized. As Hall and Jefferson put it:

> We understand the word 'culture' to refer to that level at which social groups develop distinct patterns of life, and give *expressive form* to their social and material life-experience. Culture is the way, the forms, in which groups 'handle' the raw material of their social and material existence. (Hall and Jefferson 1976: 10)

As a concept, it has been used to try to determine the relationships between 'culture', social structure and other aspects of society. However, ironically, there is no clearly defined 'sociology of culture' and many of the most important contributions to the literature on culture and society have been made by people who did not regard themselves as sociologists. The main debate arises between those who regard culture as the medium within which other developments take place, and those who regard it as a residual category in which to group all other aspects of society that are not otherwise accounted for.

Some, with Durkheim, see culture as the method by which social relations are produced and transmitted. The role of ritual and symbols in dramatizing and so reinforcing the social order has been a major preoccupation of anthropologists. However, Mary Douglas rejects the sharp division Durkheim (in common with many of his age) drew between the primitive and the modern, the former in his view being characterized, in Parsonian terms, by mechanical solidarity and the latter by organic solidarity. This is consistent with her rejection also of the structuralist belief that human thought must necessarily be couched in pairs of opposites. The belief that the anthropologist can confidently determine a single true meaning for any given symbol flies in the face of evidence that symbols are almost always complex and multi-faceted. Hence in any society the reinforcing effect of symbols is felt by their constancy, repetition and familiarity, rather than their precision (Wuthnow *et al.* 1984).

Some Marxists have in the past argued for a rather simple economic determinism, in which culture forms only part of the superstructure of society resting upon the dominant economic base. However, most modern Marxists now accept, and even argue, that the culture of a society (in the sociological sense) also affects and shapes its capacity for economic production, an idea which has long seemed obvious to non-Marxists, but which nevertheless also has Marxist antecedents, notably in the work of the Italian Marxist Antonio Gramsci. They therefore stress the power of ideas to shape events and the way in which some cultures come to dominate others. As Hall and Jefferson put it:

> Groups which exist within the same society and share some of the same material and historical conditions no doubt also understand, and to a certain extent share each other's 'culture'. But just as different groups and classes are unequally ranked in relation to one another, in terms of their productive relations, wealth and power, so *cultures* are differently ranked, and stand in opposition to one another, in relations of domination and subordination, along the scale of 'cultural power'. (Hall and Jefferson 1976: 11).

Certainly comparison of, say, the economic history of Argentina with the comparable instances of Australia and Canada suggests that a mechanistic economic explanation is inadequate and that cultural differences, in the sociological sense, have to be taken into account if the differences in outcomes are to be adequately explained (Duncan and Fogarty 1986).

Anthropologists generally follow Durkheim in seeking to explain societies in their own terms. To an anthropologist, culture refers to the entire pattern of behaviour of a society. Anthropologists therefore tend to use a very loose definition of the term, following Tylor in defining culture as 'that complex whole which includes knowledge, belief, art, morals, law, custom and any other capabilities and habits acquired by man [*sic*] as a member of society' (Tylor 1891: 18; quoted in Billington *et al.* 1991: 2).

The development of anthropology as a serious academic discipline in the nineteenth century accompanied the involuntary process of discovery of new cultures brought about by colonization. In one sense this was helpful, since it meant that much was studied and recorded that might otherwise have been lost. In another sense it was not, because the basic assumption behind colonization – that the culture of the colonizers was in some or all senses 'superior' to that of the colonized – was seldom successfully challenged. Following the path laid down by Lamartine, the French in particular adopted the notion of the *mission civilisatrice*. The justification of colonization lay in the opportunity it afforded for the colonized to gain access to the dominant culture of France, and because of the superior advantages of that culture the French had a right to spread it.

Here we are concerned with the impact of change on culture, 'the common, learned way of life shared by the members of a society, consisting of the totality of tools, techniques, social institutions, attitudes, beliefs, motivations, and systems of value known to the group' (Foster 1976: 11). Colonization is a drastic change in culture. So too is decolonization and, for that matter, industrialization. Foster notes six characteristics of cultures which are crucial to the understanding of the process of change:

- Sociocultural forms are learned.
- A sociocultural system is a logically integrated, functional, sense-making whole.
- All sociocultural systems are constantly changing: none is completely static.
- Every culture has a value system.
- Cultural forms, and the behaviour of individual members of a society, stem from, or are functions of cognitive orientations, of deep-seated premises.
- Culture makes possible the reasonably efficient, largely automatic interaction between members of a society that is a prerequisite to social life (extracted from Foster 1976: 12–24).

The problem is complicated by the fact that there is a third, very common way in which the term 'culture' is used, and indeed much more commonly and widely used. This is to designate the evidences of specialized forms of self-expression such as art, music and literature. Culture in this sense, sometimes termed 'high culture', is generally seen as being the particular province of intellectuals, who designate what is to be regarded as 'good' or 'bad' within this specialized cultural inheritance. Thus since French culture was admired and copied by other European peoples, it seemed obvious both to them and to others that it also ought to be copied by the colonized. Time has shown how successful the policy was.

'High culture', therefore, forms part (but only part) of the dominant culture in the sociological sense. But it is a particularly important part, since it embodies in the highest degree the characteristics that differentiate that culture from all other cultures (or subcultures) within that society, and so forms the core of its 'entitlement' to cultural power. This entitlement of the ruling class, and its unconscious recognition by the masses, was called 'hegemony' by Gramsci. It is the distinctive property of culture that the values and norms it conveys are internalized by members of the society in general, enabling the rulers the more easily to exercise power over them.

THE CONCEPT OF MODERNITY: COMPETING CULTURES

In the nineteenth century, the development of industrialized society in Europe was increasingly accompanied by a belief in the 'evolution' of cultures – the survival of the fittest. Imperial powers, such as Spain, Portugal, France, Britain, the Netherlands, Belgium, the United States and Russia, saw it as their 'duty' to 'civilize' subject peoples and to impose their cultural norms on them.

The main vehicle of transmission was the education system. Utilizing both the pedagogy and curriculum of the dominant culture, it subordinated indigenous values by offering those who could take advantage of the system the opportunity to share in the task of government and administration.

Critics call the policy of deliberately propagating a culture of self-defined modernity 'cultural imperialism'. They argue that although formal imperialism, in the old sense of political and military domination, has ended, informal imperialism continues. Imperialism always involved a combination of strategies: it was never simply a matter of superior force, as the history of British involvement in South Africa makes very clear. Obviously the two are closely linked, as Hoogvelt argues: 'No society can successfully dominate another without the diffusion of its cultural patterns and social institutions, nor can any society successfully diffuse all or most of its cultural patterns and institutions without some degree of domination' (Hoogvelt 1978: 109). This process of diffusion could be highly effective. Anthropologists, often inadvertently, helped the process by designating residual indigenous cultures as 'primitive' and so by implication inferior to their own. Some recognized the potential problems, though, and Malinowski was concerned about possible contamination of cultures by observation (Malinowski 1961).

Mere contact with a more powerful culture can be highly traumatic. The effect on the Inuit of the destruction of their traditional way of life has been accompanied by high levels of alcoholism and other problems previously unknown. Alvin Toffler's warning about *Future Shock* (1970) was aimed at advanced industrial societies faced with accelerating technological change. It was based on an extrapolation of what was already known about the established term 'culture shock':

> Culture shock is the effect that immersion in a strange culture has on the unprepared visitor. Peace Corps volunteers suffer from it in Borneo or Brazil. Marco Polo probably suffered from it in Cathay . . . It is what happens when the familiar psychological cues that help an individual to function in society are suddenly withdrawn and replaced by new ones that are strange or incomprehensible. (Toffler 1970: 12–13).

The impact of an externally driven rapid process of change on whole societies not used to it is potentially even more devastating, since in those circumstances there is no way back to the familiar certainties of the past. Even such an apparently straightforward matter as the rising cost of maintaining traditional customs, such as the provision by leading families in turn of a fiesta for the villagers, can have a serious effect on a delicately balanced peasant economy (Steward 1967).

However, rapid adaptation to technological change is likely to be much easier for a society which is already faced with the prospect of rapid change, and which has already come to the end of its capacity to adapt, than it is for societies which have not been forced to abandon old ways. In *New Lives for Old*, a study of the island of Manus to the north of New Guinea, Margaret Mead argued that it was far more difficult for people to adopt fragments of a culture than to take on board a whole new culture. Toffler quotes her verdict approvingly, but with reservations about the limits to adaptation (Mead 1956; cited in Toffler 1970: 329). Defeat in war afforded Japan and Korea the opportunity to compete on the basis of new technology. Already people are arguing that the collapse of Communism may enable large parts of eastern Europe to do the same. But in many Third World states the problem is rather for for the future of indigenous cultures surrounded by the modern state.

Certainly various cultures can co-exist – if enough space separates them. The Yanomami in Brazil were largely insulated from the outside world until the arrival of the *garimpieros* (gold miners). However, the 'discovery' in 1971 of the Tasaday, a Stone Age culture in the Tiruray Highlands of Mindinao in the Philippines, has now been shown to be spurious. Suspicion should have earlier been aroused by their small numbers, their improbable sex ratio and their absence of cultural traditions, to say nothing of their relatively close proximity to towns and villages.

However, Europe has been influenced by the East since Marco Polo. The British association with India influenced Britain as well as India. Modern Indians claim to have learnt their habit of bureaucracy from Britain, but the Northcote–Trevelyan reforms in the UK stemmed largely from the experience of empire. India was simply too large and too complex for its cultures to be swept away. British culture was incorporated, but did not supersede indigenous patterns, and in fact with few exceptions (e.g. the self-immolation of widows) the Raj did not seek to end traditional Indian practices. Given the small numbers of the colonizers and the practice of indirect rule, Indians had to collaborate actively in their own domination for the process to work at all. British culture was admired for its association with power, wealth and modernity. When these values ceased to be unconditionally admired, and Indian values came to the fore, the end of the Raj was at hand. However, the survival of the traditional lifestyle of 'tribals' (as indigenous people are known in India) is now threatened most by the aspirations of other Indians and the quest for 'modernity' or development.

However, relationships established with colonization do not end at independence. In his well-known attack on French policy in Algeria, Frantz Fanon (1967) argued that the psyche of black peoples in Africa had been damaged by colonization – they had been taught to regard their 'own' culture as inferior. Time has shown this to be too pessimistic a view; based, no doubt, on his own individual experience. Fanon himself was born in the French Antilles and brought up in Martinique, but his argument does not appear to have the same resonance in Africa South of the Sahara as it did in North Africa. Others have yet to explore fully the impact of the experience of empire on the colonizers themselves.

IMPACT OF TRANSNATIONAL MEDIA

To the developed world, the ready availability of many channels of information seems a most desirable state of affairs. However, there are problems seen from a Third World perspective:

1. *The need to use existing networks of communication.* Cables and satellites are very expensive and use of them is controlled by the advanced industrialized countries – though Indonesia and the Philippines have both sought to enter the world of satellite broadcasting by commissioning their own communications satellites. The world's press is largely fed both text and pictures by the US agencies Associated Press and United Press International; the view of the rest of the world is systematically affected by the pro-US bias of agency reporters and editors. British (Reuters), French (Agence France-Presse) and, in the past, Soviet agencies (Tass) have similarly played their part in defining the news agenda. But Third World agencies, with the rather limited exception, for brief periods, of the Cuban Prensa Latina, have not.
2. *The problem of finding a common language.* The effort to impose Hindi in India, initiated by Nehru, who however had made his independence speech in English, was only partially successful. The attempt of S.W.R.D. Bandaranaike in 1956 to impose Sinhalese instead of English as the sole official language of Sri Lanka backfired by alienating the large Tamil minority, who had previously made use of English to gain access to the higher ranks of the civil service and other important jobs. His assassination at the hands of a Buddhist extremist was followed within a few years by riots in which Sinhalese sacked and looted the Tamil district of Colombo. Equal rights for Tamil were conceded and English continues to be a working language of government, as it is in India and Pakistan.

   In North Africa, ironically, Arabic is already available as a common language. Yet unity is elusive and attempts to amalgamate existing states have been consistently unsuccessful. Although notions of self-interest are obviously at work here, so too has been that elusive perception of difference conveyed by dialect and idiom. Over most of Latin America Spanish serves as a common tongue, although it is resented also for the very fact that makes it universal: the fact that it was imposed from above. The Portuguese speakers of Brazil can understand Spanish, although they do not choose to speak it. In Africa both Nigeria and South Africa lack a common language and continue to find English invaluable as a working language of communication. However, in East Africa Swahili was established as a universal language before the onset of colonization.

The need for a common language is powerfully reinforced by the universality of radio in the Third World. Radio speaks directly to people over long distances. It is cheap and the modern transistor does not require mains electricity. In Latin America, apart from Cuba, the pattern is one of competing commercial stations. In Africa the service is generally state run. With the gradual economic decline of Sierra Leone, the state-owned television transmitter in Freetown broke down and was not repaired; radio, however, continued to function even in the most remote areas.

3. *The problem of competing with systems of mass cultural production.* TV is the most effective of mass media, since it does not require literacy and, though a low-content medium in terms of information, it does have a strong emotive impact through use of visual images. But the very high cost of TV production means that all but the basics of news, weather and talk programmes have until recently been very expensive by Third World standards. Only now have small, lightweight cameras become sufficiently sophisticated to enable companies to compete with imports, especially in the field of drama and serials, or, as they are commonly known, 'soap operas'.

The USA sets production standards – viewers come to expect a sophisticated product, even if the content is bland – as well as standards for structure, through the need in products intended originally for the US market to incorporate breaks for advertising. US productions build on the success and reputation of Hollywood and its experience of film (movies). As with movies, which have had a much longer history of exposure in the Third World, TV productions propagate key images of life in America. These include the following:

(a) universal wealth, which creates a demand for western products, which in turn increases dependence on imports and distorts local consumption patterns, sometimes with serious effects, as in the case of the use of infant milk formula;

(b) easy violence, from cartoons and the traditional westerns to *Robocop* and *Terminator II*. Such images may imply that low local standards in this regard are satisfactory because they also exist in the United States, despite the fact that standards in most developed countries, and especially in Japan, are very much higher. Hong Kong is a major producer of films based on proficiency in various spectacular and undoubtedly threatening martial arts, and these are clearly very popular among young viewers.

Major exporters of film in the 1990s include, as well as the USA and France, Hong Kong, India and Italy. Among Third World states, India and

Brazil stand out as major producers of TV. However, in general little of their product reaches First World screens, except on cable. The Mahabarat has had a major impact in Britain in reawakening pride in Hinduism; in India it is believed to have contributed significantly to the rise of Hindu nationalism. Mexico's state-owned Televisa dominates Mexican programming, but is becoming increasingly important (as is Spain) in productions for the Hispanic-American market, and Brazil's O Globo has grown from a newspaper into the largest TV network in Brazil and the fourth largest in the world.

OPINION FORMERS

Perspectives on the world propagated by media etc. are mediated through 'opinion formers', who reinforce stereotypical images. The question of where these opinion formers come from and how they come to perceive the world as they do is an interesting one. Broadly, centre influences periphery, although there remains a special role for churches and sects, teachers, doctors and local government officials in the local context.

Education in India is dominated by Brahmins. Though the western-educated élite help shape opinion in towns, in the countryside the traditional élites still hold sway. In Latin America education is skewed by cost towards the well-to-do; the wealthy in turn have traditionally owned/edited news-papers and increasingly dominate radio and TV.

Ideas are carried by people, so travel, for whatever reason, is important in enabling ideas to pass from one place to another. War has a most dramatic influence on all societies, both because it forces people to travel and because of the challenge it presents to traditional notions of leadership and competence. Soldiers returning to Africa (Lloyd 1971) and to India after the Second World War carried with them ideas of independence. When, as in the case of Burma or Indonesia, a country was actually invaded and occupied, the effects were even more powerful. Throughout South-East Asia the Japanese invaders transmitted a powerful message that the former colonial powers could in favourable circumstances be challenged and even defeated.

However, the transmission of ideas works all the time in urbanizing societies in a much less spectacular but probably no less efficient fashion. Those who work in towns return to the country with news and gossip about events in the wider world, but also with a certain prestige which makes their ideas more weighty.

In Islamic countries the revival of Islamic fundamentalism has demon-strated both the power of opinion formers and the ability in certain circumstances to bypass them. The power of the mullahs in generating hatred of the Shah in Iran was clearly important. But it was following the revolution that those pressing for the adoption of an Islamic Republic were able to use the traditional sermon at Friday prayers to great effect. On the other hand, criticism of the ruling élite in Saudi Arabia was not possible in this way. Clandestine sermons have therefore been circulated on audiotape and found a ready market, thus circumventing the ban on public criticism. In both Egypt and Algeria, countries which have been much more directly exposed in the past to influences from western Europe, a similar revival is also very evident, despite strong attempts by the government to prevent it, particularly in the case of Algeria, where the FIS was prevented from taking power and was then banned fom overt activity.

NEWS MANAGEMENT AND INTERNATIONAL PERCEPTION OF THE THIRD WORLD

News management does not just affect what is seen in the Third World. It also affects international perception of the Third World. Press agencies, television news and features all combine to present a very selective view.

It is, of course, natural that people all over the world are concerned with their own local needs and issues. It is also understandable that bad news tends to have a much bigger impact than good. As a result many parts of the Third World get only selective and spasmodic attention from the rest of the world, and then all too often only when some 'natural' disaster hits the headlines. Even the world's first TV station with pretensions of universality, Cable News Network (CNN), which has its base in Atlanta, GA, is strongly biased towards news from the United States itself.

In 1984 famine in Ethiopia siezed public attention in Britain when a BBC news report showed moving pictures of starving children. In fact, the famine had already lasted more than three months, but had not previously caught the public imagination. Government aid (as usual) was slow to emerge; meanwhile, led by a rock star, the public spontaneously put their hands in their pockets to subscribe, and increased government aid resulted. However, in some ways the manner in which the issue emerged did Ethiopia a disservice. The news coverage was essentially ethnocentric. Ethiopians were underrepresented in such broadcasts and their own relief efforts were minimized, although they were by far the more important. Thus were the traditional stereotypes of helpless Africans and capable and benevolent foreigners confirmed in the public imagination in the advanced industrialized countries. In 1994 the situation was not as much improved as First World television neglect would suggest. Much imported food was still needed, although the rains had come and starvation was much more localized. The government of the Derg had fallen and been replaced by a weak democratic government, hardly able to tackle the country's fundamental problems.

In Somalia in 1989 the main problem was the breakdown of public order. Emphasis on this fact ultimately led to US intervention and a futile attempt to oust one of the local warlords, General Aideed. Meanwhile, in a large part of the country, former British Somaliland, without publicity, order had success-fully been restored and famine was not a problem.

Latterly, with the end of the Cold War, US attention has refocused on the security threat allegedly posed by Islamic fundamentalism.

HIGH CULTURE

A distinctive feature of Europe has been the special role ascribed to the arts and the artist. Each of the arts has defined rules (up to a point) of appreciation, but they vary very much between one art form and another. These rules are established by an élite and subject to the whims of fashion. Breaking the rules may lead to innovation, but it can also lead to the artist losing credibility.

Relationships between First and Third World élites are complex, and this is reflected in art as in all else. Though Europe initially provided the first global culture, in the twentieth century the United States has come to provide a powerful rival and mass substitute. In the plastic arts, the obvious conse-quence has been a clear trend towards the extension and ultimately globalization of high culture made possible by technology. Since the Middle Ages 'European' culture has incorporated many significant elements from countries that are now relatively underdeveloped – steel from what is now Iraq, carpets from Turkey and Iran, porcelain and stoneware from China, textiles from India, bronze from Thailand. Such objects were first imported and admired, then, more or less successfully, copied, and finally displaced by mass products retaining an eclectic mixture of European and overseas design. In Victorian Britain the severe Gothic of the mid-century contrasts sharply with the riot of interior colour and the use of a spectacular range of elements from (among others) the Indian, Turkish, Arab and Chinese decorative arts.

In recent years there have been other influences. The tomb of Tutankhamun led to a second rediscovery of Ancient Egypt in the United Kingdom and the United States, where its spectacular quality had a powerful influence on Hollywood. The powerful impact of African art on France in the age of art deco is also significant. And if the archaising tendencies in inter-war Mexican art were often awkward, the powerful naive images associated with Diego Rivera, José Clemente Orozco, David Siquieros and others of the Mexican school of muralists spoke far more eloquently of exploitation and suffering and the need for revolutionary unity than did the Mexican politicians of the generation of the revolution.

It is, of course, the capitalist West that established the idea of an art market, creating a demand for products of the traditions not only of the developed countries, but also of the Third World. Art has become an international commodity. As a commodity, though, it has rather unusual rules, since its value varies very much with the degree of authenticity attributed to it, and this is very much a matter of opinion. The export of large numbers of objects from China and Russia since the fall of the Soviet Union has upset the market, but with the increasing globalization of trade, other traditions have increasingly attracted the attention of collectors.

Music too requires neither language nor literacy for comprehension, but here the power of modern mass culture, spread by radio, television, the vinyl disc and audiotape has been overwhelming. African rhythms reappeared at the turn of the twentieth century in American jazz; they have since been reintroduced to Africa along with (disconcertingly) another popular US musical export: Country and Western.

However, literature is not so easily transmitted, and here the relationship between the First and Third Worlds is often confused. Austin writes of the problem confronting the present-day African writer:

> Whereas African artists can draw on tradition in sculpture or dancing or music, it seems doubtful whether a novelist or poet can write in his mother tongue out of a background of general illiteracy. Where would his audience be? . . . There is said to be a continuing tradition of poetry in the Somali language, and Hausa epics are still recited in northern Nigeria. There have also been local attempts to recast village ceremonies in modern dramatic form, as in the Ogun plays among the Yoruba in Nigeria, or as Efua Sutherland has tried to do in village theaters among the Akan in Ghana. At every turn, however, the African writer is confronted not simply with illiteracy but with the prevalence of English or French or Portuguese. (Austin 1978: 137)

There is a problem of the 'cultural hegemony' of the former colonial language which has to be addressed by African writers who do use English or French. They gain access to a wider readership, but there is a price to be paid. The first generation of post-independence writers found the transition particularly difficult, as they moved from rejection of colonialism and enthusiastic support for independence leaders to disillusion with and contempt for corrupt and dictatorial regimes. The influence of Marxism on the extent to which writers felt that violence was needed for successful liberation is evident throughout; its most famous exponent and advocate, Frantz Fanon, has already been mentioned.

A distinctive feature of the Francophone, as opposed to the Anglophone writers, has been the positive emphasis on Africanness, first termed *négritude* in a poem by the Martiniquais poet Aimé Césaire in 1939. The concept was elaborated in the post-war period by Léopold S. Senghor, former deputy in the French National Assembly under the Fourth Republic and later President of Senegal.

By contrast the notion of pan-Africanism, which originated with Marcus Garvey and W.E.B. DuBois in the United States, had in a relatively short time to yield to the political realities of a divided continent. It led to a new emphasis on African identity in the Anglophone territories, which was taken up by Nnamdi Azikiwe and Jomo Kenyatta, among others, but expressed in political form by Kwame Nkrumah of Ghana, almost alone among African leaders of the independence generation. There is no exact equivalent of *négritude* in English.

By the end of the decade, the first glow of independence was already fading. Wole Soyinka expressed disillusion with new governments: what choice was there but revolution on the one hand or a comfortable symbolic position with the UN or UNESCO in the other? Chinua Achebe of Nigeria denounced the system of corruption he saw there and foresaw the military coup that was to come. James Ngugi of Kenya Africanized his name to Ngugi wa Thiongo'o and called for revolution. Ironically, white South Africa formed the one cause that united a continent.

In the nineteenth century, the small élite of Latin American authors similarly rejected their Spanish heritage; in fact the first novel published in Latin America, Fernández de Lizardi's *El periquillo sarniento* ('The itching parrot'), published in Mexico in 1816, was a violent condemnation of Spanish colonial rule in all its manifestations. Uniquely at that stage, in Mexico in the latter part of the century Ignacio Altamirano (1834–93) went one stage further. Casting the invading Spaniards as the real savages, he glorified the conquered native peoples as wise and noble. Elsewhere, however, writers ignored both, and, despite the advice of Andrés Bello, rejected the challenge to establish a new and typically 'American' literature, choosing instead to try to emulate the highly artificial forms then fashionable in Europe.

This choice reflected both the contemporary cultural dominance of France among a cosmopolitan élite and growing disillusion with the actual progress of events in the Americas since independence. The theme of the struggle of human beings against hostile nature came to the fore and has remained a key theme in Latin American writing. Parallel with it was a deep disillusion with human beings and their political achievements. In the age of the dictators, the novel was one method by which coded criticism could be made of the established order, and even then such critics often found it necessary to live abroad. One of the earliest and best-known examples of this genre, *Facundo*, was published in 1845 in exile by Domingo Faustino Sarmiento as an attack on the rule of Rosas in Argentina. More recent examples have included the Venezuelan Rómulo Gallegos' *Doña Bárbara* (1919) and the Guatemalan Miguel Angel Asturias' *El señor presidente* (1946). Better known outside the Spanish-speaking world is the Mexican Carlos Fuentes, who denounced the betrayal of the Mexican revolution in *La región más transparente* (1958). This feeling of betrayal of the promise of the region was, however, expressed even more strongly by Alejo Carpentier, who in *El siglo de luces* (1962) rejected the French revolution itself and all that stemmed from it (by implication including the very existence of Latin America).

However, whereas in the early twentieth century, regionalism was the other key feature of a realistic attempt to portray the continent as it was, in the years since 1945 the major trend has been away from harsh realism towards fantasy. Yet it is within the strange and exotic rules of what has been termed 'magical realism' that a generation of readers outside Latin America have first perceived and then tried to come to terms with the real social processes at work in its cities and countryside. The Colombia of Gabriel Garca Márquez is fiction, a product of the imagination of an outstanding writer of world stature. Yet precisely because of that, his major work, *Cien años de soledad* (1967) has an aura of reality that still today sends people in search of the 'real' Macondo.

Asia is too big and too diverse to allow us to generalize. The use of English as a medium of communication by Indian writers makes their works available to the outside world without translation, and they are increasingly attracting a huge and very appreciative readership in the First World. An example would be Vikram Seth's immense epic, *A Suitable Boy* (1993). Books by Sri Lankan writers, too, have received critical acclaim in Britain, although many of the successful such writers deal with controversial matters at home, and some may have preferred to live in self-imposed exile at least until the return of the SLFP in 1994.

However, the implied criticism of the Muslim attitude towards women in Bangladesh in Taslima Nasreen's novel, *Shame*, led to such a hostile reaction that fundamentalists held an open meeting, wrongly quoted her as condemning the Koran and pronounced a *fatwa* against her.

> The usual punishment for my so-called crime – blasphemy – is hanging. The threat makes me more determined to fight oppression. I nearly went crazy when I was in hiding after the fatwa was pronounced. There are 14 people living in our house in Bangladesh, and only one of them knew I was sheltered there. I wasn't allowed to make a sound, not even a rustle. I didn't know if it was day or night and I couldn't get food regularly. I forgot how to eat and I didn't know when I was hungry. I could only go outside at midnight, as if I was a stray cat. I didn't sleep from worry. (Taslima Nasreen, interview by Marcelle Katz, *Sunday Times Magazine*, 22 January 1995: 54)

In August 1994 she had to leave her native Bangladesh and to seek exile abroad. The hazards facing a creative writer in the Third World are many, since the difference between fact and fiction, if understood, is not always accepted as legitimate.

CONCLUSION

Again it is next to impossible to know how to attempt to do justice in outline to the rich cultural variety of the Third World. While a brief summary of the literature of Latin America may serve to illuminate its main themes, because its distinctive characteristic is its common inheritance from Spain from which it has grown, no such summary could ever do more than hint at the diversity of Africa, let alone Asia. Yet there is one thing that all this cultural diversity has in common: an underlying fear that it is threatened by the powerful forces of the North's 'cultural imperialism'. This populist leaders have quite understandably sought to resist. However, in their attempt to appropriate cultural symbols for their own personal advantage, they have also run the grave risk of stirring up sleeping resentments in a way that can in the end prove politically unmanageable.

PART III
Politics of the Third World

7 State-building

INTRODUCTION

The basic interaction of world politics is the relations of nation-states. Originally, the term 'nation-state' was employed to distinguish modern states from earlier forms of political organization covering relatively small areas, such as tribes or city-states. It is true that in modern states the majority of inhabitants generally identify themselves with one another, by the possession of a common language, religion and/or culture. A people with this sense of identity is regarded as a *nation*. However, the term 'nation-state' is a misleading one, for there is no exact correspondence between state and nation. There are states with more than one nation (Britain), nations with more than one state (ethnic Albanians, Hungarians, Serbs, etc.), states with no definite national identity (Chad) and nations with no definite state (the Palestinian Arabs) (Seton-Watson 1977). The reason why it is so popular is that in nineteenth-century Europe there emerged, with the concept of *nationalism* (see below), the belief that the only appropriate basis for a state was the nation. To this day, therefore, states which lack a sense of national identity try very hard to inculcate it, as the United States did (Lipset 1979).

As so often with composite terms, over time the newly coined expression comes to have its own meaning which is more (or possibly less, but certainly distinguishable from) the sum of the parts. We can compare the term 'Latin American', which refers to Guaraní-speaking Paraguayans, Welsh-speaking Argentines, German-speaking Chileans, Brazilians of African descent, etc., as well as Colombians from old Spanish families. Similarly, 'nation-state' may be seen as simply designating a unit approximating to the ideals of statehood as described by Michael Smith: 'sovereign territoriality, authority and legitimacy, control of citizens and their actions' (Smith 1992: 256). These elements express the international as well as the national aspect of nation-statehood. Indeed, at its simplest, full penetration of the national area and the capacity to act as a single unit on the world stage might be taken as a starting point for some kind of definition and/or classification. Even this, however, would be more rigorous than would be wise in certain instances. For example, Sri Lanka would probably fail the first of these two tests: the instruments of the state do not have full penetration of the national area, being excluded from LTTE-controlled areas in the Jaffna Peninsula and around Batticaloa.

Nevertheless Sri Lanka, despite its ethnic divisions, remains a nation-state on any meaningful definition. The great danger in seeking precision in such terms as nation-state is that so few countries would fit any reasonably parsimonious definition and a new term seems unlikely to be any more useful or, indeed, accurate.

The rather arbitrary creation of many Third World states raises the issue of nation-building (cf. Kedourie 1971; Golbourne 1979). It is necessary to establish some sense of loyalty to the new state. In the Third World, state boundaries do not unite people of common descent, language and customs. This ethnic pluralism has been the source of conflict, the most glaring examples being in Africa. Thus independent Somalia, formed by the union of former British and former Italian Somaliland, has been seeking to extend its borders to embrace ethnic Somalis in Ethiopia. Ex-President Obote slaughtered 300,000 people in his attempts to wipe out the Buganda tribe in Uganda, one of the most ethnically diverse countries in the world. More recently, in tribal slaughter in Burundi in October 1993, 100,000 people were killed and some 600,000 more fled, adding to the already immense and rapidly growing problem of refugees seeking to eke out an existence on marginal lands. Likewise, Tutsi army rebels confronted the Hutu majority that had repressed them in the Rwandan bloodbath of 1994, in which more than half a million people died and more than a million fled their country for the refugee camps in neighbouring Zaire.

The Organization of African Unity (OAU) has sensibly enough taken the view that the colonial boundaries should remain, since tinkering would open up Pandora's Box. Hence Igbo independence from Nigeria found little favour and the would-be state of Biafra was not officially recognized by any other power. However, in the brief period before it was overwhelmed by the military force of the Federal Government, General de Gaulle expressed his political support for it and France and some African nations supplied it with arms. Libya's intervention in Chad has in turn brought an armed response from Nigeria to preserve the status quo.

To build a state is to institutionalize the need for emotional/ideological penetration of society. Such a link between state and society makes possible the viability of regimes. If there is no dominant group, political institutionalization cannot occur and 'society' remains 'stateless' as in the Lebanon in the 1970s and 1980s. In addition, some peoples have senses of nation but are also stateless (for example, the Palestinians until 1993 and the Kurds today); others feel imprisoned in existing states and seek to create independent states (for example, the Sikhs in the Punjab and Muslims in Kashmir).

It is not necessary for secessionist movements to be active for the state to lack authority and efficacy. Since Indian independence there has been pressure to reorganize state boundaries on a linguistic basis. The reorganization of states in the 1950s to take account of this has been criticized for intensifying the potential for ethnic violence. Certainly it has weakened state loyalties, although there is no evidence that it has made local politicians any less keen on obtaining the favour of central government.

However, some states – Bihar, Mysore, Orissa, Uttar Pradesh and West Bengal – were already effectively monolingual. And Bihar, today, is the most violent state in India. It is the area of France but with a population of some 86 million. Two-fifths of its people are illiterates with an income below the official Indian poverty line. There are numerous murders and kidnappings. A political mafia which connects crime and politics runs the dacoits (bandits), who then flee over the Nepalese border to avoid arrest. There are 1,200 illegal gun factories which increase production at election time, and their products are often used. Caste rivalry is part of the violence of the political contest. All the main national parties are involved, notably V. P. Singh's Janata Dal, which is the dominant party in Bihar.

In such an atmosphere, Third World constitutions often seem quite unrelated to reality. Some regard them as foreign impositions, hastily put together and presented to referendum in the hope of enhancing popular legitimacy. But in reality they are compromises, as are constitutions in any other part of the world, between the desire of the central government to exert its will and the determination of peripheral regions to resist it. Hence constitutions often stress democracy and centralism when the reality is of centrifugal forces such as tribalism in Africa and political gangsterism in Asia and parts of Latin America. Subrata Kumar Mitra says of India generally:

> the resilience of the state in India can be attributed to its success in incorporating some of the key features of the Indian tradition while retaining the essential features of modernity. Primordial sentiments have been balanced with those of economic interest and ideology. The edge is taken off the potential for authoritarianism through the division of power and widespread participation. By co-opting traditional centres of power and creating new ones the modern state has found a niche for most interests and norms with a support base in society. (Mitra 1990: 91)

NATIONALISM

National sovereignty has become the core value of international relations, as witness the moral indignation which was generated in response to Iraq's invasion of Kuwait in 1990. It is also the main obstacle to the solution of international problems. Yet in a sense at the national level, nationalism looks increasingly obsolete, in the face of the developing importance of local action on the one hand and international interaction on the other. There are at least five levels of security involved. Nation-building involves generating a sense of common will and purpose, which in turn leads to a sense of community, identity, solidarity, loyalty, etc. Without some kind of common political culture, the modern nation-state is difficult to sustain. Political culture is part of national identity. But it is often fragmented in the Third World because of the way in which people feel a lack of legitimacy after independence. There is a certain moral legitimacy to be obtained from the concept of national security. The fact that there are no accepted rules is a powerful spur to corruption.

The social upheaval connected with independence can be countered with an open appeal to the historic past, especially if, as in the case of Ghana or Zimbabwe, that past is more glorious than the present (and perhaps the future). An emotional appeal to shared historical experience becomes a means both to acquire legitimacy and to delegitimize the opposition, who become subversive. However, states can also suffer harmful effects from an appeal to territorial nationalism, such as the high cost of arms to defend borders often against non-existent threats. This cost has to be seen in terms both of what other things cannot be bought, such as schools or hospitals, and also of the 'lock-in' effect that purchases of modern arms entail in terms of the need to maintain weapons systems, to replace ammunition and to buy spare parts from the foreign suppliers.

The colonial practice of 'indirect rule' left a dual legacy. This practice of indirect rule is associated particularly with Lord Lugard, the first Governor of Nigeria in 1914, and was given a theoretical justification by him in *The Dual Mandate in Tropical Africa* (1922). However, it was also used by Britain in East Africa, notably in Uganda, and was employed to some degree by most successful colonizing powers. Its effect was to leave the local élites responsible for the collection of taxes and the maintenance of law and order on a day-to-day basis. This maintained to some degree their standing in their own societies. But in the nature of things, it also made them potentially very unpopular (see Crow *et al.* 1988: 28). Generally, indirect rule seems to have been very effective in undermining any general sense of national identity, albeit by reinforcing a specific sense of identity in separate tribal areas.

RELIGION AND ETHNICITY

Like nationalism, religion penetrates fragmented societies, binds disparate elements, overlooks present problems and establishes future – and past – orientation. Often it is invoked, as in Iran, to present an ideology opposed to the West which would suggest a glorious future when compared with so-called decadent advanced societies in decline.

Religion can be a political tool as a mobilizer of masses, a controller of mass action and an excuse for repression. On the other hand, religion can also form the ideological basis for dissent. Thus in the Catholic Church in Brazil and Central America, 'liberation theology' was a response to repression, and its suppression by the Vatican has left room for the extensive penetration of both Brazilian and Central American society by Protestant fundamentalism.

Ethnic politics is a powerful force challenging the cohesion of states, and in the Third World the challenge is occurring before the state has stabilized. There are four times as many self-defined ethnic groups as states in the world. As a result, ethnic nationalism is responsible for a variety of national and international tensions, such as the revival of communal tension in India.

Hindu nationalism

Ethnic nationalism has characterized the post-colonial history of South Asia. Mohammed Ali Jinnah, leader of the Muslim League, referred constantly to the Muslim 'nation' in his successful campaign to establish an independent Muslim state of Pakistan.

In India, now, the Bharatiya Janata Party (BJP) or Indian People's Party is thriving in a Hindu nationalist surge. The BJP symbol is the lotus flower, which represents peace. However, its leaders tell their supporters to rise up and defend their religion. Political, social, cultural as well as religious organizations are parts of Hindu fundamentalism, and the BJP is only part of a much wider movement.

Its leader Lal Krishna Advani, like millions of others, was displaced at partition and resents the division of India. Tensions erupted into violence when on 6 December 1992 the ancient Ayodha mosque was stormed and destroyed by Hindu fundamentalists. They believed that they were called upon to build a shrine in honour of Lord Ram, on whose reputed birthplace the mosque had been built. This Hindu deity is regarded as the 'patron' deity of the BJP. Hence, although the BJP denied responsibility, they were not widely believed.

With the decline in recent years of Congress (I), the BJP have won control of four state governments in the last five years and are the biggest opposition party in the Lok Sabha. The real power behind the BJP is the RSS or 'The Brotherhood'. All members of the BJP are also members of the RSS. The Brotherhood was formed in 1925 and has about two million members now. It seeks to establish Hindu domination and is banned by the Indian government (*Assignment*, 'The Brotherhood', BBC Television, 1993).

Gandhi was the spiritual father of the modern secular state of India. He rallied Indians of all kinds, different religions and castes, towards the single goal of independence. In the past, low-caste Hindus would have been allied with Muslims of similar socioeconomic status. Now their attitudes to Muslims have changed and they see themselves as superior. No subsequent powerful rallying goal has been found to hold the country together. The assassin of Gandhi was a prominent member of the RSS. As with Christian or Muslim fundamentalist groups, secular assistance wins hearts and minds for the BJP. RSS volunteers provide help for the poor at mobile health clinics. Not surprisingly, where this happens, political support soon swings away from Congress to the BJP.

The VHP or World Hindu Congress is the religious wing of the RSS; it provided the religious justification for the destruction of Ayodha and it threatens to capture mainstream Hinduism. RSS women's groups teach the martial arts. This is part of the training of Hindus for a holy war against the Muslims (who comprise some 30 per cent of the population or 100 million people, and who are worse off and more poorly educated on average). Fundamentalist Hindus resent the legal appeasement of minorities (Muslim objections to maintenance sparked the most recent upsurge of such resentment). The VHP teaches that Muslims should not enjoy citizenship rights at all, let alone what it perceives as enhanced rights. It justifies this position by arguing that Indian Muslims were forcibly converted to Islam and must therefore reconvert to restore their rights.

There is already increasing segregation in BJP-dominated areas and there is likely to be more conflict in future. Delhi has limited powers against the righteous indignation of impassioned people: it was able to remove the BJP government of Ayodha, but the RSS is preparing to build a temple on the site of the mosque although the Indian government has promised that the mosque will be rebuilt. The most obvious place for a future clash is the Matura mosque, which was built by the Moghuls on the site of Lord Krishna's birthplace and is an even more sensitive issue than Ayodha.

Ethnicity

Ethnicity is often a form of political identity and, where it does not coincide with state boundaries, a source of division. Such a coincidence is much less likely to occur in new states established by external intervention. Indeed, as in Nigeria, the establishment of the state itself may threaten ethnicity, and lead to insurgency or even secession.

Ethnicity is not, however, an exclusively Third World problem. There are ethnic divisions in older states too, and as the history of Europe in the twentieth century has shown, at least as much trouble can arise from trying to eliminate ethnic differences as from having to live with them. Everywhere the problem is compounded by the fact that the nation-state is under increasingly strong attack both from without (international organizations, transnational corporations, regional economic groupings, satellite communications, global environmental concerns) and from within (ethnic nationalism).

Common ancestry is one possible basis for ethnic identity. But the anthropological evidence suggests that from earliest times people have used the notion of common ancestry as a convenient legal fiction, and certainly in the huge multiethnic states of today it is in the highest degree unlikely that cultural differences reflect real ethnic differences. For example, there is doubt even whether the Tutsi and Hutu of Rwanda and Burundi are, as they believe, different ethnic groups, or whether they merely reflect class differences. Some other factor or factors, perhaps a common language, usually a different religion, often perceived economic and/or political grievances, usually come into play to differentiate one ethnic group from another. On the basis of such cultural distinctions is a collective ethnic consciousness then made the trigger for a belief in self-determination which may in turn lead to secessionist demands. The aspects of cultural distinctness emphasized may change according to their utility. Religion divides Sinhalese and Tamils as much as language, but it is language that is stressed by the Liberation Tigers of Tamil Eelam (LTTE) in Sri Lanka, reflecting the fact that it was the attempt of Sinhalese politicians to deny Tamils the use of their language that triggered the continuing division between the two peoples, but also enabling the LTTE to claim majority status in some areas, including in ethnic headcounts Tamil-speaking Muslims, who are generally opposed to the LTTE.

In Islamic societies there is much more stress on religion. The tendency to define identity in terms of religion alone had led the Turks in particular to deny the very existence of Kurds as a separate ethnic group. Religion is for Muslims the chief source of ethnicity, the means both to mobilize and to contain societies. The consensus on religion stems from the tendency for aspects of Islamic society to be mutually self-supporting. The popular-level actions by fundamentalist groups such as the Muslim Brotherhood echoes the official level (dogma and law). Moreover, there is an important international dimension to Islamic thought and organization. There are more than 40 Muslim governments, whose agencies are supportive of Islam, wherever it exists. Muslim leaders have a political role by definition, since Islamic thought makes no distinction between the sacred and the secular.

Sri Lanka

Many villages around Batticaloa on the east coast of Sri Lanka are deserted. Their people have left in response to the activities of the Sinhalese army, which is fighting a war which has already produced a million refugees and thousands of dead.

Three-quarters of Sri Lanka's 17 million population are Sinhalese; about two million are Tamils. Tamils place great emphasis on education and seek professional jobs in the public services, especially in law and medicine. Independence in 1948 'marked no great watershed in Sri Lankan politics' (Moore 1990). Sri Lanka remained insulated from world politics for nearly three decades. However, in the meantime the disappearance of colonial rule unleashed Tamil success at obtaining jobs and at the same time promoted the rise of Sinhalese chauvinism. In 1956 Tamil riots followed the decision of S.W.R.D. Bandaranaike's government to make Sinhala the sole national language in place of English. No allowance was made for Tamil, which would have been a problem anyway, but the exclusion of English made it difficult for the Tamils to continue as they had done in the past to get jobs in the public sector. By the mid-1970s, with Mrs Bandaranaike as Prime Minister, the

Tamils felt the government was deliberately loading the dice against them, especially since at the same time it was continuing with the policy begun by the British in the 1930s of resettling Sinhalese peasants from the south and centre in the north and east.

This was increasing ethnic tensions among Tamils, who were beginning to view all Sinhalese in Tamil-dominated areas, whether incomers or not, as intruders. The result was to encourage demands for a separate Tamil state. The LTTE was formed in 1976. In 1977 an electoral landslide overturned the Bandaranaike government and installed one led by J.R. Jayawardene, who took advantage of his victory to introduce a new Constitution with himself as executive President.

In 1983, in a Sinhalese backlash, a mob rampaged through the market district of Colombo. They killed more than 2,000 Tamils and more than 200,000 were made homeless. Within a year a dramatic escalation took place in the number of incidents ascribed to the LTTE, and soon the north and east were in a state of open insurgency. The Indian Prime Minister, Rajiv Gandhi, feared the spread of separatist demands to the Indian state of Tamil Nadu. In 1987 he and the Sri Lankan government signed an accord which offered some autonomy to Tamils in the north and east in return for a ceasefire. An Indian Peace-Keeping Force (IPKF) was sent to police the agreement.

Two months later the LTTE broke the ceasefire. The Indian presence unleashed the problem of Sinhalese nationalism, and Sinhalese left-wing extremists, the JVP, began a campaign of violence intended to stop any concession to the Tamils. The new Sri Lankan President, Ranasinghe Premadasa, negotiated a new ceasefire with the LTTE on condition that the IPKF withdrew and gave the Indian government notice to go. This they did in 1990 (Saravanamuttu 1990). However, 1990 also saw the beginnings of armed attacks on the small minority of Muslims. The LTTE claims that the attacks on the Muslims were a government ploy to blacken the name of the LTTE. However, the Muslims believed they were the victims of LTTE violence and began retaliatory attacks against Tamil villages.

Then on 21 May 1991 Rajiv Gandhi was assassinated by a suicide bomber at an election rally in Tamil Nadu, one of a series of rallies which had appeared to herald his return to power. The LTTE denied responsibility, but the method was absolutely characteristic of the suicide squads of the LTTE known as the 'Black Tigers' and there is much evidence that the bomber was a member of such a squad. More than 25,000 have been killed in the separatist struggle since 1983. The LTTE had virtual control of Batticaloa for a while before the government launched an offensive to recapture it. The LTTE still does control towns around Batticaloa, the Jaffna Peninsula and other areas of the north-east, where loudspeaker systems carry LTTE propaganda to whole villages and towns while the inhabitants go about their normal business.

Ethnic nationalism is likely to increase in certain specific circumstances: for example, where a previously authoritarian state democratizes or a formerly democratic one becomes more authoritarian. It is likely to find a sympathetic response given increased international concern for human rights. When it seems likely to work in their favour, emerging regional powers like India may seek to establish cross-border connections between ethnic groups. As Rajiv did not live to find out, they may pay a heavy price for doing so. On the other hand, regimes may manipulate ethnicity to their own ends. Where a leader's ethnic base is larger than that of the opposition, he or she may strengthen relations with it when threatened. This is exactly what Premadasa did in Sri Lanka. It served to exacerbate ethnic tensions beyond the capacity of the system to manage them, and in 1993 it cost him his life.

PERSONALISM

Personalism is a means to bridge the gap between state and society. As Weber himself noted, charismatic authority was an ideal-type, a tool for comparison rather than something which could exist in its pure form. In practice there is always a tendency for patrimonial relations to co-exist within a rational-legal framework, Clapham (1982: 48) terms this condition 'neo-patrimonialism'. It is a feature particularly of Latin American polities, but is also found elsewhere. Personalism, therefore, is not just the most spectacular form of charismatic authority. It is closely linked to three related phenomena: *patrimonialism*, *populism* and *clientelism*.

Patrimonialism is the most enduring legacy of the pre-colonial society for new states and comes back into its own at independence. Many newly independent Third World states have undergone periods of unstable democracy alternating with military dictatorship. Many would argue that Pakistan, which is a most important example of this phenomenon, has become the personal fiefdom of the Bhutto family, and that politics has degenerated into factional infighting between family members. Certainly much of its social structure remains essentially feudal. Two-thirds of Pakistanis still live in rural areas where feudal justice is often arbitrarily dispensed by the local landed aristocracy. Eighty per cent of the country's politicians are of aristocratic families, such as the Bhuttos themselves, and they rely first and foremost on the support of the local people to whom they are patrons. Today the main civilian opposition comes from Al Haq's Muslim League, which is also starting to look dynastic as well as personalist.

In Africa indirect rule meant that traditional chiefs were maintained, forming a useful interface between colonial rule and the peasantry. However, they were not maintained unaltered. The colonial government frequently merged, promoted or suppressed chiefdoms. Moreover, they were not cheap to maintain, although since the costs of 'Native Administration' were borne by the people they helped administer, the full extent of them was not obvious at the time. In Sierra Leone in 1949, 46 per cent of the total cost of administration went in payments to hereditary rulers. Comparative figures for Tanganyika, northern Nigeria and western Nigeria show a very similar picture, and in Kano in northern Nigeria the salary of the Emir alone accounted for 13 per cent of expenditure in 1936–7 (Kilson 1966: 31–2; citing Perham 1937: 118).

Despite this, in the Sierra Leone Protectorate tribal allegiances remained strong and the chiefs formed a key link in the structure of the country's independence party, the Sierra Leone People's Party (SLPP). In December 1960, Sir Milton Margai 'met with twenty-five leading Paramount Chiefs to inform them of the party's plans for attaining independence and instructed them how to communicate the information to the masses. "Their duty," he directed, "was to tell all the section chiefs about independence; the section chiefs in turn should educate the town headmen who should explain to the people"' (Kilson 1966: 241). In the 1957 elections, 59 per cent of all candidates and 84 per cent of the successful candidates who contested Protectorate constituencies had chiefly ties. In 1960–1 some 35 per cent of the SLPP's officers were sons, grandsons or nephews of chiefs (pp. 232–3).

Max Weber (1964: 132, 324ff.) believed that the authority of government originally stemmed from what he termed *charisma*: that is to say, the outstanding personality or personal qualities of an individual. In more developed societies, charisma was 'routinized', or subjected to legal forms and controls. It could be either *traditional* – accepted because it had always been accepted – or *legal-rational*, which is to say, accepted as being conferred by formal rituals involving some kind of choice or recognition by or on behalf of the society as a whole. Weber therefore distinguished these three types of authority, charismatic, traditional and legal-rational, from one another, while treating them as 'ideal-types' which were not found in pure form.

Charisma refers to the possession by the leader of outstanding personal qualities recognized as such by others, and charismatic leadership has often accompanied the emergence of new regimes in the Third World. Thus Mao Zedong was hailed as a prophet, Mustafa Kemal as 'Father of the Turks' (Atatürk), Ho Chi Minh as 'Father of the Indo-Chinese People', Nkrumah as 'the Saviour, Redeemer and Messiah', and Ayatollah Khomeini as Imam. Charisma has been sought by those who lack it. Imelda Marcos, wife of the President of the Philippines, likened herself to Eva Perón (Evita) of Argentina, but the real parallel lay in the use of economic rewards for mass political support as an alternative to the generally much more costly use of force (Bresnan 1986).

Populism is a rather vague term, which refers to the way in which leaders generate support by claiming to speak in the name of those they follow. Appeals for support are direct, expressed by appearances on presidential balconies with arms and voice raised. A classic example would be Perón removing his jacket and declaring himself also to be a *descamisado* (lit. 'shirtless one' = worker). Personal appearances around the country are important, although radio and television can be and are used to reinforce the leader's image. There is little need to pay much attention to such institutional devices as keynote speeches to Congress, where they are for the most part unheard by 'the people'. Such leaders usually lack strong ideological conviction, seeing the will of the common people as being the determining factor. The key to their success is the way in which they identify issues that call forth the maximum response from their chosen constituency (Canovan 1981). Gamal Abd-el Nasser of Egypt and Saddam Hussein of Iraq are each in very different ways examples of the way in which charismatic leadership can bring forth a strong popular response, and even generate the momentum necessary for war.

The idea that political office brings with it the duty, as well as the opportunity, to use patronage on behalf of one's family, friends or tribe, which is termed *clientelism*, is often seen as being the distinctive feature of Third World politics, and is often found in connection with the illegal making of personal gain out of one's office (Clapham 1982). Clientelism is a means to sustain one's political support base during the time in which the rallying force of nationalism declines and classes have not yet developed to provide the bases for political parties. It may be based on ethnicity, as in the tribal society of West African states, where national leaders may go in for 'pyramid buying', by buying up local leaders who can deliver the necessary support at election times. Its strength depends on the fact that the patron–client bond derives from the notion of responsibility to one's family characteristic of traditional society, and so is immediately understood by all parties to a transaction, and its dangers from the way in which it lacks the traditional restraints on the individual and as a private relationship is not open to scrutiny by modern state structures.

The key features of the patron–client relationship have been defined by John Duncan Powell (1970) as follows:

> First, the patron–client tie develops between two parties unequal in status, wealth, and influence ... Second, the formation and maintenance of the relationship depends on reciprocity in the exchange of goods and services ... Third, the development and maintenance of a patron–client relationship rests heavily on face to face contact between the two parties.

Because of its unequal nature the patron–client relationship is inherently unstable, but in the context of traditional village life the fairly simple network of mutual relationships is well known and fully understood. This tendency to instability increases rapidly in the context of urban immigrants, whose desire for a job makes them vulnerable to recruitment into a much more complex network where any sense of reciprocal obligation is easily lost. At a national level the network is wide open to exploitation by wealthy landowners and entrepreneurs and by foreign interests. Bill (1972) documents how under the

Shah's 'White Revolution' the professional middle class of Iran expanded uncontrollably, generating increasing criticism of the failure of the regime to allow it to grow even faster.

State clientelism is also important. The state tends to be the largest employer in Third World countries. Hence salaries are generally the state's largest expense. This is most marked in large federal states, such as Brazil, India or Nigeria, where the lower level of regional bureaucracy also has to be maintained. The use of patronage, in the form of appointments to sinecures and posts with parastatals such as Petrobras in Brazil, forms the means by which the state is enabled to intervene in both urban and rural sectors. But there is nothing in this situation which leads us to believe that the government has any interest in reversing it; nor is there any obvious reason why those who benefit from it in the provinces should wish to do so either.

CORRUPTION

Gathering accurate information on corruption is, of course, an impossible task. Even the definition of corruption is problematic. However, the boundary is crossed when payment or reward is made directly to government officials to secure a service of some kind. A distinction can be made between payment to expedite a service to which one is entitled anyway, and payment to secure a service to which one is not entitled. But in practice both are properly regarded as corrupt. As Williams points out, there is a moral, as well as a political meaning to the term 'corruption'. It is 'used ... to describe a morally repugnant state of affairs and implicit in its use is the desire to eliminate it' (Williams 1987: 13; Wraith and Simpkins 1965; Heidenheimer 1970).

This is implicit in the most widely used definition of corruption in public office, that of Joseph Nye, who describes it as:

> behavior which deviates from the formal duties of a public role, because of private-regarding (personal, close family, private clique) pecuniary or status gains; or violates rules against the exercise of certain types of private-regarding influence. This includes such behavior as bribery (use of a reward to pervert the judgement of a person in a position of trust); nepotism (bestowal of patronage by reason of ascriptive relationship rather than merit); and misappropriation (illegal appropriation of public resources for private-regarding uses). (Nye 1967: 419)

The dangers of corruption are highest where the divisions between public and private are blurred. 'The morally corrupt society is one where moral life has, so to speak, been privatised' (Dobel 1978). The persistence of traditional culture, where the structure of government is based on reciprocal gift-giving, may contribute to a culture of corruption. Similarly nepotism, the employment of or granting of favours to relatives, is often the logical extension of extended kinship networks. The low salaries paid in the lower echelons of bloated bureaucracies of states such as India, Nigeria and Mexico, and the fact that in all societies status is measured by the conspicuous display of wealth, may contribute too.

It is impossible to tell just how much corruption costs Third World countries. However, estimates in Europe suggest that corruption in Italy accounts for some 15 per cent of gross national product, and it is likely that the rates for Third World states are much higher.

Certainly it is inevitable that under a clientelistic system there will be no hard and fast distinction between public and private, and corruption will be endemic. What seems clear is that the effects of clientelism are much more serious in authoritarian or one-party states than they are in competitive systems. Though it is probably impossible to eliminate corruption entirely, the threat of public scrutiny forms an effective brake on the more outrageous forms of corruption. Small-scale corruption may be relatively harmless, indeed it may be redistributive. However, on a large scale it can literally undermine the foundations of society. A hospital and other modern buildings collapsed during the Mexican earthquake of 1986 when traditional buildings dating back to the colonial period survived. The ruins disclosed the extent to which the theft of cement and reinforcing bars during construction had compromised the stability of the modern buildings.

In Africa, long spells of military rule have made Nigeria notorious – probably unfairly – for the depth and breadth of public corruption. 'By the mid-1970s, the corruption associated with the Gowon regime, if not with General Gowon himself, had reached amazing proportions and events like the Cement Scandal . . . confirmed popular impressions that the riches of the oil economy were being siphoned off by a parasitic élite at an alarming rate' (Williams 1987: 98). The problem was that it did not end with the return of civilian government and the end of the oil boom. Corruption was a feature of both the 1979 and 1983 elections, and within weeks of the latter the military were back in power, alleging that the main reason for siezing power was the corruption of the Shagari government.

Accusations of corruption have long been standard practice in Latin American elections, but in recent years governments have started to take legal action against particularly flagrant examples. In Venezuela, the second term of Carlos Andrés Pérez was brought to a close by his impeachment, followed by his trial on corruption charges. More recently, President Collor of Brazil, on the eve of presiding over the Earth Summit at Rio, was accused of corruption by his own brother and subsequently resigned in December 1992 under the imminent threat of impeachment. In December 1994, however, he was cleared by the nation's Supreme Court, although not without criticism of the authorities for having failed to prepare their case properly.

An additional problem of administration in many developing countries is the scale of the bureaucracy and the extent to which it diverges from the 'ideal-type' described by Weber and embodied in legislative form by the Northcote–Trevelyan reforms in the UK. In a clientelistic system, it is unlikely that personnel will be recruited on merit alone, and pay and promotion alike are dependent on the favour of the ruling élite. Few civil servants have been able to separate themselves convincingly from the political arena. Paradoxically, this situation has been worsened by the attempts of military regimes in countries such as Pakistan and Nigeria to use civil servants in the formation of allegedly 'non-political' governments. In addition, the contempt that military officers tend to have for the police reduces their status and pay, favouring a pervasive culture of low-level corruption in the enforcement of law and order, while in Mexico, as in many other Third World countries, the traffic police enhance their standard of living by arbitrary use of their power to obtain bribes from well-off motorists (*The Guardian*, 22 May 1995).

Certainly the nature and structure of the party system in the single-party states of Africa, Asia and Latin America after 1960 cannot be explained by internal factors alone, but must be sought in the wider context of world politics. For the argument often advanced in defence of these systems was that in the aftermath of colonization the emerging state simply could not 'afford' the 'luxury' of competitive politics. Hence in these cases, too, the ideological justification for the monopoly of power by the single party was that total control of the economic system was essential for the planning of future development. The trouble was, as events showed, that the silencing of criticism by opposition, far from enhancing efficiency, allowed corruption to become rampant. In an extreme case, Liberia, it led to the violent overthrow of the regime in 1980, and since then its economic base has been virtually destroyed by endemic civil war without any compensating advantage for the bulk of the population.

A Third World state's external connections also feed corruption through the demonstration effect, through the payment of bribes by foreign companies or their agents and through their support of regimes known to be corrupt.

MILITARY INTERVENTION

Many of the military coups that have deposed governments in Africa (e.g. those that brought to power Ibrahim Babangida in Nigeria, Jerry Rawlings in Ghana and Valentine Strasser in Sierra Leone) have had as one of their two or three principal avowed aims the ending of corruption. It was a scandal concerning a £300 million contract for the purchase of Jaguar aircraft that was said in some circles actually to have precipitated the fall of the Shagari government in Nigeria in 1983. The alleged 'commission' on the deal was said to have amounted to no less that £22 million (c.$40 million).

Following the intervention of General Buhari, the new military government arrested a number of prominent businessmen and others and had them tried before special military tribunals for 'economic crimes'. Charges were brought against a leading political figure, Umaru Dikko, who had already escaped abroad. As Chairman of the Presidential Task Force on Rice, it was alleged that he had received over four million naira for one rice contract alone. However, from his refuge abroad he explained that the delivery of suitcases full of money to his home did not mean that he was in any way corrupt. 'Just because money was delivered to to my house boy doesn't mean that it was for me' (*West Africa*, 25 February 1985; quoted in Williams 1987: 99). An attempt to kidnap him to face trial in Nigeria failed.

Sadly within months the new military regimes are usually at least as corrupt as the civilian governments they replace or supplant. Given that in an authoritarian climate backed by the use of force there is little incentive to audit the military budget effectively, they have proved in the main to be even more corrupt.

One of the worst examples was Argentina between 1976 and 1983, where the economic policies of the regime were disastrous and led to corruption on a scale even greater than anything that had gone before. Corruption was not confined to the looting of the property of 'subversives' and their families, nor the labelling as 'subversive' of individuals whose property was desired, but it permeated all the economic dealings of the regime. As the economy was opened up to foreign capital, loans were sought for grandiose developmental schemes, and a substantial proportion of these funds disappeared into the pockets of both civilian contractors and their military contacts. Of $20 billion added to the national debt during the period, the Alfonsn government was only able to trace $10 billion. The whereabouts of the rest remains a mystery except, of course, to those who still have it. Military intervention weakens the legitimacy of civilian government without securing legitimacy for itself, and thus paves the way for greater corruption. Its causes are so important that it will be discussed separately in Chapter 9.

AUTHORITARIANISM

As with corruption, the prevalence of authoritarianism is greater where legitimacy is less well developed. *Authoritarianism* is the belief in the principle of authority as opposed to that of individual freedom. In its most developed form this becomes advocacy of orderly government under military or other dictatorship. Although quite independent of it, it is therefore closely related to *militarism* (see Chapter 9).

With the rapid decolonization of the 1960s came first disillusion with the allegedly slow processes of democracy, and this in turn led to a wave of military coups in Africa and Asia. In a key study Linz identified the new authoritarian states as:

political systems with limited, not responsible, political pluralism; without elaborate and guiding ideology (but with distinctive mentalities); without intensive nor extensive political mobilization (except at some point in their development); and in which a leader (or occasionally a small group) exercises power within formally ill-defined limits but actually quite predictable ones. (Linz 1970: 255)

On the basis of Linz's definition, it is possible to distinguish as he does between *new* and *old* authoritarian regimes. The longer established an authoritarian regime is, the less it needs to rely on the overt use of force and the more it tends to develop new forms of legitimacy. However, for Linz authoritarian government is always a transitional state, either towards democracy or towards totalitarianism.

In addition, Sahlin (1977) suggests, it is also useful to distinguish between *protective authoritarianism* and *promotional authoritarianism*. Protective authoritarianism is the argument of those who intervene by force simply to protect the status quo and the position of those who benefit from it. Following a traditional military coup, which has only the limited aim of displacing the existing government, a period of emergency rule normally follows in which the armed forces emphasize the power available to them, their limited ambitions in making use of it, and their intention to return the country to civilian rule as soon as possible. Some regimes of this type – for example, that of Franco's Spain – do survive for a long period and, Sahlin notes, become 'old' authoritarian regimes in Linz's terms, gaining a degree of legitimacy through force of habit, and, generally, needing to depend less on the overt use of force. However, their principal aims remain the same: the depoliticization of issues and the demobilization of the masses.

Promotional authoritarianism, by contrast, is characterized by a desire to promote change, by supplanting the existing government and establishing one which will stay in power for a period of years to pursue certain stated aims. Chief among these aims is economic development, the desire for which is in itself rooted in a nationalistic belief in the value of a strong state. But this requires a certain degree of mobilization of the masses in the interests of productivity, which can most safely be achieved by appealing to nationalism. However, even this does not resolve, but only postpones, a fundamental conflict between the desire for economic mobilization and the fear of political mobilization (Calvert 1994).

COERCIVE STRUCTURES

The tendency towards authoritarianism is promoted by the crisis of legitimacy that follows independence or any other serious challenge to the continuity of the state. However, it is often in part able to rely on the tradition of paternalism. The masses, being generally ill-educated and especially so in comparison with the élite, are not seen as being really fit for self-government. Any tendency to revolt is merely seen as confirmation that this judgement is correct. At the same time in the aftermath of a major crisis, such as independence invariably entails, the 'fear of freedom' drives many members of the public to seek refuge in the leadership of a single supposedly wise figure who represents both authority and stability.

Long-serving autocrats with tame military support are noticeably less common now than they were 20 years ago, and the move away from military government which began in Latin America in the late-1970s gathered pace and has now affected almost every part of the world from Haiti to China. Twenty years ago most Third World states were characterized by military governments, personalist dictatorships or one-party rule – or a combination of these. Now Thailand, South Korea, Bangladesh, Pakistan and Nepal no longer have personalist or military governments. In Africa 25 out of 41 states have held competitive elections in the past five years, and nearly all of Latin America has governments chosen by competitive election. However, author-itarian rule does remain in Burma (Myanmar) where Aung San Suu Kyi remains under house arrest, despite the fact that as leader of the opposition she successfully won a democratic election organized by the military regime which is still holding her captive. China and Indonesia are both authoritarian, as are a number of states in South-West Asia, notably Syria and Iraq.

In liberal democracies, violence in society is controlled through the use of the *legal system*, but even there behind the legitimate authority of the government lies a very wide range of powers to control and to coerce, all backed by the sanction of force (see *inter alia* Hewitt 1982; Hillyard and Percy-Smith 1988). In the Third World, as in the First, most governments have at their disposal a substantial army, an extensive police system, and some kind of paramilitary reserve or militia that can be called upon in emergencies. However, since they tend to identify their own survival with that of the state they rule, they are much more likely to make open use of them.

The maintenance of a stable government is the fundamental assurance of the political control of a ruling élite. Losing control of government means at the least that their power will be severely curtailed, at most that it will be lost for good. But maintenance of a government is only part of political control, since it can operate effectively only if the system of relationships around it is also maintained, which is done by the use of both rewards and punishments. Rewards are available both for members and would-be members of the élite, and no less significantly for potentially useful people who might otherwise be political opponents, who may be *co-opted* into the system. As well as co-option (co-optation), rewards include promotion, pensions and honours. Punishments include demotion, dismissal, fines, banishment, imprisonment and even execution. In Ghana, Jerry Rawlings had no less than four of his predecessors shot during his first brief term in office, but even military-based governments seldom go quite so far.

AUTHORITY AND LEGITIMACY: THE SYMBOLS OF POWER

It is generally thought that authority stems from legitimacy, but the two concepts, though often confused, are in fact quite different. Legitimacy means that a government is generally recognized to have the right to do what it does. It depends, therefore, not on what the government claims, but on whether or not that claim is recognized. The fact that a government is recognized as legitimate gives it authority, which is the assurance that its commands will be obeyed. Recognition, however, can come in either of two ways. A government may be recognized as legitimate by its own citizens. Provided it is recognized as such, it does not then matter much what others think of it. To the United States Fidel Castro may be a Communist dictator, but to many Cubans he is the leader of the revolution through which they hoped to attain freedom and dignity among other states. The government of President de Klerk in South Africa lost the ability to govern effectively before the formal transfer of power to the government of President Mandela in April 1994. On the other hand, where legitimacy is weak or contested, as in 'quasi-states' such as Haiti, the fact that a government is recognized by other states may be a significant factor in maintaining it in office, though without authority.

Authority is never absolute or unlimited. To have authority to do something is to have the right to do that thing, and be obeyed. Authority can be, and is routinely delegated, divided or shared; otherwise complex governments could not work. Hence a government in all but the very smallest states has to depend on the willingness of others to implement its orders. The fact that they do so depends less on a specific act of recognition or legitimacy than on the fact that, on their own, few people regard themselves as having any alternative but to obey. All Weber's forms of authority, therefore, result in the same thing: obedience. The collective habit of obedience gives a tendency to inertia in social systems; once established, they will tend to continue unaltered until either society decides to change them or it discovers that it has forgotten any need for them. By extension, the longer a social institution continues in existence, the longer it is likely to continue.

Conquest formed the basis of colonial rule. In post-colonial states, however, paradoxically, despite their rejection of colonialism, governments claim their authority by virtue of being successors to the colonial power, notably in Nigeria and Ghana, where force has been used again and again since independence to install a series of military governments. In consequence, for many people in the Third World 'internal colonization' has simply replaced the traditional external variety. 'Internal colonization' is a term that has been used occasionally by Marxist writers, but not with a very consistent meaning. Here it is used in a very specific sense, to draw attention to the fact that large parts of many Third World states are still in effect colonized by their own ruling élite.

This process has serious consequences, since this élite is generally one of town dwellers who tend both to fear and to dislike the countryside, and to seek their entertainment in what passes for an urban environment, or abroad in Paris or Las Vegas. The view from the capital involves the colonization of the countryside by the town. The logical extension of the desire to control is the urbanization of the countryside, reducing it to orderly controllable form. The effect of this is the rapid destruction of rural habitats and ecosystems, which has reached an extreme, for instance, in the area surrounding Manila in the Philippines. Hence it is this urban perspective that lies at the basis of the environmental crisis of the Third World (see Chapter 13).

WHO MAKES THE LAW?

The symbolism of Third World governments is a fascinating study in itself, combining as it does traditional elements such as chieftainship, colonial elements derived from the imperial past, and modern notions such as the executive presidency, associated with the world superpower, the United States. Some rulers, such as Sir Dawda Jawara of The Gambia or Sir Eric Gairy of Grenada, retained the knighthoods of colonial governors. The government of India continues to operate from New Delhi, designed by Sir Edwin Lutyens to serve as the capital of the Raj, and Indian regiments use bugles, bagpipes and the regimental silver as symbols of continuity. Pakistan is the world's largest manufacturer of bagpipes as well as of cricket bats. Yet the wheel of Asoka on the Indian flag, like the Sinhalese lion of Sri Lanka or the trigrams of Korea, speaks of a much older inheritance. The shield and spears of the flag of Kenya are traditional symbols of military and so of political power, but the fly whisk carried by Jomo Kenyatta (and other East African leaders) was also a symbol of chieftainship, even if the office he held was a modern, constitutional one. The symbolism of gender relations is not overlooked – V.S. Naipaul suggests that in imposing 'his' women on macho Argentina, Perón was asserting his own ability to lead and control (Naipaul 1980). This, however, seems rather to underestimate the charismatic personality of the first of them, Evita.

By putting his own head on the coins of Ghana, Nkrumah not only demonstrated in the clearest possible way that power had passed to an African, but as earlier rulers had done, confirmed his leadership in enduring form (Clapham 1982: 62). In Kenya, Kenyatta's style was that of an African monarch:

> When Kenyatta moved between State House in Nairobi and his homes in Gatundu, Mombasa and Nakuru, it was less the seat of government that moved,

so much as an entire court. Kenyatta became the centre of governmental activity and thus access to him was the *sine qua non* of preferment for politicians, bureaucrats and businessmen alike. As discussed earlier, access to decision-makers is never unlimited and not always free in Africa. The court 'gatekeepers' of Kenya extracted sizeable entry fees and most visitors left with lighter wallets or thinner cheque books after having 'voluntarily' contributed to one of Kenyatta's favourite causes or schemes. (Williams 1987: 83)

What is clear is that in many Third World states, whether as heir of the colonial governor, or as heir of the traditional chieftain, the president rules and does not reign. Indeed this is the form of government that the citizens understand and (despite some of its obvious shortcomings) are comfortable with. The initiative in legislation lies, inevitably, with the government. Within the government, the adoption of the presidential system has placed great emphasis on the role of presidential leadership.

It has therefore also institutionalized conflict between presidents and legislatures, particularly, but not exclusively, in presidential states. Service as a legislator remains an important rung on the political ladder to preferment, and the importance to a would-be Third World politician of a strong local power base in the region/area/tribe can hardly be overstated. In return, rewards are expected by the local community as a result of support for the government, even in a one-party state.

In Latin American states, institutionalized conflict between presidents and legislatures is compounded by multiparty politics. Factional squabbling was used as an excuse for President Fujimori of Peru to close Congress in 1992 and to rule by decree. On the other hand, the fall of both Carlos Andrés Pérez in Venezuela and Fernando Collor in Brazil was made possible by their lack of an effective congressional power base.

However, there are limits on the power of other Third World governments to legislate. This is most noticeable in Muslim countries, such as Bangladesh, Pakistan or Sudan, where there has been strong pressure to make the Koran the sole basis of all law, and governments have sought to reintroduce punishments such as flogging, amputation and stoning to death, which had been abolished by the former colonial power. In 1995 the government of Benazir Bhutto in Pakistan refused to intervene in the case of a 14-year-old Christian boy sentenced to death under Islamic law for having allegedly daubed walls with anti-Islamic slogans two years earlier. Fortunately for him, on appeal to a higher court, the evidence against him was dismissed as concocted, despite well-organized demonstrations outside the courtroom calling for the sentence to be upheld. In the long run, the thing that may cause the greatest problem for these governments is the Koranic prohibition against charging interest on the use of money, since if it too is implemented, it means either that their banking systems will not function at all, or that they will be wholly in the hands of foreigners.

THE PROBLEM OF THE WEAK STATE

Many of the problems of the Third World, therefore, come down to what can be called the problem of the weak state. Populist campaigning and the emotional aspects of television are used to reinforce the illusion that choice of a single candidate or party will solve all (or at least some) of the personal difficulties of the voter. But this is just not possible.

Even if it were possible to fund the overnight improvement in the distribution of wealth envisaged (for example) at the time of the election of President Mandela of South Africa, it is hard to see how he (or any other leader in a similar position) could be in a position to deliver. And the fact is that the Third World leader is rarely in a position to ensure policies become practice, not because he or she lacks the resources, but because the leader does not have the power to see that those resources are actually allocated to the purpose for which they are intended. Even in relatively sophisticated states like Iran in the last years of the Shah, or Mexico under Gustavo López Portillo (1976–82), large sums were expended for work that was not carried out, government inspectors being bribed to ignore the obvious fact that the buildings and roads did not exist.

The reasons for the inefficiency of public administration in such circumstances have received most extended theoretical treatment from Fred Riggs (1964). Riggs derived his theory of the three stages in the development of post-colonial states from his observation of the Philippines, using an analogy drawn from optics, namely the passage of light through a prism. Traditionally, in the conciliar state, decision-making was 'fused', the decisions in different areas being incorporated in the same body in the way that white light contains all the colours. At the same time, the price of goods was strongly affected by what Riggs terms *arena factors* such as the power and prestige of certain individuals.

In a modern state, on the other hand, the competence of government is increasingly split into functional areas, each the responsibility of a different government department, and in the 'ideal-type' of the administrator this functional separation would be complete. Decision-making, therefore, is 'refracted', just as white light leaving the prism is refracted into different colours. At the same time, the price of goods is primarily determined by the market (though this for its maintenance depends on the willingness of government to guarantee its stability).

However, most developing countries have mixed institutions in which functions are incompletely separated. The analogy is with light actually passing through a prism; hence Riggs' term, 'prismatic' society. In 'prismatic' society, Riggs suggests, prices are fixed by two competing mechanisms, the bazaar, where bargaining is the rule, and the canteen, where a favoured clientele is supplied at special fixed prices. This undercuts the position of the entrepreneurs and makes them dependent on patronage for their right to bargain. In return they help generate the surplus by which a very small élite maintains its extremely favoured lifestyle. The 'pariah entrepreneur' is a very characteristic feature of such societies.

Riggs attaches particular importance to what he terms *clects*, a cross between a clique and a sect; the *dowreh* in pre-revolutionary Iran forms a particularly clear example. Clects are composed of people who have already been recruited to the patron–client system, and they consequently have a strong incentive to strengthen it in their own interests:

> Each clect draws its membership from a particular community; it applies its norms selectivistically [*sic*] to members of that community; and its poly-functional goals always include a communal-orientation as well as whatever economic, religious, political, educational, or social objectives constitute its manifest functions. (Riggs 1964: 171)

Such a society is characterized by what Riggs terms the *sala* system of administration; the term *sala* being the Spanish for a room or a hall: for example, in the presidential palace. This is an overcentralized system in which every decision is subject to the whim of the president (or other chief executive). There are three consequences: decision-making becomes, or remains, overcentralized; every decision is taken several levels higher up than is really necessary; and the top level in particular is both overworked and overpowerful. There is serious waste in public spending because money gets spent two or three times over: what Riggs terms the *canteen* system, where government controls prices, enables it to set prices low for insiders and high for outsiders. In any case, no one knows exactly how much is being spent, and in such a situation administrative and political corruption flourishes (Wraith and Simkins, 1965). In consequence, Riggs suggests, there is a strong tendency in the system toward what he terms *negative development*: that is to say, development focused on the needs and wants of the élite and not on the needs of society as a whole. Positive development, for Riggs, can only occur where there is simultaneous political, social and economic change.

In the Third World state, therefore, the formal structure of the law, courts, civil service and all else is subject at all times to the whims of the executive, who becomes the centre of all patronage and all preferment. A strong executive can, at a cost, defy powerful groups and public opinion; a weak one is likely to settle for the expedient decision. In such circumstances, state-building is difficult.

CONCLUSION

State-building is the most vital process in any newly independent Third World country. It is intimately linked to the development process because, without an adequate perception of the country as its own state, the dynamism and ambitions of the population (and in particular the entrepreneurial élite) will not be directed constructively. An identity must be forged at the collective level, just as it must for individuals. Nationalism, religion and ethnicity can either strengthen or weaken state identity, depending on how they are used. Clientelism, corruption and military intervention all act to undermine both authority and legitimacy, and in extreme circumstances can contribute to the collapse of regimes and the disintegration of the economic order.

8 Political participation

INTRODUCTION

There has been much criticism of the fact that few of the constitutions of the newly emerging states in Africa or Asia long survived independence. Much of this criticism, in English-speaking countries, was directed at the 'Westminster model' of parliamentary democracy. The fact that in 1994 parliamentary democracy was alive and well in a substantial number of Third World countries, and that the governments of both Sri Lanka and Pakistan were seriously considering reintroducing it, suggested that these criticisms might have been misdirected, even if they were not actively encouraged by the apologists for authoritarian government.

Pinkney notes that for a small number of countries 'the main problem has not been one of achieving a transition from authoritarianism to democracy, but of preserving a democratic structure which has survived continuously since independence' (Pinkney 1993: 83). He cites Jamaica, Trinidad and Tobago, The Gambia, Botswana, Mauritius, India and Papua New Guinea and some smaller island states, together with Costa Rica in Central America, which has had a stable democratic system since 1948.

Pinkney is rather pessimistic, and a closer consideration of the countries he lists does highlight the problems. In Asia, Sri Lanka has had constitutional government since 1948 and Malaysia since 1957. Both have been independent longer than Jamaica. In Latin America, Mexico has had a stable constitutional government continuously since 1948; in fact, since 1920. On the other hand, although Smaller Island Developing States (SIDS) are a better bet for democracy than their mainland counterparts, there is no guarantee of this: the Comoros (1975, 1978, 1995) and Seychelles (1977) in the Indian Ocean, Fiji (1987) in the Pacific and Grenada (1979, 1983) in the Caribbean have all suffered from armed intervention in the political process. In 1994 the government of Sir Dawda Jawara in The Gambia succumbed, at the second attempt, to a military coup.

Obviously, as the inclusion of Costa Rica makes clear, the absence of military forces, or, alternatively, their weakness, is a major factor in safeguarding democracy (see Chapter 9). Other reasons for the survival (or otherwise) of democracy can be grouped as political, economic and social. Among the political reasons are the existence of a widely accepted constitution for government, the ability of major interest groups to influence decision-making, and the emergence of broadly based and well-organized political parties.

CONSTITUTIONS

It is certainly doubtful if many of the constitutions of independence would have survived for long anyway. However, their main problem was that they were drafted by lawyers with a lawyer's concern for the *output* of government. Hence the way in which democracy was to function was left to a series of assumptions about the uses of power which were not widely shared and not necessarily understood. The result was a democracy for the élite, at best; at worst, a system in which smooth-tongued demagogues manipulated unsophisticated masses to give electoral support to an essentially authoritarian system: 'Democratic forms in a country where most of the people are illiterate, politically unsophisticated, fearful of those in accustomed authority, and at the same time easy prey to demagogues, may merely camouflage continued control by a small segment of society' (Staley 1954: 226).

Naturally, too, in different ways the various colonial powers sought to ensure as far as possible the continuing protection of their own interests. The documents therefore took little or no account of the *input* side, especially the relationship of business and financial interests to government. Business is often inimical to democracy, owing to its desire to strike bargains and gain advantages over rivals, especially when armed with the financial resources of transnational corporations. The precursors of independence were in a particularly strong position. They could use their historical position to negotiate with the former colonial power a settlement which left them in control of the key resources. Hence in many cases the new government was dominated by a single tribe or regional faction. As long as it had the necessary resources, it was then in a position to generate political support by clientelism. Where such systems have survived, therefore, there seem to have been at least two preconditions: that the resources available should be sufficient, and that they should be spent in a way that enhanced social satisfaction and not frittered away on the self-indulgence of those in power.

As an economist, Sir Arthur Lewis noted the need for firm financial managerial control of public expenditure and the need to ensure that no one person be entrusted with its authorization. However, British constitutional practice is notably lacking in any formal restraint of this kind other than that imposed by accountability to Parliament, and this mechanism could not survive the institution of the 'one-party state'. In this respect the French system, with its emphasis on financial control, was perhaps more suited to African conditions than the British, with its excessive reliance on dangerously vague notions such as trust, self-regulation and the 'old boy network'.

INTEREST GROUPS

Demands on the political system originate in the minds of individual citizens, often in a quite unformed state. They may well not be immediately recognized as political, and whether they are seen to be or not will depend on the nature of the society concerned. However, except in a very local sense, the voice of one individual in a modern society will normally carry little weight unless the demands which that individual *articulates* come from within the central élite and its decision-making body – what Easton (1957, 1965) calls 'withinputs' or 'intraputs' – or until those concerned get together with others who share a common interest and *aggregate* their demands into a programme for action. In liberal democracies, typically, demands are articulated by interest groups and aggregated by political parties. However, this model is by no means always applicable elsewhere.

It is now recognized that interest groups – people sharing a common interest – exist in all societies, although usually in a *latent* rather than an *active* state, waiting to be activated by a relevant issue. In a sense they cover the entire field of political interest articulation other than that of the individual, for the family itself can be regarded as an interest group. Many groups, especially those with better formal organization, aggregate interests also into a common action programme. But the interest group differs from the political party, to which it is closely related, by not seeking political power for itself; it seeks merely, when it acts at all, to influence decisions taken by others.

Almond divides interest groups into four categories (Almond and Coleman 1960: 33ff.): non-associational, institutional, associational and anomic.

1. *Non-associational.* People do not join non-associational groups, they are born into them, and therefore as far as politics are concerned the groups may remain latent rather than active, often for many years. They include family and kin groups, castes, classes, religious sects and ethnic groups. Membership of such groups is, at least at the beginning of their politically interested life, a given in their environment. They are defined as non-associational, therefore, indicating that they have not joined together in a specific way, they just happen to be members of this common bond of interest. Almond seems to regard the predominance of non-associational interest groups as characteristic of developing countries and criticizes India specifically for 'poor boundary-maintenance between the polity and the society' (Almond and Coleman 1960: 45). What he means by this is that in India there is a strong tendency for such groups to be significant in appointments to public offices, for example.
2. *Institutional.* Institutional interest groups include all groupings to which one belongs by virtue of economic necessity – the need to earn one's living.

They include bodies like the armed forces, police, civil servants, teachers, professional groupings generally, and other occupational groups. However, at the institutional level interest groups cease to be usually latent and shift to a more overt, participatory level. In Third World states the civil servants in general and the armed forces in particular enjoy a considerable advantage over other institutional groups, since they are state funded and enjoy special routes of access to the centres of power (see Chapter 9).

3. *Associational.* The associational category includes all interest groups which have a formal membership and an established process of entry. Straddling the boundary line between institutional and associated groups are the trade unions. It is necessary for many purposes in many countries to belong to a trade union in order to earn one's living, but in Britain they are, at least, still considered to be in some sense voluntary bodies, as in the United States. They are therefore regarded, for most purposes, as being an associational interest group. The associational category also includes most of the various forms of pressure group: that is to say, groups whose sole or principal purpose is to exert pressure upon government.

Pressure groups can in turn be subdivided into two categories: those that are designed to defend interests on the one hand, and those that are formed to promote interests on the other. Protectional groups consist of people who are actively engaged in a trade, profession or some other activity whose interests they seek to defend. Promotional groups, on the other hand, do not necessarily consist of the people whose interests they seek to promote, and often, as in the case of the international pressure group Greenpeace, they could not in fact easily do so, if at all.

4. *Anomic.* 'Anomic' refers to a state of alienation from the normal processes of society, such as was originally described by Emile Durkheim in 1893 (Durkheim 1964: ix). Anomic groups, to Almond, have only a temporary existence and no formal organization. They are 'spontaneous irruptions from the society into the polity' (Almond and Coleman 1960: 34). Riots, demonstrations, strikes, walk-outs, and sit-ins form anomic interest groupings in this sense.

In Third World countries, interest groups are distrusted, and when they take the form of ethnic or community groups there is great fear that they endanger national unity. In India, where a caste, ethnic group or region dominates the politics of a state, that group will benefit disproportionately in the allocation of appointments and contracts. Many government officials, as Weiner noted, tended initially to decry this tendency as a violation of democratic principles. They had, he suggests, a rather idealistic picture in their minds, not of the way that the British system of democracy actually works, but of how it was supposed to work. They were not well informed about the politics of the United States, for example:

It is assumed by many Indian intellectuals that the Indian population is particularly susceptible to having its passions and loyalties exploited; and indeed there is some truth in this. In the eyes of these intellectuals, the existence of community associations, and the demands made by them, result from the exploitation of community sentiments by politicians, as if politicians in 'truly' democratic societies do not behave in such a way. But the presence of a democratic framework, and especially of universal adult suffrage, requires that the local politician seek to organize interests, sentiments, and loyalties in such a way as to maximise his political opportunities. In the process he may appeal to caste, religious, linguistic, and tribal identifications as well as to secular identifications, such as peasant, worker, refugee, student, woman, and so on. Representative government is the catalyst for all kinds of organizations that bespeak a greater involvement in politics by the population. (Weiner 1962: 68)

Most Third World states are still characterized by a predominance of non-associational interest groups and a relative scarcity of formally organized associational interest groups. Theorists of democracy have identified a number of factors which appear to facilitate the emergence and/or maintenance of democracy. Two relate to the expression of interests. On the one hand, a relatively wealthy society is better able to fulfil all the demands made upon it than a poor one. By definition, therefore, many Third World states, lacking such resources, will find it difficult to satisfy these demands. On the other, the development of powerful opposition coalitions is much less likely where interests are diverse in nature and base, creating cross-cutting cleavages within society, such that no one tribe or group is able to dominate the whole. The problem is how to secure this state of affairs.

The device of the separation of powers (or the division of powers between federal and state governments in a federal system) is effective only where enough interests pull in both directions.

POLITICAL PARTIES AND ELECTIONS

A political party is a formal organization of people seeking to achieve or to retain political power.

Some writers on political parties find it hard to see Third World political parties as parties and regard them only as factions. While all political parties derive ultimately from factions, factions are temporary and their future is always uncertain. Parties, on the other hand, are characterized by permanence of structure, a deliberate attempt to win recruits and regular procedures for recruitment of political leaders. Possession of these attributes can and does lead to the formal acceptance of their right to exist in law. For this reason Sartori believes that personalist parties, which often have a very short life with little or no institutional continuity, do not really deserve the title of party at all (Sartori 1976: 254–5). Since such parties are inevitably rather common in new states, where, that is, they are allowed to exist, this presents something of a problem. It is certainly also possible for them to institutionalize over time. Such is the case with the Perónist (or, more properly, Justicialist) Party in Argentina.

It is important to distinguish, too, between political parties and party systems. The most important distinctions are those between competitive systems, in which a number of parties compete for power, and non-competitive systems, where there is only one party. Where there is more than one party, parties shape not only themselves but one another. Hence the number of parties active is certainly significant, although unfortunately it is very difficult to define.

Competitive systems are the ideal of democratic theorists. However, the public display of dissension which democracy requires comes as an unpleasant surprise to those brought up under the enforced stability of a colonial government or traditional regime. It is also true that in many democracies, perhaps the majority, elections are often accompanied by a high level of violence, and sadly more people may be killed in the quarrels that accompany an election than in the course of a military coup. Three-quarters of all military coups in Latin America in recent years have resulted in no casualties at all.

Hence, especially in the years immediately following independence, many Third World states sought to control internal rivalries by creating what is often loosely called a 'one-party state'. There are in fact three distinct types:

- Those systems where no party is allowed.
- Single-party systems.
- One-party (dominant) systems.

It is arguable that all are clearly separable from competitive multiparty systems, but in very different ways.

RISE AND FALL OF THE 'ONE-PARTY STATE'

Apologists for authoritarian rule paved the way for military intervention, especially but not exclusively in Africa. Abroad many who might otherwise have been more suspicious were influenced by enthusiasm for specific leaders, notably Julius Nyerere and his model of Tanzanian socialism.

From the 1960s onwards, the idea that only one state-sponsored party was sufficient and indeed desirable was repeatedly justified by Third World leaders on the grounds that it overcame divisions damaging to an emergent nation. The one-party state may be seen as replacing tribal loyalties and identifications in holding together a fragmented society such as that of Zaire. However, coalition-building is always vital even under single-party rule or military dictatorship. Opposition elements, such as newspapers or trade unions, may be and frequently are co-opted by government by a not very subtle combination of inducement and threat.

The weakness of authoritarian government is that it rarely meets the aspirations of the population at large. Exceptions include both Brazil and South Korea, where rapid economic growth was experienced under military government. However, there are very many cases in which the reverse happens. The development boom of the 1970s was accompanied by growth of grassroots organizations. These were often seen as subversive by Third World governments, and every effort was made to limit their effectiveness. However, in Brazil, where the number and importance of these 'base communities' is very marked, they were (and remain) strongly connected with the informal structure of the Catholic Church (see Chapter 6).

In modern times, political parties are so widespread that it is usually only under a military dictatorship, when they are forbidden to organize, that they are entirely absent. Recent examples include Chile under General Pinochet after 1973 and Burma at the present time. However, there have been other cases. A noteworthy example was that of Afghanistan after the introduction by the king of parliamentary government in 1964. Since there were no political parties, candidates ran as individuals and very few eligible voters bothered to turn out. With no basis for organization, the parliament's proceedings were chaotic. This, as was possibly intended, enabled the king and the court clique to continue to run the country without effective interference, but in the end it helped create the conditions for the Soviet-backed military coup which overthrew the king and his parliament in 1973 (Weinbaum 1972).

By contrast, the Shah of Iran in 1963 had sponsored the organization of one 'official' party, the Rastakhiz (New Iran) Party. Other parties were not banned, but strong pressure was brought to bear on members of the élite to show their loyalty to throne and country by becoming active members of the new organization (Bill 1972: 44–51). Protected at least to some extent by the complex network of family influence, many did not do so, but initially the new party seemed to be very successful; it was only later that it was shown how far its introduction had broken up the traditional structure of loyalties and so helped focus opposition to the regime on the Shah personally.

A variant of the one-party system is to be found in Morocco, where officially there are a number of political parties, but where it is known which one at any one time enjoys the favour of the king, without which nothing can be done.

The party in such cases serves merely to identify the political élite and to enable them to continue to control the political process behind a façade of democracy. The pretence is the more convincing if the government does not formally create a one-party state, and encourages the emergence of an official opposition party which it can continue to control. Such states create an illusion of democratic participation while ensuring as far as possible that it does not become a reality. S.E. Finer termed them 'façade democracies'. As shown above, the mere existence of elections and parties does not guarantee that a system will give genuine and effective participation. It is essential to look closely enough to determine how the system works in practice, and especially what other political or social structures exist to control nominally 'democratic' activity.

Between one-party (dominant) systems and single-party systems the difference in theory is great, but in practice there is a 'grey area'. In some states one party can obtain overwhelming dominance of the political system without restraints being placed on opposition parties. Once in power it then becomes very difficult to dislodge.

A striking example, as the opposition has found in recent years, is Mexico. When the Mexican Party of the National Revolution (PNR) was founded in 1929, no one was in doubt about its 'official' status. All key interests were required to form part of it, and it was financed by a levy on the salaries of state employees. However, other parties did function and in the period after the Second World War there seemed a genuine possibility that the system would evolve into a two-party system such as that of Colombia or Venezuela. However, since 1964 it has become increasingly clear that every step in that evolution so far has been strenuously and, on the whole, successfully resisted. Even under President Salinas (1988–94) the opposition found it virtually impossible to succeed even at state level, and it was not until May 1995 that an opposition party succeeded in winning the governorship of a key state, Guanjuato.

India in the years immediately following independence is another obvious example. The Congress Party enjoyed its initial hegemony owing both to its leadership of the struggle for Indian independence and the presence of Pakistan. Nehru himself strengthened this position through the international goodwill and attention India obtained as the result of advocating, on behalf of smaller and less influential countries, a theory of their place in the world which they found congenial. But at home the supremacy of the Congress Party was maintained as the result of its success in monopolizing patronage and being able to 'deliver' on its political promises. When excluded groups decided that they were not going to obtain access to patronage through the system, they were able through the democratic process to mount successful regional and ultimately national challenges. Their suspicions were confirmed by the autocratic style of Indira Gandhi and her willingness to use any means, including force, to maintain her leadership of a divided Congress. Still with the assistance of her land reform campaign, the dominant faction, Congress (I), retained sufficient credibility to recover from the disaster of the State of Emergency and its defeat at the polls in 1977. Though the party's hegemony has since been broken following the breach in its dynastic leadership of the assassination of Rajiv Gandhi, the example of the Congress Party in India seems to illustrate both the strength of one-party politics and its most obvious limitations.

Such one-party systems, on the other hand, are quite different in principle from single-party systems, where opposition parties are either banned or persuaded by a variety of means, including force if necessary, to disband themselves. A number of countries in Asia and Africa adopted the single-party model after decolonization. The nature and structure of the party system in these single-party states cannot be explained by internal factors alone, but must be sought in the wider context of world politics. Their proponents, including Kenyatta in Kenya, Nyerere in Tanzania and, more recently, Mugabe in Zimbabwe, argued that in the aftermath of colonization the emerging state simply could not 'afford' the 'luxury' of competitive politics, because total control of the economic system was essential for the planning of future development. The trouble was, as events showed, that the silencing of the opposition, far from enhancing efficiency, allowed corruption to become rampant.

In single-party states, elections are held. In the modern world there is no other universally accepted way of showing that a government is legitimate. But such elections (really plebiscites) merely act to confirm the continuity of a regime. There is no real chance of changing the office-holders. The problem is, of course, that this situation is unstable. The creation of a single party does not really end competitition for power or office; it merely creates a pretence that it does not exist, while at the same time allowing resentment to build up against the existing office-holders.

Two- (and more) party systems do not guarantee rotation in office, but they do make it possible. Theorists of democracy regard the ability of the voters to change their rulers as one of the most important advantages of the system. The amount of harm they can do is limited to their elected term, and rival groups are given a turn in managing the affairs of the state. Of course, there is a cost. Holding elections is expensive and competitive politics leads to a great deal of money being spent to win votes, although the history of the spoils system in the United States (and Japan) suggests that clientelism in itself is not a barrier to economic or political development. The short time-span of an elected government, however, may also operate against long-term development planning. Why, then, should rulers be prepared to give up their power? In Third World states, there is a very compelling reason: the fear of what may happen to them or to their families if they do not. Opposition builds up over time and giving up political power is better than facing the firing squad.

PRESIDENTIAL VS PARLIAMENTARY GOVERNMENT

Parallel with the move to institute 'one-party states' was the tendency in the years after 1960 to abandon the parliamentary constitutions inherited from the colonial period and replace them with presidential systems. Of course, almost all republics use the term 'president' to designate their head of state, the official who represents the state on formal occasions, receives ambassadors and performs a range of ceremonial duties. A presidential system is one in which the president does not merely carry out the formal duties as head of state, but also acts as head of government, chief executive and (at least in theory) commander-in-chief of the armed forces.

The system of government in which power is concentrated in the hands of an executive president was a regional curiosity before 1946. In the first three decades of the nineteenth century, presidential systems were adopted by most of the newly independent states of the Americas, with the exception of part of Haiti and of Brazil, which remained a parliamentary monarchy until 1889 (Needler 1963). Only one other presidential state dates from this period: Liberia, a colony for freed American slaves, independent in 1847. After that there was a long gap, until the rising power of the United States created Hawaii (1892; annexed by the United States 1898) and Cuba (1901).

It was only after 1946 when the Philippines, under American tutelage from 1898 onwards, became independent that the presidential system came to sweep the rest of the Third World, beginning with the Middle East and North Africa, and spreading throughout Africa South of the Sahara in the wake of the dissolution of the British, French and Portuguese colonial empires after 1960. So powerful was the urge to imitate it that even established parliamentary systems such as those of Pakistan and Sri Lanka were modified in the direction of presidentialism.

But few of the systems that have resulted are true presidential systems in the constitutional sense. Since there is no focus of power, presidential systems are dynamically unstable. The invariable tendency has been for the president to assume, often with the aid of force, control over all functions of government. To be a true presidential state, three conditions have all to be observed. The president must be elected directly by the people according to agreed rules generally regarded as fair. The president must not be an hereditary ruler, be self-appointed, come to power by a military coup, or be nominated by the chiefs of a military regime. He or she must be elected for a definite term. There is a subtle difference between being elected for a series of definite terms and being in power indefinitely, but in practice one tends to lead to the other. Consequently, constitutional provisions limiting presidential terms are normal, although they are often abused, if necessary by the systematic rewriting of the constitution. The president must not be able to dissolve the assembly, or suspend its powers during its fixed term of office. In practice this is often done, as in Uruguay in 1973, by the leaders of military or military-backed regimes, making use, in most if not all cases, of emergency powers, which will be considered further later (Weinstein 1975: 132–3).

Though there must, if government is to function at all, be a close relationship between the two areas of competence, executive and legislature, summed up in the American phrase 'checks and balances', they must be reciprocal and there must be limits on the president's ability to influence the assembly. The balance is perhaps easier to attain when, as usually happens, the president is elected at the same time as the assembly. Even then, different political parties may, as in Brazil since 1990 or in Venezuela since 1994, be chosen to represent the people in each of the branches of government.

POPULISM AND DEMOCRACY

Populism refers to the way in which leaders generate support by claiming to speak in the name of those they follow. The term arises from its use by the People's Party, which achieved some electoral success in the United States of the early 1890s for its Omaha Platform, but was eventually swallowed up in the Democratic Party (Hicks 1961). Slightly earlier, a group of intellectuals in Russia had called themselves the *narodniki* – a term usually translated as 'populist'. They, like their very different American counterparts, believed in the proposition that 'virtue resides in the simple people, who are the overwhelming majority, and in their collective traditions' (Wiles 1969: 166).

Populist movements have received particular attention in the Latin American context, where they are associated with the early stages of industrialization. There a populist movement has been defined as:

> A political movement which enjoys the support of the mass of the working class and/or peasantry, but which does not result from the autonomous organizational power of either of these two sectors. It is also supported by non-working class sectors upholding an anti-status quo ideology. (Di Tella 1965)

Dix has argued that there are two distinct forms of populism: authoritarian and democratic. For him, the authoritarian form is characterized by leadership from the military, the upper-middle-class, landowners and industry, support from a 'disposable mass' of urban/unskilled workers, and a short-term, diffuse, nationalist, status-quo-oriented ideological base. The democratic form is led by professionals and intellectuals, its support comes from organized labour and/or peasants, and its ideological base is more concrete and reformist, with its nationalism more articulate (Dix 1985). Yet in practice populist movements are both democratic and authoritarian in differing degrees.

Latin American populism, therefore, is 'urban, multiclass, electoral, expansive, "popular", and led by charismatic figures' (Conniff 1982: 13). However, as di Tella implies, it is stretching matters to suggest that populism is urban rather than rural, and in practice the term has come to refer to any movement characterized by three things:

- An assertion that the people are always right.

- A broad, non-ideological coalition of support.
- A charismatic leader, often lacking any specific ideological commitment.

Canovan derives from actual examples a typology of no fewer than seven types of populism. These, too, are 'ideal-types', and actual movements may well overlap more than one of her categories (Canovan 1981: 13). Their importance lies in precisely how clearly they demonstrate both how widespread populism is and how its main characteristic is its *fluidity*. It was this that provided a vehicle for leaders such as Gamal Abd-el Nasser of Egypt and Saddam Hussein of Iraq to mobilize the masses in support of their governments. The key to their success is the way in which they identify issues that call forth the maximum response from their chosen constituency (Canovan 1981).

The populist leader, however, speaks on behalf of the masses and seeks to control them for his or her own purposes. The leader finds out what they want, only to be able to offer it to them. To that extent, therefore, the successful populist leader takes responsibility off the shoulders of the people, whereas if they are to participate in a fully democratic society, they have to avoid the temptation to abandon the cares of responsibility to others.

EMPOWERMENT AND DEMOCRATIZATION

Empowerment, on the other hand, lies in encouraging individuals and groups actually to make their own decisions and to take part in shaping their own future.

This is not a new idea in the Third World. It lies at the root of the panchayat system in India, and in the island states of Oceania the tradition is so strong that decisions concerning the whole community are made collectively by a Council of Elders.

Empowerment, if it is to mean anything, means that people must be able to participate effectively in the making of decisions affecting them. In other words, it is not enough for them to be told what the government is going to do for them. They have to be able to initiate policies and to shape the development of policies initiated by others.

This means having the ability to participate in decision-making at all relevant levels and through a variety of channels. In most states, significant decisions are made on at least two levels: local and national. In federal states, at least three. It is also true that certain important decisions relating to the national and local economy of Third World states are taken abroad, outside the state boundaries, whether by banks, aid agencies, transnational corporations or otherwise. Nevertheless, the first step in empowerment is learning how things work on the local level. External influences are effective only when they work with local interests.

Democratization in the Third World has certainly been encouraged by the fall of Communism in Eastern Europe. However, the pressure for democratization already existed in the Third World before 1989. By 1989 most of the countries in Latin America had returned to constitutional government, and more than half the countries in Africa had held competitive multiparty elections.

Democratization movements have in the recent past been seriously hampered by their identification with anti-state activity, and in many cases concessions have been made which on closer examination often turn out to be more apparent than real. Hence the mere existence of multiparty elections does not guarantee that truly competitive politics will operate.

Singapore illustrates some of the ambiguities of the democratization process. Before 1991 the ruling People's Action Party held all the seats in Parliament. Since the election of 1991 there have been four opposition members in the 81-member unicameral Parliament, but they hardly add up to an effective opposition. Although he had had the support of the vast majority of his people since he came to power in 1959 with a programme of social reform/economic development which has been very successful for most of the population, Singapore's first Prime Minister, Lee Kuan Yew, who led the country into independence from Malaysia in 1965, had been in effect an autocrat for more than 30 years when he decided to retire. He continues to watch over his creation, a remarkably disciplined city-state, from the post of Senior Minister in the Prime Minister's office.

In consequence the impulse to democratization may produce a system where democracy is defined in very limited terms (Arat 1991). For example, equal political rights may exist on paper, but social and economic inequality may be protected from political interference. Third World democracies often have quite restrictive politics with considerable coercive power: for example, India and Kenya. The more adept regimes arrange for a public display of the trappings of democracy and may allow semi-official opposition parties to participate in doctored elections, as in Mexico.

A third possibility is illustrated by Brazil, where a mass electorate is influenced by the enormous power and highly questionable role in the Third World context of the media. Some 18 million people in Brazil get their news from the O Globo TV station each evening, and O Globo sees part of its role as manufacturing presidential candidates. But for Brazil as for some other Third World countries, the replacement of formal military government with formal 'democratic' government conceals the continuing (and possibly enhanced) importance of some groups in society, including (and perhaps especially) the military establishment. If the military have ceased to intervene, it may be because they really do not need to do so. In 1994 President Cardoso, elected with the support of O Globo, sent troops into the *favelas* (shantytowns) of Rio de Janeiro in search of drug-dealers. Ever since these depressed neighbourhoods have echoed to the sound of gunfire, but the drug problem gets no better, since the methods that are being used to counter it are entirely inappropriate.

CONCLUSION

With the fall of Communism in eastern Europe there have since 1989 been signs of a new interest among international funding and lending agencies in promoting 'good government' in developing countries. Hence political conditions are attached to loans.

Western governments and the World Bank have come under strong criticism for not attaching strong enough conditions to their loans, to mitigate their ecological and social impact. For example, the British government has been accused of wasting public money by funding the Pergau dam in Malaysia and has had difficulty in refuting the allegation that it did so only to obtain significant arms contracts from the Malaysian government. Mrs Thatcher's support for the Mahaweli project in Sri Lanka has also been criticized in retrospect, as ecological considerations have assumed a higher profile in political debate and awareness has spread of the environmentally damaging effects of large dams.

Such criticism may reduce any impact that considerations of good government might otherwise have. But there is also a sense in which any consideration of this kind has to be handled very sensitively by aid donors, if they are not to be accused of interfereing in the internal affairs of the recipient country.

Certainly many more Third World countries enjoy ostensibly democratic structures today than was the case, say, 20 years ago. However, there are factors which militate against real participation whatever the theoretical arrangements. First, democracy cannot be imposed from above, and it takes time to establish itself even in the most favourable circumstances. Second, democracy, like the market, functions less effectively in conditions of poverty, and where, for example, it means freedom to sell your vote to a corrupt local politician it has little substance. Third, even for many genuinely newly democratized countries, much energy has first to be consumed in trying to come to terms with an undemocratic past.

For the increasingly secular societies of the non-Islamic world, there is no other basis for legitimate authority than some form of democracy. How then can national history be satisfactorily explained? Democracy is no longer a decorative ideological overlay on a functional authoritarian base, it is the essence of that functioning. As Brundtland (WCED 1987) so rightly points out, without participation, development will not happen and the environment will be destroyed.

9 The armed forces and politics

INTRODUCTION

There are nearly 200 countries in the world, but only three (Costa Rica, Iceland and Luxembourg) have no military forces. In general, where there are military forces there will be military intervention, although usually of a limited kind. Even in the advanced industrialized countries, where armed military intervention is a rarity, the armed forces are a major spending department of government and, with the advantage of inside knowledge, constitute a most formidable lobby in defence of their privileges and their budget, although this is not usually regarded as intervention. For that the armed forces have to show that they are ready and willing to make use of their unique resource, the ability to use force.

And in Third World states armies are of very great importance indeed. During the 1980s they not only assumed and/or retained political power throughout the Third World, they spent at the same time an ever-increasing proportion of their countries' wealth on arms. The consequence was arrested development and (in some places) accelerated environmental degradation.

MILITARY INTERVENTION

Finer (1975) regards military intervention, in the more active sense usually implied by the term, as being the product of both the ability and the disposition to intervene. Virtually all armies, however, have the ability to intervene; the question is why and how they choose to do so.

Military intervention in politics in Third World states results both from push (propensity/disposition to intervene) and pull (stimulation/provocation) factors. Both may be needed to trigger an actual intervention, as for example when the breakdown of legitimate civilian government is accompanied by changes in the military institution.

Push factors for military intervention include the ambitions of individual officers, factional disaffection and institutional activity said or believed to be in the 'national interest'. Pull factors include the association of the armed forces with military victories, a general perception of a lack of cohesion, discipline or stability in society, and a specific perception by the armed forces of threats to the military institution or to the officer class, or to the dignity or security of the nation.

The ambitions of individual officers undoubtedly do play a part in military coups. However, their idiosyncratic nature makes it plain that they cannot of themselves be regarded as a general cause of coups. Some individual leaders, such as Gen. Soglo in Dahomey in 1965 or Lt.-Col. Lamizana in Upper Volta in 1966, have seized power in their own names. But on the other hand, some coups have resulted in the choice as leader of personnel who did not take part at all in the coup itself. Examples from Africa are the choice by his fellow officers of Lt.-Col. Gowon to replace Gen. Ironsi in Nigeria in 1966 and the summons of Lt.-Col. Juxon-Smith from London to assume power in Sierra Leone in 1967 (Wiking 1983: 134–5).

Factional disaffection is a serious problem when poorer Third World states are unable or unwilling to reward their armed forces at the level they have come to expect. The former was clearly the case in the mutiny of ordinary soldiers led by Sgt Doe which overthrew and killed the President of Liberia in 1980, and the latter in the fall of Busia in Ghana in 1972. Both are exemplified by the episode in January 1994 in Lesotho when the capital Maseru was shelled by opposing army factions ostensibly seeking OAU mediation of a pay dispute. Behind this claim, however, lay the fear of both factions that they would lose both power and perquisites following the landslide defeat in Lesotho's first free elections of the military-supported Basotho National Party, which had ruled since 1966.

Institutional activity, the most important of these factors, rests on military ethos, socialization of officers, the social standing of the military in Third World states, the organizational strengths of the military relative to other institutions, and last but not least the emergence in some cases of an ideology of military developmentalism, sometimes termed bureaucratic-authoritarianism, associated with the national security ideology of the Cold War period. The armed forces intervened in Ghana in 1966 to put an end to the government of President Nkrumah, which they regarded as 'interfering' with the army (Austin 1978: 51; Afrifa 1966).

The contagion theory of military intervention, that coups in neighbouring states contribute to the will to intervene, and the habituation theory, that coups are fostered by the tradition of past coups by the same military institution, are also aspects of military explanations. However, although neither is necessarily simply military, and the latter in particular obviously reflects the weak legitimacy accorded to civilian institutions, both are supported by statistics which show clearly that coups tend to be particularly common in certain countries and do seem to be imitated within regions (Brier and Calvert 1975).

In a number of military takeovers, external influence and encouragement can be inferred, although rarely proved. As Ruth First pointed out, even if foreign influence did play a part in African coups in the 1960s, internal factors were also at work and were at least equally important (First 1972: 17; Decalo 1976).

However, despite the argument of Samuel P. Huntington that military aid and assistance has no political effect (Huntington 1968: 192), the wave of military coups that occurred in Africa in the 1960s did receive significant foreign encouragement both before and after the event from the way in which foreign powers, especially the United States and France, provided support for military governments, military aid and training missions. Britain, too, welcomed the fall of Milton Obote, whose aircraft had been unaccountably delayed in returning to Uganda, enabling Idi Amin to seize power in his absence (Wiking 1983: 28). At the same time, post-1961 counter-insurgency training by the USA both in the United States itself and in the School of the Americas in Panama promoted the development of a virulent anti-Communism and the 'national security ideology' among the armed forces of Latin America. The latter was later summed up by the Argentine General (later President) Leopoldo Galtieri in the phrase, 'The Third World War is one of ideology against ideology', and it was to lead in that country to the atrocities of the 'dirty war'.

Civilian explanations rest on pull factors such as the weakness of civilian institutions, participation overload, lack of political legitimacy and economic instability.

The first three of these undoubtedly played a part in shaping the military assumptions of power in both Africa and Latin America during the 1960s. However, Jenkins and Kposowa (1992) found that the African military coups they studied had their roots in military centrality and ethnic competition, not in participation overload or economic dependency causing social unrest. In Latin America, following encouragement from the Carter administration in the United States, civilian institutions successfully reasserted themselves during the 1980s.

The economic failure of a civilian government affects the armed forces both directly, by leaving less money for them, and indirectly, by alienating popular support for the government (Nordlinger 1977). The impact of economic instability on the social groups of which officers are members, rather than on the military institution itself, may be important in encouraging them to take action. However, economic failure is seldom cited as a major reason for a military coup, and more often than not it has been given as a reason for the replacement of one military government by another (Wiking 1983: 116).

Sometimes the military assumption of power results from a civilian government shooting itself, metaphorically speaking, in the foot. The *autogolpe*, or 'self-coup', led by an elected leader against his own government, continues to be a problem in Latin America. Even President Fujimori of Peru refers to his illegal assumption of additional powers in 1992 as an *autogolpe*. President Itamar Franco was still being urged to close Brazil's Congress in January 1994. However, he wisely resisted the temptation to try to do so and the presidential elections scheduled for later in the year went ahead as planned.

STRUCTURE OF ARMED FORCES

Obviously the military role in the politics of any given country does depend crucially on the nature and origins of the armed forces themselves, and their relationship to the society in which they serve. In Nigeria, for example, the military takeover of 1966 owed much to the persistence of tribal conscious-ness in the army, among the northerners who felt excluded by the commercially active and politically dominant Igbo (Ibo). The first coup, in January 1966, was directed against not only the civilian government, but also the military leadership of Maj.-Gen. Ironsi. The killing of senior officers that accompanied it significantly altered the composition of the officer corps, leaving Ibo officers holding nearly every senior position. The second coup, in April 1966, led to a massacre of both Ibo soldiers and civilians.

> In general, being an Ibo was sufficient grounds for slaughter during the seizure of power in army units at the early stages, though there was more selectivity later on in preparing lists of 'suspects' for killing. It appears that non-Ibos, whether from the East, Mid-West or West were only killed if they got in the way during the seizure of power, if they were suspected of sympathy with the January coup, or if particular Northern troops by whom they were confronted made the false assumption that they were Ibo. (Luckham 1971a: 76)

The fall from power and death of William V. Tubman in Liberia in 1980 was born of resentment by the dominant tribe of the interior, the Vai, of their exclusion from power by the True Whig Party and Americanized settlers on the coast.

However, it does not follow that the military act only as the armed wing of a tribe, or indeed of a class. Even weak Third World armies are highly organized and hierarchically structured organizations, and the profound importance of the army as an institution to soldiers should never be underestimated. This is compounded by the fact that the majority of armies are dominated by a relatively small, professionally trained officer corps (Howard 1957). Its recruits are in terms of their respective societies largely middle class. Though in a number of African states they tend overwhelmingly to be drawn from a single tribe or region, this is not always the case, and in any case once recruited and trained they are bound together by important institutional ties. It is through the service as an institution, moreover, that they obtain their access to a system of substantial personal privileges, such as pensions, mortgages, credit, cheap goods, clubs and free medical attention. Most importantly, it is membership of the institution that guarantees at one and the same time a high standard of living relative to that of the societies they are supposed to serve, and also the opportunity through promotion to gain access to much greater rewards in various government positions.

Military intervention in politics is guaranteed by the need to maintain this institutional structure in the face of competing civilian interests. Its persistence is due to the complex interrelationship between the three levels of the social, institutional and personal interest of the intervenors, such that no one of them can be singled out as the cause, nor wholly disentangled from the others (Calvert 1990: 42–4).

COMPETING ROLES OF ARMED FORCES: MILITARY, SOCIAL, POLITICAL

The principal role of the armed forces is, of course, to fight the armed forces of other countries. However, for a variety of reasons this role is relatively unlikely to be dominant in many Third World states. In Latin America, distance, formidable natural barriers and relatively small armies have helped prevent all but a handful of major conflicts. In Africa, at decolonization armies were often no more than token forces. The decision of the OAU to respect colonial boundaries has meant that, despite a very considerable build-up of potential trouble, actual conflicts have been few. In both cases the majority of armed forces are too small and too dependent on supplies from abroad to present serious resistance to the armed forces of a major power. However, as noted above, the 1980s saw a very rapid arms build-up in Third World states, especially in SSA.

In South Asia, on the other hand, the long-standing feud between India and Pakistan has resulted in three major wars since 1947, and the loss to Pakistan, not only of part of Kashmir, but more seriously of its former eastern part, now Bangladesh. India has also had to face up to Chinese penetration into Ladakh. The ill-organized, tribal armies of Afghan guerrillas were able successfully to resist and eventually to defeat the invasion of the Soviet Union, then the world's second superpower. China's army has mounted a punitive expedition against Vietnam, and its navy disputes with both Vietnam and the Philippines the sovereignty of the Spratly Islands. Significantly, in each of these cases the armed forces seem for the most part to be highly professional and to have been brought in recent years under civilian control. Only in South-West Asia do large fighting forces operate under the command of authoritarian military governments, notably those of Syria and Iraq.

Governments may also be challenged from within, by insurgent movements. In Latin America, such challenges have been a major reason (some would say excuse) why armies have intervened in politics. The wave of military coups that began in 1961 initially formed a limited response to the Cuban revolution and to local circumstances (Lieuwen 1964). By 1965 the challenge of guerrilla-type movements had been effectively contained, and the attempt by some movements to switch their tactics into what was loosely and incorrectly termed 'urban guerrilla warfare' was to prove equally unsuccessful. Part of the reason was the intrinsic weakness of the movements themselves, criticized by Gérard Chaliand:

> A certain number of other sociological traits common to most Latin American societies also need to be mentioned. While these would be secondary in a major war, with the revolution held together by a central revolutionary ideology, these traits weigh against successful action in other circumstances: verbal inflation, accompanied by a slight ability to keep secrets; lack of group cohesiveness, worsened by an obsession with authority (what Latin American in charge of a dozen others resists proclaiming himself *comandante*?); machismo and fascination with death (largely products of the Hispanic tradition). (Chaliand 1977: 48–9)

However, it was perhaps inevitable that Latin American armies, encouraged by fresh supplies of arms from the United States, should have taken the credit for defeating subversion. Hence, during the transition from the first to the second phase, in the mid-1960s the doctrine took root that the only way to cope with armed insurgency was through military government, beginning in 1964 with Brazil (Philip 1984 and 1985; Black 1976; cf. O'Brien and Cammack 1985). The training in counter-insurgency provided by the United States at the School of the Americas in Panama and in the United States itself undoubtedly helped strengthen the Latin American military's perception of themselves as defenders of the nation against internal subversion.

With the return to civilian government over most of the Americas, the two major states in Latin America in which combating guerrillas remains a major task for the armed forces in the 1990s are Colombia and Peru, the former under civilian government, the latter at least nominally so. However, in other parts of the Third World governments are also faced with widespread insurgency. In Asia, insurgency and subversion are still the major concerns of the government of Burma (Myanmar) and, despite the nominal victory of pro-western forces in Afghanistan, much of the country remains effectively outside the control of the government in Kabul, although as much as one-third is now (1995) believed to be controlled by the Taliban, a fundamentalist Islamic student movement appealing to those weary of 17 years of hostilities. In Africa, the peace settlement between the government of Mozambique and the Renamo guerrilla movement is exceedingly fragile. The guerrillas, initially organized by the settler government of Rhodesia and supplied by South Africa, continue to control most of the core of the country, drawing their support (as does the government) from specific ethnic groups.

Military training may, however, even in broadly civilian societies be a valuable path to social preferment. In Latin America compulsory military training was introduced towards the end of the nineteenth century, enabling the armed forces to promote themselves as one of the major pillars of the national identity.

Historically, soldiers have played a major role in geographical surveying and the establishment of communications in remote regions. In Third World states these tasks too are still of considerable significance in the development of *inter alia*, north-western India and modern Pakistan, Iraq and Egypt. In Amazonia the Brazilian army maintains communications, surveys geographical formations, watches for infiltrators, and teaches civics classes. In the remoter regions of Ecuador, Bolivia and Peru too, the army has historically often been the sole agency of government which is actually effective over large areas (see Bourricaud 1970: 313–15).

DEVELOPMENTALISM

Not surprisingly, armies which have assumed such tasks are easily persuaded that they have a wider mission to bring about the development of their countries. In Latin America in the 'developmentalist' era of the 1960s a new phenomenon emerged, starting with Brazil in 1964, by which the armed forces seized power with the open intention of staying in power for an indefinite period, long enough to bring about the forced development of their societies. This phenomenon is often termed 'bureaucratic-authoritarianism', a term originally invented by the Argentine Guillermo O'Donnell (1988), whose views derive from Marxism and more particularly from dependency theory.

O'Donnell's theory envisages three stages of development of political systems. In the oligarchic stage, the popular sector is not yet politicized, and so is neither mobilized nor incorporated in the state structure. In the populist stage, the popular sector is mobilized and incorporated. In the bureaucratic-authoritarian state it is then demobilized and excluded. For O'Donnell the bureaucratic-authoritarian state 'guarantees and organizes the domination exercised through a class structure subordinated to the upper fractions of a highly oligopolized and transnationalized bourgeoisie' (O'Donnell 1988: 31). Within the state structure two groups have decisive weight: specialists in coercion (the armed forces), whose job it is to exclude the 'popular sector' from power, and finance capitalists, whose role is to obtain the 'normalization' of the economy, which performs the dual purpose of excluding the popular sector from economic power and promoting the interests of large oligopolistic interests. As part of the exclusion policy, social issues are depoliticized by being treated as a matter of narrow economic rationality, and direct access to government is limited to the armed forces, the state bureaucracy and leading industrialists and financiers.

However, the term 'bureaucratic-authoritarianism' seems rather to be designed to distract from its key feature, the fact that the process was directed by the army and gained its distinctive features from the army's ability to make use of force. For this reason the present writers use the term 'military developmentalism', a term which stresses its analogies with the military regimes of Egypt under Nasser, Pakistan under Zia ul-Haq or even Thailand, where a succession of military leaders have held office within a strongly formalized system of public administration, deriving legitimacy from the charismatic and traditional authority of the monarchy.

MILITARY AND CIVILIAN MILITARISM

There are two types of militarism: 'military' militarism (militarism among the military personnel themselves) and 'civilian' militarism (militarism among the civilian population) (Vagts 1959).

Military militarism is a caste pride, a pride in the glory, honour, power and prestige of the military forces. This type of militarism, however, goes well beyond the normal pride of belonging to a well-organized force, resulting in extreme cases in an exaggerated sense of remoteness and of superiority over the outside world in all aspects, so that those functions which the military does not undertake are considered to be not worthwhile for society as a whole. Military militarism, then, tends to arise in one of two sets of circumstances.

The first is when, for whatever reason, the whole end, existence and pride of the state is seen by them to be the concern of the army and the army alone. In modern Third World states this condition in its extreme form is fortunately rather rare, if only because few Third World armies can convincingly see themselves as an effective fighting force against all possible opponents. However, the Chinese army, which re-emerged as a distinct political force during the chaos that followed the Great Proletarian Cultural Revolution, has shown in its handling of the Tienanmen Square demonstrations that in the last analysis it is prepared to intervene to safeguard the state structure that it has established. There is also some evidence of military militarism as a factor in North Korea.

However, a lower level of military militarism is widespread in Third World states. The forces in such countries – whether in Asia, Latin America or Africa – have a pride in their prowess which does not necessarily derive from recent combat, as, in many cases, for geographical or other extraneous reasons, the opportunity has not arisen. Until recently, however, the fact of independence implied an important historic role for the forces. They had the role of guardians of the state thrust upon them, in their opinion, because they saw themselves as the ones who had given birth to it. Second, the forces in those countries are relatively well educated compared with their fellow-citizens, and in addition have a significant capacity for the use of force.

The alternative situation is when the military feel that they have been betrayed by their own civilians. The most striking Third World example may well still be Egypt after the humiliation of 1948, when the government of King Farouk accepted the Anglo-Egyptian Treaty. The fact that Egyptian forces were so conspicuously outclassed by the apparently amateur Israeli army (Neguib 1955) led to a process of military politicization and ultimately to the revolution of 1952. Throughout the Middle East, in Libya, Iraq and elsewhere, the military have continued to see the confrontation with Israel as justification for their continued rule, a situation deftly exploited by leaders such as Gadaffi in Libya or Saddam Hussein in Iraq.

Civilian militarism is the other side of the same coin. It may afflict either the élite or the mass of the society, or in extreme cases both. It is a feeling among civilians that the army should be rewarded with the unconditional support of the population on whose behalf it fights. In extreme cases it then becomes a nationalist pride in crude power and can lead, again in Vagts' words, to 'self-immolation on the altar of violence' (Vagts 1959: 22). In weak states, relying for the effective use of force on inadequately trained and equipped armies, this can lead to catastrophe. Thus the intervention by West African states in the civil war in Liberia did not succeed in arresting the slide of that country into chaos, but it did succeed in destabilizing neighbouring Sierra Leone. Military rule is often seen as an efficient and therefore acceptable substitute for weak and divided civilian government. Unfortunately the reality is often very different.

ARMS PROCUREMENT

Independence is often accompanied, as we have already noted, by a rise in nationalism which in turn promotes enhanced arms expenditure. Since then the costs have escalated and in most cases faster than income.

The quest for 'security' has three aspects for both politicians and military. The importance of each kind varies between these two groups, but also within them too. The three aspects are as follows:

- Defence of territory from invasion/occupation.
- Defence of raw materials and markets.
- Defence of political and social values.

The fact that military budgets are remarkably constant over time as a percentage of GNP suggests that they are not responsive to actual threats, but reflect aspects of the national political culture, such as how much the people will endure, the degree of paranoia or the salience of the presumed threat. Likewise, in the rare cases in which Third World states have significant navies or air forces, the allocations of resources between the services seem to be a consequence more of their lobbying power than of a real estimate of a strategic or tactical threat.

Vested interests include not just military establishments and the arms industry, but also scientists and engineers, diplomats and other civil servants who administer the defence establishments of their countries. Though this is more obvious in the weapons-producing countries, it is no less true of those which are buying. Thus the perception of national 'security' contributes to economic and environmental insecurity. As Brundtland says in *Our Common Future*: 'Competitive arms races breed insecurity among nations through spirals of reciprocal fears. Nations need to muster resources to combat environmental degradation and poverty. By misdirecting scarce resources, arms races contribute further to insecurity' (WCED 1987: 297). This is echoed in 1989 by Paul Shaw, a UN adviser on population and development: 'No amount of deforestation in Brazil, desertification in the Sahel, or water pollution in the Nile can compare with the cumulative effects of war' (quoted in *New Internationalist*, September 1992: 14).

It is hardly surprising that heterogeneous new states experience internal conflicts, sometimes even civil wars. These have during the Cold War period sometimes been exacerbated by great power intervention. When this takes place on opposite sides, the risk of escalation increases dramatically.

Since 1945 there have been over 120 international and civil conflicts in the South. More than 20 million people have died as a consequence. There have been hundreds of attempted coups, some much bloodier than others. There are countless refugees from conflict both directly because of fear and indirectly from the environmental degradation it causes and the consequent loss of livelihood.

However, at the same time developed countries have lost no opportunity to promote profitable arms sales to the South. Four out of five of the largest arms dealers: the United States, the United Kingdom, France and Russia, are in the North and all are members of the UN Security (*sic*) Council. Credits for such purchases are generally easy to get and it is left to future generations to pay the bill. Even as it is, the military expenditure of developing countries is some 25 per cent of the world total, and in 1986, ironically designated the International Year of Peace, this amounted to more than $900 billion. Of course, the Third World's contribution to the arms trade specifically is proportionately much greater, accounting for some 60 per cent of the $21 billion trade by 1990. These figures represent a colossal transfer of funds from the South to the North and are estimated to have added some 40 per cent to the Third World debt burden.

Third World military expenditure is highly concentrated in a few countries, but even so it is rarely proportionate to the potential threat or to the resources available. Developing countries spend more as proportions of their budgets on military activity than developed countries. Their spending on arms, for example, is three times as much as would be needed to provide health care, sanitation and clean water to all their populations. One of the most glaring examples of this obsession is Ethiopia, where under the Derg the armed forces consumed some 10 per cent of the country's GNP, while only some 1.5 per cent was spent on health. Moreover, the diversion of resources to arms is only the direct cost to development. There are also indirect costs associated with the distortion of the political culture, including the decline of democracy and participation, the growth of corruption and popular alienation from the government and society.

Third World arms production also exists and is in fact becoming an increasingly significant, although a far from desirable South–South linkage. There is already generally a redistribution of funds within the Third World from the poorer to the richer and more powerful states. Brazil stands out as the leading arms manufacturer and exporter in the Third World, with more than a million people employed in arms production. The future role of South Africa, where the ANC government has inherited a strong indigenous arms industry, has yet to be determined.

NUCLEAR WEAPONS IN THE THIRD WORLD

The idea of deterrence due to the threat of mutual annihilation is really a product of a bipolar world and relies on the rationality and stability of the actors concerned. But as Keith Colquhoun (1993: 210) has put it: 'The problem of North Korea is that the government is widely perceived to be insane.'

In 1945 only the USA had nuclear weapons. During much of the Cold War era the nuclear 'club' remained limited to the USA, USSR, UK, France and China. Moreover, the power blocs gave rise to an ideological line-up and only China could be said to have an independent nuclear capability. By the end of the Cold War a further six countries, including Pakistan, were on the verge of acquiring nuclear weapons and ten more, including India, Brazil and South Africa, had the capacity to do so.

It is clear that the original US strategy of non-proliferation has failed. This is not surprising, since successive summits were aimed primarily at reducing the inherent risks of superpower confrontation, and the United States felt it necessary to connive at the acquisition of nuclear capability by friendly countries such as Britain, France and Israel, rather than risk its overall strategic dominance. The Non-Proliferation Treaty was negotiated to try to limit superpower activity and was not really aimed at the Third World.

Since 1989 there has been a sharp change away from bipolar confrontation, but the world is still littered with the debris of Cold War; literally so in the case of the conventional and nuclear weapons of the former Soviet Union. Week by week the news of the interception of smuggled uranium consignments compounds the uncertainty about the future intentions of middle-range states such as Iraq and Iran. The US post-Cold War strategy is to keep enough nuclear weapons to confront 'any possible adversary', and this continued nuclear hegemony is thought by some to be a means to prevent proliferation. The assumption is that we have moved into an era of an interdependent world military order which is both established and hierarchical. The problem, it has often been suggested from a First World perspective, is that nuclear capacity does not necessarily follow this hierarchy.

The spread of nuclear weapons to more countries is generally termed 'horizontal proliferation' and was inherent in the nuclear game from the outset owing to the diffusion of knowledge about nuclear processes. The spread of civil nuclear technology cannot be stopped and indeed was actively encouraged by the capitalist countries as a way of building up their own nuclear capability. The inherent tendency for scientific knowledge to diffuse did the rest. Hence Argentina and Pakistan both have uranium enrichment plants which could produce nuclear weapons material rather than reactor fuel, but they have developed these capabilities themselves, having been unable to purchase such sensitive technology on the world market.

The whole world is now a single strategic arena, and military deployment of nuclear weapons in any future confrontation would be global. However, this does not mean that horizontal proliferation does in fact present serious dangers. It is not clear what the use of nuclear weapons could achieve for a Third World state that happened to possess them, given their likely political objectives. The obvious reason would be to enhance their power in relation to surrounding states. For this purpose a mere bluff might suffice, and some argue this is so in the case of North Korea. On the other hand, the normal response to fear of a nuclear attack seems to be to respond in kind, as in the case of India and Pakistan, whose relative position has not changed as a result. Moreover, the acquisition of nuclear weapons might be sought to empower a southern state in face of a threat from the North. It has been argued that customers always have some leverage against their suppliers, so they can gain a degree of empowerment through purchase. However, a more realistic perception is that any advantage gained is offset by the weakness of needing spare parts, and support services in the form of technological advice and periodic updates. If new standards are set by technology, striving to achieve them is a treadmill and certainly does not constitute empowerment.

The nuclear issue in Argentina and Brazil

Brazil and Argentina have long had the most sophisticated nuclear programmes in the South America and Caribbean region. Both countries embarked on major nuclear programmes in the 1970s, stating at the time that they needed nuclear power to meet predicted shortfalls in future energy needs.

Today, Brazil has one nuclear power plant (Angra I, supplied by the United States) and three small research reactors currently in operation. Two further plants are scheduled for start-up in 1995 and 2000, respectively (Angra II and Angra III, both supplied by Germany as a result of a 1975 transfer agreement). Also under construction is a jet nozzle uranium enrichment facility, which is not expected to reach industrial-scale production until the year 2000, and more significant gas centrifuge uranium enrichment research projects at the Aramar Research Center, Ipero and at the Institute for Energy and Nuclear Research, São Paulo.

Argentina currently has two nuclear power plants in operation (Atucha I and Embalse), with a third (Atucha II) expected to come on line in the mid-1990s. Argentina also has five nuclear research reactors presently in operation. But where the major advances in Argentina's nuclear power programme are under way are in the areas of enrichment and reprocessing technology. At Pilcaniyeu, Argentina has constructed a gaseous diffusion enrichment facility which is already operational, and at Ezeiza a small-scale reprocessing project is also under way.

Throughout this period of nuclear expansion, concerns have been expressed that because neither country was party to the Non-Proliferation Treaty (NPT) or the Treaty of Tlatelolco, which makes Latin America a nuclear-free zone, they have not made any formal commitment not to pursue nuclear weapons paths. Speculation has thus been rife about the intentions of Brazil and Argentina where military nuclear programmes are concerned.

Both Brazil and Argentina rejected the NPT because they regarded it as an inherently discriminatory treaty. The treaty distinguishes between two categories of signatory state: those states that have tested a nuclear weapon before the 1 January 1967 are classified as Nuclear Weapon States (NWS); and those states which have not conducted such a test are classified by the treaty as Non-Nuclear Weapon States (NNWS). Brazil and Argentina regarded this distinction between NWS and NNWS as discriminatory because it legitimizes the existing international distribution of power between nuclear 'haves' and nuclear 'have nots'. The two countries therefore declined to sign the treaty.

All signatories to the NPT are obliged to open all nuclear facilities operating within their territory to safeguards inspections by the International Atomic Energy Agency (IAEA). This provision, referred to as Full Scope Safeguards (FSS), enables the IAEA to maintain a comprehensive picture of all nuclear material activities taking place within the signatory state. On the basis of such safeguards, the IAEA can then assure other signatories that no diversions of nuclear materials are taking place and that the signatory is fulfilling its NPT obligations not to pursue nuclear weapons.

Brazil and Argentina similarly declined to become full parties to the Tlatelolco Treaty. Brazil both signed and ratified the treaty, but exercised the right under Article 28 of the Tlatelolco Treaty to postpone its entry into force. Argentina also signed the treaty, but withheld ratification until Brazil had adhered to it. As long as neither state was party to either the NPT or the Tlatelolco Treaty (which would also require FSS to operate), there was no comprehensive safeguards coverage over their nuclear industries. Parts of the nuclear infrastructure in the two countries were, it was true, under IAEA safeguards (as a result of obligations undertaken in past nuclear transfer agreements), but a few key installations remained outside any international inspection. It was the existence of these installations which fuelled the international speculation about the potential for these facilities being used for nuclear weapons programmes.

In the mid-1980s a major nuclear *rapprochement* began between Brazil and Argentina which has quelled many concerns about the region. In November 1985, the then respective Presidents of Brazil and Argentina, Sarney and Alfonsín, announced that the two countries were to further their co-operation in the peaceful uses of nuclear energy and to begin a programme of mutual inspection of each other's nuclear facilities. The announcement also stated that the results of the mutual inspections would not be made available to the IAEA.

Following that meeting the two countries have developed much closer nuclear links, including reciprocal visits by the respective heads of state to their most sensitive nuclear installations. When President Menem replaced President Alfonsín in Argentina, and President Collor de Mello replaced President Sarney in Brazil, these confidence-building measures in the nuclear sphere continued. On entering office, President Collor stated that he would implement a strategy of nuclear 'transparency' for Brazil's nuclear programme. This policy has included introducing greater civilian oversight of its nuclear programme and curtailment of a military nuclear programme, known as the Solimoes Project, which President Collor stated had been under way since the late 1970s. In September 1990, President Collor closed the previously secret nuclear test site at Cachimba in the Amazon forest. And at the United Nations, he also called for a ban on nuclear testing in South America and the Caribbean.

At the same time as the statements about Brazil's 'parallel' military nuclear programme were made public, the President also announced that Brazil would begin implementing a stricter policy for the export of sensitive technologies to other countries. This statement, too, has considerable arms control significance for the future, as Brazil is already a major supplier of advanced conventional technology and will soon be in a position to export several key items of nuclear technology as well.

In November 1990, this evolving policy of nuclear restraint in the region was given a further boost. It was announced that Brazil and Argentina would begin negotiations with the IAEA to establish an acceptable safeguards agreement between the two countries that would allow the IAEA to receive information about nuclear material activities within their territories. At regular summit meetings the gap between the two countries was narrowed, while the construction of the South American Common Market (Mercosur) assumed a high priority in both countries' plans for the future. In consequence of these developments, in 1994 both countries finally became full parties to the Tlatelolco Treaty. At a ceremony held in Mexico City on 18 January, both Argentina, which had ratified the treaty in November 1993, and Chile, which had ratified it in 1974 but suspended implementation, acceded to the Treaty of Tlatelolco and became full members of the Organization to Ban Nuclear Weapons in Latin America (OPANAL). Then on 30 May, Brazil signed the treaty, which was ratified by President Itamar Franco on 16 September. On 29 August, Cuba, which had previously held aloof from all such moves, finally announced its intention to sign. Hence the *rapprochement* between the two major regional powers has had positive consequences for peace throughout the entire region.

CHEMICAL WEAPONS

Chemical weapons are sometimes called 'poor man's atom bombs'. They are much cheaper, they use much more readily available and more easily disguised technology, and the major powers (officially at least) have chosen not to have them. They are for these reasons the weapons of mass destruction most obviously inclined to proliferation in the Third World. In view of the rapidly blurring boundaries between the destructiveness and grossness of nuclear and conventional weapons, the distinction no longer really makes sense.

The manufacture of chemical weapons is an offshoot of the civil chemical industry and therefore the potential exists in many moderately industrialized countries. In the Third World, the most notorious example is Iraq under Saddam Hussein, who used them against his own citizens at Halabjah and so breached what had been becoming an unwritten norm of international conduct unbroken since the 1930s.

Chemical weapons exist in countries other than Iraq. They are known to exist in the United States, France and somewhere in the former USSR. But more worrying is the extent of their probable existence in the Third World. Argentina, Chile, Cuba, Guatemala, Peru, Angola, Chad, Ethiopia, Libya, South Africa, Afghanistan, China, India, Myanmar, Pakistan, Thailand and Vietnam are all believed to have a chemical capability. Perhaps Iran does also – it is believed to have been very active in seeking supplies in 1993–4.

The problem with chemical weapons as weapons of mass destruction is that the manufacturing processes involved are relatively simple, so that an Iraqi plant could be easily disguised as a factory producing infant milk formula, for example. Detecting breaches of international agreements is therefore much more difficult than with nuclear weapons, where the tell-tale signs of reprocessing and storage facilities are hard to conceal from the circling spy satellites.

REGIONAL POWERS

The role of regional powers in Asia has been much complicated by the fragmentation of the former Soviet Union. However, one thing remains certain: in East Asia the massive size of China outweighs all others. In many ways, though, it is still very much a Third World state with a Third World army.

In South Asia, India has naturally assumed the regional role which its size and population seemed to indicate. However, despite a string of successes in the early years following independence, it received a severe setback when Chinese forces entered Ladakh in 1962: even if the actual loss of territory was insignificant, the blow to its security and even more to its morale was considerable. Its confidence revived considerably after its successful intervention in former East Pakistan in 1971, which resulted in the independence of Bangladesh. At the end of the 1980s, however, the mission of the IPKF in Sri Lanka was not accepted either by the insurgents or by the Sri Lankan government, which took the first convenient opportunity to invite it to withdraw.

In South-East Asia, Vietnam has been unable to avoid involvement in its neighbouring countries since the end of war in 1975. The brief Third Indo-China War resulted from Chinese concern about its growing military strength, and tension remains between the two countries over control of the Spratly Islands, which are also claimed by Malaysia and the Philippines. Vietnamese intervention expelled the Khmer Rouges from Cambodia in 1979, but cut short the opening to the West begun in 1976 and halted its economic recovery. It was followed by a ruthless campaign to force Vietnamese withdrawal.

In 1962 the creation of Malaysia by the incorporation of the former British North Borneo (Sabah) and Sarawak led to 'confrontation' (*konfrontasi*) with Sukarno's Indonesia. The effects of Indonesian incursions into East Malaysia were sufficiently serious to require a substantial deployment of British troops, and resulted in the loss of 114 British servicemen before the abortive coup of October 1965, which led to the death of anything up to half a million Indonesians, the ending of confrontation and eventually the deposition of Sukarno himself (Hughes 1968). With the collapse of the Portuguese empire in 1974, Gen. Suharto ordered the seizure of East Timor, where tens of thousands of Timorese have since died resisting the new colonialism of Djakarta. The annexation is still not recognized by the rest of the world, but the western powers, fearful as they were of Communist influence gaining a foothold, were not prepared in the Cold War days to do anything about it.

In South-West Asia the most active regional powers have been Israel, a military power, and Iran, an oil-rich state with substantial economic resources. Iran is a particularly interesting case. It is more than six years since the death of Ayatollah Khomeini, but his legacy is still a powerful influence.

During his leadership Iran was at war and was shunned by the rest of the world. Since his death some would argue that Iran has pursued a more moderate line, but certainly it has been building up its arsenal probably in all categories of weapons.

Iran may perceive itself as both a regional power and a leader of Islam against the rest of the world. Certainly many have perceived a desire to export the revolution to the secular states of Central Asia which have Muslim majorities. Sir Anthony Parsons, former British ambassador to Iran, sees the West as fearful of a resurgent Iran and suggests that this is due to the perception of Iran as behaving differently from the rest of the world. Iran's geographical position, controlling access to the Persian Gulf and therefore to half of the world's known oil reserves, is at once a strength and a weakness, in that it makes Iran vulnerable.

The eight-year Iran–Iraq War (1980–8) cost Iran a generation. Iranian fear of Iraq is deeply entrenched and it is perhaps not surprising that UN sources have found significant chemical, biological and nuclear weapons build-ups – mainly in consequence of 'dual-use' purchases from the West. Iranian arms procurement has also involved buying a good deal from the Islamic states of the former Soviet Union, notably Kazakhstan. It has been described as 'shop until you drop' procurement. It is world-wide, consisting of bits here and bits there with no clear plan in view, confirming that the end state of arms supply is by no means obvious when export licences are issued. The IAEA can only effectively inspect and supervise in countries not trying clandestine tactics. It is a large bureaucratic organization and its work is based on trust. It was glaringly wrong about Iraq.

Iran's justifications for its arms build-up are easy to understand: the world did not stand up for Iran against Iraq when chemical weapons were used. Israel has nuclear weapons, why should the Islamic world not have them also? 'Nuclear' is seen as 'modern' and as such can not be denied to Iran. Certainly the pursuit of atomic power has been accepted as a legitimate reason for the procurement of much technology which could have other uses – so a high-technology trade has been seen by some elements in the West both as an entitlement and/or as a possible means to bring a modern Iran into the mainstream of world affairs and thus to enhance stability (*Panorama*, 'Arming for Islam', BBC Television, 1993).

In Africa the most important regional role has been played by South Africa (an economic and military power). Nigeria (which gains its standing both from its size and from its considerable oil revenues) has also shown by its actions that it aspires to a significant regional role. In their different ways, so too have Egypt, Guinea, Senegal and Tanzania.

As a regional power, South Africa intervened in Mozambique after it had become independent from Portugal in 1975. Civil strife has continued at some level ever since. Of the rival guerrilla groups, one, the National Revolutionary Movement (MNR), had South African backing. The MNR deliberately disrupted food production, causing the 1983 famine in which more than 100,000 people died; they also poisoned wells and burned villages. Together these measures contributed to the displacement of more than half the rural population of the country, after the infrastructure on which they relied, including health clinics and schools, had been callously destroyed.

The ability of the apartheid regime to exercise regional power was considerably enhanced by its control of Namibia. The country was originally allocated to the South African government under a League of Nations Mandate, but the apartheid government refused to recognize the authority of the United Nations and treated it as a de facto territory of South Africa. This extended the reach of that government to the borders of Angola. Angered at the support given by the Angolan government to the South West Africa People's Organization (SWAPO), the armed Namibian liberation movement, the South African government had no hesitation in supporting UNITA, a guerrilla force dedicated to overthrowing the government in Angola.

In Latin America the dominance of the United States has tended to overshadow that of all other regional powers, including that of the world's most populous Spanish-speaking country, Mexico. Brazil, however, can be considered a regional power in South America, as since at least the 1920s it has been seen as an ally by the United States, and the United States has been prepared to let it act as a surrogate.

CONCLUSION

Third World states have taken an increasingly active role in regional, if not in world politics. This activity extends to armed confrontation and in a number of specific cases to armed conflict. Taking into account also civil wars and insurgencies, at any one time over the past decade there have been at least 35 wars in progress, and of those the overwhelming majority have involved Third World states.

Though fewer Third World countries are now under formal military government, the tendency for armed forces to exercise a political role has been much enhanced since the beginning of the 1980s by the militarization of the Third World. Third World countries have been the major target of the arms salespersons from the advanced industrialized countries. In many cases, notably in Britain, France and the United States, these efforts have had the vigorous support of government. However, the evidence is that arms sales of this kind, although they create a certain sense of dependence and lock the recipient country into a continuing sales drive, have won few friends. As the Gulf War demonstrated, those that are gained in this way are all too prone to turn on their former supporters if the political situation should change.

10 The international dimension

INTRODUCTION

Until 1991 the Cold War was the main factor affecting relations between the Third World and the superpowers. Not only did the superpowers themselves evaluate everything that happened in the Third World in terms of how it would affect the global balance of power, but the Third World states themselves entered actively into the game of winning superpower support. In the process a great many people were to get hurt, but it could be argued that a certain element of discipline was thus imposed on the international community.

Whatever the Cold War may have meant for Europe or the United States, for the Third World it meant one thing: foreign intervention. The forms of intervention varied from place to place and from time to time: sometimes overt, as in Lebanon in 1958 or the Dominican Republic in 1965; sometimes covert, as in Iran in 1953 or in Nicaragua after 1981; sometimes formal, as in Vietnam in the 1960s; sometimes informal, as in Honduras in the 1980s.

INTERVENTION

Intervention means coming between contending parties in such a way as to alter the balance between them (Little 1975). Hence the usual meaning in international relations is support for opposition movements or insurgents, or even the direct use of armed force to overthrow an existing government or regime. Strictly speaking, support for an incumbent government which has been formally recognized by the international community is not only not intervention, but is something that every friendly government should be prepared to give. However, support for an unpopular government to protect it against the anger of its own people does constitute intervention in the eyes of many Third World countries. In addition, there can be a number of ways in which indirect pressure can be exerted to affect the political, economic or social stability of a target state. We must therefore distinguish between different modes of intervention:

1. *Military intervention.* When other forms of intervention are not specified, use of the term 'intervention' will be understood as meaning military

intervention. Sending troops to support an incumbent government is legitimate in international law if their presence is requested, and hence is not strictly speaking intervention. Direct military intervention against a government, on the other hand, is an act of war unless sanctioned by UN or regional bodies, and not necessarily then. Invasion, bombardment or armed blockade of a country's ports are all acts of war and may invite retaliation as well as criticism by third parties. Since the 1950s, therefore, both the USA and the former Soviet Union have used indirect military intervention, including support to insurgents, military training for friendly personnel and support for military governments.

2. *Economic intervention*. This can be carried out though a variety of institutional devices. Pressure can be brought to bear either directly through increasing or decreasing bilateral aid, or indirectly (in the case of the United States, which has a preponderant say) through international lending bodies such as the IMF. Pressure can be exercised less effectively through trade restrictions such as blockades, sanctions or the imposition of tariffs, since the ideal of free trade is embodied in a series of international agreements. It is difficult in many cases to determine how far a national agenda is pursued by transnational corporations or whether they follow their own. The US corporation ITT was eager for US intervention in Chile in 1970, but the administration response was limited.

3. *Diplomatic (psychological) intervention*. Major powers can influence events by suggesting action rather than by direct intervention. They do this by developing contacts and building friendships which enable them to discourage or to encourage specific political outcomes.

4. *Cultural intervention*. It is doubtful whether this constitutes intervention at all, since cultural influences are so slow and it is often impossible to point to any one moment at which they take effect. However, since aid and trade distributes the culture of industrialized nations (see Chapter 6) along with its products, it also assists the far more pervasive force of ideological penetration by CNN and the major news agencies.

Sensitive as they inevitably were to any violation of their newly won sovereignty, Third World states generally regarded all forms of intervention as illegitimate and were inclined to extend the meaning of the term to include all actions of which they disapproved. They pressed for the norm of non-intervention enshrined in the Charter of the United Nations to be taken literally. In practice, the question of how far (if at all) intervention was legitimate was determined not by the Third World state, but by external powers such as the United States, the Soviet Union, Britain, France and Israel.

For the Third World, the problem of the Cold War was that it complicated their desire for independence by presenting them with the need to choose a position in the international arena for reasons that they felt were not of their making. In Asia independence was substantially complete by the 1970s, and by 1975 the United States had withdrawn from direct involvement. In Latin America the experience of Cuba meant that, with the rather idiosyncratic exception of Grenada between 1979 and 1983, there was no serious attempt after 1962 for an American state to choose the Soviet Union as a partner.

In Africa, however, all internal crises of independence were externalized when states called on the outside world for help. The UN operation in the Congo/Zaire in 1960 was complicated by US and French intervention, and before the decade was out the French, Russians, Americans and Chinese were all involved in various ways. In 1963 the French intervened in Gabon to reverse a military coup and to restore the government of President M'ba. In 1964 Britain sent help when the armies of Kenya, Uganda and Tanzania mutinied. It was reluctant to do the same when in the following year the European settlers of Rhodesia made a unilateral declaration of independence. Soon it became clear that the new government was receiving the tacit support of both Britain and the United States, to say nothing of South Africa. The British, French and Soviets all became involved in the Nigerian civil war after 1967. In 1975 under *Operación Carlota*, Cuban troops arrived to support the Marxist government of Angola just as large consignments of weapons began arriving from eastern Europe, and later the same year more Cuban troops were flown into Ethiopia to support the Ethiopians against the US-backed Communist (*sic*) government of Somalia.

Such unity as there was resulted from the fact of western tolerance and covert support for the white South African regime. Protected as it was behind the UN mandate territory of Namibia (former German South-West Africa, administered by South Africa as an integral part of its territory) and a screen of what were later to become the 'front-line states', namely Angola, Botswana, Mozambique, Tanzania, Zambia and Rhodesia until 1980, later Zimbabwe, the apartheid regime proved very difficult indeed to dislodge. Then revolution in Portugal in 1974 broke up the Portuguese empire from within, much as the invasion of Spain in 1808 had led ultimately to the independence of Spanish America. Marxist governments obtained international recognition in Angola, Mozambique, Guinea-Bissau and Cabo Verde. This sudden unexpected 'success' of Marxist liberation movements and the subsequent revolution in Ethiopia led to a dramatic transformation of the scene in Africa. It was followed by Soviet interventions in Angola, Mozambique and Ethiopia, seeking to support friendly governments and extend their influence in a region where the Soviet Union previously had had rather limited success in winning friends.

A number of armed conflicts were soon in progress. The Soviet Union, finding itself faced with confrontation between its former ally Somalia and the Derg in Ethiopia, had no hesitation about supporting Ethiopia, which was seen as strategically far more important. Cuban troops, serving under Soviet command, successfully recovered the Ogaden for Ethiopia, while the Somali government turned to its former antagonist the USA for help. Meanwhile the USA, hesitant about direct intervention after the fiasco of Vietnam, countered the threat of a Communist takeover in southern Africa by enlisting African groups to help undermine the Soviet-sponsored states of Angola and Mozambique, and offered indirect support to South Africa's intervention in Angola through the organization, training and supply of Jonas Savimbi and the National Union for the Total Independence of Angola (UNITA). Proxy conflicts provided an outlet for hostilities and ideological revitalization.

American politicians of all parties had been wary of intervention ever since the hurried end of the Vietnam War. Direct intervention in Africa was unthinkable. However, quite legally in terms of international law, the USA propped up pro-western states such as Kenya and Zaire. Here as elsewhere the value of development aid was far exceeded by military assistance. Arms exports were seen by some as the chief instrument of US and Soviet foreign policy towards Africa in the 1970s and 1980s.

Ronald Reagan, President of the United States 1981–9, saw all crises in the South as the product of East–West divisions. The radicalization of much of the Third World and US failure to penetrate ideologically many former European colonies was taken hard by the New Right. Reagan's State of the Union message in December 1985, with an eye specifically on Nicaragua and El Salvador, pledged US support for Third World anti-Communist guerrillas. This policy became known as the Reagan Doctrine. A major consequence was that economic aid was withdrawn and/or replaced to some extent by military aid. However, both the burden of military spending and Reaganite free-market economic policy, with the accompanying interest rises necessary to counteract US overspending, contributed to the debt crisis which broke at the beginning of the 1980s and continued to be a problem for Third World states throughout the decade.

Despite its rhetoric, by the late 1980s the Reagan administration, fragmented and discredited by the Iran–Contra scandal, had rediscovered the necessity of superpower co-operation. Bilateral talks at all levels focused on the twin problems of stopping the growth of nuclear arsenals and limiting the spread of nuclear weapons. At the same time, the superpowers increasingly found themselves with a common interest in joint diplomatic action to resolve Third World crisis points. In Washington observers began to talk about the emergence of a superpower condominium.

After the high human, financial and diplomatic costs of the invasion of Afghanistan in 1979 and the consequent loss of Third World support, the 1980s saw the rethinking of Soviet policy to the Third World. The high cost of intervention did not sit well with the economic problems facing the USSR at home. There was a movement away from support for 'wars of national liberation' and the maintenance of client states to the acceptance tacitly of diplomatic and economic expediency. Soviet aid was in any case very limited compared to that of the USA and larger OECD nations owing to the inconvertibility of the Soviet currency and its lack of purchase on the world economic system. Soviet military capacity was very limited at levels 'useful' in the Third World. (For example, when the USSR sent humanitarian aid to Peru following the earthquake of 1970, the mission had to be cut short when one of the AN-25 transports was lost in the sea off Iceland). In addition, Third World allies were ideologically untrained and not very reliable. Allende was overthrown in Chile in 1973, and Guinea began to move away from association with the USSR after the death of Sekou Toure in 1984. With three heads of government in four years, the USSR itself had also become very unpredictable! The Gorbachev government, even more than its predecessors, made good relations with the USA its top priority in foreign affairs. Faced with gathering crises at home, it withdrew from Afghanistan, yielded to the pressure for change in eastern Europe (which had repercussions in Central Asia) and limited its intervention. It did not seek to stop the US-led UN response to the Gulf crisis in 1990.

With both North-East and North-West seeking to resolve Third World conflicts and limit arms supplies to the Third World (at least in public), both sides came to recognize the value of the United Nations as a potential peace-keeper.

NON-ALIGNMENT

The Non-Aligned Movement (NAM) had its origins in the Afro-Asian Conference at Bandung in 1955 and has met triennially since 1961 (with the exception of 1967). It includes all the African states, which belong automatically as members of the OAU, most of the Asian countries and some of the Latin American republics. The original thinking behind non-alignment was to create an association sufficiently strong to avoid association with either of the two blocs. However, from the beginning the concept was regarded with great suspicion by both sides, and this suspicion was at times well justified, as, in particular, when Fidel Castro as President of the Non-Aligned Movement abused his position to call on the non-aligned at the Havana Summit of 1979 to accept the Soviet Union as their natural ally. The invitation was not well received and the Soviet invasion of Afghanistan later the same year put an abrupt stop to any further moves to revive it.

The collapse of Communism ended the moral justification for much US intervention. The change was not immediate: the new public vocabulary included phrases such as 'ensuring international stability' or 'the world-wide crusade for democracy'. But the new US administration of George Bush did not show much respect either for national sovereignty or for democracy. Its intervention in Panama in December 1989, claimed to be enhancing the cause of democracy, was carried out in breach of the charters of both the UN and the OAS, and was censured by the OAS. Then in 1991, the decision after a long period of delay to launch Operation Desert Storm on Iraq was justified as defending what Bush claimed was 'the legitimate government' of Kuwait. Though Saddam Hussein had few friends even among Arab states, and his own government had formally recognized that Kuwait was not the nineteenth province of Iraq, the Emir's government was certainly not democratic. In fact the decision to go to war had much less to do with defending democracy than with ensuring that the combined oil output of Iraq and Kuwait did not pass out of western control, while the unilateral US decision to end the war after only 100 hours has had long-lasting consequences for the stability of other smaller oil-producing states in this key region.

The USA is now a 'lonely superpower', constrained by its own internal divisions to tread a much more cautious course. Other countries have different agendas and in groups could be powerful, but Russia too is torn by internal dissension, and the decision of Chancellor Kohl to recognize Bosnia has left the European Union (EU) divided and apparently impotent. The end of the Cold War may well mean that in the future there will be no superpowers there to restrain their former client-states when local conflicts threaten to get out of hand. In a bipolar world, in a sense every conflict matters to the two camps, since victory for one is defeat for the other. In an era of multipolarity, most Third World conflicts will not matter to the First World at all. If regional leaders do not intervene, no one may do so, and this may be even more undesirable (see Tables 10.1 and 10.2).

THIRD WORLD CONFLICTS

Among Third World 'hot-spots', where intervention has continued into the post-Cold War era, are Cambodia, Cuba, Angola, Ethiopia, Liberia and Somalia.

The withdrawal of the United States from Cambodia in 1975 left the country to the Khmer Rouge. Hardened by their long and bitter struggle, the guerrillas marched into Pnom Penh and immediately instituted a reign of terror against the town-dwellers, and especially the intellectuals, whom they regarded as having collaborated first with the French and later with the Americans. Tens of thousands of skulls testify still to the ruthlessness with which the process was carried out. However, when reunified Vietnam sent troops into Cambodia to remove the Khmer Rouge and institute a Soviet-style government, the western powers, with breathtaking cynicism, switched their support to any group that could get rid of the Vietnamese, including the Khmer Rouge. Then, with the changing world balance, the Vietnamese, seeking to better relations with the USA, decided to withdraw from Cambodia. The successful UN supervision of elections in 1993 paved the way for a coalition government to assume power under the nominal authority of King Norodom Sihanouk, deposed in a US-backed military coup in 1970.

Table 10.1 *Third World conflicts 1990–5*

Country	Dates	Cause
Afghanistan	1979–92	War of *mujaheddin* guerrillas against Soviet-backed government
	1992–	Fighting between rival groups continues
Algeria	1992–	Co-ordinated anti-government activity
Angola	1975–91	South African backed insurrection (UNITA)
Azerbaijan	1991–4	Armenian secessionist movement in Nagorny Karabakh
Burma	1989–	Armed ethnic opposition
Burundi	1993–4	Ethnic violence
Cambodia	1978–91	Civil war
Chad	1975–93	Insurrection
	1971–94	Part occupied by Libya
Djibouti	1991–4	Afar insurrection
Ecuador	1995	War with Peru over boundary delimitation
Egypt	1992–	Co-ordinated anti-government activity
El Salvador	1979–91	Civil war; government backed by US
Eritrea	1994–	Insurrection backed by Sudan
Gambia	1994	Coup and counter-coup
Georgia	1991–4	Secessionist movement in Abkhasia
Ghana	1994	Insurrection in Northern Region
Guatemala	1960–94	Guerilla operations
Guinea	1994	Armed clashes with opposition forces
Haiti	1994	US intervention to restore President Aristide
India	1947–	Armed Kashmiri resistance
Indonesia	1976–	Resistance to annexation of East Timor
Iraq	1990–1	Invasion of Kuwait
	1991	Gulf War
Kenya	1994	Ethnic violence
Kuwait	1990–1	Occupied by Iraq
	1991	Gulf War
Lebanon	1982–	Part occupied by Israel and allies
Lesotho	1993–4	Fighting between rival army factions
Liberia	1990–	Civil war
Libya	1973–94	Occupation of disputed territory in Chad
Mali	1992–	Continued clashes with Tuaregs
Mexico	1994–	Agrarian insurrection in Chiapas
Morocco	1976–	War against Polisario Front of Western Sahara
Mozambique	1986–94	South African-backed insurrection (Renamo)
Nicaragua	1981–91	US-backed insurrection ('Contras')
Peru	1995	War with Ecuador over boundary delimitation
Rwanda	1990–	Insurrection by Rwandan Patriotic Front (FPR)
	1994	Ethnic violence following death of President
Sierra Leone	1991–	Insurrection backed by National Patriotic Front of Liberia (NPFL)
Somalia	1991–	Ousting of Siad Barre followed by civil war
South Africa	1990–4	Inkatha/ANC clashes
Sri Lanka	1983–	Separatist war led by Liberation Tigers of Tamil Eelam (LTTE)
Sudan	1983–	Separatist guerrillas in South
Togo	1994	Insurrection against President Eyadema
W. Sahara	1976–	Occupied by Morocco and Mauritania

Sources: *Third World Guide 93/94*; *Keesings Record of World Events*.

Sadly, since 1993 Khmer Rouge activity has increased once more, and the future of the settlement looks extremely problematic.

Another casualty of changing international alignments has been the Soviet-backed regime in Cuba. Since the end of the Cold War, the government of President Fidel Castro has lost its superpower patron and come under much external pressure from the United States, which has tightened its embargo on trade with the beleaguered island. The most serious blow was the withdrawal in 1991 of its guaranteed supply of Russian oil, which had not only fuelled its agriculture and industry, but provided a considerable surplus that could be sold abroad for hard currency. However, despite increasing diplomatic isolation and a serious economic crisis, the Cuban government survives and the US government has so far not risked direct intervention.

Even before the crisis in eastern Europe in 1989, Soviet military support for the Popular Movement for the Liberation of Angola (MPLA) had dried up and the Cuban troops that had been supporting the internationally recognized government of the country were withdrawn. Meanwhile US material and strategic support to the South African-sponsored UNITA continued unabated, and Zairian troops arrived to lend them material support. Early in 1993, UNITA held some two-thirds of the country. Though the US ambassador to the UN, Margaret Anstee, described the situation in Angola as full-scale civil war, she still argued that there was nothing the UN could do. Nevertheless by the end of the year, the UN was sponsoring peace talks.

Ethiopia received the most military 'aid' of all the African states from both the USA and the Soviet Union. However, despite all their efforts, the government of Gen. Mengistu Haile Mariam was unable to suppress the secessionist movements in Tigray and Eritraea. When their support for him became too embarrassing, Soviet and Cuban support for Mengistu was withdrawn, and he was overthrown and forced to seek political asylum in Zimbabwe in May 1991.

It was noted earlier that for a century Liberia, a state for freed slaves on the west coast of Africa, had been dominated by the settler élite at the expense of the tribes of the interior. In September 1990 the government of Samuel Doe was ousted by a military coup and the deposed president and much of the political élite were hacked to death. The USA, which had sponsored the formation of Liberia, and which benefited from the rubber produced there for the Firestone Tire Co., refused to intervene, although President Bush did send a small team of marines to rescue US citizens. The civil war which followed led to a joint military intervention by the ECOWAS states, and was apparently ended by a peace agreement signed in Benin in July 1993. However, the UN remains concerned that the armed forces appear to be still out of control, and it still receives reports of refugees being massacred.

Table 10.2 *Expenditure on defence in excess of 12% of budget in 1990 with 1992 percentage (high-income countries in italics)*

Country	1990	1992
United Arab Emirates	41.9	n.a.
Oman	41.0	35.8
Syria	40.7	42.3
Pakistan	30.9	27.9
South Korea	25.8	22.1
Israel	25.4	22.1
Burma (Myanmar)	24.7	22.0
El Salvador	24.5	16.0
Jordan	23.1	26.7
United States	22.6	20.6
Kuwait	19.9	n.a.
Thailand	17.3	17.2
India	17.0	15.0
Zimbabwe	16.5	n.a.
Bolivia	14.1	9.8
Iran	13.6	10.3
Guatemala	13.3	n.a.
Paraguay	13.3	13.3
Ecuador	12.9	12.9
Egypt	12.7	n.a.
United Kingdom	12.2	11.3

Source: World Bank, *World Development Report*, 1992.

THE ROLE OF THE UNITED NATIONS

Since the ending of the Cold War, the USA has reverted to its 1945 policy of supporting the United Nations. During the Cold War the UN's capacity for action was little used, but it is now the northern-dominated instrument of intervention. Vetoes of substantive issues in the Security Council have all but ceased; the USA and other major powers act together and their actions are legitimized because they are UN sponsored. Since only the decisions of the Security Council are binding on member states, this means that in practice the organization continues to be dominated by the advanced industrialized countries.

The UN is an *international* rather than a *supranational* organization. 'International' means between nations, with the implication of theoretical if not actual equality, while 'supranational' means something above nations which in some way limits sovereignty. However, in reality international, supranational and transnational links all act to reduce not only sovereignty (which is an old-fashioned impractical concept anyway), but also the autonomy of all but (or perhaps even) the largest states.

The UN represents states, not non-governmental organizations (NGOs). Though the latter may be bigger and of more service to the UN, they have no votes. However, they may be represented and speak at major international conferences. The member countries of the UN are organized politically into groups which frequently take up common positions to enhance their clout. Organizations of this kind, other than regional conferences, include the Non-Aligned Movement (NAM) and the Group of 77 (G77). The 'Group of 77' is an economic grouping actually made up of 126 members. All countries of the South are members except China.

The most striking feature of UN activity in the past ten years has been the dramatic extension of UN peacekeeping activity. More UN intervention has taken place since 1989 than in the whole of the previous 44 years of the organization's history. Since UN peacekeeping operations are not funded out of the UN budget, but from precepts on member states, the situation has been viewed with increasing concern by both supporters and opponents of the UN role.

It is the unusual case of Somalia that seems in the end to have brought this problem to a head. A military revolt in Somalia in January 1991, which deposed the tyrannical government of Gen. Siad Barre, had been almost universally welcomed. However, as time went on, no new government was able to gain power and the country relapsed into tribal conflict between factions led by contending warlords. At the end of 1992, following his defeat in the presidential elections, President Bush sent US marines to Mogadishu nominally to protect food aid to the starving people. Soon they were embroiled instead in a futile attempt to eliminate one of these warlords, Gen. Aideed, whom the USA accused of interfering with the aid convoys. Then in October 1993 both US and UN policy changed away from seeking to oust Gen. Aideed, to seeking a peaceful settlement with some new government which could obtain control, and the UN proceeded to halve its troops to 15,000 when US troops eventually left the country in March 1994.

The significance of this rather tangled story is that UN Resolution 794 makes no pretence that UN forces were invited into Somalia in the first place. Its justification for intervention is that its objectives were reconstruction and disarmament and not just peacekeeping, but that in the course of active pursuit of these objectives subsequent resolutions reconfirmed both the objectives and the role of UN troops. The conclusion is that UN intentions may have been worthy enough, but the extension of its powers that this implied conflicted with the norm of non-intervention and was bound to raise doubts. Additionally, the fact that the Somalis soon started complaining of human rights abuses did it no credit and set back the cause of so-called humanitarian intervention. Early in 1995 the new Republican majority in the US House of Representatives passed legislation which if law will effectively end UN intervention, since it requires the President to subtract from the cost of any contribution to UN peacekeeping budgets the cost of UN forces, and will effectively transform the US contribution into a negative balance.

REGIONAL ALIGNMENTS

One obvious way to avoid excessive dependence on or influence by great powers was to create regional organizations. However, the oldest such organization, the Organization of American States (OAS), founded in 1948 as a regional organization within the UN system, is not clearly a Third World organization. Since its foundation, as a development of the old Pan-American Union, it has been dominated by the regional and world superpower, the United States; and the parallel military alliance, the Inter-American Treaty of Reciprocal Assistance (commonly known in English as the Rio Pact) was specifically created in 1947 to form one of a network of alliances supporting the United States against the Soviet Union.

The OAS was largely by-passed in the confrontation between the United States and Cuba which led to the exclusion of the latter from the working of the organization in 1962. In the 1960s and 1970s its numbers were swollen by the accession of Suriname and the former British colonies in the region. Two were excluded because they had frontier disputes with existing members. However, both, Belize and Guyana, were admitted at the beginning of the 1990s together with Canada, which had previously chosen to stand aloof. Hence the organization, which was reorganized along UN lines by the Protocol of Buenos Aires in 1970, reproduces many of the conflicts which characterize the working of the UN itself.

The Organization of African Unity (OAU) was formed in 1963, in the first flush of independence. Despite the hopes expressed at the time by Kwame Nkrumah of Ghana, it did not aim so high as to create some form of pan-African superstate. Its three main aims were the eradication of colonialism, the promotion of economic co-operation and the resolution of disputes among member states. Originally annual meetings were held in different capitals, which nearly bankrupted the host government; since 1970 there has been an established permanent centre in Addis Ababa.

At its inception the organization created an African Liberation Committee to channel aid to liberation movements. However, most African governments have given little and in the major case, that of South Africa, the strategy of armed confrontation destabilized the 'front-line' states without any obvious effect on apartheid. The Lusaka Declaration of 1970 was a belated admission that negotiation might be a more effective way to secure the desired objection of decolonization. The collapse of Portuguese colonial rule in 1974 was followed by the alliance of the 'front-line' states to give support to the liberation of Rhodesia/Zimbabwe, but in the years that followed the South

African government successfully organized guerrilla forces to destabilize both Angola and Mozambique. In its major confrontation with South Africa, the main instruments of the OAU were a combination of sanctions and economic boycotts, but once again a significant number of African states failed effectively to implement sanctions. A few, notably Malawi under Dr Hastings Banda, openly rejected them, and Dr Kenneth Kaunda of Zambia, who consistently pressed for a peaceful transition of power in Rhodesia/ Zimbabwe, was prepared to meet South African leaders and even to support their action in intervening against the Marxist government of Angola (Tangri 1985: 142).

The OAU's Economic and Social Council was set up to promote economic collaboration, but with a few small exceptions it has been notably unsuccessful. Most African states have only slowly lost their trade and other economic links with their former colonial powers.

It is as a political organization seeking to maintain the defence of the sovereignty of existing national territories that the OAU has been most successful. An early and important decision was to recognize the existing colonial boundaries of member states. Since then it has had to deal with conflicts of three main kinds:

- Challenges to state integrity.
- Challenges to regime integrity.
- Ideological/personality disputes.

The three great achievements of the OAU have been the settlement of the 1967 frontier dispute between Kenya and Somalia, the independence of Zimbabwe (formerly Rhodesia) and the collapse of apartheid in South Africa. However, on most of the major post-colonial issues it has shown itself weak and divided, failing to contribute effectively to the settlement of the Congo/ Zaire crisis, the Nigerian civil war, the Angolan crisis and the dispute between Morocco and Mauritania over the Western Sahara. In 1982 the member states were so divided that it was unable initially to obtain a quorum to hold its annual summit.

Meanwhile a steady build-up of arms in the region led to an increasing willingness to use force. Significantly, this tended to be on an individual state or sub-regional level. Armed support for incumbents was given when Guinean troops were sent to support Siaka Stevens in Sierra Leone in 1971 and Senegalese forces to The Gambia in 1981. Armed intervention to end a state of anarchy and civil war included Tanzania's intervention in Uganda in 1979 to expel Idi Amin, and the ECOWAS intervention in Liberia in 1989, which led to the destabilization of Sierra Leone and the fall of President Momoh. Armed aggression to obtain additional territory has been rarer. Libya's intervention in Chad in 1983, which led to the virtual annexation of one-third of its territory, was countered, ultimately successfully, by US and French intervention. Only in this last case did the OAU act to set up a peacekeeping force (largely Nigerian), which was withdrawn after a few weeks for lack of support.

Its main weaknesses as an organization are nationalism, the problems it faces in getting member states to pay their contributions, and the fears of African heads of state and heads of government that they will be deposed while they are out of country. The end of apartheid in South Africa has taken away the one cause that motivated the desire for unity.

Asia is too big to have a clear existence as a continent, so there is no regional equivalent to the OAU or the OAS. Western attempts to set up regional alliances in the Middle East and South-East Asia foundered on the realities of local politics. Sub-regional organizations in the 1990s include the following:

- The *Commonwealth of Independent States* (CIS). Founded in 1991, this is the ghost of the former Soviet Union. Though rivalry between the Russian federation and the Ukraine over the Crimea and the Black Sea Fleet seems to have died down, regional rivalries seem for the time being to be sufficiently strong to forestall any greater degree of unity.
- The *Arab League*. Founded in 1945, this is effectively a regional organization for South-West Asia and North Africa. The League displays vast political differences between member states despite their religious and ethnic bonds. However, its members dominate the more recently formed Islamic Conference, which with 41 members is now the most powerful regional bloc in UN politics.
- The *Association of South-East Asian Nations* (ASEAN). Founded in 1967, this has only six members: Brunei, Indonesia, Malaysia, the Philippines, Singapore and Thailand.
- The *South Asian Association for Regional Co-operation* (SAARC). Founded in 1985, this has seven member states: Bangladesh, Bhutan, India, the Maldives, Nepal, Pakistan and Sri Lanka.
- The *South Pacific Forum* (SPF). This was founded in 1971 as an association of the self-governing states in the Pacific, and it meets annually. It has gradually superseded the older (1948) South Pacific Commission (SPC), consisting of representatives of the non-self-governing Pacific territories and their administering powers.

The, to some, extraordinary survival of the *Commonwealth* owes much to the relatively peaceful transition to independence of many of its members, and to the informality of its organization. With the accession of Namibia and the return to membership of South Africa, it now has 51 members. Fiji remains self-excluded by its refusal to accord equal treatment to its citizens of Indian origin. Hence despite the inclusion in its membership of two of the G7 nations (Canada and the UK) as well as Australia, it is very much a Third World organization, which helps account for the fact that the former British Prime Minister Margaret Thatcher so obviously had little or no time for it. The Commonwealth, however, is not a federation but a club. Its effectiveness, which is often underrated, lies precisely in the fact that it operates through informal meetings and relies on shared understandings which do not have to be put into words.

GLOBALIZATION

For the past century or more we have been witnessing a process of *globalization*, 'the process by which events, decisions, and activities in one part of the world can come to have significant consequences for individuals and communities in quite distant parts of the globe' (McGrew, Lewis *et al.* 1992: 23). Globalization is the key characteristic of the modern economic system and even, it has been argued, of modernity itself (Giddens 1990). As a result, theorists of international relations have come increasingly to emphasize the systemic factors affecting state behaviour rather than the individual decisions of states themselves.

The notion of systemic factors, however, implies the existence of an international system. By system we mean an enduring set of interactions between individuals, or, in this case, states (Nye and Keohane 1971; Keohane and Nye 1977). States are in themselves functional systems, and can be viewed either as such or as subsystems within the larger international context. Despite the formal absence of authority in the world-system, states have in general behaved in an orderly way which presupposes some notion of international order (Bull 1977). The world is a very complex place and with the speeding-up of communications during the present century we have all come to interact with one another, across national boundaries, to a much greater extent than was ever possible before. Hence despite the formal absence of global political authority, states do act together co-operatively, with each other and with a whole variety of non-governmental organizations (NGOs) and international organizations (IOs) to make decisions that for the most part are effective. Indeed, in some areas, such as TV broadcasting or air traffic control, they have no practical alternative.

The concept of system, though, is inappropriate to the Third World as such. Indeed, it is not always of much use in a regional context. There is one obvious exception: the Western Hemisphere. Not only is it isolated by water from the main arena of world politics (Calvert 1988), but it is even conceptualized by those who live there in system terms, and the notion of an 'inter-American system' has, as noted above, actually been embodied in a regional international organization. But few would concede the same degree of identity, for example, to South Asia. Differences of perception are easily illustrated:

The open invitation by Pakistan to 'foreign powers' in the early 1950s led to an Indian condemnation that has never really stopped. Yet Pakistan has argued that India's subsequent policy of non-alignment, and the need for cold war rivalry to be kept out of the South Asia region, was a rather purple Indian version of simple power politics, a cunning disguise of Indian expansionist interests dressed up in the language of moral virtues. This belief is still held to this day. A recent Pakistani commentator has pointed out that: 'It is significant that many Indians, when they speak of the *Indian* land mass cannot refrain from making it clear that what they are really talking about is the entire South Asian region'. (Hewitt 1992: 27, quoting Khan 1990)

Otherwise we are left with the rather vague concept of a world-system, and the problem with this is that, while it may in some sense be true that everything and everyone in the world influences to some degree everyone else, in practice we have to establish some limits on our inquiry if we are to make any sort of sense. What then are the transnational links that transcend the nation-state? How far are they actually able to avoid the power of the national state to regulate and to control them?

TRANSNATIONAL LINKS

Theorists of international relations no longer accept the classical view of their discipline as being concerned only with relations between states – the 'billiard ball' model. However many other links there are between people and organizations, though, the fact remains that the state system, originally evolved in Europe at the Treaty of Westphalia, continues and is likely to continue to structure all such relationships.

The first problem begins with the notion of citizenship and the requirement of an individual to have a passport and permission to enter another country. Citizens of Third World states do not enjoy the same freedom of movement as citizens of the advanced industrialized countries, and their governments are unable to give them even the same limited degree of protection that most of the industrialized countries can arrange. If they have to flee from persecution, in theory they have to be received wherever they go. In practice the industrialized countries have made matters very difficult for refugees, and by classifying all other potential immigrants as 'economic migrants' they have absolved themselves from any obligation to receive them. Only the universal human institution of the family, to a limited extent, transcends these barriers: in some, but not all, cases successful immigrants are also allowed to sponsor their relatives as immigrants.

The second problem comes from the multiplicity of currencies and the lack of an agreed world standard of value. It is true that this has in recent years been supplied to some extent by the US dollar. However, since the devaluation of the dollar by the Nixon administration in 1971, its preeminence has no longer been taken for granted, although it is still more widely available and more widely accepted than any other currency. In recent years a growing difficulty has been the growth of global currency dealing on a scale which makes even the currencies of the advanced industrialized countries vulnerable to sudden attack on the financial markets. The fact that billions can be moved in seconds renders the currencies of smaller states even more vulnerable than those of larger ones. And the global market is all too prone to sudden alarms, on the principle that it is better to be safe than sorry. The devaluation of the Mexican peso in December 1994 not only smashed the illusion of financial stability in Mexico itself, but immediately threatened the stability of the financial systems of other Latin American states, especially Brazil and Argentina, and the governments of those countries found it very difficult indeed to counter the impression that they too were in some way affected. The private citizen of a Third World state lives with this perpetual instability, which gets greater the more open his or her country is to the world market.

The third problem concerns the availability of information. As we have already noted, the provision of world news has long been dominated by the advanced industrialized countries and their news organizations. Only in the last ten years has the spread of the Internet, which celebrated its 25th anniversary in 1994, begun to erode this control. The irony is that, although the computers that have made this possible are actually manufactured and assembled in the Third World, it is the inhabitants of the developed countries who benefit from the new freedom of communication.

Similarly, it is they who have benefited most from the rapid decline of sea travel in favour of air, and of rail travel in favour of the private car. The explosion in long-haul holidays has turned Thailand into a major tourist destination and is in the process of doing the same to the Indian state of Goa. This is no doubt very enjoyable for the tourists. The impact on the economic and social fabric of the countries concerned is already causing alarm, and none more so than its most sinister manifestation, the growth of 'sex tourism', which is accelerating the global spread of AIDS.

BUSINESS AND POLITICS: TAXATION, TARIFFS AND PRIVATIZATION

The problem for Third World states of the links between transnational corporations and local interests have already been mentioned. The main issues between such corporations and governments revolve around three main issues: taxation, tariffs and privatization.

International law accepts that companies are subject to local taxation wherever they operate. However, it is quite a different matter for a weak Third World government actually to obtain the revenues to which it feels entitled. The fact the the country needs the company more than the company needs the country weakens its bargaining position. The practice of 'transfer pricing', by which goods are sold internally by one branch of a company to another, can, if judiciously employed, result in a much reduced tax bill. In extreme cases a company can, if it has sufficient resources, simply buy the outcome that it wants, preferably in a weak, undervalued local currency.

One thing at least has changed. It is no longer acceptable practice for a company that feels hard done-by to appeal to its home government for military force to be used in its defence. It is also true that they seldom need to do so.

Much economic growth in the Third World has taken place behind protective tariff barriers. The conclusion of the Uruguay Round, and the creation of the World Trade Organization (WTO), if taken literally, rule out such a strategy and leave Third World countries vulnerable to strong selling pressures from the advanced industrialized countries. However, common sense suggests that both tariff barriers and non-tariff barriers will be employed for some time yet. The fact is that for major transnational corporations they have always been manipulable by a variety of devices, even if the country concerned has not, as in many cases it has, been so keen to invite in foreign investment that it has been prepared to waive all tariffs on imported capital goods for a substantial period, typically ten years.

In the current economic climate, the nationalization of foreign-owned enterprises is unlikely to be an issue in the immediate future. Its place as a problem area has been taken by privatization.

'Privatization' now generally refers to the process by which state assets are transferred to private ownership. In this sense it is a new term, originally popularized in Britain when, following its successful re-election in 1983, the Thatcher government embarked on a crusade to divest the state of its ownership of profit-making enterprises. The sale of public enterprises has, however, gone on for many years – as long, perhaps, as public enterprises have existed. In Argentina, for example, a report by Raúl Prebisch for the interim military government of 1955–8 recommended the sale of all state enterprises except the railways and the oil industry, but no action was taken (Di Tella and Rodríguez Braun 1990: 7). Under President Frondizi, however, in order to reduce public expenditure the government sold off 40 companies previously German owned which had been expropriated at the end of the Second World War, and privatized the urban bus transport network in Buenos Aires, with according to the Minister of Economy 'excellent results' (Roberto T. Alemann, in Di Tella and Rodríguez Braun 1990: 69). At the same time, private participation was invited both by Argentina's state oil corporation Yacimientos Petrolíferos Fiscales (YPF), and by Petróleos Mexicanos (PEMEX) in Mexico, where in an act widely hailed at the time as a declaration of economic independence, British and American oil companies had been nationalized in 1938.

Despite vigorous US propaganda for private enterprise, the real shift towards privatization in Latin America did not get under way until the 1970s, when it was associated with the policies of the 'Chicago boys' in Chile. It is only since the early 1980s that it has become a major theme of Latin American economic policies (Glade 1991: 2). Its spread to the rest of the Third World has been slower, the obvious reason being that many of the poorer Third World countries have few if any major assets which a buyer would find attractive. Additionally, it is one of the ironies of privatization programmes that by the law of supply and demand, a government keen to privatize national assets can be expected to receive the *lowest* possible price for them, and many Third World governments that were originally keen to sell have at least hesitated when they found that they might end up paying out more in inducements than they were going to receive from the sale.

Were the choice of either nationalization or privatization purely a matter of economics, the question of which to adopt would be a purely technical one. Unfortunately, however, both the acts themselves and the way in which they are executed involve significant and complex ethical questions. For a Third World state a major problem is presented by potential foreign-owned monopolies. The desire of foreign corporations to bid for former public enterprises is much enhanced when a successful bid will give them exclusive economic control. However, turning state monopolies into private monopolies is likely at least to breed nationalist resentment. Alternatively, where two or more companies are bidding for a key asset, the question of which bid to choose may well be determined as much by political (or even personal) considerations as by economic ones.

CONCLUSION

Economic weakness makes Third World countries politically powerless. Opening up their economies to investment and trade promises wealth, but brings with it a greater openness to outside influences.

Because of this, purely Third World organizations have not been particularly successful at influencing world affairs, while regional organizations incorporating a substantial power are inclined to come under the influence of that power. The OAS has not for long been able to avoid the influence of the United States, and through the Francophone states France has exercised and continues to exercise a disproportionate influence within the OAU.

Though interactions between the citizens of different countries are becoming technically easier, money and political influence combine to ensure that the globalization of world politics tends to strengthen the power of the major states and/or the advanced industrialized countries, and not of the Third World.

PART IV
Policy issues

11 The right to development

INTRODUCTION

The meaning that you attach to the term 'development' depends on where you start from. It means different things to different people, even at its most mundane and practical level. For example, a resident of rural Senegal might see development as the availability of very basic services such as a reliable source of potable water; someone living in the suburbs of Greater Buenos Aires would expect rather more. Certainly both would associate the term with some sort of improvement in the quality of their lives.

In its earliest form, 'development' was seen in terms of economic changes which would seek to counter the problem of global poverty, which was being addressed for the first time in the post-war era. Poverty was believed to be measurable in economic terms, simply as the amount by which per capita income fell short of the US level, and so was easily solvable by economic changes. Today development is seen as a much more complex concept, involving consideration of not only the crude increase in production, but the nature of that production and the range of social facilities which accompany it. It is this stress on quality rather than simply quantity which separates 'development' from 'growth'.

But this still does not answer the often-asked question of whether the concept is properly an economic or a political one. Development agendas change (see the discussion on poverty and basic needs in Chapter 3). A decisive response laying strong emphasis on political or economic aspects of development usually reflects strong attachment to a particular perspective.

THEORY AND PRACTICE

The earliest considerations of Third World development were modernization theories. The best-known form is perhaps to be found in the work of the US economist W.W. Rostow (1960), who argued that in favourable conditions the less developed countries could hope to attain 'take-off' into sustained economic growth, just as the advanced industrialized countries had already done. The critique of this view from the dependency theorists and others has already been addressed in Chapter 4. The point to note here is that Rostow himself laid as much emphasis on the political as on the economic preconditions of development. Not only is this reflected in related studies such as Clement Dodd's *Political Development* (1974), but even the more sophisticated 'politics of order' theories shared this emphasis. For Huntington (1976), the key variable is political mobilization. Though, where strong institutions exist, mobilization results in democratic societies, mobilisation produces praetorianism in the absence of strong and developed (political) institutions. At this stage, however, economic development was still generally understood in terms of increasing gross national product, and relatively little attention was paid to the inequalities resulting from uncontrolled or partly controlled development.

Intergovernmental organizations would now seek to define development in a very broad way. The invention of the Human Development Index (HDI), was an attempt to measure the real impact of economic development through a small number of carefully selected indicators. The most important difference from older measures was to reject the use of fluctuating and frequently misleading exchange rate conversions in favour of purchasing power parities. There are four basic indicators: life expectancy, adult literacy, mean years of schooling and average income. From 1994 the comparisons between countries made on the basis of the HDI are made more realistic by fixing maxima and minima for each variable range (United Nations Development Programme 1994). Adult literacy cannot exceed 100 per cent, and 98.5 per cent is probably a more realistic maximum. Life expectancy is unlikely to attain 85 years in any country in the foreseeable future; nor is it likely to fall below 25. Mean years of schooling vary between 0 and 15. Such refinements reflect the growing awareness that economic growth, changes to the productive sectors and increased per capita income do not necessarily bring benefits to whole societies.

Some economies may be starting from such low bases that such changes make little difference to any section of the society. More usually the benefits which do accrue do not 'trickle down' beyond the élite or, perhaps more broadly, the urban industrial sectors. Sometimes such benefits to one sector are accompanied by negative consequences for other sectors. The growing concern with environmental degradation and its impact on the quality of all our lives (see Chapter 13) has further contributed to the tendency to broaden definitions of development to emphasize sufficiency and other non-economic factors. But of course herein lie different interests, and these definitions tend to be presented by well-meaning First World authors.

It would be hard to criticize the scope and range of the definition given by Michael Todaro:

> Development must therefore be conceived of as a multidimensional process involving major changes in social structures, popular attitudes and national

institutions, as well as the acceleration of economic growth, the reduction of inequality, and the eradication of poverty. Development, in its essence, must represent the whole gamut of change by which an entire social system, tuned to the diverse basic needs and desires of individuals and social groups within that system, moves away from a condition of life widely perceived as unsatisfactory toward a situation or condition of life regarded as materially and spiritually 'better'. (Todaro 1994: 16)

At its simplest and most cogent, the term may be best expressed as in the work of Amartya Sen (1981) as a reduction in vulnerability and as increased strength to counter problems consequent upon an enhancement of the options available. For Sen development involves the increased freedom of the population. There is in this a validity that other definitions do not so adequately express, since income as measured by purchasing power gives freedom, but the freedom it gives also embraces a series of needs within society, for participation, health, education, etc.

All the above discussion essentially takes place within a structuralist framework. That is to say, all these definitions/models of development, even dependency ones, are concerned with changes in social/political/economic *structures*. The neo-liberal model of development, on the other hand, stresses market relations, and this is still in ascendancy in the ideological ambience of international agencies like the World Bank.

GHANA: THE DESIRE FOR ECONOMIC INDEPENDENCE

The early history of independent Ghana illustrates the hopes and failures associated with the 'take-off' model of development. Ghana's future leader, Kwame Nkrumah, returned in 1947 to the Gold Coast, as it was then known, from the USA where he had been a postgraduate student and taken his doctorate. By 1949 he had formed his own political party (CPP) seeking immediate independence from Britain, which had been the colonial power for more than a century.

In 1951 the Gold Coast held its first elections. Nearly a million people voted. Although Nkrumah himself was still in gaol, his party swept to power and he became Prime Minister in an elected government which had full internal self-government, although Britain still controlled foreign and defence policy. In 1957 he became the first leader of a newly independent Black African state, and set out to turn Ghana into a modern industrial utopia.

The British had planned the Volta dam to provide hydroelectric power to smelt aluminium, but in 1956 they cancelled the project, saying it was too expensive. Nkrumah saw the Volta dam as a means to the power needed to fuel the modernization of Ghana. It would be a source of power for comprehensive development as well as the means to irrigate the Accra plains.

Eisenhower, anxious that Ghana should be pro-USA in the Cold War, suggested that US aluminium manufacturers might be interested in supporting the Volta scheme. In 1958 Kaiser Industries agreed to build a smelter in Ghana and to buy the electricity generated by the scheme. Nkrumah asked the World Bank for £30 million, the largest loan ever requested down to that time.

In accordance with the prevailing 'take-off' model of development popularized by W.W. Rostow, power on a massive scale was seen as the means to industrialization and therefore to development. In 1960 the World Bank approved the scheme in principle, but expressed some reservations about the prices Kaiser had agreed to pay to Ghana for energy to run the smelter. The World Bank took the view that these prices must be higher if Ghana was to have a chance of realizing the development plans which were an integral part of the Volta River scheme. Kaiser was determined not to pay more than the lowest rates available anywhere in the world. Nkrumah had little option but to agree to Kaiser's price, or Kaiser would pull out and the dam would not be built.

Nkrumah wanted to keep Ghana out of the Cold War tensions, but the USA saw the dam and his developmental aspirations as the means to win him over. The USA had agreed to lend millions to the scheme and used these loans to pressure Nkrumah into accepting US policies. Hence the Volta River scheme was shaped by political and economic pressures, not by Nkrumah's idealism. As an investment, Ghana was initially seen as an excellent prospect. The colonial power, Britain, had left it a good infrastructure and an educated population. Thus the dam got built.

Construction of the Volta dam took four years. The process came to illustrate the high levels of corruption in Ghana. There were not only corrupt government officials, but also corrupt foreign suppliers who would do anything to make a sale. European industrializts seeking to sell their products in Ghana found that the easy way was to offer a bribe, and bribery soon became the business culture of Accra. One result was a rush to sell Ghana anything, no matter how inappropriate. The most grandiose development schemes were encouraged by foreign suppliers and domestic vested interests, and taken up by local politicians eager to win popular support. Most proved expensive and some unviable.

The key to Ghana's strong economic position was cocoa. However, in 1964 cocoa prices collapsed and since cocoa was Ghana's main source of foreign exchange, Ghana, which had been one of the richest countries in Africa, slid into debt. Nkrumah's vision was now beginning to be seen as megalomania. Only one month after the dam was finished in 1966, the armed forces took over the government while Nkrumah was abroad. Nkrumah fled to Guinea, where he died in 1972.

Significantly, the post-Nkrumah years were also a period of economic failure. The Kaiser aluminium plant flourished and the World Bank loan was paid off with the money paid for power, but as electricity prices rose everywhere in the 1970s, Kaiser still paid very little. In 1979 Flt. Lt. Jerry Rawlings took power in the seventh coup since Nkrumah, and he was determined to get more from the Kaiser smelter. In 1983 the Ghanaian government tried to get Kaiser to renegotiate prices by allowing rumours of nationalization to circulate and by keeping the dam shut down until Kaiser agreed; two years later, in 1985, a new agreement was signed which raised prices threefold ('Pandora's Box', BBC Television, 1993).

THE RIGHT TO DEVELOPMENT?

The World Conference on Human Rights (June 1993) revealed once more the extent of the North–South divide on the issue of the 'right to develop'. However, this is only a particular example of the fact that human rights are defined differently the world over. These arguments can be divided into two main groups. Developing countries argue that political and civil rights are not separable from and certainly not more important than economic, social and cultural rights. The industrial West argues that political and civil liberties should come first. Some thinkers believe that economic, social and cultural rights cannot be regarded as true human rights, since they depend on the ability to make economic resources available.

A further question is whether collective (i.e. developmental) rights should outrank individual rights. The question is complicated by the fact that, as so often in international politics, countries have put their names to high-sounding statements of general principles which they are not always prepared to put into practice.

As early as 1948 the UN confirmed development as a right in Article 28 of the Universal Declaration of Human Rights. This commitment has been reiterated and deepened on many subsequent occasions. The 1960s were proclaimed as the UN 'Decade of Development'. The results for many Third World countries were so disappointing that a second Decade was proclaimed for the 1970s. Any hope that this might be more successful was to be abruptly cut short by the first 'oil shock' of 1973.

This was enormously ironic, since the oil crises of the 1970s were initially seen by both oil-rich and oil-poor states as an opportunity to redress the balance between the First and the Third Worlds. However, in practice it was the Third World countries, which did not have access to their own oil reserves and lacked the leverage to gain preferential access on the world market, that came off worst. In 1979 the Brandt Commission proposed a formal redistribution of wealth from the First to the Third World states by way of a 'global income tax' (Brandt 1980). However, the 1980s were a decade of neoliberal 'solutions' and high interest rates, and by 1990 the majority of Third World countries were actually worse off than they had been in 1979.

THE NEW INTERNATIONAL ECONOMIC ORDER

Eventually, with the enlargement of the United Nations, came in 1964 a response to western domination of trade in the holding of the United Nations Conference on Trade, Aid and Development (UNCTAD). That first meeting of UNCTAD, UNCTAD I, stressed the need for structural reforms in world trade if rapid development was to be achieved by the South. But although UNCTAD became a permanent organization, holding a sequence of major conferences, it had no real power, as the northern states were unwilling to consider more than minor tinkering with the existing system.

At UNCTAD III at Santiago de Chile, the President of Mexico, Luis Echeverra Alvarez, called for the creation of a New International Economic Order (NIEO). The Mexicans voiced the feelings of most Third World governments when they criticized the prevailing terms of trade. They saw themselves as being condemned by the existing system to export large quantities of primary products at low prices, and to import the manufactured goods they needed at very high ones; hence the demand for an arrangement that would link producer prices to changes in the price of manufactured goods. They were backed by the President of Venezuela, Carlos Andrés Pérez, and by most of the other OPEC states. In April 1974 the UN General Assembly, which was then heavily dominated by Third World states, endorsed the idea of the NIEO.

This resulted in the adoption by the United Nations General Assembly in December 1974 of the Charter of Economic Rights and Duties of States (CERDS). Its main planks were as follows:

- Fair terms of trade for developing countries.
- A new world currency linked to the price of primary materials.
- The abolition of IMF conditionality as a requirement for new loans.

Though the resolution to adopt CERDS was carried by 120 votes to 6 with 10 abstentions, the programme it represented was in fact, though acknowledged by President Carter, totally opposed by the governments of the United States and the advanced industrialized countries, and so was effectively a dead letter (Thomas 1985: 65–6). CERDS might, on paper, have been agreed, but not surprisingly it was never implemented. For example, it was intended that prices of primary products would be pegged to prices of manufactured goods, but this proved to be unrealistic. Manufacturers were unwilling to pay more, and competition between Third World suppliers kept prices down. OPEC had for a time been successful in driving up the price of petroleum, but similar cartels for other products failed for a variety of reasons (see Chapter 4). The United Nations called the Cancun Conference of 1981 to promote global negotiations on the NIEO, but it came to nothing.

The problem was not just economic but political. In general the USA does not feel itself bound by UN decisions with which it does not agree. The fact that it foots 25 per cent of the bill for the UN is the most powerful argument for this. The agreement by Japan in September 1994 to become the UN's second largest supporter and pay 15 per cent of the costs of maintaining the organization is likely to give Japan almost as much leverage if it chooses to use it. Not only has the United States under Ronald Reagan withdrawn from UNESCO and constantly chivvied other agencies into accepting its wishes, but on the first occasion when it was confronted with a legal challenge before the World Court to its clandestine war on Nicaragua, it refused to accept that body's jurisdiction. At the same time, by choosing to work through other groupings such as the G7 group of advanced industrialized countries, it is able to by-pass many of the constraints that the Third World domination of the UN General Assembly would otherwise impose on its freedom of action.

A New International Economic Order (NIEO) would depend on stability. To achieve this, many argue that what first would be needed is a democratization of international relations, just as democracy and participation must accompany development at a local or national level (see WCED 1987). The restoration of superpower hegemony could restore stability, but that state of affairs would be unlikely to meet the *economic* aspirations of Third World countries.

DEVELOPMENT STRATEGIES

Different Third World states have devised their own strategies for development. These routes have varied with starting point, location, tradition and ideology. For example, while some states, such as Zambia, have continued to rely on exporting primary products and some, such as Cuba, have been forced to do so, others have chosen (or perhaps 'chosen' is too strong, given the constraints) more unusual directions, like India's quest for self-sufficiency or Singapore's investment in technology and education. Some have favoured export-led growth, as in Taiwan or South Korea, taking advantage of, if not actively embracing, a free market ideology premised on the assumption that benefits will trickle down to the poorest sectors. This latter strategy is illustrated by the cases of Brazil, Chile and other countries of Latin America.

Development relies on availability of funds for infrastructural and other capital investment. Third World states generally get such funds as revenues from import/export duties, fees and taxes on transnational corporations, the profits made by state agencies for the import or export of products, foreign loans or aid, and the manipulation of exchange rates. Domestic revenues are much more difficult to extract, since local élites resist often successfully any attempt of the state to set realistic levels of personal taxation. Hence Third World regimes must necessarily be reluctant to contemplate any development strategy which hits international trade relations, and certainly their relatively small size in the main precludes the realistic possibility of economic autarky.

In some cases there may be a conflict between a Third World state's development strategy and the interests of transnational corporations. Although a state must be fairly small for transnational corporations still to have a great degree of national power, a number of them are still in that position, particularly in SSA. Generally speaking, the two parties, the state and the corporations, need each other, but the relationship is often unequal. The increasing globalization of the world economy and the deregulation of transnational activities are enhancing linkages between transnational corporations and thus increasingly marginalizing the weaker South. The figures are sobering. The annual turnover of Nestlé is more than seven times the GNP of Ghana. In 1984 no African state had an annual turnover as big as Exxon. Only South Africa, Nigeria, Egypt, Morocco and the Ivory Coast had GNPs big enough to get them places among the top 100 corporations. Transnational corporations now control more than 40 per cent of world output, and as much as 30 per cent of world trade takes place not between but within large corporations (Thrift 1986).

Why is this so? A major reason is the number of states and the relatively limited number of major corporations. There is keen rivalry between less developed countries (LDCs) to attract transnational corporations. Once they have chosen to set up operations, the governments concerned find that they cannot effectively regulate them, since it is so easy for large corporations to switch production to another Third World state. Sometimes transnational corporations transfer dangerous or polluting operations to the South. But there are always countries available to allow them to do so, in view of the very large legal and illegal returns that they expect to obtain.

In some states there have been attempts to develop different development strategies and eliminate the involvement of transnational corporations. The Bolsheviks in Russia seized their oil fields in 1917. The oil companies were slow to realize that the change was permanent, but by 1924 they were ready to compete both openly and secretly with one another to market Soviet oil abroad. However, as Stalin consolidated his grip, foreign participation in the Russian economy was ended and did not return until after the collapse of the Soviet Union in 1991. Later transnational corporations were squeezed out of the oil industry in the 1930s in Bolivia and Mexico, in the 1940s in Romania, in the 1950s in Brazil, in the 1960s in Peru and in the 1970s in Algeria, Libya, Iraq and Venezuela. However, the key to the oil industry, as John D. Rockefeller was the first to realize, is not production but distribution and marketing, and the industry continues to be dominated by the 'Seven Sisters': Exxon, Gulf, Texaco, Mobil, Chevron, BP and Shell (Sampson 1975).

By the 1970s Third World countries were finding that nationalization was a strategy fraught with dangers. In Jamaica the ownership of sugar production was taken out of the hands of Tate and Lyle and the plantations were nationalized. Twenty-three co-operatives were established by the People's National Party led by Michael Manley from 1976 on, and with the plantation workers in charge of production they succeeded in producing one-half of the country's sugar. However, several factors worked against them: plant diseases, the hostility of the USA and the IMF, and a drop in sugar prices. In 1980 the PNP lost the elections, the co-operatives were shut down, and Tate and Lyle was invited back in.

Development of stronger First World regional economic groupings – for example, the European Union and NAFTA – is also marginalizing the Third World. While North–North interdependence is strengthening, as yet South–South bonds have not been much developed. The 1950s and 1960s did see the establishment of regional and subregional links in the South, some of which were political and some economic. Regional and subregional development banks were founded. Despite this, South–South trade and communications often pass through northern facilities en route. South–South linkages without northern intervention would strengthen the southern bargaining position in relation to the North. At present the South's organizations and structures do present a common front and these can be effective, but not usually in economic matters, where individual countries short of skilled negotiators can be easily 'picked off' one by one. Often this is done by the North meeting some pressing short-term need, as in the case of the Pergau dam in Malaysia. Economies of scale for countries trying to meet broadly similar needs and facing similar problems should be possible. Further, in one sense, newer and poorer Third World states may have more choice in development strategies, since they have fewer vested interests to placate.

Development directions may be influenced either externally or internally or both. Externally they are shaped by advice and pressure from the US Agency for International Development (USAID), the World Bank, the IMF, etc. The combined effects of these powerful bodies is striking, and the example of the Caribbean Basin Initiative is instructive. During the 1980s, when the United States moved from being the world's largest creditor to being the world's largest debtor, its economy was booming as a result. The Caribbean Basin Initiative was supposed to enable it to benefit its smallest neighbours, allowing them preferential access to the US market for selected products. But at the same time, the small nations of the Caribbean, which faced a declining price for their few commodities, were being told by the international lending agencies to stop 'living beyond their means'. The combined effect of structural adjustment on their economies was to export capital to the advanced industrial economies, a situation made much worse by prevailing high dollar interest rates, which had increased so much that they significantly worsened the terms of borrowing and therefore the debts that the countries concerned had been forced to assume.

In 1987, the Caribbean as a whole paid out US$207 million more to the foreign governments, banks and multilateral agencies that are 'aiding' the region than it received from all of them combined in the same year. This net outflow of funds was mainly in the form of interest and principal payments on the region's foreign debt, which totalled US$20.9 billion in 1988. The removal of funds from the Caribbean would have been even greater had not a major portion of official debt bills been repeatedly postponed; Jamaica's debt payments, for example, have been rescheduled every year since 1979. The consequence is accumulation of arrears and even higher bills to be paid in the future. (McAfee 1991: 13)

However, no less significant are internal political considerations such as who must be consulted and who must be bought off. Vested interests are just one indigenous obstacle to development. Others may include: a lack of industry and infrastructure at independence, especially in Africa; low literacy, poor education and low school enrolment; rapid population growth and urbanization; little administrative capacity; poor financial institutions; archaic social structures; and internal conflicts. External assistance is important, but the key requirement is for self-directed development using human and material resources to satisfy local needs.

Development strategies vary, but they usually stress either import-substitution industrialization or enhancement of exports. Often Third World governments develop medium-term (5–7 years) comprehensive development plans and/or a national development ideology such as South Korea's New Community Movement. These are assertions of government control of the economy, which is not always capable of being realized in practice. Diversification is perhaps the most important part of any development strategy. It is vital to most Third World states owing to variations in the prices of commodities on the world market. However, the grandiose plans of the developmentalists often fail. The process of import-substitution industrialization can easily be hijacked by transnational corporations, as is the case in Brazil, where some 85 per cent of the pharmaceuticals industry is owned by transnational corporations. But some countries have succeeded with import-substitution industrialization. In South Korea, import-substitution industrialization has been transformed into exporting success by corporations such as Hyundai, although some argue that such development can be achieved only if repression is used to channel resources from consumption to investment.

Third World countries often target their exports on to other Third World countries. A striking example is the Brazilian arms industry. But since much of the technology needed for development, and especially that needed to get beyond import-substitution industrialization, must come from the developed countries and often from their transnational corporations, their capacity for independent action is limited.

THE GATT AND THE WTO

The General Agreement on Tariffs and Trade (GATT) was never intended to be permanent. It was an interim measure proposed by the advanced industrialized countries in 1947 at the First (Geneva) Round of trade talks, to fill the gap left in the Bretton Woods system when the US Congress refused to ratify the Havana Charter. The original idea had been to establish an International Trade Organization, with the goal ultimately of securing universal free trade. However, owing to the onset of the Cold War, the USA finally abandoned the idea in 1950. The GATT remained a temporary regime which, however, slowly extended its scope through a series of Rounds. These took longer and longer to complete, and it was only after five years of negotiating at the Eighth Round which began in Punta del Este, Uruguay, in 1986 that a Draft Act was agreed, and it was three more years before it was signed (15 April 1994). Hence it was not until 1 January 1995 that the World Trade Organization (WTO) finally came into existence, and then without agreement between the 81 member states on a Secretary-General.

The GATT was not designed to deal with Third World countries' problems. For example, balance of payments disequilibria are to be dealt with by exerting pressure to adjust on the countries that are in deficit, not on those that are in surplus. The outcome of such adjustments would appear to favour the countries of the North and their transnational corporations. Where they have not liked GATT principles, the developed countries have simply established trade barriers against them. Such groups as textile manufacturers, industrializts and farmers are well organized and powerful in the developed countries. Whatever they profess to believe, they resist trade liberalization which could favour less developed countries. The GATT (and the WTO) is based on three assumptions:

- Trading results in higher living standards.
- Free markets as the basis of international trade promote the greatest benefits.
- The distribution of such benefits is of secondary importance. It is a technical issue and is for the market to decide rather than for political solution.

Pessimists have taken the view that, on the contrary, there can only be limited growth in world demand for primary products, that less developed countries therefore have inherent balance of payments problems because imports are more elastic than exports, and hence that their fragile economies need protection in a way that stronger ones do not. *Optimists* reply that the less developed countries have comparative advantage in cheap labour and thus low unit costs. They will benefit from the opening up of their economies to world trade, as this will result in diversification, which in turn will protect them from reliance on primary products and food crops which can fail.

Overall the optimists got their way in the most recent GATT negotiations. This was to be expected, since it responded in large measure to growing protectionism and bloc-building in the developed world. The Uruguay Round liberalizes and dismantles barriers, but the Third World loses protection. The

GATT Rounds of the 1950s and 1960s opened up new markets and thus facilitated the growth of transnational corporations to the advantage of the developed nations on whose territory these companies were located (and taxed), but some semblance of balance was maintained. The GATT rules allowed less developed countries to use quotas to defend themselves against balance of payments problems. Under the Seventh (Tokyo) Round (1979) and earlier Round rules, the industrialized countries were not permitted to subsidize manufactured goods or minerals, although limited subsidies to agricultural products remained. Less developed countries were allowed to continue to use export subsidies in the short term, but with the rather open-ended proviso that these must not do any damage to any other signatory. Some less developed countries approaching the Uruguay Round thought that industrialized countries should deliver on agreements from previous Rounds before embarking on more negotiations.

This Eighth (Uruguay) Round began with background negotiations in 1982. It formally assembled for full negotiations in 1986 in Punta del Este, Uruguay, before moving to Geneva, where the bulk of the debate took place. It was eventually concluded at the end of 1993. Altogether 117 countries were involved in the negotiations, but as this number shows, many less developed countries were not members. Others had only very recently joined, such as Mexico, which had joined the organization in 1986 after years of declaring the intention of determining its own trade policy. This Round brought new areas under international jurisdiction: services, agriculture and intellectual property rights were the most important.

The OECD estimates that the conclusion of the Uruguay Round will add $270 billion to world output by 2002. However, this is equivalent to an increase in global GDP of only $40 per capita. Moreover, it is clear that the benefits, such as they are, will not be evenly distributed. Some two-thirds will accrue to the developed world, and especially to the European Union. The effects on the Third World will broadly be as follows:

- South America gains $8 billion, of which Brazil alone will gain $3.4 billion.
- India gains $4.6 billion – as much as the whole of South America less Brazil.
- The 'Asian Tigers' gain $7.1 billion between them.
- Africa loses some $2.6 billion, with Nigeria bearing the brunt of the loss, to the tune of $1 billion.

The astonishing negative impact that the new GATT is expected to have on Africa South of the Sahara (SSA) is due to the loss of trade preferences in the European market, and in particular to the consequences of the dismantling of the Lomé Convention. SSA simply does not have any alternative products with which it can take advantage of the liberalization in world trade. In summary, the GATT will contribute to the 'drawing apart' of the Third World, as one-third of benefits expected to go to the Third World will go to the wealthier parts of it and to China.

Pessimists argue that the Uruguay Round deal does not address the problems of debt and low commodity prices; that it serves the interests only of some sections of the industrialized countries and more particularly of transnational corporations. Deregulation of trade is seen as enhancing the power of international capital and giving active encouragement to the global search for cheaper labour. Thus pessimists expect negative impacts on the standard and quality of life in the Third World and for poorer sections of the First World. The environment is also threatened as investment and jobs move to areas offering the lowest production costs. Low costs often reflect the lack of environmental protection legislation in such areas, with serious consequences for especially fragile ecosystems.

In addition, less developed countries must now deregulate, and this means removing restraints on transnational corporations, such as the existing limits imposed on profit repatriation. Services, which constitute some 20 per cent of world trade – including transport, tourism and construction – are brought under the ambit of the GATT for the first time. This is thought to present another problem for the Third World, in that it undermines the development of services without advantaging those less developed countries which do not export services. As regards financial services, less developed countries which are members of the GATT must now open their markets up to US banks and insurance companies. The predictable consequence is that nascent financial services sectors in less developed countries will be destroyed as they face unconstrained competition from northern transnational corporations such as American Express. A third consequence is that they must implement patent protection laws, which will hit indigenous industries and in particular make the production of vital drugs in a generic form problematic. They will have to pay royalties on such developmental necessities as seeds and technology. Non-compliance will mean retaliatory action under the rules of the World Trade Organization, the new trade body which will have the power (which does not exist at present) to police and regulate international trade in the same way that the IMF regulates international borrowing.

Optimists argue that the South will get much more in return. They claim that northern markets will be opened up to less developed countries and that more investment will flow South. They also take the view that the alternative was far worse. To save their advantages the northern states could have imposed high tariffs and other protectionist measures which would have hit the Third World particularly hard.

TRANSNATIONAL CORPORATIONS

Because the majority of them are small companies with headquarters in one country and often only one other branch abroad, the term 'transnational corporation' is preferred both here and by the World Bank to 'multinational corporation', which implies a large enterprise with regional or even world-wide reach and many foreign subsidiaries.

Transnational corporations (TNCs) are responsible for 40 per cent of world trade, 90 per cent of world trade in commodities and 30 per cent of world food production. The largest transnational corporations are responsible for most of the world's foreign investment. The USA provides most such investment, with the UK second and Japan third. The largest firms are household names like IBM, Exxon, General Electric and General Motors.

Although more than three-quarters of transnational corporations are based in the United States or in Europe, there are also transnational corporations based in LDCs, and hence some LDC transnational corporation involvement in other less developed countries. Brazilian companies are involved in West Africa, Indian companies in Indonesia and Malaysia, and the Argentine corporation Bunge y Born in Brazil and Uruguay. The United Nations estimates that transnational corporations employ more than 60 million people world-wide.

Supporters of transnational companies use arguments associated with free market economic theories. They claim that transnational corporations fill gaps of various kinds which exist in local economies. Such corporations, they argue, enhance the earning capacity of host states and generate foreign exchange. They see them as being risk-takers that are exceptionally dynamic in promoting growth. They argue that transnational corporation investment may reduce the need of a host country to borrow abroad, or may fill a need not met by borrowing. Notably, when bank lending declined during the debt crisis of the 1980s, transnational corporation investment became still more important. Company investment not only supplements local savings, but also increases saving by increasing local income and stimulating domestic investment to provide inputs to transnational corporations.

Manufacturing output is seen as the motor of development, and some 30 per cent of LDC manufacturing output comes from transnational corporations. Some of the most successful emerging economies are to be found in the regions that have been most penetrated by transnationals: in Singapore more than 60 per cent of manufacturing output is generated by transnational corporations. Such organizations enhance the earning capacity of host states and generate foreign exchange. Local individuals and companies are paid for their part in production. While some profits are repatriated, some are reinvested in local plant and supplies, and much flows into the local economy by way of wages and salaries. Transnationals are also responsible for generating substantial additional tax revenues.

Several other aspects of TNC activity can be seen as positive. Some technical knowledge is transmitted to local employees and contractors along with managerial skills, resulting in new products becoming available locally and a more efficient use of local labour. In particular, transnational corporations are often seen as a major force in modernizing agriculture, the sector traditionally most resistant to change.

Transnational corporations frequently pay well above the going market rate in salaries and wages. Additionally, they often provide social services for their workforces, contributing to local health and education, and minimizing any drain on local provision.

Some even argue that they act as buffers, insulating the host economy from the full harshness of the international system. There is widespread agreement that they tend to have a generally liberalizing effect in the developed economies in which they are based. One of the results is that they have a strong incentive to lobby against quotas and tariffs which would limit entry of their Third World products to the advanced industrialized countries.

Opponents of TNCs take a very different view of both the economic and political processes involved.

They note that most transnational corporation investment occurs in countries which have been in a position to promote export-led growth, such as Brazil and Malaysia. Transnational corporations are conspicuously absent from many parts of Africa South of the Sahara. Zambia's economy, 70 per cent controlled by transnationals, has collapsed since 1991 as a result of a combination of structural adjustment and trade liberalization. The critics cast doubt on the real rate of return a country can expect from attracting transnational corporations. The inducements offered, such as tax concessions and stable exchange rates, can be very expensive to the host government, and in business terms hardly justify their use.

Far from adding to local capital resources, critics argue, transnationals consume them. Through their presence, foreign investment is made easy for the local foreign-oriented élite. They do not promote domestic development, but seek only to invest where they can maximize their profits. Agricultural transnational corporations do even more harm by buying up high-quality land which could better be used for domestic food production, and so indirectly increase the need to import food. Such corporations hit local economies by repatriating an excessive level of profit, at the same time minimizing their real rate of return to local economies through devices such as transfer pricing. Transfer pricing involves undervaluing transnational products in the host country, and revaluing them by the time that they have reached the home base of the corporation, by selling them on through the company's subsidiaries. As with transfer pricing, the high cost of imported inputs, whether real or as an exercise in accounting, reduces the profits which can be locally taxed.

Transnational corporations go abroad to find new sources of inputs which are declining or becoming more expensive at home. This includes labour. Skilled labour is to be found in middle-income rather than poor Third World states, so the more technical operations are located there.

Transnationals use the protection of LDC import-substitution industrialization strategies, but tend to go where new markets open up in order to exploit those temporary advantages. Hence they are more likely to invest in the top- and middle-income countries of the Third World.

As for them transferring technology to the local economy, they do often use superior technology, but this can be quite inappropriate to local conditions and invariably is much more capital intensive. LDC transnational corporations are often thought to provide more labour-intensive technologies and therefore to be more acceptable. However, in both cases the sharp end of advanced technology may be kept under wraps at home to prevent transfer, in order to preserve the corporation's competitive advantage.

Lastly, wherever they operate, transnationals may enhance the unevenness of development. Manufacturing companies charge the local population premium prices for local products carrying popular brand names. They may displace local firms. They often produce inappropriate products intended originally for the First World, and stimulate local consumption of products such as cigarettes, baby milk formula and brand-name drugs. This is the technique of 'coca-colonization'. On the other hand, mining companies and plantations worsen the rural/urban imbalance, use up natural resources much faster than otherwise would be the case and bring about environmental degradation.

An open question following the Bhopal diaster has been the question of safety. Certainly in that case the standards maintained by a local subsidiary of a transnational corporation were found to be very inadequate, and there are serious doubts as to whether such a dangerous process should have been located so close to a centre of population. However, in their defence it can be argued that generally transnational corporation standards of environmental protection and safety are higher than those of small local companies which can afford less.

THE POWER OF TRANSNATIONAL CORPORATIONS

The prejudice against transnational corporations in many Third World countries is very great. It is based on the power of a big corporation like the former United Fruit Company in a small and relatively weak country like Honduras.

The Windward Islands, Jamaica and Belize have enjoyed guaranteed UK markets, but the advent of the single European market threatens these. The producers of 'dollar bananas' (i.e., bananas grown in Central and South America), especially the three big US transnational corporations, Del Monte, Chiquita and Dole, want to increase their sales to Europe, where they already have 60 per cent of the market. Liberalization of trade under the GATT deal will mean that they get their way at the expense of the banana industries of Britain's former colonies in the West Indies.

Small producers on their family run farms in the Caribbean could not compete without some form of protection. They could not produce bananas as cheaply as the low-paid workers on the plantations of Central and South America. In fact 'dollar bananas' cost only half as much to produce and one Central America plantation can grow as many bananas as 20,000 growers in the Caribbean island states. The problem is an historical one. Although the islands were not very suitable for banana cultivation, Britain encouraged the growing of bananas in its Caribbean dependencies because it wanted guaranteed prices in the financially problematic post-war years and the islands' sugar production was in decline. There is little scope for diversification in the islands. Tourism is growing, but some form of agricultural production is vital and whatever is grown will cost more to produce than elsewhere (see also Grugel 1995).

The transnational corporations established themselves throughout Central America. Refrigeration gave them the technology they needed, and they soon had turnovers bigger than the countries in which they were operating. They were notorious for their interference in local politics. The involvement of the banana companies in local politics has many unsavoury aspects, ranging from unsecured personal 'loans' to dictators, such as the $1 million paid to Jorge Ubico in Guatemala to get a reduction in corporation taxes, to the fact that in all countries they held much land idle to prevent competition developing, while they paid minimal taxes and export duties.

Honduras is the archetypical 'banana republic'. The United Fruit Company (UFCo), now Chiquita, cynically exploited the unlimited access its weak government allowed it. The banana plantations form a vast enclave in the north-east of the country, on the shore of the Caribbean and well away from the centres of Honduras' small population. There whole towns were built by the company, linked to each other and to the company ports by company-owned railways. Both workers and other local inhabitants use company stores, company hospitals and company schools.

By contrast, Costa Rica, the second largest banana producer in the Caribbean, has avoided becoming a 'banana republic' and is a democratic and politically sophisticated country. However, its prospects now confront the interests of its banana-growers. Ecotourism is very important to Costa Rica, but the country has recently doubled the acreage given over to bananas. A chemical-free banana production system is possible, but agribusiness 'needs' take precedence over the environment. Conservation groups are very concerned. Pesticides seep into drainage systems and are threatening Costa Rica's national parks. Its coral reef is dying. In addition, Costa Rica has the highest rate of deforestation in Latin America (*Assignment*, 'Banana Wars', BBC Television, 1993).

Times of crisis weaken Third World states in the face of transnational corporations, and the debt crisis of the 1980s made transnational corporations more vital to Third World states and enabled them to rebuild their position. On the other hand, transnational corporations are mainly involved in the more autarkic sections of the Third World, because middle-income countries offer them diversified economic structures, sophisticated and substantial markets, and the skilled labour these corporations most often need. The 1960s and 1970s saw the development of a variety of controls on their activities. States prescribed the degree of local investment required, the maximum length of time an activity could be left under transnational corporation control before transfer to local interests, and so on. Such restraints on freedom of manoeuvre caused IBM and Coca-Cola to leave India in the 1970s. The ultimate weapon was expropriation, but this has been very rare outside the oil industry. There was some use of nationalization in emerging states in the 1960s and 1970s, but the number of countries prepared to confront transnational corporations was always small, and among the most notable were Chile, Cuba, Uganda, Zaire and Zambia. Generally, where nationalization has taken place, output has fallen and the expected benefits have not been for the most part realized. Most such Third World weapons against the power of transnational corporations will disappear under the new WTO regime.

AID

Foreign aid is a very new concept. It was virtually unknown before 1945. The use of economic aid as a tool of superpower competition in the Cold War established the practice, but it took much longer than that for the concept that rich countries had a duty to help poor ones to become accepted.

With the ending of the Cold War, much of the self-interest which generated aid flows between 1950 and 1980 has come to an end. The Third World is likely to be the main victim of the change. Already there is in human terms far too little economic aid, and despite their professions of good intentions at the Rio Summit and elsewhere, the budgets the advanced industrial countries devote to aid are minimal (see Table 11.1). To put the figures in perspective, the European Union (EU) uses two-thirds of its budget to subsidize European farmers through the Common Agricultural Policy (CAP) and spends only about 3 per cent of its budget on food aid.

Much excellent work is done, especially in emergency situations such as famine and earthquake, by NGOs such as Oxfam and Save the Children. But it is state action which is vital, the role of individuals and NGOs being minimal in comparison. For a variety of reasons government aid is, however, often of very little value for development purposes.

First of all, much of what is classified as aid consists of military aid. Not only does this have no value in promoting development in the target country (though it does, of course, have a significant political and economic role in sponsoring industrial concerns in the donor country), but it undermines

Table 11.1 *Countries receiving most overseas development aid, 1990*

Country	Aid ($m)	$ per capita
Egypt	5,604	107.60
Bangladesh	2,103	19.70
China	2,076	1.80
Indonesia	1,724	9.70
India	1,586	1.90
Israel	1,374	295.00
Philippines	1,277	20.80
Turkey	1,264	22.50
Tanzania	1,155	47.10
Pakistan	1,152	10.30
Kenya	1,000	41.40
Morocco	970	38.60
Mozambique	946	60.20
Jordan	891	282.50
Ethiopia	888	17.40
Zaire	823	22.10
Thailand	805	14.40
Sudan	792	31.50
Senegal	739	99.80
Ivory Coast	689	57.90

Source: World Bank (1992).

democratic freedoms and at worst has led to the most vicious abuses of human rights, such as the Indonesian colonization of East Timor.

Second, when development aid is given it is often on terms that undermine its ostensible objective. Specifically, it is often tied to bilateral trade, requiring the recipient to buy goods from the donor state. This is done both for economic reasons, since tying recipient purchases to donor products benefits the donor country's own manufacturing industries (i.e. it is in fact giving aid to itself, although there is still a transfer of goods and services to the recipient) and/or for political reasons, in that by making the recipient country a customer for its own products, it is in fact shaping the political and social development of the recipient country in a way that makes it complement its own interests.

CONCLUSION

No one in their senses would want to stop the development of the Third World; nor could anyone make a moral case for people elsewhere in the world being denied the material things that First World peoples take for granted. But the pattern of development that has been established over the years is not sustainable and has certain very obvious disadvantages. The problem of rapidly expanding populations has been met by encouraging uncontrolled and unplanned development. Those countries that have been successful in making the breakthrough into long-term growth have made industrialization a prime target and have invested heavily in education to provide a skilled workforce. Unfortunately, at the same time they have degraded the environment and made their societies overreliant on the continued expansion of production. Where plantation agriculture exists, and it is widespread, it has had serious effects on the capacity of a country to feed its own people. This mode of development, therefore, is not sustainable in its present form (Jackson 1990).

Foreign investment and the growth of transnational corporations are features of development in the Third World about which there is considerable controversy. To the proponents of the free market, they have been largely beneficial. To their critics, they have at least produced significant negative effects, and there is reason to suspect that both act to widen the gap between rich and poor countries, and between rich and poor in any one country.

12 Women and indigenous peoples

INTRODUCTION

The positions of women and indigenous peoples were established as key human rights issues for the World Conference on Human Rights (June 1993). Apart from moral and ethical questions concerning their rights as human beings, women and indigenous peoples each form a vital part of the development process, and their contributions to a sustainable form of development are integral. Environmental degradation is increased by inappropriate development, which is a consequence of poverty, and it then in turn increases the poverty from which it arises. It is most painfully experienced by the poorest elements of society. These usually include women, children and indigenous people.

WOMEN AND DEVELOPMENT

According to the old adage, women comprise half of the world's adult population, constitute one-third of the world's official labour force, perform two-thirds of all working hours, get one-third of world income and own 1 per cent of the world's property. Such inequitable distributions of work and benefits are obviously topics which social scientists would wish to probe. Essentially over the years approaches to the understanding of the situation of Third World women have reflected the changing perception of the development agenda.

The modernization approach quite simply ignored women. It was assumed that what benefited men also benefited 'their' women. Women were not recognized as constituting a distinct – and particularly disadvantaged – group.

The basic needs or anti-poverty approach to development in the early 1970s, expressed, for example, through UN Conferences on Food and Population held in 1974, for the first time drew attention to the fact that social policies, developmental or otherwise, have not been gender neutral. It was recognized that a disproportionate number of the world's poor are women and that, if considered with the dependent children for whom these poor women carry responsibility, they constitute the vast majority of the poorest people on earth. Hence their well-being is a primary ethical question for developmental schemes.

The effects of development on women and its corollary, the role of women in the development process, were therefore opened up to research and the UN declared 1975 International Women's Year, with a major conference held in Mexico City. The period 1976–85 was decreed the UN Decade for the Advancement of Women.

More radical approaches also stress that women are a separate issue on the development agenda, but they do so for functional as well as moral reasons. They argue either:

- that the involvement of women is vital for the efficiency of any developmental scheme; or
- that the empowerment of women is *the* motor force for development of any meaningful kind.

Empowerment, a concept deriving from the work of Brazilian educationalist Paulo Freire, means acquiring the awareness and the skills to take charge of one's own environment. This perspective, combining as it does elements from radical and Marxist feminist thought, often also takes on board other poor sections who suffered under colonialism, and who now continue to do so under a form of development perceived as distorted and exploitative both of people and of nature (Shiva 1988: 2).

WOMEN AND SOCIAL CHANGE

Women are disproportionately subject to the effects of social change. Modernization emphasizes capital accumulation. However, the move away from artisan production tends to disadvantage women, since as employees they are not in a position to accumulate meaningful amounts of capital, and if they are married women, their earnings essentially become the property of their husbands and contribute to his standing rather than their own. Industrializing makes them part of the labour force in a way that was not previously the case. The most conspicuous area in which this is true is in electronics and other skilled assembly work, where some 80–90 per cent are women. Women form the bulk of the labour force in the *maquiladoras* of Mexico and Central America (see e.g. Petersen 1992).

Such occupations, even at the very end of the twentieth century, however, are not typical. Some 90 per cent of the world's women still depend directly on the land for survival.

1. Women produce most of the food in developing countries, and 60–80 per cent in Africa South of the Sahara (SSA). They work longer hours and do heavier work than men. Ester Boserup popularized the view 'that African

agriculture exhibited a dualism based on gender: a cash crops sector in which *men* grow highly productive income-earning export crops, and a food crop sector in which *women* use traditional methods to produce food for their families to consume' (Boserup 1970/1989). This view has now been shown to be wrong, as it understates the involvement of women in the modern sector of the economy and ignores the fact that food crops are also grown as cash crops (Whitehead 1990: 55). But it still leaves women responsible for the bulk of food production. In China on marriage a woman ceases to be part of her birth family, symbolized by the physical removal of herself and her possessions to her husband's home, but she does not cease to work. In rural areas the planting and cultivation of wet rice is regarded as women's work and on any building site in China and Vietnam the bulk of the unskilled labour is provided by women.

2. Women are also responsible for overseeing the considerable additional contribution that children make to the domestic economy. Women and the children under their direction are usually exclusively responsible for domestic access to water.

3. Energy in the rural Third World is mainly biomass (fuelwood, crop residues and manure), which is collected by women and children. Biomass accounts for 75 per cent of fuel used in the Third World generally and 90 per cent of fuel consumed in SSA. Fuelwood collection is often blamed for deforestation. However, rural women traditionally use fallen dead wood. Fuelwood from cut trees is usually for commercial sale to urban areas. Burning dung is, of course, a contribution to agricultural underproduction, but not a very great one.

4. Women have well-developed skills in managing resources. They probably know more about sustainable development than men, as they live it more directly.

Unfortunately, the common factor in limiting the capacity of women to make their views felt and to share their skills is *lack of formal education*. There are estimated to be a billion adult illiterates in the world, of which 60 per cent are women. The education of women, their capacity to control their fertility, and their economic independence are not just concessions to a disadvantaged group. The Third World cannot afford sops. Women are functional parts of the process of development that the Third World cannot afford not to encourage. Women must play a fuller part in development in this generation and in future through their care and education of their children. Their lack of education damages their capacities as primary health carers and educators.

The reasons why women's productivity is so often underestimated are as follows:

• The assumption that they are less strong. This is not necessarily so, and in any case they usually work longer hours.

- The fact that domestic labour is not accorded its proper value. Domestic labour is still not counted in the calculation of GNP, although common sense suggests that it must account for a very high proportion of it in less developed countries.
- The fact that local economies are largely ignored in favour of urban and export markets, and that it is men who own the land on which cash crops are grown or who manage the factories in which women work.

Though women's roles are often marginal, not to say invisible, women, like men, are basic economic units. They are often wrongly perceived as dependants when in reality they are producers. Much of their time and energies have been squandered on the least productive domestic concerns, from which it should have been possible to begin liberating them.

They have not received support in their agricultural production in the form of loans, technology or training. They have not had a say in the decision-making which affects them. One result of this situation is that it is cash crops that benefit from irrigation schemes and not subsistence farming. This is a major contributory factor to the decline of food for local consumption in most Third World countries. The rural poverty of women has led to their out-migration as agricultural labourers on plantations, as export workers in entrepôt enclaves or as domestics at home or abroad. Policy-makers (who are usually male) often perceive women as burdens and do not take their needs on board. An exception is where women band together in organizations to run base communities. For example, in Brazil they have been able to overcome some of the misconceptions which govern official dealings with them, because their contribution as an organized group requires a political response from elected officials and civil servants.

Women's participation in development requires that they receive increased access to land, credit, skills, primary health care, water, sanitation and education. Amazonian women without mature sons lose their land because colonization agencies are reluctant to accept female-headed households as 'families' (Bunker 1985). There is, of course, also an ethical question as well as practical ones. It must be clear that, if development is a right, equal opportunities to achieve development should be available to all nations and also to all individuals (see also Chapter 11 on development). Without full participation in the development process, as recommended by the Brundtland Report, there cannot be the peace and stability in which development can occur.

SOME EXAMPLES OF THE POSITION OF WOMEN

Colonialism in some places distorted the traditional role of women. In pre-colonial West African societies, women were important in agricultural production, crafts and marketing. Colonialism brought cash crops grown for external markets. Women's labour remained important, but the land was owned by men who received the profits from it. At the same time, imports from mass production in Europe and North America hit craft production. There were benefits, such as education, but in Muslim areas women were often excluded from the benefits colonialism brought, and cultural norms have been powerful enough to resist legal changes for the benefit of women. This was the case, for example, when after the end of the colonial period female circumcision was officially banned in Sierra Leone by the government of Milton Margai.

In China male dominance continues in some key urban aspects, especially in heavy industry, skilled trades, management and secondary education. It is largely unquestioned in traditional rural areas where women's activities are generally restricted to the household and that household is that of the husband's family anyway. Despite legal rights, the real situation is that Chinese women do not have property, and lack the resources for independence. The 1982 census showed that 70 per cent of China's 200 million illiterates were female. During the 1980s high unemployment rates gave employers more choice in selecting workers, and women were perceived as more expensive owing to the requirement to provide for child care, maternity leave and earlier retirement. Employers were only required to make the rather cheaper provision of accommodation to male employees.

In the 'Asian Tigers' women make up the bulk of the workforce in the so-called Economic Processing Zones (EPZs):

> The EPZ economy is based on employing cheap labour for the assembly of high-volume standardised components. Such work is seen as particularly suited to women. Since the 1960s young women have been employed in EPZ factories on a large scale. They comprise the majority of child labour, often spending most of their teenage years in sweatshops making plastic toys or garments. By the 1970s they had moved on the more sophisticated assembly lines – particularly electronics and pharmaceuticals. By 1982, of the 62,617 workers employed in EPZs in Taiwan 85 per cent were women. (*New Internationalist*, 263, January 1995)

Such workers are recruited in the countryside under false promises, often, that they will gain valuable education as well as make a useful contribution to the marginal existence of the family group. While in work they live in dormitories under strict control and supervision. However, safety at work is not much of a consideration – in South Korea, for example, 10 or 12 hours' work a day is still normal, and the country has one of the highest rates of industrial accidents in the world. If recession comes, the women workers are often unaware of any rights they may possess under employment legislation and can be speedily laid off.

CHILD-REARING/CARING

Half a million women still die in childbirth each year, but African women are 200 times as likely to die from pregnancy-related causes as women in industrialized countries, where perinatal mortality is now very low owing to professional attendants, good hospital resources and advanced medical techniques. Even within the Third World there are very considerable differences in the standard causes of death. The main avoidable risk is specific to women and is *pregnancy*. In the Third World, pregnancy still carries a significant hazard of potentially fatal infection for the mother. WHO figures show that of 500,000 maternal deaths each year (deaths during or within 42 days of pregnancy from causes specific to the pregnancy), only 3,000 now occur in the industrialized countries. As with other diseases, the prevalence of neonatal diseases is now greater in the Third World than it was a century ago. The avoidance of pregnancy through birth control is therefore an important factor in enabling women to live longer, while by reducing the burdens of looking after large families, it has important additional social benefits, especially for the children of the smaller families.

In China the establishment of the Republic in 1911 meant the end of the appalling abuse of foot-binding, which was, in any case, a Manchurian custom introduced by the Ching Dynasty. After 1949 equality was a prime goal of the new Communist regime and many improvements were made in the position of women, such as the introduction of a 48-hour week, maternity leave and child care. However, after Mao Zedong's death in 1976, there was a tendency for pragmatic economic goals to push out ideological political goals. Officially the one-child policy stresses child health, good parenting and care for the elderly. The policy has been very successful in urban areas where the vast majority of children under 12 are the only children of their families. However, in rural areas where the first child is female there are fears of high levels of female infanticide, and a second or even third child may be permitted ostensibly to help provide labour on the homestead. This may be seen as official government endorsement of traditional assumptions of male superiority. In urban areas a second child may lead to loss of benefits, including the advantage of nursery care for the first child. A subsequent illegal child may mean compulsory sterilization for the woman, not for the man.

Mahatma Gandhi said that to understand India one should study its villages and its women. The respect Gandhi accorded Indian women is not necessarily echoed in Indian society as a whole. Since 1911 there has been a steady decline in the ratio of women to men, with the steepest fall in the decade 1961–71. There are now 929 women to every 1,000 men (in the UK, by comparison, the ratio is 1,060 : 1,000).

In India the killing of baby girls was once associated mainly with isolated rural communities. In Rajasthan female infanticide was a military custom. Only boys could become warriors, so girls were often killed. 'Devdasis' was the offering to God of female children as a ritual sacrifice, usually to get a son. Now that India is at peace the practice should be dying out, but it is actually spreading. Female infanticide was outlawed in India more than a century ago by the British Raj, but in India, as elsewhere, laws do not necessarily change social customs, and in recent years there have been reports of the continuance of the practice in southern India, where it is usually carried out by the grandmother. The local authorities often collude in the slaughter of baby girls. It is impossible not to notice that anything up to four out of ten baby girls are being killed soon after birth; it shows in the sex ratio of the children in the villages.

Women go on child-bearing in the hope of having a son who will bring a dowry to the family, look after his parents in their old age, preserve the family name, keep the family property intact, attend to his parents' funeral rites and light their funeral pyre. Cradle schemes now exist so that 'unwanted' girl babies may be deposited and cared for, but they are not really unwanted in this sense, and fatalism about death means that many mothers prefer to kill their girl babies and such schemes have few takers. Girls who are not killed at birth sometimes die of neglect while their brothers thrive – it is often boys who are taken to hospital when ill; girls are in some areas considered to be very lucky if they receive any medical treatment at all. Girls suffer a 30–60 per cent higher rate of mortality simply because they receive medical treatment less often when sick.

Meanwhile, modern technology has offered an alternative. Millions of women in India are now using ultrasonic scans to decide on terminations. The Indian government has recently prohibited the selective use of scans to determine the sex of babies, but in the nature of things it may be difficult to prove. There is no shortage of ultra-sound equipment, even though India suffers a huge deficit in medical technology. More than one million female foetuses are destroyed after scans in India each year. Sex determination has become big business, and science has become a tool of a traditional prejudice. Scientists have made it easier not to give birth to girls, and it has therefore also become less acceptable to do so. There is a shortage of some 25 million women in India already, and the use of selective abortion will increase this imbalance – the sex ratio of newborn children is now 100 girls : 116 boys. Sex determination tests have been banned in one state but to little effect; there are proposals to extend this ban, but it will not work without a change in attitudes.

The main problem is the rising cost of dowries, or rather the high costs of 'gifts' on marriage now that dowries are no longer legal, since there is now much less restraint on the parties involved. Girls are a very expensive liability for their parents, and to have even one in a family can mean financial ruin in the future. In Tamil Nadu, where expensive rituals accompany the growing-up of girls, a 'dowry' can cost as much as 15 years' income and the daughter of parents who cannot pay may be outcaste. Dowries were made illegal 30 years ago and were in any case largely confined to the upper castes, but the institution has now spread to the poorest villages. With the demonstration effect of western television programmes, families are making demands for still bigger dowries to meet their aspirations to western luxuries. Where marriages are arranged, dowries often represent a simple transfer of capital from one family to another. The dowry may be used as an on-going form of blackmail, and daughters may be returned unwanted to their parents when their husbands' further financial demands are not met. Worst of all, some women are extremely cruelly treated for not bringing larger dowries, or to extort more money from their families. The extreme case is bride-burning, where the bride is set on fire with paraffin, to simulate an accidental fire in the cooking area. Officially bride-burning claimed 2,449 women's lives in 1991, but the real figures are undoubtedly much higher (*Assignment*, 'Let Her Die', BBC Television, 1993).

Deliberate cruelty of this kind is, of course, relatively rare. Much more common is the impact of cultural norms promoting inequality. These norms are sustained as much by the women who are disadvantaged by them, as by the men who might be perceived as benefiting. It is women who struggle to feed their families, even actually eating afterwards in many cultures. As it is women who generally organize food in any household, it seems natural to them to feed their families first and more adequately than they do themselves. Seventy per cent of pregnant women suffer anaemia caused by malnutrition. This is not really surprising, as even early studies (e.g. Sinha 1976: 13) show the extent of inequality – in Hyderabad the calorie intake for pregnant and lactating women was only 1,400 per day against the average Indian requirement of 2,200 calories per day.

IMPACT OF SAPs ON WOMEN

In the 1980s Structural Adjustment Packages (SAPs) were oriented to markets and in particular to the removal of what were considered to be distortions in them. This had a detrimental effect on the standing of women. Women were largely excluded from national markets, and the food subsidies and other support for the poorest sectors from which they might hope to benefit were precisely the 'distortions' to development identified by the market liberal approach to development, and their removal was the main target of such adjustments. In addition, when SAPs require cuts in Third World expenditure, (male) vested interests and (male) national pride ensure that disproportionately large military budgets are protected. In turn, since protection for military personnel is built into those budgets, social services are hit hardest. There are a few exceptions, such as Uruguay, but in general a reluctance to cut social services is seen by international lending agencies as unwillingness to comply with the terms of loans, and can lead to serious consequences for the credit-rating of the governments that try to evade these requirements.

Women are an 'adjustment variable' on whom SAPs impact particularly hard. The problem is that austerity measures intensify as they pass down social structures. The semi-autonomous and wholly privately funded UN agency with responsibility for the children of the world, the UN International Children's Emergency Fund (UNICEF), estimates that a 2–3 per cent decline in national income in developing countries hits the poorest sections to the tune of 10–15 per cent. At the same time SAPs hit the public sector, and women are disproportionately likely to be employed as teachers, nurses, etc. This was especially true of Nigeria in the 1980s. In Nigeria women had moved into a rapidly expanding public sector during the petroleum bonanza of the late 1960s and the early 1970s. When negotiations with the IMF broke down, a World Bank-backed indigenous SAP was devised. This aimed, among other things, to reduce the public sector, and the immediate result was the loss of many of these new public-sector jobs.

SAPs also raise food costs. Between 1980 and 1983, 76 per cent of IMF-supported programmes included increased indirect taxation, 46 per cent increased tariffs and only 13 per cent increases in direct personal or corporation taxes, the least regressive of the alternatives available.

SAPs have diverted women from their families to marginal economic activities, and thus have contributed to social problems such as child abandonment and delinquency, as in Brazil. Both directly and indirectly, therefore, they have lowered standards of health care and nutrition for mothers and children, causing lower birth weights, poor child health and lower intelligence, building up problems for the future. In Chile child mortality was increased by cutbacks in the child-feeding programme in 1983, although these have since been reversed. And the long-term effects are also significant: SAPs hit education budgets and girls' secondary education is generally seen as the area most easily sacrificed. The sad thing is that it would not cost much to protect the living standards of the poorest sectors during SAPs. They have so little to protect, but they do not make the decisions.

Because of the impact of SAPs on most disadvantaged groups, UNICEF has recommended changes: more medium-term financial support and less shock, the encouragement of policies that do not hit vulnerable groups, sectoral policies confining adjustment to the productive sectors, policies to enhance efficiency and equity of the social sector, compensatory programmes and the monitoring of living standards. The World Bank is now well aware of the impact of SAPs on women and other vulnerable groups. In April 1987 it issued *Protecting the Poor during Periods of Adjustment*, but argued for compensatory measures to be added on rather than changing the basic nature of SAPs.

INDIGENOUS PEOPLES

In 1992 the United Nations responded to the growing indigenous movement by establishing the Working Group on Indigenous Populations and declaring 1993 the International Year of Indigenous People. The end of that year saw the UN launch the Decade of the World's Indigenous People.

It is hard to define indigenous peoples as such, since from earliest times human beings have been moving about the planet. However, where such groups are clearly recognized to exist, they have the following characterisitics:

• They tend to have a timeless relationship with their lands.
• They are descendants of the original inhabitants of the specific lands they relate to, although many will not now be living on their original land.
• They share a common culture, language and ancestry.

Perhaps the simplest definition would suggest that indigenous peoples exist wherever traditional, sustainable lifestyles survive in continued opposition to the encroaching power of the modern, internationalized state. It is precisely this confrontation that brings indigenous peoples to the attention of the outside world. In extreme cases, such as the rising in the southern Mexican state of Chiapas in 1994, it takes the form of physical conflict.

Indigenous people probably comprise some 4 per cent of the world's population, an estimated 300 million people in 70 countries, but they are very loosely defined and there is much variety. On the broadest definitions, in the Americas Amerindians still comprise some 70 per cent of the population of Bolivia, 45 per cent in Peru, 40 per cent in Ecuador, 30 per cent in Mexico. However, even where, as in Guatemala, they are substantially in a majority, they are noticeably worse off than the rest of the population. In Guatemala, Indian life expectancy is 11 years less than for Ladinos (people of part-European descent). Even in Paraguay the infant mortality rate in Guaraní communities is as high as 50, compared with 10 per thousand among Criollos and Mestizos (people of whole or part European descent).

The Yanomami or Yequana, who live in southern Venezuela/northern Brazil, are hunter-gatherers who move every four years to build a new maloca or communal house, thus opening up new family plots for cultivation and avoiding soil degradation. The Demini Health Project, which has been jointly funded by the British government and Oxfam since late 1970s, has helped contain malaria in the region. But in recent years there have been increasing epidemics among the Yanomami owing to the influx of Brazilian *garimpeiros* (gold prospectors) into their tribal areas. Hence it is hoped that what remains a short-term emergency programme at present will become a Primary Environmental Care Programme (PEC) – PECs help indigenous people to meet their developmental needs while caring for the local environment. The British/Oxfam involvement led to Brazilian government demarcation of Yanomami tribal areas and the granting of secure title to nearly 100,000 square kilometres of ancestral lands in May 1992, when press attention was at its height with the approach of the Rio Summit. However, although the invasion of the *garimpeiros* is threatening the health and security of the Yanomami as well as that of their environment, the Brazilian government has not taken the measures necessary to halt this influx and prevent the devastation in the long-term. Indeed it is doubtful whether it has the ability to enforce its will over such a vast and remote area.

As noted above, the entry of Mexico into the North American Free Trade Agreement (NAFTA) on 1 January 1994 was accompanied by an unwelcome reminder of Mexico's indigenous past, an uprising by the self-styled Zapatista National Liberation Army (EZLN) in the state of Chiapas. Chiapas, in the extreme south of Mexico on the border with Guatemala beyond the Isthmus of Tehuantepec, is Mexico's poorest state, as was noted by the UN *Human Development Report* (United Nations Development Programme 1994). It has an infant mortality rate of 94 per thousand. Sixty per cent of its population is living below the official poverty line, and half the population has no access either to drinking water or to electricity.

The problems of Chiapas stem from two causes: existing inequality and the impact of recent programmes for rapid development. The land reforms of President Lázaro Cárdenas in the 1930s might have had some impact on the traditional pattern of land tenure, but the quasi-feudal oligarchy resisted successfully, aided by the local bishop. Since then peasants of Mayan descent who have sought title to their lands have been evicted and have faced violence, disappearances and killings at the hands of the local bosses or their *pistoleros* (strong-arm men). Many have been displaced and some 200,000 landless families now work on the coffee and cocoa plantations. In the 1960s the state was linked for the first time to the rest of the country by good roads (Vogt 1969). Settlers began to pour into the state in a bid for land colonization, and tensions rose. The PRI government has installed corrupt generals to control the province and built an enormous army base in the town of San Cristóbal. Much development funding was given to Chiapas, but the oligarchy and the new settlers benefited and the former inhabitants were still deprived.

The Papuan people of Irian Jaya, the eastern province of Indonesia, are being forced to use violence to defend their tribal identities. They confront a well-equipped army only as a simple people with home-made weapons. Their land is the western half of the island of New Guinea (cf. Rappaport 1968), seized in 1963 by Indonesia, against the wishes of the native Papuans, who are seen as primitives in Jakarta. Their lifestyles are being marginalized by imported Javanese who it is hoped will speed up the process of change. The case of East Timor, seized by Indonesia after the collapse of the Portuguese Empire in 1975, is similar.

Malaysia exemplifies many of the various pressures threatening indigenous peoples. Paul Harrison cites the case of the Semai of Musoh, whose population density is already beyond what is sustainable by hunter-gathering alone. Despite this, they still operate a relatively ecofriendly lifestyle, supplementing hunting and gathering with the keeping of chickens and goats. Traditionally, the Semai make use of slash-and-burn techniques to grow hill rice and cassava and then shrub crops. The land is then left for 10–20 years before being brought back into cultivation. 'Such forest peoples tread lightly on the earth. They impoverish no soils, destroy no ecosystems. Their survival does not demand the destruction of any other species' (Harrison 1992: 3). But this delicate balance is threatened now. The tribal lands are already surrounded by encroaching Malay and Chinese agriculture. Meanwhile the Semai naturally want the trappings of modern life, such as bicycles and radios, and to buy them they take (or allow others to take) more from the forest than they need. Semai children supply butterflies for sale in the tourist shops of the nearby Cameron Highlands. Their parents are beginning market gardens to supply urban Malaysia, and logging is starting up too (Harrison 1992: 1–6).

The Malaysian Minister of Finance, Anwar Ibrahim, has been quite blunt about his attitude towards indigenous peoples: 'the best course for indigenous peoples is to accelerate their integration into the global society'. However, the Penan hunter-gatherer tribespeople of the Sarawak rainforest of East Malaysia, who shoot monkeys and birds with blow-pipes, do not agree. They have sought to stop foreign logging companies ending their way of life through their policy of 'clear-felling' the mountain forest, and have met violence and tear gas for their trouble. Needless to say they were not invited to take part in the Malaysian government's International Seminar on Indigenous Peoples.

A new dam project would flood some 73,000 hectares of this prime forest and displace 6,000 tribal people, who are expected to be relocated to the oil palm plantations in other parts of Sarawak. The local community are not expected to benefit from the electricity produced by the dam, which is expected to be fed 600 km under the sea to West (Peninsular) Malaysia.

In Tripura in India, secessionist feeling grew as Bengali settlers fleeing the anti-secessionist violence of the Bangladeshi security forces, who drove them from their homes in the Chittagong Hills, were encouraged to settle in tribal areas to the detriment of the identity and culture of the tribal peoples.

In 1979 it was ruled that resettlement and rehabilitation of the 'tribals' displaced by the Narmada River project must keep in step with the other two aspects: environmental protection and construction. It has not done so and the scheme is being delayed, but for the most part the problem of tribals has been minimized by the denial of title to lands occupied for centuries to many of the displaced indigenous people. Protesting tribals have been fired on by police.

Indigenous people's calls for rights are often interpreted as secessionist movements and therefore resisted. Also indigenous people often occupy the most resource-rich regions, and therefore there is intense outside interest in exploitation of their homelands. However, they are also often the world's most fragile environments.

The preservation of indigenous peoples with their way of life intact presents the rest of the world with a moral dilemma. Not all the traditional aspects are good, and some elements of modernity, such as an expanded trade and protection against imported diseases, may be vital to preserve the traditional. Perhaps the only way forward is some blending together of past and present. The demonstration effect will in any case ensure that indigenous peoples (or at least the youngsters) will crave the trappings of development: the radios, television sets, CD players, bicycles, cars, etc. Those who enjoy such things, or who have experienced them and rejected them, are hardly in a position to argue that such experience should not in principle be available to all who want it. It may be possible to feed that demand in some way that minimizes damage to local tradition and cultures, as well as to sensitive environments. While rejecting US influence, the Peruvian government found it expedient to allow the sale of locally bottled 'Inca Cola'.

13 Environment and development

INTRODUCTION

All our basic needs have sources in the natural world. The natural world, however, is finite. Human beings are, therefore, now faced with a two-pronged crisis. On the one hand, in the near future more and more resources that we now take for granted are going to start to run out. On the other, our environment is becoming increasingly contaminated by the waste we produce.

The combined pressures of the increasing awareness of coming scarcity and the build-up of toxicity have increased the salience of the environment as an issue. Even more, it has given rise to *ecopolitics*, defined by Guimaraes (1991) as 'the study of political systems from an ecological perspective'. Social, cultural and political understanding is as important as natural science when considering ecosystems and their capacities.

ENVIRONMENTAL DEGRADATION

The late 1980s saw the change from the environment as a local and regional issue to a global one (Tolba 1988; Hurrell and Kingsbury 1992). Initially this formed part of the globalization of security concerns. Security had historically always been defined primarily in military terms.

Jessica Tuchman Matthews (1993) says: 'Global environmental trends shift the balance [of power] . . . No more basic threat to national security exists.' However, although interest coalitions straddle the North–South divide on some environmental issues, the politics of the environment still mainly reflects a North versus South division. It is, sadly, not the spectacle of human misery as much as potential threats to global stability consequent on resource scarcity which invokes the concern of the First World. At the same time, national economic advantage gets in the way of a coherent world policy. Agreements tend to be compromises between vested interests. They are not intended to save the world and they will not do so.

The 1972 Stockholm Intergovernmental Conference on the Human Environment established that the problems of the environment were urgent, and sought to identify those which were global problems. The work of the conference resulted in two documents: the Stockholm Declaration of basic environmental principles that should govern policy; and a detailed Action Plan. This in turn led to the creation of the United Nations Environment Programme (UNEP), whose director, Maurice F. Strong of Canada, who had been Secretary-General of the Stockholm Conference, was in due course to become Secretary-General of the United Nations Conference on Environment and Development (UNCED), which met at Rio de Janeiro in 1992.

The message that the environment was too big and too important to be dealt with by national governments was unwelcome to many of those governments, and in the ten years that followed the majority of them were very slow to accept that it had any relevance. However, some progress was made. In 1972 the Convention on International Trade in Endangered Species of Wild Fauna and Flora (CITES) was concluded and a World Heritage Convention was held. But a potential setback to the cause of the environment came in 1974 with the adoption by the General Assembly of the otherwise welcome Charter of Economic Rights and Duties of States (CERDS). It laid heavy emphasis on the 'rights' of states to development, but lacked any reference to environmental criteria. This was paralleled in the late 1970s and early 1980s by increased emphasis on free market 'solutions' in the advanced industrialized countries, accompanied by their abdication of responsibility for the outcomes of economic processes. At this stage the trend was away from international consensus.

The crucial turning-point came in 1983 when the Secretary-General of the UN asked the Prime Minister of Norway, Gro Harlem Brundtland, to form a commission to investigate how a planet with a rapidly accelerating population growth could continue to meet basic needs. The Brundtland Commission (properly the World Commission on Environment and Development) was charged with formulating realistic proposals linking development issues to the care and conservation of the environment, and raising the level of public awareness of the issues involved. With the publication in 1987 of its report, *Our Common Future*, the concept of 'sustainable development' became central to future thinking. It was the realization of the extent to which matters had worsened since 1973 that was to lead directly to the Earth Summit.

The biggest shock to world public opinion had come from the discovery of the 'ozone hole' over Antarctica, which led in 1987 to the conclusion of the Montreal Protocol to the Vienna Convention on the Protection of the Ozone Layer, with the aim of regulating the use and release of ozone-depleting substances such as chlorofluorocarbons (CFCs) and halons. The belated realization both that ozone depletion was accelerating, and that it was also taking place, though at a slower rate, in the Arctic, where it posed a much greater threat to major concentrations of the world's population, led to urgent measures to extend the Montreal Protocol. As a result, the problem of the ozone layer was not directly addressed at Rio, though it was very much a matter of concern to delegates from the Southern Hemisphere.

Many other developments, however, did contribute to the agenda for the Earth Summit. In 1987 UNEP called attention to the alarming rate of extinction of species. It was estimated that, if the current rate of extinction continued, up to one-third of all species could be lost for good within 40 years. The international nature of the trade that was leading to extinction called for an international convention on biological diversity (*biodiversity*), and in 1988 the General Assembly established an *ad hoc* working group on biodiversity. In 1990 the Committee of Experts became the Intergovernmental Negotiating Committee (INC) on Biological Diversity.

In 1988 the Intergovernmental Panel on Climate Change (IPCC), which had been set up by the World Meteorological Association and UNEP, reported that if nothing was done to arrest the rising level of 'greenhouse gases' in the atmosphere, the global mean temperature would continue to rise by about 0.3°C per decade. A global temperature rise of one degree Celsius by 2025 would place serious strains on the capacity of agriculture to modify its procedures, and would risk flooding, by the melting of the polar icecaps, of low-lying areas and small islands. At the Second World Climate Conference General Assembly in 1990, 137 countries called for negotiations for a framework convention on climate change, and by Resolution 43/53 the General Assembly established an Intergovernmental Negotiating Committee (INC) on Climate Change to prepare a draft.

Both climate change and biodiversity were linked to a third major area of concern, the accelerating rate of destruction of forests. Forests act both as 'carbon sinks', returning to the earth the carbon dioxide liberated by the burning of fossil fuels and so acting naturally to arrest global warming, and as a rich habitat for a diversity of species. Their destruction, on the other hand, releases significant additional volumes of carbon dioxide. In addition, their sustainable management could in time prove to be of immense and increasing value to the rising populations of the developing states. Sadly, their governments have been unable or unwilling to act to prevent their hasty destruction for short-term gain or ground clearance. In the early 1980s it was estimated that some 27–40 million hectares were being lost annually; by the late 1980s this figure had doubled.

Several other areas of concern were side-tracked along the way. Notably, the poorer African states of the Sahel had been calling for global action on desertification. There was no doubt about its importance to Africa: television had beamed pictures of starving children in Ethiopia, Sudan and Somalia on to TV screens throughout the developed world. What was at issue was its urgency as a global question. The UN Plan of Action to Combat Desertification (PACD), instituted by UNEP and approved by the General Assembly in 1977, had never been effectively implemented, largely because of the lack of effective resources. However, reluctance to support it had recently been reinforced by new satellite pictures which proved conclusively that the general advance of deserts, though widely accepted, was a myth (Pearce 1992).

SUSTAINABLE DEVELOPMENT

The suggestion that there is a choice between environment or development is, like many political arguments, a false alternative. It is no longer possible (if it ever was) to have one without the other. The world is a closed system and everything affects everything else. In short, what is needed is *sustainable development*.

The Brundtland Report defined sustainable development as: 'development that meets the needs of the present without compromising the ability of future generations to meet their own needs' (WCED 1987: 43). Sustainable development does not use non-renewable resources faster than substitutes can be found, or renewable resources faster than they can be replaced; nor does it emit pollutants faster than natural processes can render them harmless.

It was the World Commission which first popularized the term sustainable development. They defined it in terms of two criteria: intra- and intergenerational equity. The next generation must be left a stock of quality assets, and not simply left to scrabble among the scraps. It was hardly surprising, given the numerical majority of the Third World states in the UN, that when the World Commission was established, with commissioners from 21 countries, most of them were from the Third World. In the words of Gro Harlem Brundtland: 'the "environment" is where we all live; and "development" is what we all do in attempting to improve our lot within that abode' (WCED 1987: xi).

At the moment, however, unbalanced development is a major cause of the destruction of the environment. The poor can hardly be blamed for exploiting their environment in a way that destroys its long-term potential, when the rich, including transnational corporations, are doing the same thing on a much more massive and destructive scale. Deteriorating terms of trade and the burden of debt on the Third World states increase pressure for exploitation by making short-term returns the most urgent consideration. The implication is that, in any plan for sustainable development, the future development needs of the South must be allowed for. Development cannot be sacrificed for environment any more than the other way round. The North–South gap cannot be perpetuated if the world is to remain stable. Therefore, sustainable development must meet the economic, social and environmental needs of all the world's peoples.

Brundtland's call for sustainable development is now an article of faith in the First World, but too often it has been seen as open to a much more limited interpretation, that of growth as usual, but slower. The Brundtland Report itself is a compromise. It is weak on the subject of population growth and does not really suggest a solution to the problem of rich-world resource consumption. Moreover, the depreciation of natural resources is not taken into account in calculating GNP. Economists have already been able to demonstrate 'the physical dependency of economic activity on the sustainability of crucial natural-resource systems and ecological functions, and to indicate the economic costs, or trade-offs, resulting from the failure to preserve sustainability and environmental quality' (Barbier 1989: xiv). If new measures were to be devised, it would be easier to see where sustainability was attainable and where not.

Following the Earth Summit in 1992, the UN created a new Commission on Sustainable Development in December 1992 to oversee implementation of its most radical document, Agenda 21, a plan for the twenty-first century. Introducing the proposal to the General Assembly, the Secretary-General, Boutros Boutros-Ghali, said in November 1992: 'The challenge after Rio is to maintain the momentum to sustainable development, to transform it into policies and practice, and to give it effective and coordinated organizational support . . . The UN must put its development objectives on a par with its political and social commitments.'

The Prince of Wales (1993) argues that, for sustainable development to be possible, the Third World needs the following:

- Developed countries to put their own houses in order on pollution.
- A reversal of the flow of funds from South to North.
- Different terms of trade that allow the South to sell more expensive goods to the North.
- The end of subsidies on agriculture etc. which make Third World products uncompetitive.
- Shared technology.

The technology that will most benefit the Third World (and the First) need not be complicated – in fact, the simpler and more trouble-free the better. The Prince, for example, recommends the use of photovoltaic cell technology as a non-polluting source of electricity to run 'the five great liberators of development':

- Cookers, which conserve fuelwood resources.
- Refrigerators, which keep food from spoiling.
- Water pumps, which avoid diseases associated with scarce surface water supplies and save so much female time.
- Radios, which provide cheap links to the outside world.
- Lights.

Michael Grubb (1992) says: 'With the continuing pressure of public opinion and steady penetration of environmental concerns into governmental thinking sustainable development is on the agenda to stay.' However, the inertia shown by First World governments since that time suggests that his optimism was rather premature.

GLOBAL WARMING

During the last glaciation, which ended only some 12,000 years ago, the average temperature was only 4°C lower than it is today. It is believed that an increase of 2.5–5.5°C on the present figure would raise sea levels initially only due to the expansion of water at higher temperatures. Although the temperature increase from global warming is expected to be greatest at the poles, the vast ice sheets of Antarctica will take a long while to melt.

The main 'greenhouse gases', the increased emissions of which cause this rise in temperature, are as follows:

- Carbon dioxide from burning fossil fuels and burning off the world's forest cover, especially in the tropics. Some 8.2 billion tons of CO_2 are being given off into the atmosphere each year. This is thought to contribute more than half of the global warming effect.
- Methane from the decomposition of organic matter. Rice (paddy) fields are a major source. So too are cattle, so the conversion of tropical rainforest to poor-quality ranching land, as in Costa Rica, has a double effect. Cattle, being ruminants, generate far more methane than goats, pigs or human beings. A great deal of methane is held in suspension in the permafrost and the sea bed, and is likely to be liberated if global warming takes place, thus accelerating the effect.
- Nitrous oxide, especially from motor vehicles but also from the overuse of chemical fertilizers.
- Low-level ozone mainly from reaction of sunlight and pollution from motor vehicles (high-level ozone molecules, in the outer atmosphere, form an essential shield against radiation and are therefore crucial to our survival).
- Chlorofluorocarbons (CFCs) synthesized by human endeavour. Although 'thoroughly' tested when discovered in the 1930s, nobody dreamt then that they would contribute disproportionately to the earth's warming, let alone that they would have damaging effects on the upper atmosphere.

In all, 157 governments signed the Climate Convention at Rio. Of these one country, the United States, is responsible for no less than 23 per cent of global CO_2 emissions. Other major contributors are the former USSR (19 per cent) and Europe (15 per cent). Their responses have been particularly disappointing, and it is not just political neurosis that has led some Third World countries to feel that they are being required to conserve their rainforest to allow the rich countries to go on burning fossil fuels (Leggett 1990).

The fact is that more than two-thirds of the global production of greenhouse gases is due to burning of fossil fuels. Only six countries agreed to cuts in their emissions of CO_2. The maximum was Germany's target of a reduction of 25–30 per cent by 2005, which will be partly met in any case by phasing out inefficient plant in the former East Germany. For the United States, similar cuts in CO_2 would mean cuts in GNP of the order of 3 per cent p.a. – less than the military budget. However, the United States did not agree to sign the Framework Convention until it had succeeded in weakening it to the point of meaninglessness. The Berlin Conference of 1995 showed that even the relatively weak targets established by the major states had not been achieved, except where (as in the case of the UK) economic recession had fortuitously cut back emissions.

As things stand, a sea level rise of only around 20 cm is expected to take place by 2030. However, floods and storms can be confidently expected to make matters worse. The Maldives, to take an extreme case, have no land more than 2 metres above sea level. A 1-metre rise in sea level would cost the Maldives $10,000 per person to defend against. Even their situation, however, could be better than that of the populations of the world's great river deltas in the South, which are home to and rich food production areas for millions of people in the Third World. They will not have the means to defend their land against even small rises. Some 95 per cent of Bangladesh is already at risk from flooding. Monsoon shifts may be catastrophic for it as for some other tropical areas, although they are unlikely to experience much temperature increase.

An awkward problem is that environmental degradation will not affect all countries equally. Global warming will actually benefit some in the short term, since rainfall increases will not be uniform. Climatic zonal shift will be devastating for many animal and plant species owing to the lag between climatic change and species evolution. Even the most conservative estimates of the likely effects of global warming imply a rate of change that would be at the limits of what species have hitherto found it possible to accept.

FOREST

In 1950 just over 100 million hectares of forest had been cleared. By 1975 this had more than doubled. Between 1950 and 1975, 120 million hectares of tropical forest were destroyed in South and South-East Asia alone. In India 1.3 million hectares are lost each year to commercial plantations, river valley and mining projects. Each year 12–20 million hectares disappear, and losses sustained at this level would mean total destruction of the rainforest well before 2050. Globally ten trees are cut down for every one planted.

Central America and Amazonia are losing more than 2.5 million hectares of forest each year to cattle-ranching (even without small-scale slash and burn which may clear an even greater area). The fact that Brazil is the largest Third World debtor and one of the fastest-growing economies in the world has been a dangerous combination for its rainforest (Guimarães 1991; Hall 1991).

Successive Brazilian governments have not sought to protect Brazil's forests. They have been much more concerned with northern markets – the Amazon has been seen as a huge resource available to large-scale enterprise, and extraction has accelerated. It has also been viewed as somewhere to relocate millions of displaced people, who then slash and burn the forest to gain two or three years of crops. Sadly the red laterite soils of southern Brazil, northern Argentina, Paraguay and West Africa, on which some of richest forest resource grows, are very thin and particularly vulnerable. Once uncovered, they soon bake hard and, where not washed away into the rivers first, become impervious to rain. Soon the disappointed settlers begin the trek back to the big cities that they were heading for in the first place.

The loss of trees has the following results:

- Loss of soil nutrients.
- Loss of biodiversity – some 50 per cent of species live in the rainforest.
- Fuelwood shortages.
- Soil erosion and thus river silting, which results in flooding and droughts, and damage to dams, HEP installations, etc.

Deforestation and consequent soil damage add every year to the numbers of refugees on the move, for example, from Haiti. Its most dramatic consequence is drought. The moisture given off by forests actually helps precipitate rain clouds. Drought is not new to countries like Sudan and Ethiopia, but massive recurring famine in their newly treeless wastes is. Every year 12 million hectares of land become desert.

Forest is frequently the aspect of the environment most accessible to debt–equity swaps. The World Wide Fund for Nature buys up Third World debt, which is then paid to WWF in local currency and the funds used on local environmental schemes such as those in Ecuador. The activities of NGOs must, however, overcome nationalistic and selfish First World responses. For example, Japan protects its own rainforest while importing hardwoods from South-East Asia.

BIODIVERSITY

The problem of biological diversity (Wilson 1988) affects all of us on three levels:

- There are different types of ecosystem.
- There is a multitude of different species.
- There is a great deal of genetic variation of individuals within species.

With extinction running at between 1,000 and 10,000 times the 'natural' rate, species losses are estimated at somewhere around 50,000 a year. Certainly more than 100 species a day, or four per hour, are being lost for ever. There is no return from extinction – and ultimately that applies as much to human beings as to any other living creatures.

Though these are 'conservative' guesses, it is quite clear that extinction rates are not constant, but actually accelerating. The loss of between 2 and 8 per cent of currently existing species can be expected over the next 25 years. Much of what is lost in this time will never have been 'discovered' by human beings.

Biological diversity is not an optional extra but a matter of sheer self-interest. Biodiversity is an essential feature of the natural world, which enables species to respond to challenge. It is biodiversity, ironically enough, that enables the malaria parasite to survive the onslaught of the so-called wonder drugs. At the same time, the variety of the natural world offers us all sorts of medicinal and biochemical possibilities to combat disease. Quinine, still an effective drug against some kinds of malaria, was first introduced to Europeans by the Jesuits in the tropical rainforest of Paraguay.

For similar reasons, we need to conserve the wild relatives of major food crops, such as wheat or maize, in case, as happened with the potato in Europe in the years 1846–8, our cultivated varieties should suddenly succumb to an attack from a new pest or disease.

These varieties are to be found mainly in what is now the Third World. But biodiversity is big business for the transnational corporations based in the developed countries. At the Earth Summit, President Bush of the United States failed to sign the Convention on the Conservation of Biological Diversity (which President Clinton has since signed), arguing that there was no agreement on what biodiversity was or how its benefits should be shared. The United States took the view that anything enhanced by human endeavour should be patentable (and indeed the new GATT deal appears to make it so). The states of the South disagreed, believing that the countries where new discoveries are made have a right to the lion's share of the rewards of development. But though they have the biodiversity, many of them have neither the will nor the strength to conserve it, with the result that some at least of it will be lost to the whole world.

DEMOCRACY AND PARTICIPATION

The Brundtland Report rightly saw democracy and participation as integral parts of sustainable development. Without the active participation of every member of the community, sustainability cannot be achieved. Rio was a reminder that the environment cannot be safeguarded without development and justice for the South. The relationship between the three can be represented by a triangle, each influencing the other two (see Figure 13.1).

Democracy, often taken for granted in the industrialized countries, has in the Third World both a local and a global meaning.

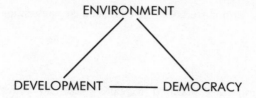

Figure 13.1 *Environment, development and democracy.*

The Mexican novelist, Carlos Fuentes, has pointed to the Zapatista insurrection in Chiapas as indicative of what could be expected without full participation and democratic rights (*The Guardian*, 15 January 1994). Base communities need incentives to improve their local environments. Security of land tenure gives the peasantry a stake in the long-term future.

On the global level, it is salutary to remember that the ratio of the per capita wealth of Europe to that of India in 1890 was about 2:1. Today it is 70:1. Hence global solutions to the environmental crisis have to be sought in a democratic atmosphere through global institutions. But the decision-making required is very complex, and at every stage it interacts with national and local politics.

THE EARTH SUMMIT

The Earth Summit or 'Eco 92', the United Nations Conference on Environment and Development (UNCED), held in Rio de Janeiro from 3 to 14 June 1992, was the largest high-level conference ever staged. Over 120 heads of state and heads of government took part in the 'summit segment' presided over personally for much of the time by President Fernando Collor de Mello, and some 20,000 people in all were involved in the preparation, planning and administration of the event. Its purpose was of appropriate importance: to concert measures to save the planet for future generations.

The publicity surrounding the Earth Summit aroused unrealistic expectations. Being an international conference, it could not and did not fulfil the hopes of those – probably the majority of the world public – who expected it to produce concrete results. It is hard for the general public not to believe that, given that many of the world's leaders are powerful separately, they will be even more powerful together. But the Earth Summit was not an 'Earth Senate'. Both the constitutional position of international decision-making and the way in which decisions are arrived at are significantly different from the way in which things are done in a national context. The very fact that the summit took place was itself significant. Beyond that, anything that could be achieved in the way of agreement was positive.

The similarities and differences can be seen at each stage of the decision-making process.

Initiation

The Earth Summit was planned to take place 20 years after the 1972 Stockholm Intergovernmental Conference on the Human Environment, at which many of the issues to be discussed had first been raised. One obvious difference was that it was much larger. There were as many national delegates at Rio (8,000) as there had been delegates and officials of all kinds in Stockholm. Another major difference lay in the formal representation at UNCED of non-governmental organizations (NGOs), who had their own offices in the sector of the complex dedicated to national representation.

It was back in 1989 that the UN General Assembly, in Resolution 44/228, had decided to convene UNCED, and urged the nations of the world to send representation at head of state or head of government level. In Resolution 45/211 of 21 December 1990 and Decision 46/468 of 13 April 1992, the General Assembly fixed the time and place of the conference. However, it is a well-established principle of international conferences that as little as possible must be left to chance. The idea of the world's senior statespersons turning up at Rio and having nothing to sign was not to be contemplated.

The European Community favoured the idea of an Earth Charter, a relatively brief statement of principles. Four in particular were suggested:

- The *precautionary principle* was that action to arrest the causes of environmental damage should not be delayed to wait for full scientific knowledge.
- The *principle of prior assessment* called, on the other hand, for full assessment of the risks before any activity likely significantly to damage the environment was allowed to proceed.
- The *principle that the polluter pays* focused on the need for individuals or companies polluting the environment to meet the public costs of cleaning it up.
- The *principle of non-discriminatory public participation* called for all people to be fully informed about potential interference with their environment and to have a right to have their views taken into account in the making of policy.

Between 1990 and 1992 four Preparatory Committees (Prepcoms) met to organize the business of the conference. The last of these, Prepcom IV, met in New York from 30 April to 8 May 1992. At this committee, a statement of general principles such as are outlined above was drawn up, and this formed the basis of what was to become the Rio Declaration. However, it had already become clear that the areas in which agreement had seemed most likely –

biodiversity, climate change and forestry – were each becoming deeply embroiled in controversy. Prepcom IV was unable to resolve some of the most serious disagreements, which were remitted to discussion in committee at UNCED. Finally, informal pre-conference consultations took place at Rio, under the chairmanship of Professor Celso Lafer, the Brazilian Foreign Minister, on the two days preceding the opening of the conference, to consider procedural and organizational matters (United Nations 1992c).

Decision

It is at the point of decision that the structure of international decision-making shows its most obvious weaknesses. In the international community, however, diverse and interpenetrated, the states remain for legal purposes 'sovereign'. This means that the only 'legislation' recognized by international law consists of treaties – international agreements freely entered into by the contracting powers. Hence the failure of any power to accede to a treaty seriously weakens its effectiveness as an instrument of global policy-making.

On some matters, states have little or no difficulty arriving at an agreement. The establishment of the Universal Postal Union, the first and arguably the most successful of all international organizations, shows that where the states concerned have everything to gain and little or nothing to lose from agreement, they have no difficulty arriving at a consensus.

Sadly, the only major treaty that has secured this degree of universal agreement is the Charter of the United Nations itself. But the Charter is not a philosophical treatise. It is the product of hard bargaining and national self-interest, and it is of course the very ambiguities of the Charter, which they can exploit in their own self-interest, that make it acceptable to both the former and would-be Great Powers. On the other hand, the United Nations today is very different in most respects from the nascent organization of Lake Success. Membership of the UN (unlike its predecessor, the League) is seen by the vast majority of its members, the new states, as a sign of full membership of the world community. For some it has been more than that, a guarantee of their territorial integrity and even their right to exist.

Decision-making within the UN system is therefore characterized by three factors:

- *The juridical equality of sovereign states*. Each state has to be treated exactly the same as each other state. Hence each delegate who speaks is thanked for his or her 'important' statement, even if, as in at least one case at Rio, the delegate concerned simply reads out a civil service brief on the history of environmental politics since 1972.
- *One state, one vote*. Decisions of all bodies other than the Security Council, where the five permanent members continue to exercise the

veto, reflect the desires and wishes of the developing South rather than
the developed North.

- *Voluntary consensus.* However wide the consensus, no decision (other
  than of the Security Council) is mandatory, unless the states concerned
  freely enter into a treaty obligation by signing and ratifying a
  convention or other agreement.

In practice, therefore, the politics of UNCED reflected the basic world
divisions between North and South. Certainly the two formal treaties, the
Framework Convention on Climate Change and the Convention on Biological
Diversity, though formally binding, lacked specific deadlines and so fell far
short of what might have been hoped.

Worse still, the United States signed the Framework Convention on Climate
Change only because it had first been watered down and all binding
commitments removed. Malaysia refused to sign it, asserting its right to
'exploit' (i.e. destroy) its remaining tropical rainforest if it chose. Hence there
was no agreement on a forestry convention which would check the
destruction in time to forestall irrevocable loss on a massive scale (it was
forecast that Malaysia would have successfully destroyed all the rainforest in
Sabah and Sarawak in just eight years, by the end of the century). Instead
there was a vague Statement on Forest Principles and a call for governments
to meet again to iron out the remaining difficulties.

Some optimism was generated by agreement on the Rio Declaration and on
the formidable list of further problems to be investigated, termed 'Agenda 21'.
Both represented a massive step forward in public awareness of the
underlying problems. Both, however, were above all the product of
compromise.

A formal declaration is a *sine qua non* of a major international conference.
The industrialized countries had favoured a brief form of words reaffirming
the Stockholm Declaration of 1972. However, the 'Group of 77' developing
countries (whose numbers had by 1992 reached 128) wanted a public
recognition of their specific concerns, especially

> their sovereign right to development, acknowledgment that the industrialized
> countries were primarily responsible for current environmental problems, and
> the need for new financing and technology to enable developing countries to
> avoid taking the same polluting route to development as did the developing [*sic*]
> countries. (United Nations 1992b)

Agenda 21 was described by UNCED's Secretary-General, Maurice Strong, as

> an action plan for the 1990s and well into the 21st Century, elaborating
> strategies and integrated programme measures to halt and reverse the effects of
> environmental degradation and to promote environmentally sound and sustain-

able development in all countries. This Agenda comprises some forty chapters and totals over 600 pages. It is the product of intensive negotiations among Governments on the basis of proposals prepared by the UNCED Secretariat, drawing on extensive inputs from relevant United Nations agencies and organizations, expert consultations, intergovernmental and non-governmental organizations, regional conferences and national reports, and the direction provided through four sessions of the Preparatory Committee of the Conference. (Strong 1992)

Role of governments

The central problem of UNCED was the conflict between North and South. This replicated on a global scale the conflict of interest between 'southern' political élites and the masses of their own countries.

The problem began at home. The massive security presence mounted to 'protect' the delegates looked impressive, and incidentally served to disguise the serious economic and social problems of Brazil itself. However, it could not disguise the fact that the opening of the conference coincided with the onset of a major political crisis. On 24 May, on the eve of the conference, President Collor had been accused of corruption, in an article in the news magazine *Veja*, by his brother Pedro. On 27 May, as the delegates were beginning to arrive, the Chamber of Deputies approved the establishment of a special commission of inquiry into the charges. By the end of 1992 he had been impeached and deposed by a Congress dominated by his political opponents.

Before this all happened, Collor had of course taken the opportunity to tell the world just how much Brazil (and by implication its President) was doing about the environment (Collor 1992). However, his own 'green' credentials were rather dubious. Although no longer official policy, the destruction of the Amazon rainforest at the hands of would-be settlers continued, while the *garimpeiros* (gold prospectors) invaded Indian lands, carrying with them disease and other problems. The spectacle of the burning of the rainforest diverted attention from some very uncomfortable arithmetic. It was the 23 per cent of the world's population that consumed 77 per cent of the world's energy resources that had created and was continuing to accelerate the problem of global warming. Left to themselves, the world's own ecosystems could have coped with emissions of greenhouse gases from the countries of the South. However, if these countries were, in the coming 30 years, to maintain a reasonable standard of living for their populations, it was all but certain that they would have to do so by burning fossil fuels. Even if they were to do so, however, they would not attain the limits recommended by the IPCC for the maintenance of climatic stability. Hence there was nothing that the developing countries could do, or not do, on their own to prevent the onset of catastrophic instability. Only by a substantial reduction in greenhouse emissions from the developed North could that risk be postponed and/or averted.

The plenary sessions

The ostensible purpose of an international conference is to confer. Hence the public face of the conference consists of a series of speeches, made in plenary session with observers present, televised to the outside world and reissued as press releases. These speeches serve at least three different purposes.

- To state (or restate) a government's official position as part of a negotiating process within the conference itself.
- To use the occasion to strengthen the political position of a government with its own public at home.
- To present the public face of the government concerned to the outside world.

The 19 plenary sessions of UNCED were divided into two segments. In the first segment, from 3 to 11 June, the world's environment ministers held the floor, together with representatives of UN agencies and NGOs. Heads of state and heads of government then arrived for the 'summit segment', which took place over two full days, 12 and 13 June, and involved 102 statements from heads of state or government or their personal representatives. During this time the two treaties that had been agreed and were open for formal signature were signed in a series of carefully timed individual ceremonies held in the hall outside the plenary session. A final meeting of heads of state or government was held in the late afternoon of 13 June, around an enormous circular table specially constructed for the purpose. The last day, 14 June, was given over to the formal closing ceremony.

At nine in the evening, as the afternoon plenary session came to an end and the other delegates drifted off to their dinners, the Main Committee began its sessions, which were not open to the public. Its chair was Ambassador Tommy Koh of Singapore, who had been elected by acclamation at the inaugural session on 3 June. The task of the committee was to resolve the fate of the many passages in the working documents which had been bracketed at the request of one or another national delegation. Bracketing a passage in this way meant that the wording was disputed, and some particularly controversial passages had two sets of brackets round them, indicating that some thought that the passage was too strong and others thought that it was too weak.

From 3 to 6 June, the Main Committee reviewed the texts of the Framework Convention on Climate Change and the Convention on Biological Diversity. These were discussed in parallel with the relevant sections of the text of Agenda 21. On 7 June, which was a Sunday, the whole of Rio, as usual, went to the beach. Over the next two days there were numerous consultations by the contact groups.

On 10 June, the committee met at 3 p.m. to a warning from the chair that the following day was the final deadline for the completion of its work. Asking his colleagues to refrain from extensive debate, Ambassador Koh said: 'If we continue to bargain here, the whole conference is in jeopardy. We must not let this conference fail' (*Earth Summit Bulletin*, 2 (9), Thursday, 11 June 1992). Then, in a marathon session that resumed at 8 p.m., lasted all night and broke up just before six in the morning of 11 June, the Main Committee concluded its discussions. In this session, delegates approved the text of the Rio Declaration in its final form, to be signed by political leaders later in the week, after references to 'people under occupation' had been deleted from Agenda 21 to satisfy the USA and Israel. They reviewed all 40 chapters of Agenda 21 and sent it forward with four major areas of dispute unresolved, all relating to finance: the date by which developed countries should renew their commitment to contribute 0.7 per cent of GNP for development; whether or not the Global Environment Facility of the World Bank (GEF) funds should be disbursed 'without imposing conditionality'; the governance criteria of the GEF; and the extent to which the IDA, the funding mechanism used for the poorest countries, should be replenished. Ambassador Ricúpero of Brazil was entrusted with the responsibility of co-ordinating ministerial discussions on these outstanding points.

Agreement on the Declaration on Forest Principles, however, proved impossible, the 8 preamble points and 17 principles having attracted 11 sets of brackets. This was remitted to ministerial-level consultations under the co-ordination of Klaus Töpfer, German Federal Minister for the Environment, Nature Conservation and Nuclear Safety.

'Applause marked the end of the all-night meeting as dawn broke over Rio Centro [*sic*]', wrote Martin Khor. 'The Main Committee's work is finished, the diplomats now take a back seat, and the political leaders are taking over from today' (Khor 1992).

The summit segment

By prior agreement in the summit segment, speakers were limited to seven minutes, and to save time, they were not seated on the platform in advance, as would normally have been the case.

On the first day, special attention focused on the appearance of the President of the United States, George Bush, who was scheduled to speak immediately after lunch, at 3 p.m. However, as so often in the past, President Castro of Cuba stole the show in the morning. Though outwardly a hang-over from the past, wearing an extraordinary multicoloured, central European-style military uniform wholly at odds with the new democratic, civilian Latin America of the 1990s, he spoke incisively. In complete contrast with his traditional oratorical style, he used only four of his allotted seven minutes to punch home two simple messages: that it was the imperialist countries that had wrecked the world and that they should pay to put it right. 'Less luxury and wastage in a few countries would amount to less poverty and hunger in a large part of the Earth' (*Earth Summit Bulletin*, 13 June 1992). Castro's speech aroused loud applause, but was aimed far beyond the hall, to the world public whose sympathy he was hoping to elicit. Yet Castro's own policies had throughout his career been based on the same strategies of industrialization and monoculture he was now criticizing, and he had left behind him in Cuba an economy devastated by the collapse of the Soviet Union, whose only hope for survival, let alone recovery, seemed to lie in the rediscovery, of all things, of dollar tourism.

Among his audience was an old antagonist, President Bush of the United States. Bush had not had a good morning. For weeks he had been using the threat not to attend to further the US agenda. His late decision to come after all had been accompanied by a decisive public rejection of the Biodiversity Convention. Next his ill-timed stop-over in Panama to meet President Endara (who had prudently decided not to come to Rio) had led to violent rioting in Panama City. The problem, of course, was the continued misery of the Panamanian population, few of whom had benefited from the many promises made at the time of the 1989 intervention, which had in any case been widely feared and disliked throughout Latin America. It was the news of the riots that blanketed the headlines on Bush's arrival in Brazil.

Bush's late decision to attend the morning session, however, even though he was not scheduled to speak until after lunch, brought him into the hall only a few minutes before Castro's speech. He was so busy glad-handing other delegates that he probably did not have his mind on what had actually been said, and delegates were surprised to see him warmly applauding Castro's denunciation of capitalism.

Bush's own speech, when it finally came, brought groans of disappointment from delegates. The President gave a vigorous defence of the US environmental record, arguing, aggressively, that it was 'second to none' in protecting its own natural habitats and wildlife. 'I didn't come here to apologize', he said. He then tried to claim credit for his (belated) decision to sign the Convention on Climate Change, and after his government had already done so much to render it ineffective, boldly called for a further meeting to be held by the end of the year to make it effective. He claimed that US measures to conserve biological diversity would in fact exceed the terms of the Biodiversity Convention, but that he still would not sign it. Finally, he offered no money.

Only one representative of the major economies received a warm welcome from delegates. This was President Mitterrand of France. It was no coincidence that he was the only one of the Group of Seven to be specific about his country's commitment to aid to the South, although it was only to raise France's existing contribution to world development of 0.56 per cent of

GNP to the target of 0.7 per cent by the end of the century, when it was unlikely that he would still be in office.

There were two obvious weaknesses in the position of the South at Rio, neither of which is likely to be solved. First, there were a wide range of special interests to be served among the very large number of states that might (or might not) be counted in that category. Second, a strong tendency in the UN for states to caucus by region was replicated at UNCED. For example, only a few of the new island states of the Caribbean voiced the fears of their Pacific and Indian Ocean counterparts, that within a generation the rising sea level caused by global warming could threaten their livelihoods if not their actual existence as states. The President of the Republic of the Maldives, Maumoon Abdul Gayoom, said that he expected his country to be seriously damaged by 2030 and to cease to exist altogether by 2100. However, Michael Manley of Jamaica had been succeeded in March by his former deputy, Percival Patterson, thus depriving the Commonwealth Caribbean of their most experienced radical voice, and their contribution to the public debate was muted. Patterson, who had been forced out of Manley's cabinet for alleged corruption as recently as December 1991, made a good plea for the implementation of the Law of the Sea Convention, but predictably placed the responsibility for global warming on the developed countries. The Prime Minister of Barbados, Erskine Sandiford, treated the assembled delegates to an ode in honour of the occasion composed entirely by himself.

Africa South of the Sahara was universally recognized as the world's most seriously deprived region. As noted above, its main preoccupation, drought and the issue of desertification, was sidelined at UNCED, despite being the subject of Chapter 12 of Agenda 21, 'Management of Fragile Ecosystems: Combating Desertification and Drought'. Continuing negotiations, which were hoped to result in the conclusion of a Convention to Combat Desertification, were finally concluded in June 1994 and the convention is expected to receive the necessary fifty ratifications by 1997. However, a convention which is limited to the world's poorest countries and lacks adequate means of financial support is unlikely to be any more effective than its predecessor (Manu 1993).

In an intermediate position were two groups of countries which shared many of the preoccupations of the southern states, but differed from them in important economic or political respects.

The governments of eastern and eastern-central Europe took the line that they were mature states capable of dealing with their own environmental problems. Their leaders had a (rather endearing) tendency to explain why their states were particularly important, on account of their peculiar terrain, unique mix of species or otherwise. The environmental arena, for them, was clearly one in which they could project their own independent national identity as players in the game of world politics.

Among the Middle Eastern states, Saudi Arabia, Kuwait and the United Arab Emirates stood out as states which commanded a significant surplus of economic resources and were able to act as alternative sources of funding to Third World states.

Implementation

The Earth Summit can fairly be evaluated not as an event in itself, but as a beginning of a much longer process of global self-education. One of its most important results was the provision by each country of a report on the state of its own environment. Often these were the first reports of their kind, and so of immense value in establishing the dimensions of the problem. Its importance, however, will in the end have to be measured in terms of the willingness or otherwise of the world's powers to recognize their own problems and to implement the programme so clearly set out for them. The first signs have been far from encouraging.

No one at Rio, least of all the authors of the numerous drafts of Agenda 21, thought that the 'major shift in priorities' it called for would be either easy or quick, involving as it did 'the full integration of the environmental dimension into economic and sectoral policies, decision-making in every sphere of economic and environmental activity and a major redeployment of human and financial resources at both national and international level' (UNCED 1992: 19).

Critics argue that no real action resulted. Basic policy differences were highlighted, especially those between the USA and the Third World, but they were not resolved. The same patterns of production and consumption continue, and in any case commitments made were not in proportion to the size and severity of the problems we face. Up to $2.5 billion in additional finance to begin funding the $400–600 billion estimated price of Agenda 21 may have been pledged as a result of Rio, but a minimum of $10 billion extra would be needed to reckon it a success. The debate over how to fund it was, as we have seen, split along North–South lines with Third World countries seeking, but not getting, assurances that official development assistance funding would not simply be diverted for the purpose. As UNCED Secretary-General Maurice Strong said of the possibilities of implementing Agenda 21: 'The real question is political will.'

Agenda 21 is above all a *social programme*. Social programmes take time and money to implement.

> The priority actions of Agenda 21 are grouped within the context of principal substantive social themes, including a prospering (revitalization of Growth with Sustainability), a just (Sustainable Living for All) and a habitable (Human Settlements Development) world. They entail promotion of a fertile (Efficient Resource Use), a shared (Global and Regional Resources) and a clean (Managing Chemicals and Waste) world, through wide and responsible participation at local, national and global levels. (UNCED 1992: 19)

To deal with the obvious question first, the new and additional cost of implementing Agenda 21, if all activities had begun at once and were fully implemented between 1993 and 2000, was estimated at an average annual figure of $125 billion. Although this looks a large amount, in relation to the current expenditure of the developed countries it is in fact minimal – less than 1 per cent of GNP (UNCED 1992: 17).

Unfortunately, it was already clear before the delegates left Rio that the developed countries, led by the United States, were simply not prepared to pay up. Worse still, the economic ideas which they were advocating were only likely to make things worse. Advocacy of the 'free market' was in practice accompanied by a clear tendency to try to define the parameters of the market in a way that sacrificed long-term stability to short-term returns.

The problem for Third World countries was not so much that the so-called free market that they had embraced so enthusiastically would not work, but that it would not work in the way that they hoped. Specifically, the beneficiaries were likely to be the larger, low-cost producers; the losers, the smaller, weaker economies. The result would be the further erosion of their already dubious ability to resist short-term demand for environmental degradation. Second, the action of the market promised to be much too slow to prevent irrevocable damage to the environment – the extinction of species, in particular, could not be averted once their numbers had declined below a critical level, and until that level was reached, there was insufficient motivation, under the unchecked market system, to halt the decline. In the last year before the formal implementation of CITES, South Korea imported 300 *tons* of tiger bones, representing the death of half of all the known Siberian tigers left in the wild. In March 1994 the UN Food and Agriculture Organization (FAO) reported that 'severe' political and economic conse- quences could be expected to follow the potentially catastrophic decline of species in nine of the world's 17 main fishing grounds. In August 1994 Britain sent two fishery protection vessels to protect British vessels fishing for tuna in international waters after they had been attacked and their nets cut by Spanish fishermen.

Some hope remained, for the Commission on Sustainable Development proposed to monitor the implementation of Agenda 21. This was established by the UN Economic and Social Council (ECOSOC) on 12 February 1993. It consists of 53 members chaired by Razali Ismail of Malaysia, and will meet annually for two to three weeks. The first session was held in New York in June 1993 (*UN Chronicle*, 30 (2), June 1993, p. 66).

Regional pressures for action are another area in which a greater degree of success may be expected. The Preparatory Committee (Prepcom) for a Global Conference on the Sustainable Development of Small Island Developing States met in August 1993. The conference itself took place in Barbados in April 1994 and produced a Programme of Action (*UN Chronicle*, 30 (2), June 1993, p. 80; *The Network*, 37, May 1994, p. 1).

Since the end of the Rio Conference, additional states have adhered to the Conventions on Biodiversity and Climate Change. However, the way in which they are to be implemented remains complicated and the procedures dismayingly slow. The chosen funding mechanism for the two conventions is the Global Environment Facility (GEF) of the World Bank, as agreed by an Eminent Persons Meeting in Tokyo between 15 and 17 April 1992. Following receipt of the Tokyo Declaration on Financing Global Environment and Development in June 1992 (United Nations 1992a), later the same month 32 governments reached agreement on the restructuring of the GEF 'to ensure an equitable representation of the interests of developing countries while giving due weight to the funding efforts of donor countries' (Global Environment Facility 1992a). Study of the projects listed in the first three tranches shows a wide distribution of funds both geographically by region and country, and across three of the four main areas to be covered: global warming, biodiversity and management of international waters. No projects were listed for the fourth area, ozone depletion. However, by June 1992 only a small selection, all but one from the first tranche, had actually been approved, examples being 'Emissions of Global Warming Gases from Rice Soils', 'Protected Areas and Wildlife Conservation in Vietnam' and 'Environmental Management in the Danube River Basin' (Global Environment Facility 1992b).

Part of the problem appears to lie with the inherent nature of environmental problems.

1. *Environmental effects are typically both weak and slow-acting.* Only in the case of serious airborne pollution, such as Chernobyl, are the effects sufficiently strong and immediate to trigger a response. The time spans involved are typically very long compared with the expectation of political office.

2. *Environmental effects typically occur across land frontiers and therefore involve only pairs of states.* Hence though security regimes typically involve a number of potential contending parties, in most environmental matters the zone of potential conflict is very limited. Even the Mexican border zone with the USA is small relative to Mexico as a whole, and hence for many political purposes can be ignored. However, what makes the potential for conflict between Mexico and the United States so great is that on both sides a legal near-vacuum exists. For example, as regards both the use of aquifers and the control of groundwater resources, 'it is fair to say that the legal and institutional situation is chaotic' (Utton 1990: 76).

3. *Environmental effects are typically transitive.* Or, as Carroll (1990: 76) put it:

> A transboundary environmental problem arises when all or most of the benefits of any pollution-emitting activity accrue to one nation, while all or

most of the costs of that activity accrue to the nation across the border. It is the existence and location of the border, therefore, and the imbalances or asymmetries in costs and benefits that result between two (or more) nations, which defines the existence of a transboundary environmental problem, and not necessarily the actual environmental impact of the activity in question.

Hence there is not the same perception of threat on one side as there is on the other. Accordingly, the pressure for some kind of solution is not evenly distributed, leading countries to try to solve their environmental problems at the expense of their neighbours. In extreme cases this can amount to a regional phenomenon. As is well known, nuclear reactors are perfectly safe. But in the Third World as in Europe there has been a very marked tendency for countries to situate their nuclear power stations on their (land or water) frontiers, facing their neighbours but as far away as possible from their own centres of population.

4. *Environmental causation is complex and still in many important respects imperfectly understood.* It is therefore all too easy for politicians to find scientific findings to support their own prejudices.

This said, structural factors in the nature of international decision-making were also to blame for the failure of UNCED to measure up to the (unrealistic) expectations encouraged by the world media. Special responsibility, however, must attach to the First World leaders of the world community, who so signally failed to measure up to the moment. It was, of course, not purely the leaders of the G7 countries who were at fault – within a year of the conference, even Gro Harlem Brundtland was under attack for her government's wish to resume whaling in the North Atlantic. However, it was an obvious irony that in general it was the smaller countries who were prepared to do most and the larger ones who could or would do least.

14 Conclusion

THE COLLAPSE OF THE 'SECOND WORLD'

Some writers, as we have seen, reject the concept of the Third World simply because, with the collapse of the 'Second', the term now seems odd. However, the most worrying thing about the changes in eastern Europe and northern Asia is precisely that they are tending to reinforce, not reduce, the yawning gap between the rich countries and the poor ones.

Some of the eastern-central European countries seem likely to find their common European home within the European Union. Obvious candidates are the Baltic states, the Czech Republic, Hungary and Slovenia. However, outside the boundaries of the former Austro-Hungarian Empire the picture is rather of a precipitate decline into the Third World status that the poorest country in Europe, Albania, already holds. In fact Richard Perle's sarcastic description of the former Soviet Union as 'Upper Volta with rockets' seems now to have been uncomfortably close to the truth.

The interesting and worrying thing is, therefore, that within the territories of the former Soviet Union and its satellites, we seem already to be witnessing the same process of 'pulling apart' that is characteristic of the Third World. The same economic and social problems are also already developing.

MODERNIZATION IN ASIA

Other writers argue that the emergence of the NICs (or NIEs) is an Asian phenomenon, based on a very special combination of local circumstances, and not easily replicable elsewhere. Far-reaching land reform in the 1950s in Taiwan and South Korea created a loyal class of small farmers and at the same time a substatial pool of industrial labour. Autocratic government, a large public sector controlling key industries and a command economy directing heavy subsidies into the manufacture of goods for export are distinctive features of the Asian NICs. So too are long working hours at low rates of pay for millions of workers, and heavy costs borne both by individuals and by the local environment. South Korea has the highest rate of industrial accidents in the world.

Some of these features are shared by other Asian developing countries. India, Malaysia, Thailand and the Philippines are much less autocratic, but in their different ways they have all encouraged the emergence of a low-wage, export-oriented economy. However, as we have seen, where there is a reasonably equal distribution of wealth, the society as a whole does benefit and the general standard of living improves. It is quite possible that in the twenty-first century Asia will again become what it once was, the most advanced region of the world in economic terms.

THE DECLINE OF AFRICA

In Africa, on the other hand, the situation is bleak. North of the Sahara, Islamic fundamentalism is spreading rapidly in Egypt and Algeria. It is possible that this could result in improved conditions for some of the poorest sectors, but so far it looks more likely to mean a retreat into insularity and isolationism which damages whole societies. Any attempt at bloc-building by Muslim countries would undoubtedly provoke similar responses elsewhere. It would certainly provide a convenient excuse to pander to the increasingly inward-oriented perspective of key sectors in the United States.

South of the Sahara, there has been no significant economic advance over the last ten years. One bright spot is in the far South, where the independence of Namibia and the orderly ending of apartheid in South Africa offers that possibility of co-operative economic development which has for so long been denied by political considerations.

THE DEINDUSTRIALIZATION OF EUROPE

The problem with the assumption that export-led growth is the route to economic development is that there has to be a market big enough to absorb the products. In the nineteenth century, Britain prospered on free trade. When other industrialized countries put up tariff barriers, the markets of the empire were big enough to allow trade to continue, at least for a time. The United States created a single internal market as early as 1791, and from that time on was able to develop behind the shelter of tariff protection.

However, the industrialization of the Third World in recent years has been accompanied by the deindustrialization of Europe. As transnational corporations have moved production out into Third World countries, to profit from their low wages, unemployment in Europe has risen to levels which have not been sustained for so long in recent times. At the same time, wages have become depressed, to the point at which Timex watches were assembled in Scotland and not in a Third World country, as long as labour costs were low enough to make the operation profitable, because the workforce was skilled enough to make sure that the work was done to a sufficient standard.

Such developments hardly suggest that Europe will be able to offer a big enough market for all the new goods that the Third World plans to put on sale. In fact, the markets of the developed world seem to have become saturated for some products already. People only need so many washing machines, refrigerators, vacuum cleaners, cars and television sets. Already the market for personal computers is getting very crowded. Prices are falling, quality and reliability have gone up to very acceptable levels, and after the first flush of enthusiasm for new electronic gadgetry it is clear that customers are becoming much more choosy. Hence Newly Industrializing Countries face the unpalatable truth that, if they are going to succeed, they are going to have to sell their goods to the Third World itself. Whether they can succeed in doing so depends not merely on their own efforts, but on the creation of markets for those goods consequent upon development, on a scale probably immensely damaging to the global environment we all have to share.

THE FUTURE OF THE PACIFIC RIM

With the emergence of the United States as a world superpower in 1945, Americans recalled the old belief that the major centre of world civilization tends to move in a westerly direction. At the beginning of the 1990s this interesting, but fallacious historical notion received a new twist with the emergence of the concept of the Pacific Rim as the new centre of world economic activity.

It is true that the United States, Japan, China and the NICs are all situated on the edge of the Pacific. So too are Mexico and Chile, which have both at different times been tipped for future NIC status. Given the size of the Pacific, a great many of the world's countries are bound to be found on its shores. However, it is not the fact that they are on the edge of the Pacific that is the common factor among the most rapidly developing of these states, but the fact that they are attached closely to the mainland of Asia.

FIRST WORLD AND 'FOURTH WORLD'

Finally we have to recall that for Africa South of the Sahara, the 1980s were a lost decade, during which development went backwards. The poorer countries of the Third World are slipping behind, not catching up. The 'pulling apart' of the Third World is continuing. Yet the boundary between the Third World and the Fourth does not always run between countries. Often it forms a series of invisible barriers between the rich and the poor of a single country, or of a group of countries.

Those of us who have the good fortune to live in the First World have to some extent relied on the disparate and in many cases powerless nature of countries of the Third World. The reality of encroaching environmental problems, if not catastrophe, changes this situation. It is no longer possible to remain unconcerned about the plight of other people because their existence does not really impinge on ours. The futures of their children and of ours are now recognizably bound together.

It is, of course, true that many people in First World countries have more pressing problems than the apparently rather remote dilemmas which surround our relationships with other parts of the world, and they have in many cases too little to be expected to make any significant contribution to a more equal world by giving up material possessions. Nevertheless the quality of all our lives ultimately depends on our recognizing our interdependence. Above all, the First World must acknowledge the special responsibility it now has for helping the Third World to achieve a quality of life appropriate for *all* human beings at the end of the twentieth century.

References

Adams, Nassau (1993), *Worlds apart: the North–South divide and the evolution of the international economic system*, London, Zed Press.

Adams, Patricia (1991), *Odious debts: loose lending, corruption, and the Third World's environmental legacy*, London, Earthscan.

Afrifa, Col. A.A. (1966), *The Ghana coup 24th February 1966*, London, Frank Cass.

Almond, Gabriel A., and Coleman, James S. (1960), *The politics of the developing areas*, Princeton, NJ, Princeton University Press.

Andreski, Stanislav (1968), *The African predicament: a study in the pathology of modernisation*, London, Michael Joseph.

Amin, Samir (1990a), *Delinking: towards a polycentric world*, London, Zed Press.

Amin, Samir (1990b), *Maldevelopment: anatomy of a global failure*, London, Zed Press.

Arat, Zehra F. (1991), *Democracy and human rights in developing countries*, Boulder, CO, Rienner.

Austin, Dennis (1978), *Politics in Africa*, Manchester, Manchester University Press.

Baker, Sophie (1990), *Caste: at home in Hindu India*, London, Jonathan Cape.

Baran, Paul A. (1957), *The political economy of growth*, New York, Monthly Review Press.

Barbier, Edward B. (1989), *Economics, natural-resource scarcity and development: conventional and alternative views*, London, Earthscan Publications Ltd.

Beauclerk, John, and Narby, Jeremy, with Townsend, Janet (1988), *Indigenous peoples: a fieldguide for development*, Oxford, Oxfam.

Beer, Christopher E.F., and Williams, Gavin (1975), 'The politics of the Ibadan peasantry', *The African Review*, 5 (3), pp. 235–56.

Bernstein, Henry, Crow, Ben, Mackintosh, Maureen, and Martin, Charlotte, eds (1990), *The food question: profits versus people?*, London, Earthscan.

Bill, James Alban (1972), *The politics of Iran: groups, classes, and modernization*, Columbus, OH, Merrill.

Billington, Rosamund, Strawbridge, Sheelagh, Greensides, Lenore, and Fitzsimons, Annette (1991), *Culture and society: a sociology of culture*, Basingstoke, Hants., Macmillan Education.

Black, Cyril E. (1976), *Comparative modernization: a reader*, New York, The Free Press.

Bonilla, Frank, and Girling, Robert, eds (1973), *The structures of dependency*, Stanford, CA, Institute of Political Studies.

Boserup, Ester (1981), *Population and technology*, Oxford, Basil Blackwell.

Boserup, Ester (1989), *Woman's role in economic development*, London, Allen and Unwin, 1970; new edn, London, Earthscan.

Bourricaud, François (1970), *Power and society in contemporary Peru*, New York, Praeger.

Bradley, P.N. (1986), 'Food production and distribution – and hunger', in R.J. Johnston and P.J. Taylor, eds, *A world in crisis? Geographical perspectives*, Oxford, Basil Blackwell, pp. 89–106.

Brandt, Willy (1980), *North–South: a programme for survival. The report of the Independent Commission on International Development Issues under the Chairmanship of Willy Brandt*, London, Pan.

Bresnan, John, ed. (1986), *Crisis in the Philippines: the Marcos era and beyond*, Princeton, NJ, Princeton University Press.

Bretton, Henry L. (1973), *Power and politics in Africa*, London, Longman.

Brier, Alan, and Calvert, Peter (1975), 'Revolution in the 1960s', *Political Studies*, **32** (1), pp. 1–11.

Brown, G. Gordon (1957), 'Some problems of culture contact with illustrations from East Africa and Samoa', *Human Organization*, **16** (3), pp. 11–14.

Bull, Hedley (1977), *The anarchical society*, London, Macmillan.

Bunker, Stephen (1985), *Underdeveloping the Amazon: extraction, unequal exchange and the failure of the modern state*, Urbana, IL, University of Illinois Press.

Cairncross, Alec (1994), 'Forget Bretton Woods – recovery was born in the USA', *The Guardian*, 22 July.

Calvert, Peter (1985), *Guatemala: a nation in turmoil*, Boulder, CO, Westview.

Calvert, Peter, ed. (1988), *The Central American Security System: North/South or East/West?*, Cambridge, Cambridge University Press.

Calvert, Peter (1990), *Revolution and Counter-Revolution*, Milton Keynes, Open University Press.

Calvert, Peter (1994), *The international politics of Latin America*, Manchester, Manchester University Press.

Canovan, Margaret (1981), *Populism*, London, Junction Books.

Cardoso, Fernando Henrique (1972), 'Dependency and development in Latin America', *New Left Review*, 74, pp. 83–95.

Cardoso, Fernando Henrique, and Faletto, Enzo (1979), *Dependency and development in Latin America*, Berkeley, CA, University of California Press.

Carroll, John E. (ed.) (1990), *International environmental diplomacy: the management and resolution of transfrontier environmental problems*, Cambridge, Cambridge University Press.

Chaliand, Gérard (1977), *Revolution in the Third World: myths and prospects*, Hassocks, Sussex, Harvester Press.

Chilcote, Ronald H. (1978), 'A question of dependency', *Latin American Research Review*, **12** (2), pp. 55–68.

Chilcote, Ronald H., and Edelstein, Joel C., eds (1974), *Latin America: the struggle with dependency and beyond*, Cambridge, MA, Schenkman.

Clapham, Christopher, ed. (1982), *Private patronage and public power: political clientelism in the modern state*, London, Frances Pinter.

Clapham, Christopher (1985), *Third World politics: an introduction*, London, Routledge.

Colburn, Forrest D. (1994), *The vogue of revolution in poor countries*, Princeton, NJ, Princeton University Press.

Collor, Fernando (1992), *Agenda for consensus: a social-liberal proposal*, Brasília, Governo do Brasil, 1992.

Colquhoun, Keith Colquhoun (1993), 'North Korea: the dangerous outsider', *World Today*, November, p. 210.

Conniff, Michael L., ed. (1982), *Latin American populism in comparative perspective*, Albuquerque, NM, University of New Mexico Press.

Crabtree, John (1987), *The great tin crash: Bolivia and the world tin market*, London, Latin American Bureau.

Crow, Ben, Thorpe, Mary, *et al.* (1988), *Survival and change in the Third World*, Cambridge, Polity Press.

Crowder, Michael (1967), *Senegal*, London, Methuen.

Danida – Danish Ministry of Foreign Affairs (1989), *Environmental issues and human health*, Copenhagen, Department of International Development Co-operation.

Decalo, Samuel (1976), *Coups and army rule in Africa*, New Haven, CT, Yale University Press.

Decalo, Samuel (1980), 'Regionalism, political decay, and civil strife in Chad', *Journal of Modern African Studies*, **18** (1), pp. 23–56.

De la Court, T. (1990), *Beyond Brundtland: Green development in the 1990s*, London, Zed Press.

Dicken, Peter (1986), *Global shift: industrial change in a turbulent world*, London, Harper and Row.

Dickenson, J.P., Clarke, C.G., Gould, W.T.S., Prothero, R.M., Siddle, D.J., Smith, C.T., Thomas-Hope, E.M., and Hodgkiss, A.G. (1983), *A geography of the Third World*, London, Methuen.

Di Tella, Guido, and Rodríguez Braun, Carlos, eds (1990), *Argentina, 1946–83: The economic ministers speak*, London, Macmillan with St Antony's College, Oxford.

Di Tella, Torcuato (1965), 'Populism and Reform in Latin America' in Claudio Véliz, ed., *Obstacles to change in Latin America*, London, Oxford University Press, pp. 48–51.

Dix, Robert (1985), 'Populism: authoritarian and democratic', *Latin American Research Review*, **20** (2), pp. 29–52.

Dobel, J.P. (1978), 'The corruption of a state', *American Political Science Review*, **72** (3), pp. 958–73.

Dobyns, Henry F., Doughty, Paul L., and Lasswell, Harold D. (1971), *Peasants, power, and applied social change: Vicos as a model*, London, Sage.

Dodd, C.H. (1974), *Political Development*, London, Macmillan.

Dore, Ronald (1987), *Taking Japan seriously: a Confucian perspective on leading economic issues*, Stanford, CA, Stanford University Press.

Dos Santos, Theotonio (1969), 'The crisis of development theory and the problem of dependence in Latin America', in Henry Bernstein, ed., *Underdevelopment and development: the Third World today*, Harmondsworth, Middx, Penguin, 1973, pp. 55–60.

Dos Santos, Theotonio (1970), 'The structure of dependence', *American Economic Review*, **60**, May, pp. 291–336.

Dreze, Jean, and Sen, Amartya (1989), *Hunger and public action*, Oxford, Clarendon Press.

Duncan, Tim, and Fogarty, John (1986), *Australia and Argentina: on parallel paths*, Carlton, Victoria, Melbourne University Press.

Durkheim, Emile (1964), *The division of labor in society*, trans. George Simpson, New York, The Free Press.

Easton, David (1957), 'An approach to the analysis of political systems', *World Politics*, 10, pp. 383–400.

Easton, David (1965), *A systems analysis of political life*, New York, John Wiley.

Fanon, Frantz (1967), *The wretched of the earth*, Harmondsworth, Middx, Penguin.

Finer, Samuel (1975), *The man on horseback: the role of the military in politics*, 2nd edn, Harmondsworth, Middx, Penguin.

First, Ruth (1972), *The barrel of a gun*, Harmondsworth, Middx, Penguin African Library.

Firth, Raymond (1936), *We the Tikopia*, London, Allen & Unwin.

Foray, Cyril P. (1977), *Historical dictionary of Sierra Leone*, Metuchen, NJ, London, Scarecrow Press.

Foster, George M. (1967), *Tzintzuntzan: Mexican peasants in a changing world*, Boston, MA, Little Brown.

Foster, George M. (1976), *Traditional societies and technological change*, 2nd edn, New York, Harper and Row.

Frank, André Gunder (1966), 'The development of underdevelopment', *Monthly Review*, 18 (4), pp. 17–31.

Frank, André Gunder (1967), *Capitalism and underdevelopment in Latin America*, Harmondsworth, Middx, Penguin.

Frank, André Gunder (1969), *Lumpenbourgeoisie: lumpendevelopment, dependence, class, and politics in Latin America*, New York, Monthly Review Press.

Frank, André Gunder (1970), *Latin America: underdevelopment or revolution*, New York, Monthly Review Press.

Frank, André Gunder (1974), 'Dependence is dead, long live dependence and the class struggle: a reply to critiques', *Latin American Perspectives*, 1 (1), pp. 87–106.

Frank, André Gunder (1981), *Crisis: In the Third World*, London, Heinemann.

Fukuyama, Francis (1992), *The end of history and the last man*, London, Hamish Hamilton.

Furtado, Celso (1970), *The economic development of Latin America: a survey from colonial times to the Cuban Revolution*, Cambridge, Cambridge University Press.

Gamer, Robert E. (1976), *The developing nations: a comparative perspective*, Boston, MA, Allyn and Bacon.

George, Susan (1993), 'The debt boomerang', *New Internationalist*, May.

Ghosh, Jayati and Bharadwaj, Krishna (1992), 'Poverty and unemployment in India', in Henry Bernstein, Ben Crow and Hazel Johnson, eds (1992), *Rural livelihoods: crises and responses*, Oxford, Oxford University Press.

Giddens, Anthony (1990), *The consequences of modernity*, Cambridge, Polity Press.

Glade, William (1991), 'The contexts of privatization', in William Glade, ed., *Privatization of public enterprises in Latin America*, San Francisco, CA,

International Center for Economic Growth, Institute of the Americas and Center for US–Mexican Studies.

Global Environment Facility (1992a), *A Bulletin on the Global Environmental Facility*, no. 5, May.

Global Environment Facility (1992b), 'A selection of projects from the first three tranches', Washington, DC, GEF/UNDP, Working Paper Series no. 2, June.

Golbourne, Harry, ed. (1979), *Politics and state in the Third World*, London, Macmillan.

Goldthorpe, John (1975), *The sociology of the Third World: disparity and involvement*, Cambridge, Cambridge University Press.

Goode, W.J. (1970), *World revolution and family patterns*, Glencoe, IL, The Free Press.

Goodman, David, and Redclift, Michael, eds, *Environment and development in Latin America: the politics of sustainability*, Manchester, Manchester University Press.

Grubb, Michael (1992), 'The road from Rio', *World Today*, 48 (8/9), August/September, pp. 140–2.

Grugel, Jean (1995), *Politics and development in the Caribbean basin: Central America and the Caribbean in the New World Order*, Basingstoke, Hants, Macmillan.

Guimarães, R.P. (1991), *The ecopolitics of development in the Third World: politics and environment in Brazil*, London, Rienner.

Hall, Anthony L. (1991), *Developing Amazonia: deforestation and social conflict in Brazil's Carajás programme*, Manchester, Manchester University Press.

Hall, Stuart, and Jefferson, Tony, eds (1976), *Resistance through rituals: youth subcultures in post-war Britain*, London, Hutchinson in association with the Centre for Contemporary Cultural Studies, University of Birmingham.

Hardoy, Jorge E., Mitlin, Diana, and Satterthwaite, David (1992), *Environmental problems in Third World cities*, London, Earthscan.

Harris, Nigel (1986), *The end of the Third World? Newly industrialising countries and the decline of an ideology*, London, I.B. Tauris.

Harrison, Paul (1993), *The Third Revolution: population, environment and a sustainable world*, Harmondsworth, Middx, Penguin.

Hayter, Teresa (1983), *The creation of world poverty: an alternative view to the Brandt Report*, London, Pluto.

Heidenheimer, A.J. (1970), *Political corruption*, New York, Holt Rinehart.

Hewitt, Vernon Marston (1982), *The international politics of South Asia*, Manchester, Manchester University Press.

Hicks, John D. (1961), *The populist revolt*, Lincoln, NB, University of Nebraska Press.

Higgins, Graham, *et al.* (1982), *Potential population supporting capacities of lands in the developing world*, Rome, FAO.

Hilling, David (1978), 'The infrastructure gap', in Alan B. Mountjoy, ed., *The Third World: problems and perspectives*, London, Macmillan.

Hillyard, Paddy, and Percy-Smith, Janie (1988), *The coercive state*, London, Pinter.

Holmberg, Allan R. (1971), 'Experimental intervention in the field', in Henry F. Dobyns, Paul L. Doughty and Harold D. Lasswell, eds, *Peasants, power, and applied social change: Vicos as a model*, London, Sage, pp. 21–32.

Hoogvelt, Ankie (1978), *The sociology of developing societies*, London, Macmillan.

Horowitz, Donald L. (1971), 'Three dimensions of ethnic politics', *World Politics*, **23** (2), p. 232.

Howard, Michael, ed. (1957), *Soldiers and governments*, London, Eyre and Spottiswode.

Hughes, John (1968), *The end of Sukarno: a coup that misfired – a purge that ran wild*, London, Angus and Robertson.

Huntington, Samuel P. (1965), 'Political development and political decay', *World Politics*, 17, no. 3, pp. 386–430.

Huntington, Samuel P. (1968), *Political order in changing societies*, New Haven, CT, Yale University Press.

Huntington, Samuel P. (1976), 'The change to change: modernization, development, and politics', in Cyril E. Black, ed., *Comparative modernization: a reader*, New York, The Free Press.

Hurrell, Andrew, and Kingsbury, Benedict, eds. (1992), *The international politics of the environment*, Oxford, Clarendon Press.

Ianni, Otávio (1975), *A formaçao do estado populista na América Latina*, Rio de Janeiro, Civilizaçao Brasiliera.

Insight (1986), *Sri Lanka*, Singapore, APA Productions.

Jackson, Ben (1990), *Poverty and the Planet: a question of survival*, Harmondsworth, Middx, Penguin.

Jaguaribe, Helio (1967), *Problems do desenvolvimiento Latino-Americano*, Rio de Janeiro, Ed. Civilizaçao Brasiliera.

Jenkins, J. Craig, and Kposowa, Augustine J. (1992), 'Political origins of African military coups: ethnic competition, military centrality and the struggle over the postcolonial state', *International Studies Quarterly*, **36** (3), pp. 271–91.

Kamrava, Mehran (1992), *Revolutionary politics*, London, Pinter.

Kamrava, Mehran (1993), *Politics and society in the Third World*, London, Routledge.

Kedourie, Elie (1971), *Nationalism in Asia and Africa*, London, Heinemann.

Keohane, Robert O., and Nye, Joseph S. (1977), *Power and interdependence: world politics in transition*, Boston, MA, Little Brown.

Kerr, Clark, Dunlop, John T., Harbison, Frederick H. and Myers, Charles A. (1960), *Industrialism and industrial man: the problems of labor and management in economic growth*, London, Heinemann.

Khan, Z.A. (1990), *Pakistan's security*, Lahore.

Khor, Martin (1992), 'Rio Declaration, Agenda 21 passed to Ministers after all-night meeting', *SUNS at the Earth Summit*, 11 June.

Kilson, Martin (1966), *Political change in a West African state: a study of the modernization process in Sierra Leone*, Cambridge, MA, Harvard University Press.

Kitching, G. (1982), *Development and underdevelopment in historical perspective: populism, nationalism and industrialization*, London, Methuen.

Laclau, Ernesto (1977), *Politics and ideology in Marxist theory: capitalism–fascism–populism*, London, NLB.

Lasswell, Harold D., and Kaplan, A. (1950), *Power and society: a framework for political inquiry*, New Haven, CT, Yale University Press.

Lasswell, Harold D., and Holmberg, Allan R. (1966), 'Toward a general theory of directed value accumulation and institutional development', in H.W. Peter, ed., *Comparative theories of social change*, Ann Arbor, MI, Foundation for Research on Human Behavior.

Leggett, Jeremy, ed. (1990), *Global warming: the Greenpeace report*, Oxford, Oxford University Press.

Lewis, Sir Arthur (1965), *Politics in West Africa*, London, Allen and Unwin.

Lewis, Oscar (1962), *The children of Sánchez: autobiography of a Mexican family*, London, Secker and Warburg.

Lieuwen, Edwin (1964), *Generals versus presidents: neomilitarism in Latin America*, London, Pall Mall.

Linz, Juan J. (1970), 'An authoritarian regime: Spain', in E. Allardt and S. Rokkan, eds, *Mass politics: studies in political sociology*, New York, Free Press, p. 254.

Lipset, Seymour Martin (1979), *The first new nation: the United States in historical and comparative perspective*, New York, W.W. Norton.

Lipton, M. (1977), *Why poor people stay poor: urban bias in world development*, London, Temple Smith.

Little, K. (1965), *West African urbanisation*, Cambridge, Cambridge University Press.

Little, Richard (1975), *Intervention: external involvement in civil wars*, London, Martin Robertson.

Lloyd, Peter C. (1971), *Classes, crises and coups: themes in the sociology of developing countries*, London, Paladin.

Lovelock, James (1979), *Gaia: a new look at life on Earth*, Oxford, Oxford University Press.

Lovelock, James (1986), 'Gaia: the world as a living organism', *New Scientist*, 18 December.

Luckham, Robin (1971a), *The Nigerian Military 1960–67*, Cambridge, Cambridge University Press.

Luckham, Robin (1971b), 'Comparative typology of civil–military relations', *Government and Opposition*, 6, pp. 5–35.

Lugard, Sir Frederick D. (1922) *The Dual Mandate in British Tropical Africa*, Edinburgh: William Blackwood and Sons.

McAfee, Kathy (1991), *Storm signals: structural adjustment and development alternatives in the Caribbean*, Boston, MA, South End Press in association with Oxfam America.

McGrew, Anthony G., and Lewis, Paul G. *et al.* (1992), *Global politics: globalization and the nation-state*, Cambridge, Polity Press.

Malinowski, B. (1961), *The dynamics of culture change*, New Haven, CT, Yale University Press.

Manu, Christopher (1993), 'The road to the Desertification Convention', *Resources*, 4 (2), pp. 7–10.

Matthews, Jessica Tuchman (1993) in Glyn Prins, ed., *Threats without enemies: facing environmental insecurity*, London, Earthscan.

Mead, Margaret (1956), *New lives for old*, New York, New American Library.

Mehta, Gita (1990), *Raj* (novel), London, Mandarin.

Mehta, Gita (1993), *A River Sutra* (novel), London, Heinemann.

Mitra, Subrata Kumar (1990a), 'Between transaction and transcendence: the state and the institutionalisation of power in India', in Subrata Kumar Mitra, ed., *The post-colonial state in Asia: dialectics of politics and culture*, New York: Harvester Wheatsheaf, pp. 73–99.

Mitra, Subrata Kumar, ed. (1990b), *The post-colonial state in Asia: dialectics of politics and culture*, New York, Harvester Wheatsheaf.

Monbiot, George (1992) in *Oxfam/Guardian Supplement*, June.

Moore, Mick (1990), 'Sri Lanka: the contradictions of the social democratic state', in Subrata Kumar Mitra, ed., *The post-colonial state in Asia: dialectics of politics and culture*, New York, Harvester Wheatsheaf, pp. 155–91.

Myrdal, Gunnar (1968), *Asian drama: an enquiry into the poverty of nations*, Harmondsworth, Middx, Penguin.

Naipaul, V.S. (1980), *The return of Eva Peron*, London, André Deutsch.

Needler, Martin C. (1963), *Latin Americam power in perspective*, Princeton, NJ, Van Nostrand.

Neguib (Naguib), Muhammad (1955), *Egypt's destiny*, Garden City, NY, Doubleday.

New Internationalist (1990), 214, December.

Nordlinger, Eric A. (1977), *Soldiers in politics: military coups and governments*, Englewood Cliffs, NJ, Prentice Hall.

Nye, Joseph S. (1967), *Pan-Africanism and East African integration*, Cambridge, MA, Harvard University Press.

Nye, J.S., and Keohane, R.O. (1971), *Transnational relations and world politics*, Cambridge, Cambridge University Press.

O'Brien, Donal B. (1971), *The Mourides of Senegal*, Oxford, Oxford University Press.

O'Brien, Donal B. Cruise (1978), 'Senegal', in John Dunn, ed., *West African states: failure and promise – a study in comparative politics*, Cambridge, Cambridge University Press, pp. 173–88.

O'Brien, Philip, and Cammack, Paul, eds (1985), *Generals in retreat: the crisis of military rule in Latin America*, Manchester, Manchester University Press.

O'Donnell, Guillermo (1988), *Bureaucratic authoritarianism: Argentina, 1966–1973, in comparative perspective*, Berkeley, CA, University of California Press.

Parsons, Talcott (1964), *Essays in sociological theory*, New York, The Free Press.

Pearce, Fred (1992), 'Last chance to save the planet?', *New Scientist*, 30 May.

Perham, Margery (1937), *Native administration in Nigeria*, Oxford, Oxford University Press.

Petersen, Kurt (1992), *The Maquiladora revolution in Guatemala*, Occasional Paper Series 2, Orville H. Schell, Jr, Center for International Human Rights at Yale Law School.

Philip, George (1984), 'Military–authoritarianism in South America: Brazil, Chile, Uruguay and Argentina', *Political Studies*, 32 (1), pp. 1–20.

Philip, George (1985), *The Military and South American Politics*, London, Croom Helm.

Philips, Herbert P. (1965), *Thai peasant personality: the patterning of interpersonal behavior in the village of Bang Chan*, Berkeley, CA, University of California Press.

Pinkney, Robert (1993), *Democracy in the Third World*, Milton Keynes, Open University Press.

Postel, Sandra (1989), *Water for agriculture*, Washington, DC, Worldwatch Institute, Worldwatch Paper 93.

Powell, John Duncan (1970), 'Peasant society and clientelist politics', *American Political Science Review*, 64, 411–25.

Prebisch, Raúl (1950), *Economic development of Latin America and its principal problems*, New York, United Nations Department of Economic Affairs, ECLA document E/CN 12/89/Rev.1.

Prescott, J.R.V. (1965), *The geography of frontiers and boundaries*, London, Hutchinson.

Prince of Wales (1993), 'Introduction' in Glyn Prins, ed., *Threats without enemies: facing environmental insecurity*, London, Earthscan.

Randall, V., and Theobald, R. (1985), *Political change and underdevelopment*, London, Macmillan.

Rappaport, Roy A. (1968), *Pigs for the ancestors: ritual in the ecology of a New Guinea people*, New Haven, CT, Yale University Press.

Redclift, Michael (1984), *Development and the environmental crisis: red or green alternatives?*, London, Methuen.

Riggs, Fred (1964), *Administration in developing countries*, Boston, MA, Houghton Mifflin.

Roett, Riordan (1985), 'Latin America's response to the debt crisis', *Third World Quarterly*, 7 (2), pp. 227–41.

Rostow, W.W. (1960), *The stages of economic growth*, Cambridge, MA, Harvard University Press.

Rostow, W.W. (1971), *Politics and the stages of growth*, Cambridge, Cambridge University Press.

Roxborough, Ian (1979), *Theories of underdevelopment*, London, Macmillan.

Sahlin, Michael (1977), *Neo-authoritarianism and the problem of legitimacy: a general study and a Nigerian example*, Stockholm, Reben and Sjögren.

Sampson, Anthony (1975), *The Seven Sisters: the great oil companies and the world they made*, London, Coronet.

Saravanamuttu, P. (1990), 'Instability in Sri Lanka', *Survival*, 32 (5), pp. 455–68.

Sartori, Giovanni (1976), *Parties and party systems, a framework for analysis*, Cambridge, Cambridge University Press.

Schmandt, Jurgen (1994), 'Water and development in semi-arid regions', paper presented to the XVI World Congress of the International Political Science Association, Berlin, Germany, 21–5 August 1994.

Schmitter, Phillippe, ed. (1979), *Trends towards corporate intermediation*, Beverly Hills, CA, Sage.

Schumacher, E.E. (1974), *Small is beautiful: a study of economics as if people mattered*, London, Sphere.

Scutz, Barry M. and O'Slater, Robert, eds. (1990), *Revolution and political change in the Third World*, London, Adamantine.

Scott, J.C. (1976), *The moral economy of the peasant: rebellion and subsistence in Southeast Asia*, New Haven, CT, Yale University Press.

Sen, Amartya (1981), *Poverty and famines: an essay on entitlement and deprivation*, Oxford, Clarendon Press.

Seth, Vikram (1993), *A suitable boy* (novel), London, Phoenix House.

Seton-Watson, Hugh (1977), *Nations and states: an inquiry into the origins of nations and the politics of nationalism*, London, Methuen.

Shaw, Paul (1992) quoted in *New Internationalist*, September, p. 14.

Shiva, Vandana (1988), *Staying alive: women, ecology and development in India*, London, Zed Press.

Sierra Leone: National Reformation Council (1968), *Report of the Forster Commission of Inquiry on Assets of Ex-Ministers and Ex-Deputy Ministers*, Freetown, Government Printer.

Sinha, R. (1976), *Food and Poverty*, London, Croom Helm.

Smith, Michael (1992), 'Modernization, globalization and the nation-state', in Anthony McGrew, Paul G. Lewis, *et al.* (1992), *Global politics*, Cambridge, Polity Press.

Smith, Tony (1979), 'The underdevelopment of development literature: the case of dependency theory', *World Politics*, 31 (2), pp. 247–88.

Somjee, A.H. (1991), *Development theory: critiques and explorations*, Basingstoke, Hants., Macmillan.

South Commission (1990), *The challenge to the South: the report of the South Commission*, London, Oxford University Press.

Staley, Eugene (1954), *Political implications of economic development*, New York, Harper.

Stepan, Alfred, ed. (1973), *Authoritarian Brazil*, New Haven, CT, Yale University Press.

Stepan, Alfred (1978), *The state and society: Peru in comparative perspective*, Princeton, NJ, Princeton University Press.

Steward, Julian H. (1967), *Contemporary change in traditional societies*, Urbana, IL, University of Illinois Press.

Strong, Maurice F. (1992), foreword to *The global partnership for environment and development: a guide to Agenda 21*, Geneva, UNCED, April.

Sunkel, Osvaldo (1969), 'National development policy and external dependence in Latin America', *Journal of Development Studies*, 6 (1), pp. 23–48.

Tangri, Roger (1985), *Politics in sub-Saharan Africa*, London, James Currey.

Thomas, Caroline (1985), *New states, sovereignty and intervention*, Aldershot, Hants., Gower.

Thomas, Caroline (1987), *In search of security: the Third World in international relations*, Boulder, CO, Rienner.

Thomas, Caroline (1992), *The environment in international relations*, London, Royal Institute of International Affairs.

Thomas, Caroline, and Howlett, Darryl (1992), *Resource politics: freshwater and regional relations*, Milton Keynes, Open University Press.

Thrift, Nigel (1986), 'The geography of international economic disorder', in R.J. Johnston and P.J. Taylor, eds, *A world in crisis: geographical perspectives*, Oxford, Basil Blackwell.

Timberlake, L. (1985), *Africa in crisis*, London, Earthscan.

Todaro, Michael (1994), *Economic development*, London, Longman.

Toffler, Alvin (1970), *Future shock*, London, The Bodley Head.

Tolba, Mostafa, ed. (1988), *Evolving environmental perceptions: from Stockholm to Nairobi*, London, Butterworth.

Tylor, E. (1891), 'Culture defined', in L.A. Coser and B. Rosenberg, eds (1964), *Sociological theory: a book of readings*, London, Collier–Macmillan.

United Nations (1992a), *Adoption of agreements on environment and development: note by the Secretary-General of the Conference*, A/CONF.151/7, 4 June.

United Nations (1992b), *Earth Summit: press summaries*, New York, United Nations.

United Nations (1992c), *Report of the pre-conference consultations held at Riocentro Conference Centre*, A/CONF.151/L.1, 2 June.

United Nations (1992d), *Report of the United Nations Conference on Environment and Development*, A/CONF.151/26 (Vol. IV), p. 4.

United Nations (1992e), Protocol and Liaison, Provisional List of Delegations to the Conference on Environment and Development, A/CONF.151/INF/2/Add.3, 6 June.

United Nations Conference on Environment and Development (UNCED 1992), *The global partnership for environment and development: a guide to Agenda 21*, Geneva, UNCED, April.

United Nations Development Programme (1994), *Human development report, 1994*, New York, Oxford University Press.

United Nations Economic and Social Council (UNESCO 1991), *Environmentally sustainable economic development: building on Brundtland*, Paris, UNESCO.

UNICEF (1990), *State of the world's children*, London, Oxford University Press.

United Nations Population Fund (UNFPA 1992), *The state of world population 1992*, New York, UNFPA.

Utton, A.E. (1990), 'Problems and successes of international water agreements: the example of the United States and Mexico', in John E. Carroll, ed., *International environmental diplomacy: the management and resolution of transfrontier environmental problems*, Cambridge, Cambridge University Press, pp. 67–83.

Vagts, Alfred (1959), *A history of militarism, civilian and military*, London, Hollis and Carter.

Vajpeyi, Dhirendra (1994), 'To dam or not to dam? Social, economic and political impact of large hydro-electric projects: case studies of China, India and Brazil', paper presented to the XVI World Congress of the International Political Science Association, Berlin, Germany, 21–5 August 1994.

Vogt, Evon Z. (1969), *Zinacantan: a Maya community in the highlands of Chiapas*, Cambridge, MA, The Belknap Press.

Wallerstein, Immanuel (1974), *The modern world system*, New York, Academic Press.

Weber, Max (1964), *The Theory of Social and Economic Organisation*, trans. by A.M. Henderson and Talcott Parsons, New York, The Free Press.

Weinbaum, Marvin G. (1972), 'Afghanistan: nonparty parliamentary democracy', *Journal of Developing Areas*, 7 (1), pp. 57–64.

Weiner, Myron (1962), *The politics of scarcity: public pressure and political response in India*, Chicago, IL, University of Chicago Press.

Weinstein, Martin (1975), *Uruguay, the politics of failure*, Westport, CT, Greenwood Press.

Whitehead, Ann (1990), 'Food crisis and gender conflict in the African countryside', in Henry Bernstein, Ben Crow, Maureen Mackintosh, and Charlotte

Martin, eds, *The food question: profits versus people?*, London, Earthscan, pp. 54–68.

Wijkman, Anders, and Timberlake, Lloyd (1984), *Natural disasters: acts of God or acts of Man?*, London, Earthscan.

Wiking, Staffan (1983), *Military coups in sub-Saharan Africa: how to justify illegal assumptions of power*, Uppsala, Scandinavian Institute of African Studies.

Wiles, Peter (1969), 'A syndrome, not a doctrine: some elementary theses on populism', in Ghita Ionescu and Ernest Gellner, eds, *Populism: its meaning and national characteristics*, New York, The Macmillan Co.

Williams, Gavin, and Turner, Terisa, 'Nigeria', in John Dunn, ed. (1978), *West African states: failure and promise – a study in comparative politics*, Cambridge, Cambridge University Press, pp. 132–72.

Williams, Robert (1987), *Political corruption in Africa*, Aldershot, Hants., Gower.

Wilson, E.O., ed. (1988), *Biodiversity*, Washington, DC, National Academy Press.

Wolf, E.R. (1969), *Peasant wars of the twentieth century*, New York, Harper and Row.

World Bank (1990), *World development report 1990*, Oxford, Oxford University Press.

World Bank (1992), *World Development Report 1992*, New York, United Nations.

World Bank (1994), *World Development Report 1994*, New York, United Nations.

World Commission on Environment and Development (1987), *Our common future* (The Bruntland Report), Oxford, Oxford University Press.

World Health Organization (1993), *World health statistics annual 1993*, Geneva, World Health Organization.

Worsley, Peter (1967), *The Third World*, 2nd edn, London, Weidenfeld and Nicolson.

Wraith, Ronald, and Simpkins, Edgar (1965), *Corruption in developing countries*, London, Allen and Unwin.

Wuthnow, Robert, Hunter, James Davison, Bergesen, Albert, and Kurzweil, Edith (1984), *Cultural analysis: the work of Peter L. Berger, Mary Douglas, Michel Foucault and Jürgen Habermas*, London, Routledge and Kegan Paul.

Zolberg, Aristide (1966), *Creating political order*, Chicago, IL, Rand McNally.

Index